Logical Form in Natural Language

⌐⌐ Bradford Books

Daniel C. Dennett. BRAINSTORMS. 1979.

John Haugeland, Editor. MIND DESIGN. 1981.

Fred I. Dretske. KNOWLEDGE AND THE FLOW OF INFORMATION. 1981.

Jerry A. Fodor. REPRESENTATIONS. 1981.

Hubert L. Dreyfus, Editor, in collaboration with Harrison Hall. HUSSERL, INTENTIONALITY AND COGNITIVE SCIENCE. 1982.

Morris Halle and G. N. Clements. PROBLEM BOOK IN PHONOLOGY. 1983.

Jerry A. Fodor. MODULARITY OF MIND. 1983.

Robert Cummins. THE NATURE OF PSYCHOLOGICAL EXPLANATION. 1983.

Stephen P. Stich. FROM FOLK PSYCHOLOGY TO COGNITIVE SCIENCE. 1983.

Jon Barwise and John Perry. SITUATIONS AND ATTITUDES. 1983.

Izchak Miller. HUSSERL, PERCEPTION, AND TEMPORAL AWARENESS. 1984.

Norbert Hornstein. LOGIC AS GRAMMAR. 1984.

Myles Brand. INTENDING AND ACTING, 1984.

Zenon W. Pylyshyn. COMPUTATION AND COGNITON. 1984.

Ruth Garrett Millikan. LANGUAGE, THOUGHT AND OTHER BIOLOGICAL CATEGORIES. 1984.

Daniel C. Dennett. ELBOW ROOM: THE VARIETIES OF FREE WILL WORTH WANTING. 1984.

Robert C. Stalnaker. INQUIRY. 1984.

William G. Lycan. LOGICAL FORM IN NATURAL LANGUAGE. 1984.

Logical Form in Natural Language

William G. Lycan

A Bradford Book
The MIT Press
Cambridge, Massachusetts
London, England

This book was set in Palatino by Village Typographers, Inc., and printed and bound by Halliday Lithograph in the United States of America.

Library of Congress Cataloging in Publication Data

Lycan, William G.
  Logical form in natural language.

  "A Bradford book."
  Bibliography: p.
  Includes index.
  1. Languages—Philosophy.   2. Semantics.
3. Pragmatics.   4. Language and logic.   I. Title.
P106.L88   1984   401   84-11292
ISBN 0-262-12108-5

I dedicate this book with love and gratitude to my parents
William H. Lycan and Janet G. Lycan.

Contents

Preface

This book has been long—far too long—in the making. I have been thinking about truth-theoretic semantics and about the relation between semantics and pragmatics since hearing Donald Davidson, Gilbert Harman, David Kaplan, Barbara Partee, and others lecture on them in 1971, at the Council for Philosophical Studies' Summer Institute in the Philosophy of Language, and I have foisted early versions of most of my present chapters on (now) generations of graduate students in philosophy and in linguistics, whose responses over the years, positive and negative, have helped mightily to shape the result.

Some of the problems I shall here attack are no longer topics of febrile interest to linguists; but not, I think, because they have already been solved or dissolved. I believe the approaches I shall offer are as advanced and plausible as anyone's (which is not to say that in every case the degree of advancement and plausibility is huge). Serious problems remain, but I hope that my work will serve as a springboard for more definitive solutions to come.

My overabundant notes, collected at the end of the book, are mainly scholarly and dialectical; the text may be read smoothly without them. I have included them in part to indicate the vast and often unexpected complexity of some of my subject-matter, and in part (of course) to protect myself against premature criticism. Mature and postmature criticism will have to take care of themselves.

I owe profound thanks to many people, particularly to my former colleagues at Ohio State: Mike Geis, Arnold Zwicky, and David Dowty, who are unrivalled as interdisciplinary mentors; Dick Garner, with whom I was privileged to teach the joint seminar that directly inspired this book; and especially Steve Boër, coconspirator and linguistically kindred spirit for over a decade. I am doubly grateful as well to Gilbert Harman, for his advice and encouragement over the years despite his almost total disagreement with the views I defend here, and for his useful criticisms of an earlier draft. Lynne Rudder Baker, Dick Grandy, Ernie LePore, and Steve Schiffer also commented helpfully and at length on drafts at various stages. Finally, like any Bradford author, I want to express my great appreciation to Harry and Betty Stanton for their expert help, for their kindness and (especially) patience, for their faith in this project, and for being Bradford Books.

Acknowledgments

Much of this book was written during a Faculty Development Quarter in 1976 and a Faculty Development Leave in 1979–80, provided by the Ohio State University. I am also grateful to the University of Massachusetts at Amherst for appointing me as Visiting Adjunct Professor during the latter period.

Sections 1 and 2 of chapter 6 are based on Boër and Lycan, "A Performadox in Truth-Conditional Semantics, " *Linguistics and Philosophy,* Vol. 4, No. 1 (1980), pp. 71–100; copyright © 1980 by D. Reidel Publishing Company, Dordrecht, Holland. Sections 1–3 of chapter 9 are based on an article that appeared in Vol. 59, No. 3 of THE MONIST, 1976, LaSalle, IL 61301. Material reprinted by permission.

Logical Form in Natural Language

Introduction

This book has three main purposes:

1. To detail the complicated anatomy of the notion of linguistic meaning. Each of the major theories of meaning that have flourished in this century has focussed on one important aspect of linguistic significance, usually at the expense of the others: truth-conditions, verification-conditions, "use" in language-games, illocutionary force, perlocutionary effect, speakers' intentions, communicative potential, representational and/or conceptual role, etc. Each of these aspects is indisputably or at least arguably real; therefore, I contend, theories *of* them should be regarded as mutually complementary components of linguistic theory, rather than being treated as rival theories directed toward a common subject-matter. However, I shall argue that the notion of a *sentence's truth-condition* lies at the core; each of the other aspects derives in its own way from that notion. I shall attempt to show how they all fit together.

2. To explore the interface between "languages" considered as formal systems and the linguistic activities of actual, living human beings in "total speech situations." (a) I shall consider a number of *prima facie* differences between formal languages and natural languages, having chiefly to do with the context-bound nature of the latter's distinctive features, and try in each case to reconcile them. (b) I shall investigate a number of specific sorts of linguistic phenomena that have threatened to erode the traditional distinction within linguistics between semantics and pragmatics, and motivate what I think is the best way of drawing that distinction.

3. To defend the autonomy of linguistic semantics as a branch of scientific psychology, both against various popular claims that "semantics" ultimately collapses into a diffuse pragmatics or into anthropology and against the Quinean contention that semantics cannot be scientific because it uncovers nothing factual.

Before getting on to these formidable tasks, I shall establish a crude starting point in the traditional threefold division of linguistic semiotics: syntax, semantics, and pragmatics. *Syntax* is the study of grammar and grammatical properties, aimed at parsing sentences of natural languages into structures of interconnected "parts of speech" in a way relevant to displaying their meanings; more recently and more elegantly, at marking off the class of a language's well-formed strings. *Semantics* is the study of the meanings of words and sentences, in abstraction from the various speech contexts in which they might be called upon to serve. *Pragmatics* is the study of the uses of sentences in context, and of how gaps in sentences' abstract meanings may be filled in by context.

Until the 1940s, philosophers of language concentrated almost exclusively on semantics in the foregoing sense, i.e., on the "cognitive" or "locutionary" meanings of sentences taken in the abstract, often identified with the structures of eternal "propositions." Wittgenstein and Austin then called our attention to the enormity of this abstraction, and to the almost total dependence of sentence-meaning upon contextual features of utterance. Thus began the battle between semantics and pragmatics, with pragmatics getting the best of it for some twenty years. Syntax was effectively ignored by both sides until its dramatic resuscitation by Harris and Chomsky in the late 1950s (it is remarkable that although for centuries philosophers had inquired into the nature of meaning, reference, truth, and entailment, no one had asked what it is for a string of "words" to be *grammatical* or well-formed); but even then syntax played no part in philosophers' accounts of meaning and use. Following the demise of verificationism, the dominant strategy was to explicate meaning in pragmatic terms of some sort—"use" in the Wittgensteinian sense (cf. Waismann (1965)), illocutionary act potential (Alston (1963)), or speakers' communicative intentions (Grice (1957, 1968)). But syntactic concerns soon asserted themselves. I now offer a quick historical sketch of the relevant developments in philosophical linguistics since the 1950s.

Background

I. Semantics prior to the 1960s.
Since Frege and Russell, philosophers have had the idea that sentences of natural languages have "underlying" semantic structures or logical forms, which diverge sharply from their superficial grammatical forms and whose features explain the sentences' otherwise puzzling logical and semantical properties.

II. The origin of generative syntax.
1. Chomsky, trained both in linguistics and in philosophy, tried in *Syntactic Structures* (1957) to give a rigorous and systematic explica-

tion of the notion of *grammaticalness* or syntactic well-formedness in natural languages.

(a) A syntax or a *grammar* for a natural language was conceived as a set of rules that picks out all and only the well-formed sentences of that language.

(b) Due to humans' ability to acquire infinite or at least indefinitely broad syntactic "competence" in a very short time and on the basis of only a tiny amount of linguistic input, an adequate grammar for a natural language must in practice be recursive.

2. A traditional Chomskian grammar (only caricatured here) consisted of a *phrase structure* component, which generated trees terminating in "kernel sentences" (alternatively, labelled bracketings of kernel sentences), and a *transformational* component, which turned those trees into other (usually more complex) trees.

3. The trees thus generated, along with the generative process itself, served as the syntactic analysis of the sentences that were their terminal strings. The tree or labelled bracketing that is both the output of the phrase structure component and the input to the transformational component in the generation of a particular sentence was called the "deep structure" of that sentence. The bracketing of deep structures was done in terms of fairly traditional grammatical categories.

The Convergence of Syntax with Semantics

I. Trends of the 1960s.
1. The (reputedly) autonomous syntax of *Syntactic Structures* began to be polluted by semantical notions. The syntax/semantics boundary blurred.

(a) Syntacticians had to import notions such as those of reference, meaning, and entailment to explain apparently syntactic phenomena.

(b) They also began to bite off more and more phenomena, some obviously semantic to begin with.

(c) In addition, they made increasing use of the concepts and the notation of formal logic, both to help in the aforementioned explanations and because some surface constructions of natural languages mirror logical locutions (connectives, quantifiers, etc.).

2. Though philosophers had long had the idea of sentences' having "logical forms," no one had ever been able to say anything about the actual *connection between* a sentence and "its" logical form (or rather, between the sentence and the formula of some canonical idiom that directly expresses that sentence's logical form), i.e., between semantics and surface structure.

(a) Theorists now noticed that syntactic transformations are the sort of things one might use to map natural-language sentences and logical forms into each other, and that these transformations can in principle be rigorously formalized.

(b) Under the influence of the "Ordinary Language" movement of the 1950s and early 1960s, philosophers also began to interest themselves in syntactic problems, first in connection with traditional philosophical issues and then for their own sake.

3. "Deep structures" began to look less and less like bracketed natural-language strings (easily mappable into surface structures by fairly straightforward transformational operations), and more and more like formulas of formal logic, which naturally required more complicated and more abstract series of transformations to "get them to the surface" or transform them gradually into surface structures.

II. The basic idea of Generative Semantics.
1. The hypothesis was formed (McCawley (1967), Lakoff (1971), Harman (1972a, 1972b)) that "deep structure" simply *is* semantic structure or logical form. Deep structures were to be notated explicitly in an enriched version of ordinary formal logic (which version was sometimes called "Natural Logic").

2. The "phrase structure component" that generated these deep structures was now tacitly taken simply to be the set of formation-rules for the canonical idiom in which the deep structures were written. Transformations operated directly on deep structures. (This was as before; the novelty was just that syntacticians had not previously thought of transformations as operating directly on *semantic* structures. Semantic interpretation had been provided, or rather not provided, by a separate (and highly *ad hoc*) "semantic component."

3. It was assumed that grammatical transformations preserve the semantic properties of semantic structures or logical forms throughout the trip to the surface. (This requirement had been anything but met by the transformations of *Syntactic Structures,* one of which (T_{not}) even took a kernel sentence onto its semantic denial.) Thus, natural-language sentences get their meanings, entailments, etc., from their underlying structures—ultimately, from the truth-theoretic interpretation of the underlying canonical idiom itself, this being already well understood by logicians. Moreover, a semantics for a natural language is generative, in that it rides piggyback upon the generative processes of syntax transformationally understood; hence the rubric "Generative Semantics." Generative Semanticists and their descendants have continued to hold that (i) there is no syntax

without semantics and (ii) there is no semantics without formal truth theories or simulacra of the same.

4. The syntax/semantics convergence, and the rapprochement between linguists and philosophers, persisted (at least so far as the philosophers are concerned), to the extent of seemingly erasing all hope of more than a difference of emphasis or tendency. The result was a fairly unified field of study that, for want of anything more lurid, we may call "linguistic semantics."

5. Beginning in the late 1960s, the line between syntax/semantics and *pragmatics* began to blur in a disturbingly reminiscent way. Some theorists heralded the collapse of that distinction, predicting with apparent approval that it would go the way of the distinction between syntax and semantics. Others (philosophers at first but more recently many linguists also) have tried to resist or forestall that outcome, and that is one project I shall be continuing here.

III. More recent developments.
1. Since around 1970, both linguists and philosophers have perceived a growing need to introduce intensional devices into the canonical idiom in which logical form is expressed. Primarily because of the work of Hintikka and Montague, semantic theories have tended more and more to be based on rich intensional logics. Since by far the most illuminating truth-theoretic interpretation of intensional logics (conceived by Carnap (1947), von Wright (1951), Hintikka (1957, 1961), Kanger (1957), and Kripke (1959, 1963, 1965)) is that based on possible worlds, the meanings of natural-language sentences are now given largely in terms of worlds, indeed often simply *identified with* set-theoretic structures involving worlds. Interestingly, "deep structures" written in the vernacular of intensional logic can approximate natural-language surface grammar more closely, thus reversing the Generative Semanticists' trend toward more and more abstract and complicated transformational derivations.

2. In the past few years, syntactic research has fragmented into numerous alternative formats and programs: trace theory, Arc-Pair Grammar, Realistic Grammar, game-theoretic syntax, Generalized Phrase Structure Grammar, and so forth. The extent to which these programs are mutual competitors is unclear to me, as are some of their respective semantic underpinnings. Thus, I cannot say how far my extended discussion of truth-theoretic semantics will interest working practitioners of those approaches. But I would be surprised if a defense of truth-theoretic foundations for linguistics did not apply at least obliquely to the newer syntactic programs as well as

to the more traditional Generative Semantics, Montague Grammar, Cresswell Grammar, *et al.*

The idea of assigning meanings to sentences of natural languages by associating the sentences with truth-theoretically interpreted formulas of a logical system has been articulated most explicitly and defended most vigorously by Donald Davidson and by Gilbert Harman, though it is imperative to note that Harman himself abandoned and rejected the "Davidsonian program" as early as 1974. (I shall deal in chapter 10 with his reasons for this apostasy.) It is to their works that I shall turn in order to bring out the fundamental connections between linguistic meaning in general and the notion of "truthconditions" as it is understood by logicians. In chapter 1 I shall set out and elaborate the metatheory defended by Davidson and Harman—hereafter, "the Metatheory"; in later chapters I shall examine it and develop it systematically in my own way. It must be noted that I am not particularly interested in Davidsonian exegesis. Nor do I agree with all of the views that Davidson expresses along the way in his writings on truth and meaning, some of which are more closely associated in the public eye with Davidson than are the views I do agree with. The Metatheory as I shall state it is all that concerns me, and the "Davidsonian program" will suffer considerable adjustment and readjustment at my hands.

When Davidson first introduced his semantic program, audiences had a hard time keeping in mind that a "theory of meaning" in his sense is a theory of the meanings of the expressions of a particular target language, part of a whole "theory of" that language. What philosophers had traditionally called "the theory of meaning," a branch of philosophy, would be a meta-metatheory relative to an enterprise of the sort Davidson envisions.[1] What, then, is a "theory of meaning" *for* a particular natural language such as English supposed to accomplish? Davidson himself has maintained no firm answer to this question (see Davidson (1976)).

The meaning that concerns me is public linguistic meaning, since English and other natural languages are public languages. Accordingly, a theory of meaning for English is designed to explain the linguistic abilities common to English speakers. But "linguistic abilities" is a notably open-ended term, and I propose to leave it so; language use is the most complex, the most versatile, and at the same time one of the most automatic and reflexive of human activities, and it would be foolish to prejudice our discussion of meaning by adopting a circumscribed set of abilities narrowly delineated at the outset. However, I take the paradigm of language use to be its use in communication, and the abilities I have most firmly in mind are communicative abilities. In particular, I think a theory of meaning for a language should explain how, upon hearing a fellow organism emit a stream of noises, an English-speaking subject immediately acquires a belief of the form, "He has said that *p*."[2] It should also help to explain how, upon hearing the noises, the subject typically acquires the belief *that p*. Further, it should figure in explanations of why speakers produce the utterances that they do in particular circumstances, though obviously more than knowledge of meanings alone is involved here, and as we shall see in chapter 10, the role of a speaker's linguistic knowledge in the respective etiologies of the speaker's utterings is a vexed one.

I
Semantics

Chapter 1
Meaning and Truth

A practitioner of the Davidson-Harman approach, attending to a particular language such as English, attempts to associate, with each well-formed sentence of that language, one or more formulas of a specific canonical idiom. The canonical idiom is an interpreted and fully disambiguated formal theory, normally a natural extension of first-order quantification theory, complete with its own formation-rules and formal semantics. Let us call these associated formulas "semantic representations" (SRs) of the English sentence under investigation (the "target sentence"). Each semantic representation will correspond to what is commonly called a "reading" of the target sentence.

The Metatheorist claims that the SR correlated with a given reading bears the following relations to the target sentence on that reading:

(a) The SR gives the *logical form* of the target sentence, in more or less the traditional sense of that term. The correct assignment of an SR to a sentence both disambiguates that sentence and systematizes and accounts for the sentence's "felt implications" on the reading in question. We account for our feeling that a sentence S_1 "implies" a sentence S_2 by uncovering the logical form of each, and then showing that the SR of S_2 is contained in or implied by the SR of S_1 in virtue of the semantical rules of our canonical idiom;[1] if some "felt implication" strongly resists this kind of structural explanation, the Metatheorist will commonly subsume it after the fact under a "nonlogical axiom" or meaning postulate. Finally, the assignment of an SR can be expected to remove conceptual puzzles and confusions in the classical way (Russell's procedure in "On Denoting" being a paradigm here), and in general to shed light on a variety of standard philosophical issues. *Prima facie,* then, the notion of an SR as representing logical form is closely bound up with that of meaning. There is an obvious but so far very unclear sense in which, if we discover the real logical form of a sentence, we discover its meaning, presuming that we are antecedently familiar with the meanings of its primitive predicates and other nonlogical terms. So it is natural to say that the logical form of a sentence combined with the interpretation of its nonlogical terms *is* the semantic structure of that sentence in some distinctive and useful sense of that term. However, it remains to explain why this should be so.

(b) According to Davidson, the answer is that an assigned SR performs all the aforementioned semantical functions by virtue of being itself a *truth-conditional* structure, and is a truth-conditional structure by virtue of being a formula of a formal language (our canonical idiom) that admits of a Tarskian truth-characterization. The recursive truth definition for this formal language is of course the semantical foundation of the language's formation- and inference-rules. (Davidson seems to claim in (1967b) that a Tarskian truth definition for a language tells us all we need to know about the meaning of any expression of that language, though especially in his later writings such as (1976) he disavows the thesis that a theory of truth *is* a theory of meaning. Harman does not make that identification himself in (1972b) and indeed goes on to attack it in later writings, particularly (1974).) In the next section I shall return to the idea that a sentence has its semantical properties in virtue of having a distinctive set of truth-conditions,[2] and try to spell it out in a plausible way; I shall then spend the rest of this book elaborating this idea and examining and evaluating its consequences.

(c) SRs also serve as the input to a set of syntactic transformations that serve to define well-formedness for the target language; this claim is at the core of the Metatheory, though it is unemphasized by Davidson. Transformations (on the broadest possible understanding of that notion) operate directly on SRs, mapping them ultimately onto their respective target sentences, this mapping being many-many—hence ambiguity and synonymy in natural language. If we take the bedraggled term "deep structure," in an unrealistically non-theory-laden way, as meaning merely whatever structure serves both as the output of the semantic component of a grammar and as the input to the transformational component, claims (a) and (c) taken together amount to the striking thesis that classical logical form and modern deep structure are one and the same. (Harman offers technical arguments for this thesis in (1972a) and (1972b); see also McCawley (1967, 1972a, and 1972b).)

(d) Since according to the Metatheory syntactic transformations preserve truth-conditions, a target sentence (on a reading) inherits its truth-condition from that of its SR (relative to that reading). Our understanding of an English sentence and its logical relations is thus to be explained as being the product of our implicit mastery of the truth-conditional interpretation of the canonical idiom that underlies English combined with our even more implicit practical grasp of the transformations that produce actual English sentences from semantic structures.

Of course, given a particular English sentence, there are any number of different possible canonical languages in which we might choose to represent that sentence; and, even when a particular canonical idiom has been fixed, we still have our choice of many different possible translations of the target sentence into that preferred idiom. How are we to find the correct theory of logical form for the body of sentences that concerns us, amid all these possibilities? In (1972b) Harman offers and motivates a set of desiderata, or principles of theory-preference, designed to choose between alternative proposals. Particular theories of a certain fragment of a natural language are to be compared with respect to these principles:

(1) A theory of logical form must assign forms to sentences in a way that permits a (finite) theory of truth for the language. This theory of truth for the 'object language' is to be formulated in a 'metalanguage' that contains the object language and has the same logic as the object language. Furthermore, the theory of truth must satisfy a condition resembling Tarski's "convention T". In particular, it must entail all appropriate instances of "x is true if and only if p", where "x" is replaced by a name descriptive of the logical form of a sentence "s" of the object language and "p" is replaced by "s" itself [= "T-sentences"].

(2) A theory of logical form should minimize novel rules of logic. In practice, this means that rules of logical implication should be kept as close as possible to the rules of ordinary (first order) quantificational logic (with function letters and identity). . . .

(3) A theory of logical form should minimize axioms. Other things equal, it is better to account for obvious implications by rules of logic alone than by rules of logic plus nonlogical axioms.

(4) A theory of logical form should avoid ascribing unnecessary ontological commitment to sentences of the language. Other things equal, one theory is better than another to the extent that it interprets sentences as implying the existence of more ordinary sorts of things. . . .

(5) A theory of logical form must be compatible with syntax. Logical forms assigned sentences by the grammar should be the same as (at least part of) the underlying structures assigned sentences by a transformational grammar. A good grammar can

> be incorporated into a good theory of logical form as the device
> that assigns logical forms to sentences. (1972b, p. 42)

Principles (1)–(5) are not arbitrary *a priori* dicta; they are empirical
rules of thumb, motivated by broader empirical considerations of a
more familiar type. For example, principle (1) is espoused because
Tarski's formal semantics is the only one we have that yields a *recur-*
sive characterization of truth-conditions of the sort needed to account
for the production of an infinite store of possible sentences using
only finite apparatus, and to exhibit the dependence of the meanings
of those sentences on the meanings of their parts. Principle (2) is
simply a conservative bromide, open to differing interpretations and
in need of careful scrutiny.[3] Principle (3) seems a trivial consequence
of the general admonition against *ad-hoc*-ness, since nonlogical
axioms are essentially *ad hoc* devices. Principle (4) follows from the
(not uncontroversial) "principle of charity," according to which we
should try to avoid ascribing wildly deviant or bizarre beliefs to another person if there is an alternative hypothesis that accounts more
or less well for his behavior but is more flattering.

Principle (5) is a bit less straightforward in its methodological intent. As it stands, it states a clear constitutive condition on the final
form of an official theory, but the phrase "compatible with syntax"
does not give us much help in actually proceeding with the construction of such a theory while it is in its early stages of development. A
very strong methodological interpretation of principle (5) would be,
"Do not accept a proposed assignment of an SR to a target sentence
unless you already have an independently motivated syntactic derivation that takes that SR as input and yields the target sentence as
output." This rule may have been satisfied once or twice in the entire
history of linguistic semantics, if that. A very weak interpretation of
(5) would be, "Accept a proposed assignment of an SR to a target
sentence only if there is no conclusively damning reason to doubt
that any plausible derivation connects that SR to that sentence." This
rule is virtually always satisfied, given the precarious state of work in
syntax to date. Clearly what is needed, and what Harman intends in
the way of methodological advice, is a rule that is comfortably intermediate in strength, e.g., "Other things being equal, assign SR_1
rather than SR_2 to your target sentence if there is reason to think that
SR_1 lends itself more readily to an independently plausible syntactic
history of that sentence." (This rule gains its appeal chiefly through
vagueness, of course; a fully articulate methodology would have to
elaborate it in considerable detail.)

I believe the general scientific idea behind principle (5) is that of *robustness:* the epistemic status and the perceived reality of a theoretical posit increase sharply with the number of mutually independent routes of epistemic access that lead to it.[4]

Harman's rules are not very precisely stated (to say the least), and their respective motivations are not as clear as one would like. But we may take them for now in the spirit in which (I think) they were meant, as slogan formulations thrown on the table for further discussion. It seems to me reasonable to suppose that some such set of principles, better articulated, could be derived from the more general canons of theory-preference that govern all explanatory reasoning (if only *they* were better articulated).

The Metatheory, then, is a program for linguistics, in which traditional philosophical considerations of truth-conditional structure and logical form are blended with technical concerns of syntax. The first manifestation of this program actually to be pursued by linguists was Generative Semantics, a splendid idea that, although fruitful and productive of countless logicogrammatical hypotheses, established no firm results and gasped its last sometime during the mid-1970s.[5] More recent semiotic formats, such as Montague Grammar and Cresswell Grammar, are for our purposes instances of the program as well.[6] In a pellucid discussion (1979, chap. 1), David Dowty has shown Generative Semantics and the going versions of Montague Grammar to be special cases of Montague's "Universal Grammar" (Montague (1970);[7] see also Cooper and Parsons (1976)); I intend my discussion in this book to apply to any semantical format that associates sentences of a natural language on some principled grounds with formulas of a logical system that are themselves semantically interpreted by explicit truth definition. With considerable trepidation, I shall continue to use the word "transformation" to mean whatever sort of formal operation figures in connecting a target sentence with a semantically appropriate SR, despite the accretion of undesirable traditional associations that it carries along, for I can think of no better term; I hope my disavowal of the traditional associations will stick.[8]

Several instances of Universal Grammar, ostensibly governed by the Metatheory, have achieved impressive early successes in illuminating both logical and grammatical issues. It would be premature to try to predict just how much further progress to expect. One must also be cautious in specifying the exact nature of the "successes" and "progress" in question—just what phenomena are being explained, just what sense of "explain" is in play, and so on. As will be made manifest in the course of this book, the answers to questions of this sort have never been settled; to quote an anonymous referee, "[w]ith-out a satisfactory theory of transformations, the [Metatheory] is little more than wishful thinking guided by philosophical intuition."

2. Semantics and Truth

Why focus on truth? Why should we think that the notion of truth plays the central role in a theory of meaning for a natural language? One might argue the reverse—that since truth *presupposes* mean-ingfulness, truth could not very well be used to explicate the notion of meaning. But the idea is not so unnatural. Meaning, like any semantical notion, is somehow a relation between language and re-ality. Paradigmatically, a sentence is meaningful because it repre-sents the world as being a certain way, or alternatively because it corresponds to a factual state of affairs that either does or does not obtain. To represent the world as being a certain way, or to corre-spond to a state of affairs that does or does not obtain, is to be true under certain conditions and not others. Thus, a sentence is mean-ingful in virtue of being true under certain conditions and not others (and when a sentence is true, there is a fact in the world that makes it true). Further, as Davidson and many earlier philosophers have agreed, to *know* the meaning of a sentence is to know the conditions under which the sentence would be true; this is no merely theoretical claim, but can actually serve as a practical test of semantic com-petence. So it is unsurprising that meaning and truth-conditions should be thought to go hand in hand, even though the foregoing ideas have proved hard to spell out metaphysically. Still, some more rigorous motivation is required if we are to focus on this affinity between meaning and truth-conditions and give it pride of place in our semiotic program. Davidson himself offers a more specific and serious line of reasoning in (1965), (1970), and particularly (1967b). It is familiar enough by now that only a brief rehearsal is needed here:

Suppose we set out to give a theory of meaning for a particular natural language such as English or Russian. What form would such a theory take? Davidson offers and motivates a number of guidelines and constraints, of which two may be considered fundamental. The first is that the theory should assign a meaning to *each* (grammatical) sentence of the target language; it must be complete in this sense. The second constraint is that

> [s]ince there seems to be no clear limit to the number of mean-ingful expressions, a workable theory must account for the meaning of each expression on the basis of the patterned exhi-

bition of a finite number of features. But even if there were a practical constraint on the length of the sentences a person can send and receive with understanding, a satisfactory semantics would need to explain the contribution of repeatable features to the meaning of sentences in which they occur. (1970, p. 18)

What Davidson has seized on here (following Ziff (1960, sec. 64)) is the semantical analogue of a key insight of Chomsky's: just as any acceptable grammar of English must contain a recursive element in order to explain speakers' ability to classify novel and arbitrarily long strings of words as grammatical or ungrammatical, a similar recursion must play a central role in our theory of meaning for English, or we will be unable to explain how a speaker—particularly a small child who has a tiny finite vocabulary and only a very limited amount of accumulated linguistic input—is able to understand (know the meaning of) a potentially infinite number of sentences of English; in fact, without such a recursion, this potential infinity of output given a small finite input would seem to be simply an impossibility.[9] Nor is the lexical finiteness an accident of the speaker's biography; Davidson insists (see particularly (1965)) that no natural language *could* have more than finitely semantic primitives. The reason is that since semantic primitives must be learned separately and one at a time by a student of the language, a language having nonfinitely many primitives could not be learned (in its entirety) at all. Thus, any speaker of English must have mastered (whether innately or by experience) a fairly simple and manageable set of recursive rules that yield the meanings of complex expressions, given only the meanings of simpler ones and a few modes of concatenation. Once having discovered and articulated this set of recursive rules and a specification of the meaning of the semantically primitive vocabulary elements of English, we as theorists would be able to generate a pairing of English sentences with their meanings—instances of the schema "*s* means that *p*."

It is at this fairly uncontroversial point that Davidson makes his move. The connective "means that" in the foregoing schema is problematic; in particular, it is venally intensional (see (1967b, 455)). Davidson boldly proposes to expunge the problem, by replacing "means that" with the uprightly extensional "is true iff." This amounts to the claim that a theory of *truth* for a language—that is, an assignment of truth-conditions to every sentence of that language— will suffice as a theory of meaning for the language. Nothing more is required, Davidson suggests; there is nothing worth knowing, or even perhaps knowable, about meanings that is not vouchsafed us by a correct and complete theory of truth. This is quite a strong claim, but if true, it is welcome, since thanks to Tarski the idea of a theory of truth-conditions at least for a formal language is clear, well-motivated, and formally implementable. Davidson gives several closely related reasons for accepting it.

(I) In Davidson's words,

> [A] theory [of meaning] will have done its work if it provides, for every sentence s in the language under study, a matching sentence (to replace 'p') that, in some way yet to be made clear, 'gives the meaning of' s. One obvious candidate for matching sentence is just s itself, if the object language is contained in the metalanguage; otherwise a translation of s into the metalanguage. (1967b, p. 455)

But this is just what a theory of truth does: it correlates ⌜s is true⌝ with s's disquotation. Moreover, the truth definition is recursive, as we earlier required of a theory of meaning for a language, and it shows how the truth-conditions of complex sentences depend on the truth- and satisfaction-conditions of simpler expressions. So there is *prima facie* reason to think that what is most valuable in the notion of meaning can be captured by a theory of truth-conditions.[10]

(II) A Tarskian truth definition for a language meets another requirement that we would want to put on a theory of meaning as well. The truth-conditions it assigns to sentences of the language "draw [only] upon the same concepts as the sentences whose truth conditions they are" (1970, p. 19). This is because Davidson's individual meaning-assignments turn out simply to be T-sentences: instances of "s is true iff p," where "s" is replaced by the structural name of a sentence and 'p' by that very sentence or by its "translation" into the metalanguage. In particular, what replaces 'p' will involve no obviously semantical notions (unless, of course, such a notion or term occurs in the target sentence itself). One reason for insisting on this is that incorporating a semantical notion (such as "means that" again) into assigned truth-conditions would probably create intensionality and reintroduce the problems that Davidson is precisely concerned to avoid. Another is that circularity would threaten, since it is just such notions that we are trying to explicate, albeit in our target-language-relative way.[11]

(III) We know the converse of Davidson's thesis is true: any adequate theory of meaning for a language should yield a truth definition for that language, since we would expect any correct assignment of a meaning to a sentence *a fortiori* to determine that sentence's truth-condition. So if a truth definition does everything that we preanalytically asked a theory of meaning to do, it seems reasonable to conclude that a theory of meaning is not anything *over and above* a truth definition, that they are one and the same (especially since any attempt to say that meanings are anything over and above truth-conditions will virtually demand the invocation of mysterious new and unexplicated notions). To see the coincidence more clearly, imagine a case of radical translation. If a veteran radical translator welcomes us to his chosen valley and proudly sets out (in English) the truth-conditions of all sorts of Native strings, and if his account checks out against our observations of the native's patterns of assent and dissent, and if into the bargain the translator can show us how he derived each statement of truth-conditions from a finite set of axioms each of which makes mention of a presumed morpheme of Native, then surely we would say that the translator had succeeded in decoding the language and had come to understand it.[12] What more, after all, could be required?[13] Davidson adds,

> . . . a theory of truth shows how we can go from truth to some-thing like meaning—enough like meaning so that if someone had a theory for a language verified only in the way I propose, he would be able to use that language in communication. (1973, p. 84)

(IV) Davidson does not stress the point, but of course a truth the-ory for a natural language predicts and explains (at least some) felt semantical features of sentences, such as ambiguity, entailment, synonymy, and logical truth, just as grammar predicts felt syntactic features—and in the most respectable possible way, by means of the rigorous formal semantics underlying the canonical metalanguage. Not all types of theories of meaning can make this claim, since some may specify the meanings of each sentence of the target language without being able to connect the notions of entailment or of logical truth to that of sentence-meaning in any serious way. And it is hard to admit that a theory predicts and explains the central semantical features of sentences and yet deny that that theory is a theory of meaning, unless one adds a fairly specific commentary on what one thinks has been left out. (Incidentally, it should be clear by now that Davidson has in mind a relatively narrow sort of "meaning," corre-sponding roughly to what has been called "propositional con-tent," "locutionary meaning," or sometimes—unfortunately—"lit-eral meaning." Wider concerns for illocutionary, perlocutionary, contextual, conversational, figurative, and emotive significance are in abeyance for now.)

(V) A further advantage in a theory of meaning whose job it is to spit out T-sentences is that the theory has infinitely many empirically testable consequences, viz., the T-sentences themselves. We can easily confirm our theory's predictions in virtue of our knowledge of our own language, if our own language is the target language. Davidson makes much of this claim.[14] It is not clear to me why any theory that entailed instances of "*s* means that *p*" would not have this same advantage equally; I suppose his point is that he does not see how any theory other than a Tarskian truth definition could do this at all. We shall examine Davidson's claim to "empirical bite" in chapter 2.

Still another attractive feature of Davidson's proposal, at least to those of a Russellian turn of mind, is that a theory of meaning that consisted of a Tarskian truth definition would (in principle) be elegantly formal (cf. point (IV)). The mathematical rigor of the Tarskian semantics for the theorist's canonical metalanguage would be forced up through the T-sentences until it pervaded all the blooming, buzzing complexities of the target language, a natural human language, itself; thus, the language would be given as secure a semantical foundation as can be given even for the most crisply formulated formal systems. Such a semantics could, for example, be taken cleanly over into a natural-language-understanding computer program; though decades too late, the Artificial Intelligence community would finally be able to build a machine that speaks Vietnamese. But two difficulties immediately confront the idea that a natural language such as English could be formalized in this way. Both were pointed out by Tarski himself.

First (1956, p. 30), the language would have to be distorted beyond recognition in order for us to be able to apply a simple Tarskian truth-characterization to it; Tarski's theories deal only in simple configurations of predicates, quantifiers, and truth-functions. Davidson considers this point (1967b, p. 460) and replies that the needed reformation of the target language would not have to be "out of all recognition":

> Pick [a formal language] as much like English as possible. Since this new language has been explained in English and contains much English we not only may, but I think must, view it as part of English for those who understand it.

If we have a Tarskian truth definition for this "new" formal-yet-English language, then we have a truth definition for at least a large chunk of English *per se*.[15]

By itself this line is highly dubious. If one looks at the truth-conditional structures actually posited by Davidson, Harman, and other practitioners of their methodology when doing substantive empirical work on English, one will be struck by the appearance of long rows of chicken-scratches, punctuated only occasionally by capitalized predicates of what might pass for English. And it is just not true that these structures are written *in* English. What is important, though, is that they can double as deep structures; they are capable of *generating* English surface strings *via* (one hopes) established syntactic transformations. Suppose we have a formal language, accompanied by a Tarskian truth definition for it. And suppose it should just happen to turn out that that formal language was an ideal medium in which to write notational equivalents of syntactic deep structures.[16] Then (given a well-justified English grammar) we would have a ready-made set of transformations that would map the sentences of the formal language onto English surface structures; if the transformations could be run in reverse, we would have a corresponding way of recovering the logical formulas from English sentences as well, and then by proceeding further backward through the truth definition for the formal language, we would map the English sentences conversely into truth-conditions and thus fix their meanings. So there is no reason to be disturbed by the superficial dissimilarity of English to the formal language that Tarski himself was able to treat.

It is important to note that this augmentation of a truth-based semantics by a syntactic component plugs a large hole in Russell's original conception of "logical form": Russell solved semantical problems by hypothesizing that sentences "had" logical forms that differed strikingly from their misleading surface-grammatical forms, but he never tried to answer the obvious question of what it is that makes a sentence's logical form *that sentence's* logical form; what is the metaphysical ground of this privileged relation between an English sentence and a formula of a logical theory (for Russell, PMese)?[17] The answer is supplied by a correct grammar for English that is justified independently and that connects English systematically to the logical theory. If the grammar has "psychological reality," then the metaphysical ground of the connection between sentences and their logical forms is ultimately a matter of brain structure. (This claim will be discussed in part III.) Psychologism aside, I believe it is vital that any theory of "logical form" provide some account of this connection, on pain of indeterminacy. More will be said of this general point in the next chapter.

Unfortunately, the dissimilarity of English surface grammar to the syntax of quantification theory was not Tarski's only basis for doubting that his method of truth-characterization could be extended to

English; the Liar Paradox drove this doubt home, and that is the second of the two difficulties he raised. Unlike standard formal languages, English contains its own truth predicate, or seems to (1956, p. 31). Is a truth definition for English not then doomed to incoherence?

Davidson has two possible replies. First, he may say that at least a theorist can give a fascinating and illuminating theory of *almost* all of English. The homegrown semantical terms, such as "true," that cause the problem are comparatively few and far between.[18] For that matter, we could impose a type theory on English and contend that "real" English contains no semantical terms, though there is a closely related language, MetaEnglish, some of whose terms characterize expressions of English, and which happens to be spoken just by people who also speak English. This would be artificial but not terribly counterintuitive. But the following objection threatens: Speakers are able to apply semantical terms such as "true" also to sentences that contain "true," so it must be supposed on the present strategy that speakers of English and MetaEnglish also speak a third language, MetaMetaEnglish, some of whose terms characterize expressions of MetaEnglish, and we are off and running. The regress of metalanguages is not vicious in itself; presumably all those distinct languages (*qua* denumerable sets of finite morpheme sequences) do exist in Plato's Heaven. The problem is that the regress leads to a clash with Davidson's crucial observation that a natural language may have only finitely many semantic primitives. Now, no one of our hierarchy of metalanguages contains more than finitely many primitives, so technically our type-theoretic ploy does not violate the letter of the finiteness constraint. But it does violate the spirit of the constraint and succumbs to the same sort of argument: a speaker would have to be thought of as understanding *each* of the metalanguages in the hierarchy, all at once, and since each metalanguage contains its own semantically primitive truth predicate, the speaker would still have to have learned more than finitely many semantic primitives (even though they are considered expressions of distinct languages), which is impossible. So let us turn to Davidson's second possible reply.

He might make a more serious effort to explicate semantical locutions in English as they stand. In fact, Harman has offered an ingenious theory of truth predicates in the object language (1972b, sec. 6), though Melvin Ulm has argued that Harman too ends up having to posit nonfinitely many primitive truth predicates, thus violating the finiteness constraint (see Ulm (1978); Ulm's argument is similar to my foregoing objection to the type-theoretic approach, and no doubt inspired it). We might also want to introduce a third truth-value (e.g., "anomalous") and devise a truth theory for English that would mark all and only the paradoxical strings as "anomalous," though Kripke (1975) points out the difficulty of this and chooses instead to interpret "true" by means of a partial function.[19] In any case, fear of the semantic paradoxes ought not to inhibit work in truth-conditional semantics on ordinary, nonsemantical target discourse.

If all English surface grammar mirrored the constructions of standard first-order logic, the task of giving a truth definition for English would be a simple one. What makes theorizing in the Davidsonian mode hard is that English contains many important surface locutions that are not, on their face, quantificational and/or truth-functional at all. (Harman tackles some of them in the middle sections of (1972b).) Either these must be shown to reflect underlying constructions that *are* quantificational nonetheless (cf. the treatment of certain adverbs in Davidson (1967a) and in Harman (1972b, sec. 3), respectively), or new logical devices such as intensional abstractors of various types must be invented and added to the canonical idiom in order to handle the troublesome locutions (cf. the contrasting treatment of adverbs in Clark (1970) and Parsons (1972), disparaged by Harman in (1972b, sec. 3)). Either of these tasks demands ingenuity and skill. Still, a multiplicity of theories may be obtained concerning the same surface locution, and it is the function of Harman's five principles of theory-preference and others like them to "tamp down" alternatives and (with luck) select the best.

Davidson has made a strong case, I think, at least for the claim that a theory of meaning for a language ought to contain a Tarskian truth definition for that language. I shall not yet try to evaluate his further thesis that a truth definition *exhausts* all that could reasonably be asked of a theory of meaning, since the term "meaning" has not been given any fixed use. In the course of this book I shall be arguing that "meaning" as used preanalytically is a vague (and indexical) umbrella term that covers a surprising number of distinct and only loosely related notions; philosophic appeal to the preanalytical idea of "meaning" is therefore both fruitless and positively harmful. Much more will be said on this topic in my concluding chapter.

Chapter 2

T-Sentences

In this chapter I shall say more on the nature and the role of T-sentences.

1. "Empirical Bite" and the Threat of Trivialization

T-sentences of and about English often look trivial to people who already speak English; students reading Davidson frequently complain that the T-sentences he mentions are "tautologous" or the like. Of course this is a mistake. Any such T-sentence states a brutely contingent fact about a string of English words and must be substantively learned, either directly or (much more likely) by inference from Tarskian base clauses that are learned, by anyone who undertakes to master English. The reason English T-sentences sound uninformative to people who already understand English is that such people already know the axioms and routinely (if tacitly) compute the truth-conditions of target sentences by derivation from axioms.[1] An easy way of seeing that T-sentences are highly substantive is to consider a truth definition for German that is written in English, containing such T-sentences as " 'Der Schnee ist weiss' is true iff snow is white." An even easier way of seeing it is to consider a T-sentence of a truth theory for a language that one does not know at all, being assured by a bilingual speaker of that language that the T-sentence is true. The suspicion of triviality will evaporate.

Nevertheless, two commentators on Davidson have argued more sophisticated versions of the triviality charge. Edwin Martin (1972) and Stephen Stich (1976) each contend, on the basis of distinct but related arguments, that a truth theory for English in MetaEnglish can easily be constructed that meets Davidson's condition of learnability by a finite human speaker but does absolutely nothing to illuminate the structure of the target language or the meaning of a target sentence, even when one fully appreciates the relevant derivations. Thus, if Martin and Stich are right, a truth definition *per se* does nothing to reveal meanings; moreover, Davidson's claim that a truth definition is necessary for an adequate theory of meaning becomes vacuous because of the trivially ready availability and hence point-lessness of such a truth definition. So their arguments demand re-sponse. I shall concentrate on Stich's, which I take to be the more formidable of the two, adverting to Martin's where appropriate. But let us begin by looking at a suggestion that I have often heard in informal discussion: that we know all the instances of Convention T simply in virtue of having assimilated Convention T itself as a schema, and not in virtue of having implicitly mastered all the com-plexities of English syntax and semantics.[2] We might try to enforce this intuition as follows: Suppose the expression "si eurt ffi" is a phrase of a language called Erewhon, and means (in English) "is true iff." This is all I know of Erewhon, and I assume the reader does not know any more than that either. Now, take any sentence of Erewhon, such as "Wons si etihw." None of us knows what that sentence means, since all we know of Erewhon is the phrase "si eurt ffi." But on the basis of the latter knowledge we can construct a T-sentence for "Wons si etihw," written in MetaErewhon:

(1) "Wons si etihw" si eurt ffi wons si etihw.

And we know merely in virtue of its form that this T-sentence is true. The argument generalizes: Given that we have a truth predicate for a language, we automatically and trivially know of each T-sentence for that language that that T-sentence is true. Therefore, knowledge of T-sentences plays no significant role in semantical understanding, since we know the T-sentences without having the faintest idea even how to express their target sentences in our own language.

This argument is seductive, but ineffectual. Knowing that " 'Wons si etihw' si eurt ffi wons si etihw" is true is not the same as knowing that "Wons si etihw" is true iff ϕ, where 'ϕ' is replaced by some English equivalent of "Wons si etihw," any more than knowing that "Kaherizash kazink kazoo" is a true sentence of Scribo (say, on the grounds that a Scribo speaker who is a reliable authority on his sub-ject has asserted it) suffices for knowing that ϕ, where 'ϕ' is replaced by an English equivalent of "Kaherizash kazink kazoo." Of course we can know of any T-sentence that it is true, without understanding its semantics or even understanding *it;* what we cannot know with-out a Tarskian truth theory for the containing language is the T-sen-tence itself.

Let me expand on this for a moment. One thing Davidson is con-cerned to explain, as I understand him, is how speakers *know that* ϕ, where 'ϕ' is a schematic letter that takes T-sentences as substituends. A speaker's being able to "produce" in some purely mechanical sense a T-sentence such as " 'Donald is wrong' is true iff Donald is wrong" (cf. Martin (1972, pp. 126–128)) does not even begin to explain how that speaker knows *that* "Donald is wrong" is true iff Donald is wrong. Nor, for that matter, does the speaker's even knowing that the T-sentence he produces is true. Suppose a speaker knows that " 'Donald is wrong' is true iff Donald is wrong" is a true sentence. How would the speaker then come to know that "Donald is wrong" is true iff Donald is wrong? The speaker could derive this second bit of information from the first only with the aid of a meta-T-sentence: " ' "Donald is wrong" is true iff Donald is wrong' is true iff 'Donald is wrong' is true iff Donald is wrong." But our problem was to explain how the speaker knows any T-sentences in the first place.

Appeals to a speaker's knowing (however "tacitly") *that* such-and-such have fallen on deaf ears in recent philosophy of grammar, and rightly so. It is absurd (in part because both gratuitous and pointless) to think that a speaker bears any epistemic relation to the syntactic processes that structure his utterances. A grammar is merely a third-person functional analysis of the speaker's syntactic ability and habits; at best it describes a form of "knowing how." Now, why should a semantics be required to do more? Martin is concerned to assimilate semantics to syntax in this regard; therefore, he might respond that it is as fanciful to require that a competent speaker have propositional knowledge of T-sentences as it is to suppose that speakers have such knowledge of syntactic transformations. After all, few ordinary speakers are semantically articulate. Indeed, Michael Devitt (1981) has expressly attacked the idea that "semantic propositional knowledge" figures in linguistic understanding, on the very plausible grounds that a child or other primitive speaker might understand most sentences of his natural language perfectly well and yet lack any overtly semantical concepts such as (in our case) truth (pp. 97ff.).

There are three initial reasons for dissatisfaction with this response: (i) Some speakers *are* semantically articulate, or can easily be made so, and do know that ϕ, where 'ϕ' is replaced by any of an indefinite number of T-sentences. This propositional knowledge needs explaining, over and above the speakers' manifested semantic ability alone, since articulate speakers have it simply in virtue of knowing English and a rudimentary metalanguage (the same is not true of the speakers' grammars). (ii) Martin seems to assume that what primarily interests Davidson is speakers' ability to go around spitting out T-sentences. But he thereby misapprehends Davidson's purpose. T-sentences are important to Davidson because he wants a semantical *theory* to entail them. What interests him about the be-havior of ordinary speakers is their ability to spit out *the target sentences themselves in appropriate circumstances* and to respond ap-propriately to the tokenings of other speakers (see chapter 9). And this ability seems to involve (to put it crudely) looking at states of affairs in the world and correlating them with the target sentences. These "correlations" that speakers make may be correct or incorrect, so it seems perfectly natural, if psychologically problematic, to talk of the speakers' tacitly knowing that ϕ, where 'ϕ' is replaced by a T-sentence. And it is just such knowledge that a mere T-sentence-emitting device will be unable to explain. (iii) Plausible as it is, I think Devitt's argument must be resisted. His suggestion is that someone might understand enormous parts of English, say, without having the concept of truth. I am not so sure. The reason is that if David Lewis (1969, 1975) is right, part of what is required for a lan-guage L to be *my* language (hence for it to be understood by me) is that I observe and expect other speakers to observe a "Convention of Truthfulness and Trust" directed upon that language; I try to restrict my utterances to truths of L and expect others to do the same. If this is right, then in order for me to have English as my native tongue, I must in some sense have and apply the concept of truth in English, however tacitly.[3]

Stich's version of the trivialization charge avoids the objection I have made against the naive idea of simply schematizing T-sen-tences; Stich offers an actual (deductive) Tarskian truth definition for a fragment of English, which truth definition is constructed in a triv-ial, mechanical way that robs it of any semantic explanatory power even though it is both deductive and finite. Before we can evaluate this argument, however, we must appreciate a somewhat different difficulty for Davidson that does seem to me to constitute a flaw in his program.

The Metatheory has it that the truth-condition assigned to a target sentence is just that which has been assigned to that sentence's logi-cal form (SR) by the formal truth definition for the canonical idiom in which the SR is written, it being assumed that the syntactic trans-formations that generate the target sentence from its SR *preserve* truth-conditions. The sentence of our metalanguage that states this truth-condition (the right-hand side of the relevant T-sentence) will tend to mirror the grammatical structure of the SR and therefore (since logical form notoriousiy differs from surface form) will *not* mirror that of the target sentence, whether our metalanguage is itself a formal language or just a technical version of English. For example, consider the analysis of English action sentences that Davidson proposes in (1967a). That analysis assigns to the English sentence "John walked in the street" a truth-condition something like "There is an event e such that e is a walking and e is past and John is e's protagonist and e takes place in the street." Clearly the resulting T-sentence,

(2)   "John walked in the street" is true iff there is an event e such that e is a walking and . . . [etc.],

does not meet Harman's requirement that its right-hand side be the very sentence mentioned on its left-hand side; more importantly, it does not even meet the weaker requirement that its right-hand side be a metaphrase translation of the sentence mentioned on its left-hand side. Our T-sentence's right-hand side is more like a good old traditional *philosophical analysis* of our target sentence. It seems, then, that Davidson and we have been equivocating on the term "T-sentence": a truth theory may systematically entail assignments of truth-conditions to target sentences and yield "T-sentences" in that weak sense, without entailing actual instances of the schema " 'p' is true iff p." Let us call a typical output of such a theory an "impure" T-sentence and call an actual instance of " 'p' is true iff p" a "pure" T-sentence.

We might suppose that pure T-sentences might be derivable in some standard way from impure T-sentences, perhaps with the aid of the assumption that syntactic transformations preserve truth-value. But this does not seem to be the case. Take the impure T-sentence (2), concerning "John walked in the street." Suppose we have a syntax that shows how to derive this target sentence from the logical form exhibited on the right-hand side, and suppose we do assume that the transformations of this syntax preserve truth-value. I still do not see any way of deriving the pure T-sentence

(3)   "John walked in the street" is true iff John walked in the street,

without confusing use and mention at some point.

Thus, a Davidsonian theory of a language yields only impure T-sentences at first go, and there is no reason to think that pure T-sentences will be obtained by further deduction. Now, Davidson's vaunted claim to "empirical bite" is based on his theories' ability to entail pure and hence uncontroversial T-sentences for testing, the virtue of pure T-sentences being that they are highly substantive *and* at the same time obvious to ordinary speakers. Impure sentences are just as substantive, but are not obvious. For one thing, as Stich observes, ordinary speakers untrained in logic will not even understand the formal notation in which the official theorems of our truth definition will be written. For another, impure T-sentences are likely to be controversial even among people who do understand them; it is hard to think of even a single case of traditional philosophical analysis that prevails uncontested, and I see no reason to expect that individual impure T-sentences will fare any better. For that matter, plausible-seeming impure T-sentences can easily be false, and their falsity may remain undetected indefinitely. (For example, for years it went unnoticed that the then standard lexical-decomposition analysis of "x killed y," roughly,

(4) $(\exists z)(DO(X,z)$ & $CAUSE(z,$
      $COME\text{-}ABOUT(NOT(ALIVE(y))))))$,

is too weak.) Thus, impure T-sentences resemble theoretical claims themselves more than they count as observational consequences whose correctness can be checked immediately against experience. The moral, I think, is that Davidson's pride in his theories' "empirical bite" is largely unearned. Unless someone can find some further uncontroversial assumption(s) that will allow us to obtain pure T-sentences given impure T-sentences, we shall just have to settle for theories that are not nearly as testable as Davidson intended.[4]

However, there are two consoling qualifications to be noted: (i) We still have plenty of empirical checks on our truth theories besides their entailed T-sentences, even though the latter are what Davidson has emphasized. A truth theory predicts felt implications, felt equivalence, felt ambiguities, and other semantic properties. And a semantics fashioned according to the Metatheory contains a complete syntax for English and so predicts grammaticality/ungrammaticality and other syntactic properties as well; this alone is a quantum jump forward from traditional Russellian analysis. So the loss of pure T-sentences does not push the linguist entirely back into his armchair. (ii) The observation that pure T-sentences (unlike impure ones) are "obvious to ordinary speakers" is a bit misleading. Pure T-sentences written in English are obvious to speakers of English only because such speakers understand both target language and metalanguage. In general, no T-sentence—pure or impure—will be directly testable by any person unless that person understands both target language and metalanguage; so perhaps it is not so embarrassing that our official impure T-sentences can be effectively tested only by informants who understand the formal notation in which they are written. Once this limitation is understood and accepted as inevitable, impure T-sentences themselves will not be totally useless in empirical confirmation, for we do usually understand their right-hand sides and we do have some intuitions about whether the assigned truth-conditions do match their respective target sentences, even if those intuitions are somewhat suspect in that they are harbored by philosophers and linguists. Methodologically, perhaps we should reinstate a weaker version of Harman's principle (1), to the effect that T-sentences ought to be kept as "pure" as possible, which is tantamount to keeping them as testable as possible. This would still help to "tamp down" semantical theories.[5]

Let us now finally consider Stich's trivialization argument. As his example Stich chooses the class of action sentences (merely because that is a fragment that has interested Davidson) and offers a simple-minded, mechanical truth definition for it. Though his truth definition is totally unilluminating with regard to the real semantic properties of the target sentence, he argues that it is empirically as well-confirmed as Davidson's own theory of the same target sentences in (1967a). Moreover, it has not been shown that anything in Davidson's methodology establishes a preference for his theory over Stich's, and so one is tempted to infer (though Stich does not draw this conclusion explicitly) that Davidson's theory *qua* finite and deductive entailer of T-sentences is totally unilluminating also, and the idea that a semantics for English *qua* Tarskian truth definition alone could explain our understanding of the target sentence is an illusion.

Stich notes (p. 217) that not all the expressions of the semantical metalanguage Davidson uses in writing (impure) T-sentences for English are entirely ordinary expressions of English themselves. For example, Davidson's theory of action sentences makes use of somewhat artificial nominalizations of English verbs, as in "There is an event *e* which is *a walking* by John and which took place in the street." Stich adds that in order for us as theorists to understand new primitives of our own theories such as "is a walking," we must learn to use them when they are first introduced into the theories. Thus, he points out, it seems we are entitled to introduce whatever primitives we like into our canonical metalanguage, if (a) we have a firm *enough* intuitive grasp of their meanings that we will be able to understand and test the resulting T-sentences, and (b) the introduction of the new primitives will help us arrive at a simple and empirically adequate truth theory for our fragment.

With this justification, Stich introduces a new primitive into *his* metalanguage: the predicate "Wahr." "Wahr" attaches to the name of a sentence of the target language, and the resulting predication will be true iff the target sentence named is a true one. This metalinguistic turn is a surprise; is Stich going to explicate action sentences by assigning them SRs that refer to and predicate things of sentences?

Never mind. Let us just see how the truth definition works out. Stich stipulates that two principles govern "Wahr" and the quote-name-forming operator that generates substituends for "Wahr (———)":

(5) a. (n)(y)(If n = ′ ′ ′ ⌢y⌢ ′ ′ ′ and y is a sentence in English, then Denotation(n) = y).

  b. (S)(n)(If n is the quote-name of an English sentence and S = 'Wahr'⌢n, then S is true iff Wahr(Denotation(n))).

Now, how shall we deal with a sample action sentence and display its truth-condition using Stich's theory? Take "John walked in the street." Stich proposes to translate this sentence by a simple syntactic operation into our canonical metalanguage and then to derive a T-sentence written in that metalanguage that assigns an empirically adequate truth-condition. The operation takes any target sentence and translates it as the result of prefixing "Wahr" to its quote-name. (We know that this syntactic operation will preserve truth-value, because of the way in which "Wahr" was intuitively explained when it was introduced.) Thus, Stich's translation scheme will take "John walked in the street" over into his canonical "Wahr('John walked in the street')." We may now use Stich's truth theory to derive an impure T-sentence. Let n be "John walked in the street." Then

(6) Denotation(" 'John walked in the street' ") = "John walked in the street." (By (5a))

Now

(7) "Wahr('John walked in the street')" is true iff Wahr(Denotation(" 'John walked in the street' ")). (By (5b))

Substituting on the basis of the foregoing identity,

(8) "Wahr('John walked in the street')" is true iff Wahr("John walked in the street").

From this T-sentence for our canonical metalanguage and the fact that Stich's translation preserves truth, we may conclude

(9) "John walked in the street" is true iff Wahr("John walked in the street"),

an assignment of a truth-condition to our original target sentence. Stich's theory could be used in this way to derive an assignment of a truth-condition to each sentence of English; thus, he claims, his theory "entails all the T-sentences" just as Davidson's event theory does, and very simply too. The fact that Stich's theory does nothing at all to reveal the actual semantic structure of action sentences and has nothing to do with the way in which English speakers actually interpret and understand action sentences just goes to show that Davidson's theory does not do these things either merely in virtue of yielding a Tarskian truth definition that meets Davidson's fundamental constraints (completeness and finiteness).

There are two reasons why Stich's argument should not elicit pessimism. First, there certainly is a difference of principle between what Stich has done here and what Davidson has achieved in the case of action sentences. We know that "John walked in the street" *is* Wahr, when we do, only because we already know that "John walked in the street" is *true*, that being the only handle we were given on the term "Wahr" when it was introduced. This is why, as Stich intends and avows, his entailed "T*-" or impure T-sentences are unilluminating as a theory and completely useless from the standpoint of testability. But we seem to be able to know that there occurred a walking by John that took place in the street, quite independently of our knowing of any sentence of our target language that it is true. This is one difference that makes Davidson's theory nontrivial. It is also just what Stich evidently means to deny:

> . . . it is by a wholly analogous procedure that Davidson introduces his three-place predicate 'kicked' [in the analysis of 'Shem kicked Shaun,' or his predicate 'is a walking' in the analysis of 'John walked in the street,'] as well as such oddities as his two-place predicates 'At' and 'Through' [and 'In']. Our grasp of these unfamiliar lexical items is secured by pairing canonical sentences containing them with vernacular sentences whose truth value they share. (p. 217)

Unless I have misunderstood Davidson, Stich is wrong about this. It would be strange if we did secure our grasp of the quaint predicates of our Davidsonian metalanguage by explicating them in terms of object-language sentences' being true. How *did* we come to understand such predicates as "Kicked(x,y,z)" or "e is a walking"? Presumably by slight deformation of their English ancestors, attendant upon a small shift of ontological set. "Think now that 'John walked in the street' describes an *event*, which we might refer to using a derived nominal such as 'John's walking in the street.' That event is an event of a certain familiar kind—it's 'a walking,' if you like." Philosophers perform this useful sort of grammatical distortion all the time, in pursuit of one ontological readjustment or another, and have no trouble understanding the results thereafter. We understand terms like "is a walking" by analogical extension of our understanding of their original, natural forms, aided by preexisting parallels in natural English (e.g., the ordinary nominalization of "Shem killed Shaun" into "the killing of Shaun by Shem"). I could not say how all such analogical extensions work in detail, but I do not see why we should accept Stich's assertion that we understand new canonical terms instead by having them defined for us in terms of the truth of sentences of the target language.[6]

Stich's truth theory differs from Davidson's in another way (this is my second objection): though it entails impure T-sentences, it does not make any of the further empirical predictions that Davidson's theory makes rather elegantly.[7] The truth-conditions it assigns to action sentences (or to sentences of any other complex kind, even simple conjunctions) do nothing at all to predict or explain felt implications, since all the interesting semantic material that has anything to do with these implications is packed irretrievably inside the relevant quote-name. Therefore, Stich's theory is neither illuminating nor testable on the matter of felt implications, whereas Davidson's is both. More generally, Stich's proposal does absolutely nothing to *clarify* the troublesome construction of either the target language or the home language, or to reveal how the expressions involved make their respective semantical contributions to sentences in which they occur. This too distinguishes the case of semantics from that of syntax; a grammar does reveal and explain syntactical contributions as fully as anyone might wish.[8] And the foregoing two points about semantics show why Stich's "theory" is negligible compared to Davidson's. Finally, Stich sells the Metatheory a bit short by neglecting the importance of mapping target sentences and logical forms into each other by means of already existing syntactic transformations. Thus, Stich appreciates neither a theory's yield of *syntactic* predictions nor the strong form of compositionality imposed on the theory by the interlocking of semantics with syntax.[9]

I conclude that Davidson's program for semantics survives attempts to trivialize it, even though the theories it induces will not have *all* the "empirical bite" Davidson has claimed for them. But the enterprise of writing truth definitions for natural languages will be seen to run into difficulties of a more specific and technical sort. I shall discuss one of these in the remaining section of this chapter, and then move on in chapter 3 to an instance of the main sort of problem that interests me: the accommodation by the Metatheory of contextual factors and the playing off of semantics against pragmatics.

2. Ambiguity

The remaining problem I have in mind is raised by K. Parsons (1973) (and echoed by Tennant (1977)). It is that when a natural-language sentence is ambiguous and must be assigned more than one truth-condition, things go awry. I shall focus just on what I take to be Parsons's main argument against the Davidsonian program as it stands. She points out (p. 383) that a pure T-sentence directed upon a target sentence containing an ambiguous term gives the wrong truth-condition for that target sentence no matter which natural suggestion we follow regarding the assignment of an extension to the ambiguous term. Let us examine this claim.

Ambiguity is a semantical property that of course is *not* preserved by syntactic transformations throughout an SR's trip to the surface, since one important function of running the transformations in reverse (i.e., of assigning logical forms to surface structures) is that of disambiguation. (This recalls the problem of "empirical bite" that we addressed in the preceding section.) Clearly the (primitive) expression of our canonical idiom will be univocal, since by hypothesis that idiom is a regimented and logically perfect formal language. We may imagine that those expressions are spelled as their English counterparts are, but with subscripts added. Thus, the surface structure "T is a bank" must be regarded as having (at least) two possible syntactic derivations or transformational histories, one that derives it from the logical structure "$BANK_1(T)$" and one that derives it from "$BANK_2(T)$" (these being distinct logical structures, since "$BANK_1$" and "$BANK_2$" are distinct lexical primitives). Now, on the Davidsonian program as we presently understand it, the truth-condition assigned to a target sentence is just the truth-condition assigned to that sentence's SR by the formal truth definition for our canonical idiom; and since our formal metalanguage will have to be at least as rich as the canonical idiom itself, it will have to be a disambiguated language too, or at least contain distinct metalinguistic counterparts of "$BANK_1$" and "$BANK_2$," if not those very terms themselves. Therefore, it seems our truth theory for the target language will assign alternative truth-conditions to "T is a bank," one being "T is a $Bank_1$" and the other being "T is a $Bank_2$."

Now, as things stand, we would expect our truth theory to entail each of the following T-sentences:

(10) "T is a bank" is true iff T is a $Bank_1$.

(11) "T is a bank" is true iff T is a $Bank_2$.

But (10) and (11) jointly entail the falsehood "T is a Bank$_1$ iff T is a Bank$_2$." How may we avoid generating unwelcome biconditionals of this sort?

Obviously sentences are not true or false *simpliciter*, but only relative to a disambiguation; they are true or false *on a reading*. One and the same sentence can be true on one reading and false on another. What is "a reading"? Given our semantic-syntactic format to date, the easiest thing to say is that sentences are true or false relative to *derivations*, that is, relative to transformational histories. Let us add a "history" parameter to our truth predicate: "T is a bank" is true *on H_1* iff T is a Bank$_1$, but "T is a bank" is true *on H_2* iff T is a Bank$_2$.

Though straightforward and natural, this solution is not at all satisfactory, for several reasons. First, in adding "H" we have sabotaged the still fairly nice empirical character of (some) T-sentences; for a person would have to know at least the outlines of a derivation of a target sentence in order to test the relevant T-sentence for any value of H. Perhaps we should therefore cease to identify "readings" with derivations and interpret them in a less theory-laden way. Certainly there are behavioral marks of target-language ambiguity in radical translation situations. Suppose the native we are translating applies the (apparent) morpheme "nosdivad" consistently to fried foods and also to prime numbers, but to nothing else, and suppose that frequently when we ask "Nosdivad here?" the native balks and seems to want clarification. It seems reasonable in such a case to conclude that "nosdivad" is ambiguous in Native between "fried food" and "prime number." But as Parsons points out, any way we find of spelling out the idea of truth "on a reading" will have to work without overt or covert appeal to the notion of a sentence's having different meanings, for it is just that notion that our truth definition is supposed to help characterize.[10]

Harman has reminded me (in correspondence) that the variable in the left-hand side of Convention T is supposed to be replaced by a *structural-descriptive* name of a target sentence; he adds that such a name will describe whatever structure is relevant to semantics. This is an important clarification, since until now we have assumed that the (quote-)name that replaces the variable describes only surface structure, or even just spelling. Harman's point would obviate the ambiguity problem, certainly, and without requiring us to posit a "reading" parameter for the truth predicate. So let us look further at what it involves.

What, and how much, structure *is* relevant to semantics? In Parsons's case we would have to see only to disambiguating surface *words*, but what about target sentences that are syntactically rather than lexically ambiguous, such as the venerable "Flying planes can be dangerous," "John saw her duck," "They are visiting doctors," "The mouse tore up the street," and "The shooting of the hunters was deplorable"? It seems our structural-descriptive sentence-names will have to expose their referents' transformational histories, and *a fortiori* their logical forms, in order to disambiguate those target sentences fully. For our purposes, we could simply regard the variable in "*s* is true iff *p*" as ranging over *pairs* of target sentences and SRs from which they can be generated. Thus, a T-sentence might be

> (12) ⟨"The mouse tore up the street," "(∃e) (TEARING-UP(e) & PROTAGONIST(the mouse, e) & PAST(e) & RECIPIENT(the street, e)"⟩ is true iff there is an event *e* such that *e* is a tearing up and the mouse is the protagonist of *e* and *e* is past and the street is the recipient of *e*.

But the SR that is the second member of a pair named on the left-hand side of such a T-sentence is written in our canonical idiom, which is an artificial formal language for which we have stipulated a Tarskian interpretation. Thus, to use a phrase of Stich's, we "already know" that that SR has the truth-condition expressed on the right-hand side of the T-sentence, and our theory's predicting that it does is no substantive empirical virtue. If our modified T-sentence is to serve as a point of empirical contact with the world, then, this must be still in virtue of what it says about the target sentence that is the first member of our designated pair. Intuitively, what it says is that *insofar as* that target sentence can be generated from the SR with which it is paired, and insofar as it can have that SR as its logical form, it has the truth-condition expressed on the T-sentence's right-hand side. But this too is trivial. Since we "already know" (because we have stipulated) that the SR has the truth-condition in question, we "already know" that, *if* our target sentence (or any other sentence) has the SR as its logical form, it has that truth-condition also.

Harman might reply that the pair-name that replaces '*s*' encapsulates the information that the target sentence does have, or can have, the SR as its logical form. If we understand the pair notation in this way, our T-sentence will make the appropriately substantive prediction about the target sentence's truth-condition after all. But our T-sentence will also be substantive in an undesirable way: it will contain the factual claim that the mentioned canonical formula *is* the target sentence's SR on one of the target sentence's readings. On the present modified way of formulating T-sentences, therefore, the foregoing example is a substantive piece of theory and not an observation sentence that we can use to *test* our theory by measuring it against the judgments of ordinary English speakers.

Such a T-sentence does intuitively make one prediction that ordinary speakers can test, though: our pairing implies that the target sentence *can* have the truth-condition expressed on the T-sentence's right-hand side, one of its readings; and that prediction is both nontrivial and "observational," so something of Davidson's intention can be salvaged. But how are we to express that prediction more precisely? We cannot very well write *it* as an elaborately modified sort of T-sentence. " 'The mouse tore up the street' can be made true by the fact that *p*" introduces opacity on the right-hand side and the unclear metaphysical notion of "a fact" as well. I am not sure how best to express the idea that our target sentence "can on one of its readings have" the truth-condition expressed by our original T-sentence, except by reverting to the jargon of our theory and phrasing the idea in terms of transformational histories and the truth-conditions of SRs. I hope that there is a better solution than this, but in what follows I shall just go back to relativizing our truth predicate to "readings," by way of labelling the problem.

The apparatus we have developed so far enables us now to address a "counterexample" or puzzle case put forward by Hintikka (1975a). Hintikka calls our attention to the target sentence "Any corporal can become a general." According to the Metatheory on its strictest interpretation, our theory of meaning for English should entail

(13)   "Any corporal can become a general" is true iff any
       corporal can become a general,

which entails

(14)   "Any corporal can become a general" is true if any
       corporal can become a general,

which is a superficial grammatical variant of

(15)   If any corporal can become a general, then "Any
       corporal can become a general" is true.

But, Hintikka contends, (15) is false. The surface interaction of "if" with "any" at the head of the antecedent clause forces an existential rather than a universal reading of the antecedent, as in

(16)   If there is any corporal who can become a general, then
       "Any corporal can become a general" is true,

which is false. Hintikka concludes that the Metatheory leads to falsehood because of its neglect of the "interplay" between the quantifier (which Hintikka argues is *itself* everywhere a universal quantifier) and its surface-grammatical environment.[11]

As Hintikka goes on to observe, any reader who is already well immersed in the Davidsonian program will feel cheated in one way or another by this argument. Hintikka responds to several *prima facie* objections, including the obvious retort that (15) is ambiguous between a reading on which it does follow from (13) but is true and a reading on which it is false but does not follow from (13). He cites two principles concerning the behavior of the word "any" in rebuttal of the claim that "any" is ambiguous (the principles are that "any" always reflects a universal quantifier, and that it normally takes wider scope than "if").

Even if "any" itself is lexically univocal, we may not legitimately infer that a clause in which it occurs (as in (15)) is univocal, precisely because scope options may be available. Indeed, we need not actually pinpoint a specific ambiguity in order to verify our suspicion that we are the victims of a sleight-of-hand. Let us try to cast Hintikka's argument in the vernacular of our own semantical format to date. On our approach, the right-hand side of a T-sentence will be a fully disambiguated formula of our canonical idiom that is or represents the logical form of the target sentence mentioned on the left-hand side, as determined both by semantical and by syntactic evidence. What might we expect the logical form of "Any corporal can become a general" to be? By itself that sentence is unambiguous (at least with regard to "any"); it has no existential reading. Therefore, letting "Cx" abbreviate "x is a corporal" and "Gx" abbreviate "x can become a general," a plausible T-sentence directed upon "Any corporal can become a general" would be

(13')   "Any corporal can become a general" is true iff $(x)(Cx \supset Gx)$.

Certainly there is no additional true T-sentence to the effect that our sentence is true (on a different reading) iff $(\exists x)(Cx \supset Gx)$ or iff $(\exists x)(Cx \; \& \; Gx)$. Now let us unleash Hintikka's argument: Our theory of English entails (13'), we may suppose. (13') in turn entails

(14')   "Any corporal can become a general" is true if $(x)(Cx \supset Gx)$,

which is a superficial grammatical variant of

(15')   If $(x)(Cx \supset Gx)$, then "Any corporal can become a general" is true.

However, (15') is true, not false, and is not equivalent to (16) on any reading of either. Therefore, it seems Hintikka's objection does not work against our version of the Metatheory, even if it does work against the versions that may have been suggested (or even intended) by Davidson in his writings.

Hintikka seems to anticipate a confrontation between his argument and a theoretical format such as ours:

> . . . the force of my counterexample is not destroyed by the cheap expedient of formulating the Tarski condition ["π is true if and only if p"] by using a formalized language instead of English as the metalanguage in which [T-sentences] . . . are formulated. This attempt will lead to expressions whose truth-value has not been determined, for the original sentence p will of course have to figure in a substitution-instance of the schema ["π is true if p"]. . . . Hence these substitution-instances . . . will then be mixed expressions containing both formalized connectives and English words like 'any' and 'can'. There simply are no grounds for deciding how 'any' behaves vis-à-vis such foreign elements as formalized connectives, and consequently no satisfactory solution is available in that way. (p. 210)

I do not follow this point, if Hintikka indeed means it to be addressed to a response of the type I have just made to his original argument. The relevant substitution-instance of "π is true if p" in my response is (14'). The original sentence or formula "$(x)(Cx \supset Gx)$" does figure in (14'), though the target sentence itself is only mentioned. Is (14') "hence" a "mixed expression containing both formalized connectives and English words like 'any' and 'can'"? Not unless one counts the English words appearing inside mention-quotes (or spelled using Tarski's concatenation sign) as genuine occurrences of those words that mix semantically with the formalized connectives on the right-hand side of (14'), which seems just wrong. Perhaps Hintikka's point is rather that "there simply are no grounds for deciding" whether a formula of our canonical idiom *is* the logical form of the target sentence in question and so should be appearing as the right-hand side of the relevant T-sentence. But if the methodology sketched in chapter 1 is viable, as it seems to be, there are such grounds. Our evidence for assigning "$(x)(Cx \supset Gx)$" to "Any corporal can become a general" as its logical form is (a) equivalence felt by anyone who knows both English and elementary predicate logic, (b) confirmed predictions of entailment relations, truth-values in counterfactual situations, and the like, and (with luck) (c) an independently recoverable syntactic history that generates the target sentence from the formula.

Hintikka anathematizes our use of a disambiguated canonical idiom as a "cheap expedient." Relative to Davidson's program as originally conceived, advertised as affording T-sentences of 100% purity, this slighting characterization is fair. But we have already seen independently that such purity cannot in principle be achieved. No obtainable truth theory for English is going to permit the derivation of *absolutely* pure T-sentences if it assigns truth-conditions to target sentences on the basis of those sentences' logical forms; and Parsons's problem requires still further sullying precisely in order to bracket ambiguities. Perhaps these facts are to be regretted as weakening "empirical bite," but they are facts and our truth-theoretic format has incorporated them. The result (that our T-sentences will be written in a disambiguated formal language) is thus a natural and unavoidable feature of the containing enterprise itself, and thus is no "cheap expedient" given the already established limitations of that enterprise. [12]

Parsons's problem about ambiguity constitutes our formal theory's first brush with the human facts of natural language and its context-relativity; sentences of natural languages display (sometimes massive) ambiguity, whereas formulas of formal languages do not. The next six chapters will explore more such confrontations and try to reconcile the crystalline abstract character of formal semantics with the rough, gritty, smelly realities of human linguistic activity. (Prefatory note: Readers who wish to hear more about non-truth-functional sentence operators and possible-worlds semantics should turn to the Appendix at this point (unless they would prefer to wait a while before even looking at another T-sentence). Readers who go on to chapter 3 and find it too finicky to be interesting should skip down to chapter 4.)

II
Pragmatics

Chapter 3

The Parameters of Truth

---

1. Deixis

Davidson (1967b) points out a problematic way in which natural languages differ from standard formal languages: they contain deictic elements, such as demonstratives, personal pronouns, and tenses, which cause sentences' truth-values to fluctuate from context to context. The specific difficulty this creates is felt when we try to offer a "pure" truth-condition for a sentence containing such an element:

> " 'I am wise' is true if and only if I am wise," with its bland ignoring of the demonstrative element in "I" comes off the assembly line along with " 'Socrates is wise' is true if and only if Socrates is wise" with *its* bland indifference to the demonstrative element in "is wise" (the tense).
>
> What suffers in this treatment of demonstratives is not the definition of a truth predicate, but the plausibility of the claim that what has been defined is truth. For this claim is acceptable only if the speaker and circumstances of utterance of each sentence mentioned in the definition is matched by the speaker and circumstances of utterance of the truth definition itself. (p. 463)

If the theorist formulating a truth-condition for "I am wise" has a particular utterance of that sentence in mind that has been made by someone other than the theorist himself, the resulting pure T-sentence may easily be false. But if the theorist has no particular tokening of the target sentence in mind and is assigning his pure truth-condition out of context, the resulting T-sentence will still be false or truth-valueless because of the truth-valuelessness of its left-hand side prior to contextual disambiguation.

To avoid disconfirmation of this sort, Davidson proposes to add two argument places to the truth predicate employed in T-sentences, relativizing truth to a speaker and a time. Thus, the theory will entail sentences like the following (pp. 319–320):

(1) "I am tired" is true as (potentially) spoken by p at t if and only if p is tired at t.

(2)   "That book was stolen" is true as (potentially) spoken by
p at t if and only if the book demonstrated by p at t is
stolen prior to t.

Davidson remarks that his relativization is "not puzzling." This is
not entirely accurate, as we shall see, but for now we may agree at
least that the impurities introduced into our T-sentences' right-hand
sides are fairly harmless from the standpoint of "empirical bite" (cf.
(1973, p. 85)).

A first question about Davidson's formula, "as (potentially) spoken by," concerns the role of the parenthesized "potentially." Why
does Davidson include it? Presumably because he wants a truth
definition for a natural language to encompass all the grammatical
strings of that language and not just those that happen to have been
tokened by real speakers in the actual history of the human race. If
this is his motive, then his person parameter "p" must be taken to
range over *all* persons (or potential speakers) and his time parameter
"t" to range over all times at which utterances might have been
made. This makes truth a counterfactual relation between sen-
tence(-type)s, persons, and times, *tout court*: S would be true if spoken by p at t iff q.

This last counterfactual formulation is ambiguous. Its most natural
reading is (S is spoken by p at $t > S$ is true in p's mouth at t) $\equiv q$, $>$
being the subjunctive conditional operator. But this will not do. Let S
be the target sentence "I am not speaking now," and replace "q" by
"p is not speaking at t"; the result is

(3)   ("I am not speaking now" is spoken by p at $t > $ "I am
not speaking now" is true in p's mouth at t) $\equiv p$ is not
speaking at t,

which is false (its counterfactual left-hand side is false but its factual
right-hand side remains true).[1] Perhaps Davidson's subjunctive operator should instead take the entire T-sentence-like biconditional as
its scope:

(4) S is spoken by p at $t > (S$ is true in p's mouth at $t \equiv p$ is
not speaking at t).

This interpretation of Davidson's counterfactual formula yields the
right result for "I am not speaking now," namely,

(5)   "I am not speaking now" is spoken by p at $t > $ ("I am
not speaking now" is true in p's mouth at $t \equiv p$ is not
speaking at t),

which is true; if p were (foolishly) to utter our target sentence at t, the sentence would be false in p's mouth, and p would be speaking at t, so happily both sides of the biconditional would be false. But this second interpretation faces problems of its own: (i) Since $>$ induces referential opacity throughout its scope, the truth-conditions assigned to indexical target sentences on the present proposal would be opaque, and hence not "fully explicit" (see the Appendix), and hence not ultimate truth-conditions in the sense we intend. (ii) Since our counterfactual formula concerns only a hypothetical state of affairs in which "I am not speaking now" *is* uttered, it does nothing to accommodate the fact that in some sense that sentence is true *of p* at t if p is not in fact speaking at t. (More on this below.) (iii) Fairly cumbersome extra apparatus would have to be added to a Tarskian theory of a language in order for an extension of that theory to entail subjunctives like our counterfactual formula. It is not clear what the axioms of the extended theory would look like.

I have characterized Davidson's move as making truth a counterfactual or subjunctive relation between a sentence, a person, and a time. But there is no particular reason for insisting that the relation be subjunctive, even though Davidson's own formulation has suggested this. In fact, our three difficulties are swept aside at one stroke if we simply eliminate the subjunctive element and take truth to be a straightforward extensional relation between a sentence, a person, and a time, as in

(6)   "I am tired" is true with respect to (or *of*) p and t iff p is tired at t.

There is no opacity here; the intuitive fact that "I am not speaking now" is true of a nonspeaking person is accommodated; and it is easier to imagine simple axioms that could be added to a truth theory for English in order to generate relativized T-sentences of this sort.

Actually our achievement so far is pathetically small. We have pointed the way toward writing T-sentences for first-person indexicals, but we have not yet even addressed demonstrative pronouns, much less all the other multifarious sorts of deictic elements with which natural language abounds. Our new extensional interpretation of Davidson's strategy, applied to Davidson's own account of demonstratives (neglecting tense for now), yields modified T-sentences such as

(7)   "That book was stolen" is true of p and t iff the book demonstrated by p at t was stolen.

T-sentences containing the technical predicate "is demonstrated" are somewhat impure (given the indefinitely many types of contextual "demonstration" that occur in human speech, "demonstrate" here must be regarded as a heavily theory-laden term); and it is unpalatable to have to introduce an anthropological predicate of this sort into a formal truth theory. But the complications are only beginning. Even if we settle for handling demonstrative pronouns in our modified Davidsonian way, we have yet to address ourselves to second- and third-person pronouns, tense, spatial indexicals, discourse indexicals, and so forth. Can all these different sorts of deictic elements somehow be explicated in terms of the speaker and the time determined by a context? How many further parameters must be added to our truth predicate?

Montague, Scott, and others[2] have solved this problem of the proliferation of parameters by relativizing truth simply to an "index," viz., to an n-tuple whose members are all the objects determined by a context that can affect the truth-values of sentences relative to that context. An "index" was originally taken to be an octuple whose members are a world, a time, a place, a speaker, an audience, a sequence of indicated or demonstrated objects, a discourse-segment, and a sequence of assignments to free variables; other contextual factors may be added as needed. The truth predicate itself need have only one argument place added. An example of a resulting T-sentence is

(8)   "I am here now" is true of (or "at") $\langle w,t,l,p,a,i,d,s \rangle$ iff p is at l at t.

It is a bit disturbing that an n-tuple of this type has no definite number of members, even though we have avoided the more crucial awkwardness of not knowing how many argument places our own truth predicate has. We cannot rest content with the canonical eight members, as Lewis (1972) points out; for there are more than eight distinct types of contextual factors that affect the truth-values of English sentences, and they cannot be explicated in terms of a small set of basic factors (such as speaker and time) unless we sully the right-hand sides of our T-sentences by injecting any number of corresponding technical terms into them. Lewis mentions[3] a sequence of "prominent objects," a causal-history-of-acquisition-of-names coordinate, and a "delineation" coordinate for resolving vagueness. There are plenty of others: restriction classes on quantifiers,[4] demonstrative elements for ordinary proper names (even the highly distinctive name "William Lycan" is deictic, as a matter of fact), and hidden parameters of all sorts.[5]

The difficulty of determining the number of members in an "index" is not a terribly serious theoretical problem, so far as I can see. Every contextual factor we can discover that does affect truth-value is one that real speakers and hearers do in fact negotiate, or it would not have occurred to us as an example. If speakers and hearers do negotiate it, then they have the resources for negotiating it, however arcane it may be. If English speakers and hearers in fact have all the context-interpretive skills requisite to negotiating all the discoverable factors, then (however many and various these factors may be) there is some definite number of them, even if as theorists we cannot say in advance what this number is. Therefore, we can be confident that the addition of members to our "indices" would come to an end at some point; the Montague-Scott method will work in principle, and the indices we actually represent in our ongoing truth theory for English may be regarded as proxies for the full-scale versions, proxies that suffice to represent at least all the elements of the full-scale versions that we are interested in at the moment.[6]

A more serious difficulty for the Montague-Scott approach is revealed by a return to our trick target sentence, "I am not speaking now." Montague, Scott, *et al.*, would write a T-sentence for this item as

(9)   "I am not speaking now" is true at $\langle w,t,l,p,a,i,d,s \rangle$ iff p is not speaking at t.

Now, a T-sentence of this type captures the intuitive fact (noted above) that "I am not speaking now" is true of or "at" a person who is not speaking. But it does nothing to illuminate (or even predict) the crucial and distinctive fact that that target sentence is false whenever uttered (and, accordingly, would never seriously be tokened by anyone who understands English). Tyler Burge (1974) puts forward a compelling general thesis that subsumes this point:

> . . . sentences containing a demonstrative element are on some occasions not just *true of* or *false of* objects, but are *true* or *false*. Thus, we should alter the traditional notion that truth is a property only of closed sentences. (p. 213)

On the Montague-Scott approach, truth and falsity *tout court* are entirely undefined even for utterances or utterance-tokens produced on particular occasions; sentence-types are true or false "at" one index or another, and that is the end of the matter. In this way, Montague and Scott treat indexical sentences as though they were simply open sentences. "I am not speaking now" will be like any other deictic sentence—true at some indices, false at others. But what of the highly salient fact that "I am not speaking now" is *false*, period, whenever it is tokened?

What is needed is a notion of truth that applies to particular utterances. But truth in this contextually fixed sense and truth in the context-relative sense must be interdefinable; it is unthinkable that they are unrelated in meaning. We have two choices: to define context-relative truth in terms of contextually fixed truth, or vice versa (there being no third notion in play). The former strategy would bring us back to counterfactual formulations (e.g., "An indexical sentence-type S is true at $\langle w,t,l,p,a,i,d,s \rangle$ just in case, were p to utter a token of S at t, p's utterance would be true"), and counterfactual formulations of this sort have been seen to lead to trouble. It seems better instead to define truth for particular utterances in terms of context-relative truth. An utterance will be true just in case the context in which it occurs determines a particular sequence of contextual elements fitting the form of an "index," relative to which sequence the sentence-type of which the utterance is a token is true.

Burge rightly complains of Davidson's analysis that it "does not bring out any feature common to the logical or grammatical form of sentences containing 'I' and the tenses, on one hand, and sentences containing other demonstrative constructions, on the other" (p. 207). He adopts a conditional format for T-sentences,[7] using the vernacular of Davidson's theory of action verbs. Simply paraphrased, his T-sentence for "That dog is an animal" reads, "For any x and y, if x is an act of reference by p at t to y with 'that$_9$' [a particular occurrence of the demonstrative "that"] in 'That dog is an animal,' then 'That dog is an animal' is true with respect to p and t if and only if the object which is y and which is a dog is an animal" (p. 211).[8] Burge expands this treatment to include the first-person pronoun by adding a special clause; we might express the resulting T-sentence as, "For any x and y, if x is an act of reference by p at t to y with 'I$_n$' in 'I am F,' *and y* $= p$, then 'I am F' is true with respect to p at t (or, the token of 'I am F' produced in the tokening that contains x is true) iff the thing which is y is F." And he expands the treatment to include tense by the same expedient (p. 217). We may expect Burge to handle other deictic elements in the same way, viz., by adding distinctive special clauses to the antecedents of his conditionalized T-sentences. The T-sentence for a target sentence containing fifteen or twenty deictic elements of various kinds would be quite complex.

How will Burge's approach handle "I am not speaking now"? Burge treats sentences containing indexicals simply as open sen-

tences whenever they are not being tokened (p. 213), so he captures
the intuition that our trick sentence is true of anyone who is not
speaking. What if the sentence is tokened? Burge will presumably
add another special clause to a new conjunct of the antecedent of the
relevant T-sentence in order to accommodate the indexical "now":

(10)   For any x_1 y, x_2, and t', if x_1 is an act of reference by p
       at t to y with 'I_n' in 'I am not speaking now,' and $y = p$,
       and x_2 is an act of reference by p at t to t' (occurring
       in the same tokening as x_1) with 'now' in 'I am not
       speaking now,' and $t' = t$, then 'I am not speaking now'
       is true with respect to p and t (or, the token of 'I am
       not speaking now' produced in the tokening that
       contains both x_1 and x_2 is true) iff the thing which is y
       is not speaking at the time which is t'.

If we add a few obvious auxiliary assumptions (such as that a person
who performs an act of reference is speaking at the time), we obtain
the desired conclusion that if a person p utters our target sentence on
any occasion, then p's utterance is false; cumbersome though it is,
Burge's strategy explains this.

But we ought to be able to do something about the cumbersome-
ness. If a sentence does contain fifteen or twenty distinct deictic elements, the Burgean T-sentence directed upon it will be impossible to
state on a single page, since (a) a separate conjunct is required in its
antecedent for each element and (b) "special clauses" must be added
to most of the required conjuncts. There is a second source of dissatisfaction with Burge's method as well: on that method, facts such
as that "I" always refers to the speaker and that "now" refers to a
time interval within which it occurs are incorporated into the semantics of English and surface in the T-sentences generated by our
truth theory, *via* the "special clauses" that Burge adds *ad hoc* to the
already special conjuncts of their antecedents. But this is peculiar.
Facts such as those are facts about the dependence of extension on
context; to know that "I" always denotes the speaker is to know a bit
of the pragmatics of English, intuitively speaking, not semantics. To
put the point in a slightly different way: Semantics need not and
should not attempt to explain its own primitives. We should take
specifically semantic relations, such as denotation and satisfaction,
as primitives in semantics, and leave the explication and contextual
computation of them to philosophy and to pragmatics, respectively.
If we can do this, we will also expunge anthropological notions such

as "referring to y with" and "being in p's present at" from truth definitions themselves and thereby streamline our truth theory considerably.

Developing a suggestion of Harman's, I propose to relativize our truth predicate itself to a context C and to invoke an assignment function α that takes a sentence and a context as input and yields a sequence of denotata for the sentence's deictic elements in that context.[9] Indeed, we may think of α as a complete valuation function for all the referring terms in our target language if we like, including nondeictic names if any. A typical truth theorem might be

(11) "I am tired now" is true in C iff α("I," C) is tired at α("now," C).[10]

And we may subsume our denotation function "Den," presupposed above, under α also:

(12) "Jones is tired now" is true in C iff α("Jones," C) is tired at α("now," C).

This establishes our context-relative notion of truth. We obtain the notion of contextually fixed truth by noting (following Scott Weinstein) that any actual utterance context determines a sequence of persons, objects, times, etc., as a designated value of α. The utterance of "I am tired now" produced in a particular context C* will be true (*tout court*) iff α("I," C*) is tired at α("now," C*).

This method of assignment functions keeps our semantics simple and our T-sentences as pure as they could have been in any case: no "special clauses" are needed. It nicely localizes the problems of indexical relativity. It also affords a convenient way of understanding a number of different recent enterprises in pragmatics and in the philosophy of language: viz., we may see these enterprises respectively as theories of *how to compute* α for arguments of particular types. For example, rival theories of reference for proper names may be understood as being rival theories of how α is to be computed when α takes a proper name as input (one theory tells us to find a description that the name is abbreviating in the context and then to find the object that uniquely satisfies the matrix of that description, another theory tells us to find the dubbing that figured in the etiology of the use of the name in that context and then to find the object dubbed in that dubbing, and so on). Our commonsense pragmatic account of the use of personal pronouns tells us how to compute α for "I" (find the utterer), "you" (find the utterer's audience), "it" (a very complex rule here), etc. A theory of ostension tells us how to compute α for demonstratives (also a very complicated business, given the prevalence of deferred ostension).

Let us make sure that in moving to the method of assignment functions we have not sacrificed any of the advantages of earlier strategies. We have preserved the generality, or potential generality, of the Montague-Scott and Burge approaches. We have avoided, or at least swept under the rug, the minor problem of determining the precise number of context-dependent features. We have captured the sense in which indexical sentences are true of or "at" randomly chosen objects (since α takes any sequence of appropriate objects as an argument until a particular context has fixed a designated sequence). We have accommodated Burge's insight that indexical sentences when tokened have contextually fixed truth-values. Now, can we explain the anomalousness of "I am not speaking now," "I do not exist," and the like? A T-sentence for the former will be

(13)   "I am not speaking now" is true in C iff α("I," C) is not speaking at α("now," C).

And our pragmatics will contain a valuation rule for "I" to the effect that α("I," C) = the utterer in C. "I am not speaking now" is false whenever uttered because for any C, α("I," C) is speaking at α("now," C).[11] "I do not exist" will be seen to behave similarly once we have given an explicit account of tense.

A feature of all the approaches to representing deixis that we have surveyed so far is that relevant features of context are presented as *entities* to which reference is made—persons, places, time intervals, and so on. This feature will cause us some trouble in the next section, but for now I conclude that the method of assignment functions is the best approach to deixis of those we have considered. Let us now see how we might apply it to tense.

2. Tense

In relativizing truth entirely to indices, Montague and Scott say nothing about the exact relations that they presume to hold between the members of an index and the deictic elements occurring in a sentence being evaluated with respect to that index. Therefore, Montague and Scott have made no commitments concerning the actual syntactic and semantic structures of target sentences that they propose to treat (though they would have to do so if they were to spell out a sample T-sentence for each of our common deictic constructions). Our method of assignment functions has already made a substantive commitment that puts at least a weak constraint on our semantical treatments of the constructions. α as I have described it is a *valuation* function, and thus has been construed as assigning individual denotata to English words as if those words were free variables or individual constants. Thus, the method requires that we suppose all such words to be singular terms denoting contextual features considered as entities: "that" is a singular term that denotes an object; "I" is a singular term that denotes a person; "now" is a singular term that denotes a time interval; and so on. So far our commitments seem harmless enough, since all these semantical claims are fairly obviously true. But it will not always be so congenial to see deictic elements as reflecting this kind of singular reference from the target language into the world.

Consider past tense, as in "That book was stolen." Superficially, anyway, the tense of that sentence is marked by the auxiliary "was" and the suffix "en." Adhering to our standard procedure, we will expect α to look at the surface construction "was ... en" and somehow relate it (given a context) to a "time." To *what* time, since our target sentence does not allude to any particular past time? Our original picture of the functioning of α does not fit the case of past tense. Of course, we can try to make it fit. Let us hypothesize that a surface tense indicator such as "was ... en" *lexically decomposes*; in particular, let us suppose that "was ... en" is (somehow) transformationally derived from a more complex underlying construction that contains a quantifier: $(\exists t)(\text{EARLIER-THAN}(t, \text{now}) \& \ldots)$. Thus, the logical form assigned to our target sentence would be something like

(14) BOOK(that$_1$) & $(\exists t)$ (EARLIER-THAN(t, now) & $(\exists e)$
      (STEALING(e) & VICTIM (that$_1$, e) & AT(e,t))).

(I adopt Davidson's "event" analysis for the action verb.) This proposal has some semantic merit, or at least squares well with what we think the target sentence means; there is even some syntactic reason to accept it.[12] The actual syntactic derivation would be awkward, however; somewhere in our sentence's syntactic history some rule or rules would have to fuse the time quantifier and the primitive predicate EARLIER-THAN and the bound time variable together and lexicalize the result as "was ... en." If this should prove to be what actually happens, our problem about applying α to our target sentence's tense is solved. We would simply look at the surface element "was ... en," read backward through the transformations, find that the indexical element underlying it in semantic structure is our old friend "now," and let α assign "now" a denotatum in the context as usual (viz., the time at which the utterance occurs).

Until now, for naturalness of exposition, I have talked as if α took surface English words such as "I," "that," and "now" as arguments. If this were so, then we would be regarding α as itself being a composite function, consisting of a function from English words to specially flagged free variables of our canonical idiom and a function from the free variables to denotata, for on the Metatheory, expressions of English have the semantical properties they do only in virtue of bearing determinate syntactic relations to expressions of a truth-defined formal language. In the case of "I," "that," and "now" themselves, the first of these two component functions is a trivial lexicalizing operation; "I" is seen to reflect a variable flagged as a first-person pronoun, "that" to reflect a variable flagged as a demonstrative, and "now" to reflect a variable flagged as an indicator of the present time.

This model breaks down in the case of "was ... en." The first component function would have substantive syntactic work to do; it would have to compute "was ... en"'s lexical decomposition, reversing the fusing transformation and perhaps others and recovering the occurrence of the underlying indexical "now." Worse, what would be recovered *is* "now" rather than an indicator of any past time; the second component function would assign the time of utterance to "now" and hence to "was ... en" *via* the first component function. Thus, α, which is supposed to be a valuation function, would end up assigning "was ... en" a "denotatum" that is intuitively wrong. But notice that *any* denotatum that α might assign to "was ... en" would be intuitively wrong, since past tense does not pick out any specific time prior to the time of utterance. Thus, past tense is just not indexical in the same way in which "now" is,[13] and so its failure to fit our two-stage conception of α is no embarrassment to that conception in particular. It requires a new model altogether.

We may still ask whether the two-stage conception of α should be retained in any case. My view is that it should not. One reason is (again) that α's job is to provide (partial) semantic interpretation, thereby plugging holes in sentences' logical forms. According to the Metatheory, semantic interpretation attaches primarily to SRs and only by syntactic extension to the natural-language sentences whose SRs they are; indeed, more generally, the job of syntactic transformations as I conceive them is only to translate already fully interpreted logical forms into sentences of natural language. To continue to think of α as taking surface elements as arguments would be to blur this autonomy or role (if only terminologically, since of course our composite function from surface elements to denotata *exists* in any case). This concern becomes a bit more telling when we recall

those surface singular terms that (unlike "was ... en") do have denotata of their own but that have those denotata only in virtue of
undergoing substantive syntactic decomposition. An example would
be a context-bound description, such as "the fat one" in "The fat one
looks like the guy that robbed my ice-cream truck"; it is plausible to
think that that phrase contains an underlying demonstrative.[14] A
better example would be a singular term containing a hidden parameter, such as "the woman on the left" (left of what?). Each of these
two sample phrases denotes what it denotes only in virtue of its
grammatical relation to a logical constant occurring in its containing
sentence's SR, and the second, for that matter, denotes something
distinct from what α is going to assign to that underlying logical
constant. Indeed, if we understand the second description in Russell's way, that description will not be *assigned* a denotatum at all,
even though it has one. These facts make it even clearer that α oper-
ates *in propria persona* on constituents of logical form rather than directly on surface elements. Let us therefore jettison the first "stage"
of our original conception and identify α with the second stage alone;
α shall take flagged free variables of our canonical idiom as its arguments. A hearer takes in "That book was stolen" and decodes it into
its SR in the ordinary way. The SR will contain a free variable "n" as
argument and assign it the time of utterance as its value. Similarly,
"The woman on the left stole it" will be decoded into an SR containing a hidden parameter. α will take this parameter as argument and
assign it a contextually appropriate value, such as another woman.
(Actually, there will be a second parameter as well, denoting our
vantage point.) In each case the semantic interpretation or truth-
condition of the SR will be completely determined by α before it begins its trip to the surface.

Our lexical decomposition hypothesis concerning "was ... en"
would incidentally solve a problem that was first put to me by
Michael DePaul and is also raised by Burge (p. 217). Our sentence
"That book was stolen" may be tokened as a reply to a question, such
as "Why did the librarian get so upset last Monday?" In order for
"That book was stolen" to be a *true* answer, it does not suffice that
the book was stolen in 1914; the book has to have been stolen on or
just before the Monday in question. How is our T-sentence to display
this? The answer is that we can restrict the time quantifier we have
already posited, and speak in effect of there being a "time" *within a
certain salient period* prior to now; and that is just the idea we want.
This feature is a mark in favor of our hypothesis. It is thus not unreasonable to suppose that "was ... en" is the surface reflection of a
restricted time quantifier, the parameter of restriction being assigned

a denotatum (a reference-class) by α as usual. (Burge chooses instead to posit an underlying interval demonstrative flagged for pastness (pp. 217–18).)

But our hypothesis has two related drawbacks. First, as I have mentioned earlier, we ought to have metamethodological qualms about allowing a part of our methodology (our format for writing T-sentences) to prejudge a substantive claim within the science whose methodology it is. Our use of assignment functions to accommodate the context-relativity of tensed sentences depends on a substantive semantical claim (our hypothesis), plausible or not, and it is in fact a controversial one. Second, according to the Metatheory that claim must be backed by a determinate syntax, and though there is some syntactic evidence in its favor (see note 12), no credible transformational history leaps to mind (are there *really* rules of quantifier-crunching, EARLIER-THAN-obliterating, etc.?).[15] These difficulties are much exacerbated by the fact that "was . . . en" and other tense markers are only the tip of a huge iceberg. Fillmore (1975) catalogues and discusses any number of covertly deictic elements in surface English (including verbs such as "come," "go," "bring," and "take," adverbs and prepositions that hide subtle spatial orientation parameters, and more) that would require very specific semantic treatment and bluntly *ad hoc* syntactic analysis if they were to be treated by our method of assignment functions as I have presented it so far.[16]

David Lewis has offered what may seem to be a competing and superior account (1980). In developing this sophisticated successor of the Montague-Scott approach, Lewis supposes that a tense marker such as "was . . . en" reflects an operator whose function is to "shift" individual features of context. Thus, "That book was stolen" is derived from the application of "It was the case that" to "That book is stolen," where ⌜It was the case that s⌝ is true at t iff s is true at some time prior to t. Time is a "shiftable" contextual feature for us, in that English contains an operator whose job it is to shift it[17] ("shiftability" is thus language-relative). An "index" is now taken to be *any* n-tuple whose members are specifically shiftable contextual features of the appropriate sorts. Lewis (following Hans Kamp (1971) and David Kaplan (1977)) argues for *double* indexing: he claims that target sentences generally are true or false only relative to a context *and* to an index in the new, broader sense. A context determines an index (the "index of" that context), but some indices do not correspond to any (actual) contexts (consider one whose speaker coordinate did not even exist at its time coordinate); the argument for double relativity is that (i) contexts are needed to assign referents to straightforward indexical terms like "I" and "now," (ii) "indices" in the new sense are needed to account for the shifting of contextual features by special operators, and (iii) neither can do the other's job.

Lewis's account predicts the correct truth-value for "That book was stolen" without a lexical decomposition hypothesis: "That book is stolen" is assigned a truth-value relative to any index containing the demonstrated book as a member (or at least any containing the book and a time at which the book exists). "That book was stolen" is adjudged true on an utterance-occasion iff "That book is stolen" is true relative to at least one index whose time precedes the time of utterance. That is all there is to it; no commitment is made concerning either the semantic or the deeper syntactic analysis of "was ... en" (though Lewis does evidently presuppose that *present*-tense verbs such as "is" reflect singular references to the present time). Is Lewis's approach not then more economical and less tendentious?

Interestingly, the truth-*condition* that Lewis ends up assigning to "That book was stolen" is equivalent to that determined by the method of assignment functions combined with our lexical decomposition hypothesis: "That book was stolen" is true at C and at C's index i_C (hence at C, period) iff "That book is stolen" is true at C and at some index i' that differs from i_C only in that its time coordinate is an earlier time than is i_C's time coordinate. But this is just to say that "That book was stolen" is true (in C) at t iff "That book is stolen" is true at some time t' prior to t, that is (again adopting Davidson's analysis of action verbs),

(15) BOOK (that$_1$) & $(\exists t')$(EARLIER-THAN(t',t) &
       $(\exists e)$(STEALING (e) & VICTIM (that$_1$,e) & AT(e,t')))),

the general form of our own truth-condition for "That book was stolen."

All the better, one might suppose, for both Lewis's approach and ours; the two at least superficially distinct approaches have led to a single result. But Lewis's approach based on shiftiness has dispensed with my tendentious semantic and syntactic assumptions. Same result with lighter baggage; should not Lewis's approach be preferred outright?

The trouble is that if we simply rest content with Lewis's method we will merely have replaced tendentious syntax by unknown or unspecified syntax. According to the Metatheory, an English sentence such as "That book was stolen" is the output of a syntactic process whose input is that sentence's logical form; it is in this way that we transcend Russell's difficulty of lacking any determinate relation in nature that makes that logical form *that* sentence's logical form (cf. chap. 1, sec. 1, and the Appendix). If we were to adopt Lewis's method rather than our lexical decomposition hypothesis, then, we would simply be presupposing that "was ... en" somehow decomposes into a time quantifier, EARLIER-THAN, etc., without explicitly saying that it does.[18] Lewis's method, if folded into our overall semantical format, is a notational variant of our own approach.

There is an alternative interpretation, which is much more likely to represent what Lewis himself has in mind. Probably he intends the operators that shift contextual features to be semantic and syntactic primitives. For example, "was ... en" would reflect a sentence operator in logical form, PAST, which operator is awarded its own clause in the recursion that defines truth for the containing canonical idiom; that clause would read something like,

(16)   ⌜PAST S⌝ is true at t iff $(\exists t')$(EARLIER-THAN(t',t) & S is true at t').

This puts us back in the business of assigning pairs of distinct logical forms to each target sentence (cf. Harman (1972b, p. 301)). The official logical form or syntactic "deep structure" would be quite shallow; "was ... en" would be derived directly and unproblematically from the underlying PAST + VP. But the logical formula that expresses the fully explicit truth-condition for the whole target sentence (recapitulated a few paragraphs back) would be much "deeper" and less pure, and would bear no apparent syntactic connection to the "official" logical form. Moreover, like the possible-worlds analysis of "BELIEVE(S,p)" (see the Appendix), it would be doing all the semantical work; the target sentence's interesting semantical properties would be explained by this second, deeper logical structure and not by "PAST(p)." (As before, the "official" logical form is not taken seriously, and we sacrifice the identification of underlying syntactic structure with logical form.) Thus, it seems to me, this interpretation does not improve the status of Lewis's method with regard to either psychological reality or "empirical bite"; it replaces our tendentious syntax, not by unspecified syntax, but by nothing.[19]

It may be replied that my demand for a psychologically real connection between surface structure and logical form is unrealistic and unreasonable; perhaps we should be content with a "pure" (as opposed to an "applied") semantics that makes no claim to psychological reality and little claim to "empirical bite," but merely predicts truth-values and felt implications of complex sentences. An instrumentalistic account of this kind would be highly congenial to Quine or to anyone else who already believes that sentences' "semantic properties" are indeterminate and obtain only relative to a stipulated

interpretive scheme; it should be *un*congenial to anyone who holds
that sentences of natural languages have meanings and other semantic properties as a matter of fact and that the job of a linguistic
semantics is to get at these and use them in the explanation of behavioral regularities. Perhaps instead we should maintain (following
the last line of defense that I hypothetically attribute to the possible-worlds theorist in the Appendix) that the connection between
"PAST(p)" and "$(\exists t')$(EARLIER-THAN(t',t) & AT(t',p)" is simply a
matter of word-meaning, hence a lexical convention; as before, then,
the psychological basis of the connection is not syntactic, but is the
sort of psychological mechanism that underlies one's grasp of any
convention, whatever sort that is.

   Yet I am not sure that my own account and the present variant of
Lewis's differ more than terminologically. Any psychological realist
(i.e., any semanticist who intends his theory as a functional description of a real mechanism hypothetically operating within speakers)
presumably holds that in some sense we think in SRs—that some or
all of our mental operations are defined over formulas of the canonical idiom that underlies the public languages we speak. But when we
voice our thoughts we utter, not logical formulas, but English sentences. Therefore, some psychological mechanism takes (if you like)
mental tokens of SRs and turns them into our familiar surface structures.[20] Does it matter whether we call this mechanism "the activa-
tion of a convention" or a "syntactic transformation"? Well, perhaps
it does, depending on what cognitive science will ultimately discover
about the psychological basis of conventional association on the one
hand and about the psychological realization of syntax on the other.
For example, there might turn out to be a systematic learning-
theoretic difference between the two that would decide our question
one way or the other. I should say the empiricalness of the question
remains itself an empirical question.

3. Vagueness and Hedging

We have seen two types of context-relativity in virtue of which natural languages differ from formal languages: sentences of natural
languages frequently stand in need of syntactic or semantic disambiguation by context, and their truth-values frequently fluctuate as a
result of contextual changes in the referents of indexical terms. There
is still a third type of context-relativity that marks natural languages
off from formal languages; its source is the fact that their terms are
commonly *vague*. The prevalence of vagueness in natural language
makes itself felt in each of two ways: (i) Within a given context,

speakers' judgments of a particular sentence's truth-value may be hesitant in a certain characteristic way and/or qualified by the sort of expression commonly called a "hedge." (ii) One and the same sentence's truth-value may be felt to fluctuate from context to context, not because of any obvious deictic element reflecting a hidden free variable or parameter, but because contexts themselves impose differing *standards of strictness* on discourse taking place within them. Accordingly, a truth-based formal semantics for a natural language must find a way of representing, predicting, and accounting for these two sorts of phenomena.

Much has been written by philosophers and logicians on the topic of vagueness, particularly on its role in traditional philosophical puzzles such as the Sorites Paradox, but the only linguist I know who addresses himself specifically to the treatment of vagueness in truth definitions for natural languages *tout court* is George Lakoff (1973a). Availing himself of the resources of fuzzy logic and fuzzy set theory, developed chiefly by Zadeh (1965, 1971, and elsewhere) (see also Goguen (1969)), Lakoff makes an impressive start. I shall summarize what I take to be the high points of Lakoff's discussion and then comment on some problems that I think will cause some trouble for his account; I believe the problems can eventually be overcome.

Lakoff begins by citing evidence of empirical studies to the effect that ordinary speakers treat class or category membership as being a matter of degree, even in the case of natural kinds. Informants ranked birds, for example, on a continuum of "birdiness," and vegetables on a continuum of vegetableness.[21] If category membership is a matter of degree, Lakoff argues, then so is *truth:* if a chicken is a bird, not unequivocally, but only to a degree of (say) .6, then a sentence such as "Henrietta is a bird [Henrietta being a chicken]" is *true* only to a like degree. This in turn suggests that sentences in general are true only (relative) to degrees; some perhaps are unequivocally or absolutely true, but this is only the limiting case of a real-valued continuum of trueness and falseness.

If truth is not simply a binary matter but comes in real-valued degrees ranging from 0 to 1, then any notion that is defined in terms of truth must be understood accordingly. This includes obviously semantic notions such as entailment, as well as more commonsensical concepts such as knowing, being right, being a reliable informant, lying, and any further concepts defined in terms of these. The social repercussions of Lakoff's thesis may be serious,[22] but fortunately we need deal only with the semantic difficulties in particular. Thanks to fuzzy techniques, logic can be extended in suitable ways: "degrees of entailment" can be defined in terms of degrees of truth; binary

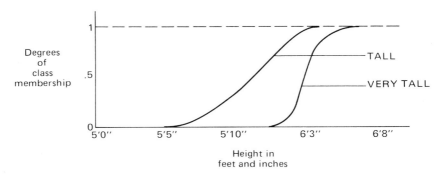

Figure 1

truth-functions can be shown to be merely degenerate cases of real-valued truth-functions, and so on.[23] Interesting and important new light can be shed on the semantic properties of tautologies and contradictions (p. 465).

Lakoff takes as his paradigm of a vague notion one that depends for its satisfaction on some fairly crisply measurable real-valued magnitude. For example, a person is *tall* to such-and-such a degree (is a member of the class of tall things to that degree) depending on that person's *height* as measured in some chosen unit of length by a real number. A person's degree of tallness, and the truth of the claim that that person is tall, can be plotted as a function of the person's height; a 5'3" American male is tall to degree 0 or vanishingly close to it; a 6'8" human person of any nationality or sex is absolutely tall, tall to degree 1 (or tall, period); a person of intermediate height is tall to a degree somewhere in between.

It is at this point that Lakoff brings out the role of "hedges." He construes them, not implausibly, as expressing functions from degrees of class membership (themselves the values of functions from magnitudes such as height) to new degrees of class membership. An obvious example is the word "very," which we may regard as being an intensifier. The graph in figure 1 represents the algebraic effect of applying "very" to "tall." "Very" serves to boost the requirements for being tall; it is harder to be *very* tall than merely to be tall (i.e., it requires a greater height). Other hedges, Lakoff says, are *de*intensifiers; an example might be "on the . . . side." The values of "on the tall side" would be shifted to the left from the values of "tall" itself, just as the values of "very tall" were shifted to the right; the curve generated by "on the tall side" is flattened a bit, just as that generated by "very tall" is steepened. Still other hedges have mixed intensifying and deintensifying effects.[24] Lakoff defines a "hedge" as an operator "whose job is to make things fuzzier or less fuzzy," but this is a slip, I think; a hedge such as "very" or "on the . . . side" does not change "tall"'s (original) *degree of fuzziness* (this notion being so far undefined for Lakoff's purposes), but simply shifts the degrees of class membership conferred by a given value of the underlying magnitude.[25]

The exact effect that a hedge has on its operand(s) may be determined by multiple combinations of factors (Lakoff brings out some typical such factors on pp. 477ff.). Further, Lakoff argues, the effects of standard hedges are themselves context-dependent (pp. 484ff.): the hedge "technically" depends on whose technical standards are relevant; "strictly speaking" and "loosely speaking" depend on a set of background interests relative to which "strictness" is defined; and so on. Lakoff does not pretend that the incorporation of vague locutions and hedges that operate on them is simple or trivial, but only that such things can be represented within a slightly elaborated truth-conditional format, using formal resources that already exist.

I want to raise four questions concerning Lakoff's program; I am hopeful that they can be answered satisfactorily, though I am not at all sure how the answers will go. The first is this: Can every fuzzy predicate be regarded as expressing a function from some underlying real-valued magnitude to a degree of class membership? "Tall" fits into this paradigm well, since height is a magnitude that we are used to characterizing by means of numerals. But it would be risky to assume that all fuzzy predicates work in this way. Consider the adjective "smart"; it is fuzzy, as shown by its occurrence in constructions like "Jones is sort of smart," "Nancy is smarter than Bill," "If you were even a little bit smart you'd buy University of North Carolina stock," "Peter is marginally smart," etc. Is smartness a function into degrees of class membership from an underlying real-valued magnitude? To affirm this, I should say, is to take a stand on the bitterly controversial IQ issue, viz., to claim that degrees of smartness are the values of a function from real numbers that number quantities of intelligence. Or consider "good" in its aesthetic sense, as in "Tallis's *Lamentations of Jeremiah* is pretty good" and "Technically speaking, Golding's *Free Fall* is a good novel." Are degrees of aesthetic goodness based on the values of some underlying magnitude (even one that varies from art work to art work)? It does not seem so. For some fuzzy concepts there will be no Lakovian graphs even though there will be degrees of instantiation. This does not affect Lakoff's account of hedges, since hedges spit out degrees of class membership as values given degrees of class membership as arguments, regardless of the ways in which the latter have been determined. Lakoff's graphs would be replaced by a much more complex and sophisticated account of the multifarious factors that determine degree of class membership.

Turning now to the second question: What of compositionality? It is not generally noticed that a single sentence may contain many, many fuzzy terms and hedges in rich and complex mixtures. Take the comparatively ordinary sentence, "I guess I'd have to say that that very bald man punching Eskimo Nell is a philosopher, in an odd sort of way." "Have," "bald," "punching," and "philosopher," at least, are vague here; "very" and "in an odd sort of way" are presumably predicate-modifying hedges; "I guess" and "I'd have to say that" are sentential hedges. Each of the vague terms makes its semantical contribution to the truth-value of the entire sentence in a way that comes in degrees: a thing is not simply within or simply outside the extension of "bald," period, but within it to such-and-such a degree, and that fact must be represented by the recursive rules that tell us how the truth-value of a clause in which "bald" occurs depends on the (degree of) satisfaction and nonsatisfaction of "bald." As we have seen, the semantical role of a predicate-modifying hedge such as "in an odd sort of way" is to shift its operand's degree of satisfaction to a new (here, higher) degree, and thereby affect the truth of the whole containing sentence. Presumably the function of a sentence-modifying hedge is to shift its operand's degree of truth to a new degree (typically a higher one). Therefore, the degree of truth ultimately assigned to the foregoing target sentence in context is a complicated function of the degrees of satisfaction and the types of shiftiness attaching to its individual semantic contributors (each of which itself may be a complicated function of any number of recondite factors; again see Lakoff, pp. 477ff.). An adequate fuzzy semantics for English would have to specify all these complex dependencies, and this is no easy job. Fuzzy propositional logic is a beginning. Fuzzy predicate logic and fuzzy set theory are well under way. But truth-functions, predication, and set abstraction may not be the only syntactic/semantic devices at work underneath natural languages; there may be sentence operators, predicate modifiers, and other things, any of which might admit of vagueness. Any new *kind* of operator superadded to standard predicate logic and set theory will demand a new, distinctive fuzzy logic of its own, and any such logic will have to interpenetrate with the best going fuzzy logics already in force. Fuzzy semantics as a whole must be fully compositional: for each semantic primitive that admits of vagueness of any sort, our truth theory must supply a fuzzy valuation; any relevant recursive rule in the truth theory must accept semantic values ranging between 0 and 1 as input; a recursive rule must be written for each different hedge in the target language; and the result must be the full determination of an overall degree of truth for any grammatical string in the target language given any set of fuzzy values for that string's primitive elements.

I have said that guaranteeing compositionality is not an easy job. But Frege and Chomsky never promised us a rose garden. Notice too that the job must be a possible one, since as hearers we *do* in effect compute degrees of truth for English sentences in context on the basis of the degrees of satisfaction (or whatever) of their parts; therefore, there must be a way in which we do it and hence a way of doing it. I find it hard to imagine a way that differs much from Lakoff's, elaborated in the directions I have indicated.[26]

My third question concerns *prima facie* distinctions within the class of ostensible degree predicates. Are all degree predicates fuzzy? It seems not; for not every predicate that admits a *comparative* construction (and hence may be satisfied to one degree or another) yields a fuzzy truth-value. Even when one thing may be more F (or F-er) than another thing, it still may be that sentences of the form "X is F" are absolutely true or false, since "X is F" may be ruled absolutely true iff X is F to any degree > 0 and absolutely false otherwise. An example might be the predicate "morally wrong"; an act is morally wrong if it is wrong even to the smallest degree, even though some acts are more heinous than others. Or consider the predicate "takes up space": an object takes up space, period, if it takes up any space at all, even though some objects take up more space than others.

Even within the class of genuinely fuzzy predicates, important distinctions can be made. Some predicates, like "tall," express simply functions from a real-valued underlying magnitude. Others, like "bird" and "vegetable," are more complex; multiple criteria govern a thing's degree of membership in their extensions, and these criteria are not easily articulated, much less weighed against each other.[27] Still others are *elaborately* elusive family-resemblance terms ("game," "work of art," "philospher," etc.), of the sort that may make us despair of finding an algorithm that determines membership in their extensions; in a finished lexical semantics, I suppose, these would receive "paradigm-case" analyses based on broad ranges of informants' judgments.[28]

My fourth question concerns the best way of dealing with the context-bound nature of vagueness in writing T-sentences. So far we have (*faute de mieux*) allowed context to disambiguate sentence-types by fixing the value of a "reading" parameter attaching to our truth predicate; and we have handled all other contextual variation in truth-value by relativizing truth to our assignment parameter α. Can we represent the resolution of vagueness, in terms of contextual "standards of strictness," within this already existing framework, or must we introduce new apparatus? Lewis simply adds a "standard of strictness" coordinate to each of his indices, but Lakoff evidently thinks yet another parameter of truth is needed, for he advocates speaking of truth *to such-and-such a degree,* effectively making truth a relation between a sentence-type and a number. It would be nice to be able to avoid the latter expedient, since the ordinary notion of truth has already suffered considerable attenuation at our hands.[29] Contextual resolution of vagueness is not a matter of syntactic ambiguity, so the relativization of truth to "readings" does not seem to bear on the present problem; can we then (following Lewis) subsume the resolution of vagueness under our contextual assignment of denotata (or extensions) to terms appearing in logical form?

It seems clear that context does not determine any one "standard of strictness" relative to which sentences are fully evaluated. This is because a sentence may contain vague terms and hedges of various distinct sorts, and there may be no single notion of strictness that applies to all of them at once. Since vague terms come in so many varieties, and membership in their extensions is determined in so many different ways, it is unlikely that a single parameter, when fixed by context, would suffice to fix determinate membership values for all the vague terms and determinate curves for all the hedges in a sentence simultaneously. Context would have to specify a multiplicity of appropriate "standards of strictness" and probably a number of different weighting-schedules for sets of family-resemblance criteria if we were to obtain a determinate context-bound truth-value for even a moderately complicated sentence of ordinary language.

As I have said, we need not be utterly daunted by the complexities involved here, for we already know that they are to be found in (psychological) nature in any case. We might then suppose that they can still all be packed into α: energetically, α would assign a fuzzy extension to any vague term in context, and might also assign values to individual hedges that would fix their respective curves exactly in context (presuming that the exact curves represented by hedges themselves fluctuate a bit from context to context). Thus, once all these context-determined values had been forced up through our combinatorial semantics and syntax, a numerical truth-value for their containing sentence would be determined as well; α would have done its appointed work.

But there is a further, deeper reason why this picture is inadequate to the facts of natural-language use. Consider a vague predicate such as "bird," and suppose there were a set of contextual "standards of strictness" packed into α in the way I have suggested. Then we would expect that, once a particular context had fixed that parameter and thus "resolved" the vagueness of "bird" for that context, an informant inside the context would issue a determinate (absolute) judgment regarding a thing's membership in "bird" 's extension. In some cases this is so. In a technical discussion among ornithologists, Charles (a rooster) would be counted unequivocally as a bird, and perhaps so too in a context featuring very loose talk and rough characterization; in a discussion among bookmakers speculating on the migratory habits of various species, Charles would simply not be counted as a bird and indeed would be treated straightforwardly as a nonbird. But (here is the point) context does not always determine an absolute judgment in this way. There are contexts, quite ordinary ones, in which, were a perfectly competent informant asked whether Charles is a bird, the informant would hesitate, stall, and hedge.[30] In such a context, Charles is still a member of "bird" 's extension *only to a degree*. The same point may be made with regard to the truth of sentences: the sentence "Charles is a bird" in one of our nondetermining contexts would still be true only to a degree, even after all the "standards of strictness" operative in the context had imposed themselves. Thus, a contextual "standard of strictness" itself plays a role no different from that of an ordinary hedge: it can *shift* a thing's degree of membership in an extension, and/or shift a sentence's degree of truth; it *can* shift these degrees onto the absolute values 0 or 1, but it need not shift them that far. Contextual "standards of strictness" are just silent hedges, then, and do not always "resolve" vagueness in the open-and-shut way Lewis seems to intend. Even in context, vagueness sometimes remains even though a fully and perfectly meaningful sentence has been uttered.

We were considering whether the resolution of vagueness might not be subsumed under the relativization of truth to our assignment function α. But this notational economy would be possible only if truth (*simpliciter*) were determined by the set of "standards of strictness" thus encapsulated in α, and we have just seen that that is not the case. Even in context, a sentence may still be true only to a degree.[31] And so it seems we must complicate our format for T-sentences and follow Lakoff in adding a new "degree" parameter to our truth predicate. We now take truth to be a relation between a sentence, a "reading" R, a context C, and a number d that is the "degree" in question.[32] But there is one familiar old relativization yet to be recognized.

4. A Final Parameter

It is a commonplace that the truth of a sentence is relative also to the *language* ("L") of which the sentence is a grammatical string. Normally this need not be acknowledged explicitly in each T-sentence, since the whole containing semantics that is spitting out the T-sentences already is the semantics *of* the target language. On the other hand, the T-sentences themselves in isolation must be considered open sentences unless the parameter "L" is somehow specified.[33]

We usually think of giving a semantics for "a natural language," of which English, Japanese, and Kwakiutl are examples. But "natural languages" are notoriously hard to individuate. Are High German and Switzerdeutsch parts of the same language? Do West Germans and East Germans speak the same language? What about BBC English and "ghetto English"? It is customary to distinguish "dialects of" the same language, and the question of whether we have two distinct languages or two dialects of the same language will in many cases be purely verbal; that issue need not trouble us. Even different speakers of the "same dialect" will differ in many of their speech habits, both semantic and syntactic. Thus, we speak further of individual speakers' "idiolects" and of two speakers' idiolects being members of the same dialect, however broadly or narrowly we choose to individuate "dialects."

Even an individual person's speech habits change over time, so that a person speaks one idiolect at one time and another at another. Therefore, the most concrete possible object of study for the linguist would be *one speaker's idiolect at a particular time.* Indeed, it is tempting to observe (whether pejoratively or not) that this is typically what a linguist does study, since linguistic semanticists rarely conduct empirical surveys of syntactic and semantic intuitions, but simply consult their own intuitions in the privacy of their armchairs. Were a solitary master linguist to construct a complete semantics for the language he speaks, based empirically on his own various linguistic intuitions, he would have given a theory of his own idiolect, provided (as is unlikely) that it had not changed during the course of his research.

Of course, this never happens either. Linguists do not work alone, and for the even remotely foreseeable future will never construct *complete* semantic theories anyway. Then what about the currently existing linguists we all know? What language are they studying?

Not just "English" *tout court,* for except by *ad hoc* stipulation there is no such thing as "English" *tout court.* Not anyone's idiolect at a time, since every linguist has some maverick linguistic intuitions that the majority of his colleagues feel free to ignore. Therefore, the linguists must be studying some idealized abstraction, suspended somehow between their respective idiolects. (Of course the abstraction *might* correspond precisely to the actual idiolect of some person at some time, but this would be purely accidental.) Perhaps they are studying an imaginary idiolect, or the idiolect of an imaginary person, which is useful in that that idiolect is very similar to those of each of an enormous number of actual Earth people. The speech habits and verbal behavior of an "English" speaker such as you or me can be explained and understood by reference to the mechanisms of the imaginary idiolect plus notings and explanations of the various relatively small differences between us and the imaginary speaker. This is imperfect science, but also the only linguistic science that will ever be carried out in "real time."

In any case, our truth predicate must be relativized to the imaginary idiolect L, in addition to reading, context, and degree; truth is a pentadic relation.

Chapter 4

Implicative Relations and "Presupposition"

1. Implicative Relations

A main function of a logical theory as applied to a natural language is to capture the "felt implications" that hold between sentences of that language. As we have seen, this is particularly true when the logical theory is actually serving as the canonical idiom in which SRs for the natural language are written. Normally a logical theory will define just one strong implicative relation, viz., entailment, and explain "felt implications" as entailments holding within the target language.

But natural languages are not so simple. A number of intuitively different sorts of "implications" can hold between English sentences, and we are reluctant to call them all entailments, or at least entailments of the ordinary sort. Three sorts of allegedly nonentailed "implicata" come to mind: (1) The *"secondary meanings"* that can be conveyed by speakers in context that do not seem to be part of logical form in the strict and narrow sense. For example, Jones says, "There's the door," meaning that Smith should leave forthwith; Professor Barkpoop writes in a letter of recommendation, "Brown reads texts with care and summarizes their contents accurately," meaning that Brown has never had an original philosophical idea in his life. (2) The *"suggestions"* and *"invited inferences"* carried by certain forms of words in certain contexts. For example, "Marsha watched the Education School burning and smiled with satisfaction" suggests (but does not seem to entail) that Marsha smiled with satisfaction *because* the Education School was on fire. "If you mow the lawn, I'll give you $5" suggests or invites the inference[1] that if you do not mow the lawn I will not give you $5, but obviously does not entail that. (3) *"Presuppositions."* For example, the sentence "The president of the United States Philosophy Corporation is fat and smokes a fine Havana cigar" presupposes that there is a United States Philosophy Corporation; "Carl realizes that his sister has lost her marbles" presupposes that Carl's sister has lost her marbles. "Presuppose" here allegedly contrasts with "entail": a sentence is not false when its "presupposition" fails, but defective in some other way; typically it is said to lack a truth-value entirely.

Now, intuitively, "implications" of each of these three sorts are *parts of the meanings of* the sentences that do the implicating, in the sense that one would not fully understand those sentences if one did not follow and grasp the implications in question. But according to our Metatheory, sentences' meanings are represented, and entirely represented, by the SRs or logical forms assigned to them by our truth-conditional semantics; semantics *is* the theory of meaning. Therefore (any number of linguists have concluded), our semantic apparatus must be modified in such a way as to accommodate our three nonentailing implicative relations. For example, some have proposed that we move to an elaborate three-valued logic in order to represent "presupposition"; others have suggested that we simply append a *list* of a sentence's "presuppositions" and other non-entailed implicata to that sentence's SR in our semantic theory.

Though phenomena of the three types listed above are indisputably real, I believe the argument I have just sketched rests on a great and toxic mistake. The word "meaning" is a slippery one, and we must not assume (as the argument does) that everything that one might call "part of the meaning" of a sentence in context must be represented in the same way; in particular, we must not suppose that all aspects of "meaning" are somehow locked within logical form itself. The sense in which an SR or logical form "gives the meaning of" its target sentence is a very spare sense indeed, contrary perhaps to what was suggested by the Davidsonian arguments outlined in chapter 1; it corresponds to the rather strict traditional notion of "locutionary meaning" or "propositional content." There are other *types* of meaning as well, and I shall be arguing throughout the rest of this book that "meaning" is merely a loose and misleading umbrella term that takes in all these entirely different aspects of linguistic activity at once. For now, let us look a bit more closely at our "non-entailed implicata" and see exactly what aspects of their parent sentences do generate them and how they do so.

2. "Secondary Meanings," "Invited Inference," and Grice

Certainly it is crucial for an overall theory of linguistic activity to explain how "secondary meanings" are conveyed by speakers in context. But this very characterization of the explicandum suggests, I think correctly, that the phenomenon of "secondary meaning" *is* a matter of what speakers do in context—that is, it is a pragmatic matter rather than one of logical form. In his now well-known pioneering work on "conversational implicature" (1961, 1975, 1978), H. P. Grice has made enormous progress in revealing the pragmatic mechanisms that in fact generate "secondary meanings" of the sort exemplified above. He begins by offering some general pragmatic rules or "conversational maxims" that greatly facilitate communication and that we all tend to obey. Some of these maxims are:

(1)　a. Make your contribution to a conversation as informative as is required (for the current purposes of the exchange). [The Maxim of Strength]
　　　b. Do not make your contribution more informative than is required.
　　　c. Do not say what you believe to be false.
　　　d. Do not say that for which you lack adequate evidence. [The Maxim of Evidence]
　　　e. Be relevant. [The Maxim of Relevance]
　　　f. Avoid ambiguity.
　　　g. Be brief (avoid unnecessary prolixity).

These rules are regarded by Grice as corollaries of a more general instruction that he has called the "Cooperative Principle":

(2)　Make your conversational contribution such as is required, at that stage at which it occurs, by the accepted purpose or direction of the talk-exchange in which you are engaged.

(2) and its subordinate maxims are taken, plausibly, to be conventions that serve as valuable auxiliaries to the prior conventions that govern syntax and meaning. Their main function is to expedite the giving and/or receiving of information, in more or less obvious ways.

Using the maxims, we can construct detailed explanations of a person's inferring the truth of a sentence S_2 from someone's assertive utterance of a sentence S_1 even though S_1 does not entail S_2. Grice in fact outlines the general form for such explanations:

He has said that p; there is no reason to suppose that he is not observing the maxims, or at least . . . [the Cooperative Principle]; he could not be doing this unless he thought that q; he knows (and knows that I know that he knows) that I can see that the supposition that he thinks that q is required; he has done nothing to stop me thinking that q; therefore he intends me to think, or is at least willing to allow me to think, that q; and so he has implicated that q. (1975, p. 50)

An explanation of this form, although it assumes that the explainer knows the normal (literal) sentence-meaning of the sentence that replaces "p," does not ascribe the explainer's inference of the sentence replacing "q" to any connection between the latter sentence and the meaning or semantic properties of the former. The explainer merely engages in some straightforward, informal, commonsensical reasoning based on his knowledge of (2) and its corollaries (1a–g). Derivatively, we may define the following relation between sentences, which can be called conversational implication, though perhaps the definiens is too strong to be satisfied very often by pairs of sentences taken entirely out of context (cf. Grice's notion of "generalized" implicature):

> (CI) S_1 *conversationally implies* S_2 iff any normal speaker of L who utters S_1 in a normal tone in a normal context conversationally implicates that S_2 is true (i.e., iff S_1 and S_2 could replace "p" and "q," respectively, in a correct application of the Gricean explanation-schema to the context of S_1's utterance).

Now, Grice's explanatory schema is perfectly adapted to explaining the sorts of phenomena I have subsumed under the heading of "secondary meaning." It predicts, given the locutionary meaning or logical form of the sentence a speaker uttered and some facts about the containing context, what the speaker meant to convey over and above (or besides) the literal content of the sentence in question. By uttering the sentence "There's the door" to Smith in appropriate surroundings, Jones conversationally implicates that Smith should leave, *via* (1e), the Maxim of Relevance. By writing "Brown reads texts with care and summarizes their contents accurately," Barkpoop conversationally implicates that Brown is unoriginal, *via* the Maxim of Strength. Thus, the facts of "felt implication" here are nicely accounted for without recourse to any tampering with logical form, or any other sullying of the distinction between semantics in our austere sense and pragmatics. Grice's method shows how a sentence can be used to convey a certain "secondary meaning" without entailing that "meaning" or in any other way having it as part of its logical form. (Notice, incidentally, that "secondary meaning" is first and foremost a property of utterances, or better, of speakers, and not a property of sentence(-type)s. *In uttering* "There's the door," *Jones* meant that Smith should leave, and perhaps *by his utterance* of that sentence Jones meant that Smith should leave. We might even say that Jones's *utterance* in that context meant that Smith should leave, but this is stretching it; there is no interesting sense at all in which the sentence-*type* "There's the door" has as a meaning, or as part of its meaning, or as one of its meanings, that Smith (or anyone) should leave. We shall return below to the distinction between sentence-meaning and speaker-meaning.)

This brings us to our second kind of nonentailing "implication," so-called "invited inference." The phenomena here are more complex than in the case of "secondary meaning" and call for a somewhat more elaborate theoretical apparatus, but can equally well be handled as part of everyday pragmatics and do not call for any modification in our semantical format. I shall not go into detail, since Steven Boër and I have done so in an earlier work (1973), but simply remark that the phenomena usually comprehended under this label are easily explained in terms of conversational implicature plus a transparently simple additional mechanism: the tacit use of background assumptions. In any conversation or other discourse, much background information is taken for granted, and vast funds of background assumptions are shared (Robert Stalnaker (1978) calls all of this material "common ground"). Sometimes when we utter a sentence we intend our hearer to conjoin that sentence with some obvious piece or pieces of background information and draw an obvious conclusion; hearers do just this, constantly and quite unconsciously. People tend to infer a sentence S_2 directly from S_1, not always because S_1 entails S_2, but because for some third sentence S_3, $\ulcorner S_1 \ \& \ S_3 \urcorner$ entails S_2 and S_3 is so deeply entrenched in their consciousness generally or is so fundamental an element of the context at hand that they make inferential use of S_3 without even realizing that they are drawing on a suppressed assumption. This perfectly legitimate but routinely unacknowledged use of background information, perhaps augmented by Gricean reasoning, is what normally licenses "invited inference." For example, what prompts us to infer "Marsha smiled because the Education School was on fire" from "Marsha watched the Education School burning and smiled with satisfaction" is our common knowledge of probable causes. Suppose we hypothetically cancel or suspend our knowledge of the effects of burning, of Marsha's attitude toward the Education School, and of the connections between the satisfaction of a person's desires and the behavior of her physiognomy; then there is no temptation at all to infer a causal connection just from the conjunctive nature of our target sentence (compare "Marsha watched the Education School burning and nibbled her spinach pie"). Causal inferences are "invited" only through background assumptions, perhaps with the aid of the Maxim of Relevance, and not in virtue of logical form in particular. The same is true of so-called "conditional perfection," illustrated by the case of "If you mow the lawn, I'll give you $5." We infer "If you don't mow the lawn, I won't give you $5" (our target sentence's converse) *only* because we know independently that people do not usually hand out money for services not rendered and that there would be little point in my uttering our target sentence to someone if that person knew that I was going to give him $5 anyway. Compare "If you fail the midterm, you'll fail the course," from which it would be rash at best to infer that if the hearer passes the midterm he will pass the course (even if he fails the final).

Neither "secondary meaning" nor "invited inference" requires any change in our basic truth-conditional format for semantics; each can be happily accommodated within a very simple and natural pragmatics. Our third type of nonstandard implicative relation, however, is felt by some linguists to require such a change, for failure of a sentence's "presupposition" is said to affect that sentence's truth-value in a direct but nonstandard way.

3. "Presupposition"

A decade ago, linguistic semanticists and philosophers of language alike seemed to agree that the notion of "presupposition" is both rich in intuitive content (thus available as an important source of *data* for syntax and semantics) and crucial for our understanding and theorizing about the meanings of utterances (thus *theoretically* important in syntax and semantics). Readers of the literature would come away with the impression that we have a vast stockpile of relatively hard data concerning the presuppositions of sentences and that, though we have yet to get quite as clear about what "presupposing" is as purist metatheoreticians might like, the intuitive notion that we have will do well enough to go on with, and we may continue to appeal to data concerning presupposition in framing syntactic and semantic arguments on diverse topics. Though much examination and analysis of the notion has taken place since 1970 or so, this basic position remains relatively unchanged in practice.

Here are some examples of pairs of sentences the like of which have been adduced under the rubric of "presupposition" (as distinct from entailment):

(3) a. Sam realizes that Irv is a Martian.
     b. Irv is a Martian.

(4) a. Fred regretted leaving home.
     b. Fred left home.

(5)   a. Bring me the avocado in the brown paper bag.
      b. There is an avocado in a brown paper bag.

(6)   a. Few girls are coming.
      b. Some girls are coming.

(7)   a. If Irv were a Martian, I'd be running away from here.
      b. Irv is not a Martian.

(8)   a. Have you stopped beating your wife?
      b. You have beaten your wife.

(9)   a. I hope I can disprove Gödel's Theorem.
      b. It is possible to disprove Gödel's Theorem.

(10) a. I promise to bring back your toilet-seat.
      b. I intend to bring back your toilet-seat.

(11) a. Fred, who was fat, could not run.
      b. Fred was fat.

(12) a. Camille is pretending to be sick.
      b. Camille is not sick.

(13) a. John managed to get out of the phone booth.
      b. John tried to get out of the phone booth.

(14) a. She was poor but she was honest.
      b. Being poor tends to preclude being honest.

(15) a. Melvin is a bachelor.
      b. Melvin is an adult.

It may be clear that the first member of each of these pairs somehow suggests or "implies" its fellow. What is not at all clear (and would be naive to assume) is that there is a single distinctive and important relation that is instantiated by all these pairs. In fact, the differences between the pairs are more interesting than the similarities. It is now more or less standard to distinguish "semantic" from "pragmatic" presupposition (Stalnaker (1972), Keenan (1971), Karttunen (1973), Thomason (1973), Atlas (1975), and others); it is common knowledge that there are at least two such notions that are not quite the same. Roughly, a notion of "presupposition" is *semantic* iff the implications in question are a function of semantic status, semantic properties, propositional content, or logical form, whereas it is *pragmatic* iff the implications in question arise only in virtue of contextual considerations, the roles of the relevant sentences in standard speech acts, Gricean conversational matters, simple matters of background knowledge on the part of particular speakers, etc. (the differences between even the subspecies of "pragmatic presupposition" are more striking than the similarities, though they go virtually unremarked even now). But even this vague distinction is not often taken seriously in the literature—thus, Karttunen writes:

> For the time being, let us simply assume that we understand what is meant by a presupposition in the case of simple sentences . . . and turn our attention to more complex cases.
> . . . we may even forget about the distinction between semantic and pragmatic presuppositions. What is said about one kind of presupposition will apply to the other as well (I hope). (1973, p. 171)

To judge by the foregoing characterization of the distinction, Karttunen's hope is a wild one.[2]

If either notion of "presupposition" requires complication or modification of our semantic format, it is (by definition) the semantic notion rather than any of the multifarious pragmatic ones. Attempts to define "semantic presupposition," though haphazard, have centered around roughly Strawson's notion: a sentence S_1 semantically presupposes a sentence S_2 iff S_1 necessitates S_2 and S_1's denial necessitates S_2 (thus, if S_2 is not true, then S_1 is neither true nor false).[3] This notion visibly contrasts with that of entailment (which supports contraposition) and if admitted to our semantical format would require the adoption of a three-valued logic plus apparatus for determining which "felt implications" were entailments and which were "semantic presuppositions" in the sense defined.

In our monograph, *The Myth of Semantic Presupposition* (1976) (henceforth, *MSP*), Steven Boër and I have attacked the notion of "semantic presupposition" on a number of fronts, and tried to demonstrate its uselessness for and perniciousness within linguistics; see also Kempson (1975) and Wilson (1975). Our arguments have been hailed in conversation and in print with a good deal of approval and verbal agreement, but to my mind have not had the effects on theorizing that they were intended to have, or even much practical effect at all. My project in the remainder of this chapter will be to reemphasize the morals that Boër and I intended should be drawn from our investigation, to strengthen the arguments for our hostile and nihilistic conclusions, to respond to some criticisms, and to exhibit some more of the harmful effects produced by tolerance of "presupposition" talk in linguistic semantics.

Our principal claims in *MSP* were these:

(I)   The term "presupposition" is viciously misleading and is not scientifically well-behaved, in that the class of sentence pairs that have been subsumed under it is very far from constituting a natural kind.

"Presupposition" is an ill-conceived umbrella word that is used to cover any number of importantly distinct and largely unrelated notions (from formal semantics, the theory of conversation, speech-act theory, the theory of speaker-meaning, the psychology of inference, and more). A single term devised to comprehend all these notions, or probably even two or more of them, would figure in no interesting (and true) linguistic generalizations.

(II)   The various implicative notions have in fact, indeed epidemically, been conflated and licentiously interchanged in the literature, with the result that any number of theoretical issues have been stymied and several pseudoissues brought unhappily into being.

A striking symptom of the prevailing confusion is that linguists very commonly introduce their use of the term "presuppose" by explicit reference to a formal version of Strawson's notion and then without the slightest hesitation, acknowledgment, qualm, or return to the definition, go on to make claims for or raise questions about their own notions that are obviously and wildly at odds with Strawson's notion.[4]

(III)   Though several of the various pragmatic notions collected under the only slightly more refined heading of "pragmatic presupposition" are individually clear, manageable, and theoretically important, the Strawsonian notion of "semantic presupposition," once clarified, is empty (or all but empty) and useless for the purpose of understanding the workings of natural language.

Many so-called "semantic presuppositions" are just entailments; the denials of the allegedly presupposing sentences do not in fact necessitate the alleged presupposita. Other allegedly presupposing sentences do not even themselves necessitate their alleged presupposita.

(IV)   The notion of "truth-valuelessness" engendered by the notion of "semantic presupposition" is unmotivated, specious, and pernicious to the study of natural language. Neglecting cases of indexicality and cases of vagueness as discussed in chapter 3, we should hew to the line of bivalence in the semantic analysis of English.

This is not to suggest that there is anything *formally* wrong with a mathematical notion that corresponds to Strawson's, or that there is anything at all wrong with three-valued logics (or seventeen- or five-hundred-fifty-two-valued logics) in themselves, but only that none of them is the logic of English.

Claim (I) I consider a very important contention, and it is the one most commonly glided over by readers of *MSP*. People quite frequently come up to Boër or me at meetings and say things like, "Your breakdown of all the different kinds of presupposition there are is terrific; you've given a wonderful master theory of presupposition." As (I) gently suggests, to say this is to miss our point quite badly. That point (I now decline to speak softly) is that people should *stop using that word. It has caused nothing but trouble and error.* Nor should any essentially equivalent bastard term be introduced. Rather, we should simply adopt more specific and precise terms for each of the distinct but undisputedly real implicative relations that have formerly been forced into each other's company under the label of "presupposition," and use those terms exclusively.[5] (We offered such a set of terms in section 2.2 of *MSP*; perhaps a better set might be devised.) Of course, one might reserve a term such as "Strawsonian presupposition" or even "semantic presupposition" for a single clarified version of Strawson's notion, if one supposes (contrary to claims (III) and (IV)) that there are any instances of that relation in English.

I shall now try to bring out more clearly the reasons for my hostility to the notion of "semantic presupposition" in particular (even after it has been sharply distinguished from other implicative relations and clarified as nicely as one could wish).

4. The Unnaturalness of "Semantic Presupposition"

Let us begin by looking at the notion of "truth-valuelessness" more closely than has been done to date. My purpose in this section is to express skepticism about it, skepticism that is the more crucial in that "truth-valuelessness" is the central notion in any semantic theory of presupposition.

It is not in doubt that there are truth-valueless sentence(-type)s. Questions, imperatives, and (some say) explicit performatives are not thought to have truth-values (actually I shall challenge this commonsense view in chapter 8). I become skeptical only when this harmless truth-valuelessness is extended to cover declaratives of the familiar sort—sentences that look like fact-stating sentences. Even within this class, we recognize a subgroup of uncontroversially truth-valueless sentences: those that contain hidden parameters so far unspecified. Thus,

(16)   Rex is big

lacks a truth-value until we explicitly or contextually specify a reference-class ("Big for a what?"). Similarly, Boër and I have argued (1975) that a sentence like

(17)   Perry knows who Clark Kent is

lacks a truth-value until some purpose or "project" has been specified. And Ethical Relativists contend, though rarely on syntactic or semantic grounds,[6] that a moral judgment such as

(18)   Murder is wrong

has a truth-value only relative to some person or group.

This sort of truth-valuelessness is easily understood: it is simply that of the open sentence. The string

(19)   He is sick

is truth-valueless in exactly the same way. But truth-valuelessness of this type is a purely syntactic and semantic matter, and is resolved in something like the way I have described in chapter 3. It does not depend on any background information concerning further contingencies in the world; and that is precisely what the alleged truth-valuelessness resulting from presupposition failure does depend on. Presupposition theorists surely do not mean to suggest that "presupposition" failure somehow implants a hidden parameter in the allegedly presupposing sentence that is not there when the putative presuppositum is true. Thus, the truth-valuelessness in terms of which semantic presupposition is defined is of none of the foregoing familiar types.

It is clear on reflection that "truth-valuelessness" in the Strawsonian sense is no ordinary, commonsensical notion. It is quite a technical one. Although speakers of plain English may balk when queried, "Is S_1 true or is S_1 false?", finding themselves unable to respond either "It's true" or "It's false" without further explanation, clarification, or qualification, this mulish behavior is hardly tantamount to responding "Neither—S_1 lacks a truth-value!" or the like. To take a native's inability to choose one of the two truth-values on the spot as indicating either that he believes S_1 to lack a truth-value or that S_1 in fact lacks a truth-value is to make a highly substantive explanatory claim, a hypothesis that must be compared to alternatives. And in every such case, I contend, there are plausible alternatives in the offing; Boër and I brought out and defended some of them in *MSP*.

This point undermines the first of Strawson's two arguments against Russell on the topic of nondenoting singular terms (offered, incidentally, in the article (1950a) that gave rise to talk of truth-valuelessness in the first place). Strawson asks us to suppose that someone has uttered

(20)   The king of France is wise

"with a perfectly serious air." Now:

> Would you say, 'That's untrue'? I think it is quite certain that you would not. But suppose he went on to ask you whether you thought that what he had just said was true, or was false; whether you agreed or disagreed with what he had just said. I think you would be inclined, with some hesitation, to say that you did not do either; that the question of whether his statement was true or false simply did not arise, because there was no such person as the king of France. (p. 183)

I have indicated my rejection of Strawson's contention that we have "pure intuitions" of truth-valuelessness. (If an informant were to respond to our query "that the question . . . did not arise," the most likely possibility would be that he had read Strawson somewhere.) Still, it is true that no normal speaker would respond simply, "That's false."

So let us agree that

(21)   That's false

would be inappropriate at best if tokened in response to (20). Strawson concludes without further deliberation that (21) itself is false. But, as I have pointed out and shall elaborate below, falsity is only one of many, many different varieties of inappropriateness, in-felicitousness, or unacceptability; and there may well be some more plausible account of the inappropriateness of (21). In fact, there is what I believe to be a more plausible alternative: the trouble with responding to (20) by tokening (21) alone is that in so limiting one's answer one violates either Grice's Maxim of Strength or his Maxim of Relevance; one who believes that there is no king of France is in a position rather to assert the far stronger

(22)   That's false, since there is no king of France,

and therefore such a speaker sins (according to the Maxims) in not doing so. (Notice particularly, in addition, that (22) is perfectly acceptable to a normal speaker in the circumstances envisioned.) This explanation of the inappropriateness of (21) is not only compatible with but entails the truth of (21) and the falsity of (20).

It must be pointed out that what I have said here is entirely compatible with the contention, often attributed to Strawson, that when we utter a sentence whose "presupposition" has failed, we do not succeed in thereby making a statement. Whether or not a speaker has made a statement is a question of illocutionary force and hence of pragmatics; thus, so far as has been shown, it is irrelevant to the question of whether the sentence uttered is in fact true. (It is easily seen that anyone may utter a sentence that is in fact true without thereby making a statement—as when he utters it within quotation, on stage, to practice elocution, or to activate a phonetically coded door-opening device.) Therefore, even if it could be established in particular cases that a speaker had failed to make a statement in or by uttering some sentence, that still would not show that the sentence was truth-valueless. The most we could conclude is that the sentence's truth-value just did not matter in the context in question (I shall amplify this point below).

I have argued that ordinary speakers are not normally capable of making intuitive judgments of truth-valuelessness (as distinct from refraining from making any judgment at all), and that the notion of "truth-valuelessness" is a theoretical artifact of linguistic and philosophical semanticists. It ought to be noted in addition that to take truth-valuelessness seriously is to require some significant departure from the simple traditional format of standard logic. Logicians who are willing to take this step are forced to invent three-valued logics (cf. Woodruff (1970)) and/or fancy semantical machinery such as van Fraassen's method of supervaluations (1966), in each case courting justified charges of arbitrariness in settling the numerous don't-cares that arise in the newly amplified models. To say this is not to raise any direct objection to hypothesizing truth-valuelessness; there are deviant logics of the sorts I have mentioned that can be made as elegant and as mathematically satisfying as anyone could wish. The point is only that "truth-valuelessness" as a semantical notion needs considerable formal spelling out before it can soberly be understood.[7]

One would expect from the foregoing points (that "truth-value-lessness" is not a concept pretheoretically possessed by laymen, and that its logic is neither simple nor uncontroversial) that it may be hard even for the semantic theorist to form an intuitive judgment, with regard to a given sentence in a context, concerning whether that sentence has a truth-value in that context. And this expectation is richly borne out, in my experience anyway. Although there are intuitively clear cases of true sentences (in particular contexts) and clear cases of false sentences (in particular contexts), I have yet to see a clear case, in any context, of a *truth-valueless* sentence that is not an instance of one of the familiar and unexciting types mentioned above. Whatever theoretical function the notion of truth-valuelessness may serve, that notion is no raw and intuitive one; by itself it yields no data.[8]

There is a deeper objection to be put as well. It is in the nature of a declarative sentence to portray or represent the world as being a certain way. Now either the world *is* as it is portrayed, or, for whatever reason, it is not. If the world is that way, then our declarative sentence is true. If the world is not that way, then our sentence is untrue. One is tempted to infer straightaway that it is false; but John Martin prudently cautions us against making this inference without further ado.

> There is a distinction to be drawn between two broad classes of non-true sentences that is both intuitively recognizable and theoretically productive. . . . There are equally weighty conceptual reasons for restricting application of 'false' to one of these subcategories of non-truths as there are for bivalence. (1979, p. 254)

I have already given counterarguments against the "intuitive recognizability" of his distinction and (in *MSP*) against its alleged theoretical value; but I agree that the dilemmatic argument sketched above does not by itself conclusively demonstrate the bivalence of English. A further consideration is needed to bring out what I have referred to as the "unnaturalness" (and am willing to refer to as the "perversity") of the notion of truth-valuelessness that figures in "semantic presupposition."

The consideration I have in mind is akin to Wittgenstein's denial in the *Tractatus* that any proposition's having sense could depend on any other proposition's being true (§§2.0211, 2.0212).[9] Even if I can perhaps make sense of the idea of a fully determinate, eternal, and complete proposition's lacking a truth-value (which I still have trouble doing), it is prohibitively hard for me to think that such a proposition's having a truth-value at all somehow depends on the truth of some second, contingent proposition. Like Wittgenstein, I have no knockdown argument to show that this idea is incoherent, but it strikes me as quite bizarre. Why should a proposition—an object whose very function it is determinately to represent the world as being a certain way—be truth-valued *at all* only at the whim of some other (contingent) proposition, i.e., only depending on the world's being some other, further way? It is as if a number's being rational or irrational at all were to depend on some other number's being rational.

If the foregoing three points are right (that the kind of truth-valuelessness required by "semantic presupposition" is a theoretical artifact, that it complicates logic, and that it is—upon reflection—quite strange), then clearly whatever utility the notion of "semantic presupposition" has is theoretical utility, as opposed to reportive utility. To repeat: a field linguist may report, as a datum, that a native informant refused to commit himself to a judgment of truth or to a judgment of falsity; but the linguist may not report, as a datum, that the native committed himself to a judgment of truth-valuelessness, unless (as is both unlikely and irrelevant) the native is himself a professional linguist or philosopher or has been force-fed on the spot by such a person.

What, then, can "semantic presupposition" do for semantic theory? In the course of a series of eight case studies in *MSP*, Boër and I found no legitimate theoretical job for Strawsonian presupposition to do. If there is any such job, then as Garner (1971) has insisted, the best way to get at it is most likely to investigate systematically the consequences of "presupposition" *failure*. Are there any sentence pairs $\langle S_1, S_2 \rangle$ of which we would want or need for any theoretical reason to say that if S_2 is false, S_1 lacks a truth-value?

In some cases of alleged semantic presupposition, the penalty for the failure (falsity) of S_2 is simply the falsity of S_1. In other cases, the penalty is the violation of Grice's Maxim of Strength. (Notice that as a by-product of this sort of violation, the presumed truth—far from the truth-valuelessness—of S_1 is assured. To violate the Maxim in uttering S_1 is to utter S_1 when one is in a position to assert some stronger truth, i.e., one that entails S_1 but is not entailed by it; and only truths are entailed by truths.) No doubt, in still other cases, the penalty will be that S_1 is *infelicitous;* but infelicitousness entails nothing about truth or falsity, as we shall see. In still other cases, the penalty will be that whoever tokened S_1 (or possibly someone else in the speech situation) has a false background belief; but that result too is consistent with S_1's being either true or false.

The arguments for all these claims are to be found in *MSP;* I shall not reiterate them here. Thus, I do not claim to have said anything in this chapter that would convince a devout believer in semantic presupposition to abandon the faith. What I do want to do in the remainder of it is to explain why the notion of semantic presupposition has seemed so plausible to linguists and philosophers alike, and in particular why the idea of truth-valuelessness is as current as it is.

Thus, my purpose here is diagnostic, and I hope the diagnosis will prove therapeutic as well.

5. Three Influential Errors

In this section I shall review three polluted sources of philosophical intuition—three types of mistakes that, once made, have given rise to claims of semantic presupposition. The first, theoretically negligible but significant in particular cases, is the ignoring of arcane but perfectly clear counterexamples to claims of necessitation. Semantic presupposition requires necessitation, and necessitation requires the absolute inconceivability of counterexamples. One can easily find counterexamples to an enormous number of alleged semantic presuppositions in the literature (see particularly, for example, Lakoff (1972)). Thus, even many of the data that are claimed to indicate semantic presupposition are spurious at the very outset. Indeed, as Boër and I remarked in section 3.3 of *MSP*, some of even the commonest claims of semantic presupposition can be refuted out of hand when it is pointed out that the denials of the allegedly presupposing sentences "imply" the alleged presupposita only *cancellably* (in the sense of Grice (1961, p. 128)) and that their conjunction with the denials of the presupposita simply does not result in contradiction. Consider the following standard examples:

(23) a. It's false that it was John who caught the thief.
      b. It's false that John is aware that Mary is pregnant.
      c. It's false that Irv knows that Sam is a Martian.
      d. It's false that it is significant that Mary is pregnant.

The important thing to notice is that the various "implications" carried by these denials can all easily be cancelled, as in the following examples:

(24) a. It's false that it was John who caught the thief, because no one caught her.
      b. It's false that John is aware that Mary is pregnant, because she isn't.
      c. It's false that Irv knows Sam is a Martian, because Sam isn't one.
      d. It's false that it *is* significant that Mary is pregnant, because she isn't.

(24a–d) may be a bit strange, but they are fully intelligible and, more to the point, they are clearly *not contradictions*. Now, the notion of *necessitation* is an apodeictic one and does not admit of (noncontradictory) cancellation in this way. Therefore, the "implications" of (23a–e), cancelled in (24a–e), respectively, are not necessitated by (23a–e). By definition, then, no semantic presuppositions are involved in these cases. And their very cancellability in context should be enough to tip us off that the notions we are dealing with are context-bound, pragmatic.

In making the present point I am assuming that the position of the operator "It's false that" in (23a–d) and (24a–d) is to be taken at face value, i.e., that the negation in question has the widest possible scope. (23a–d) are semantic denials or "external negations." It is to the distinction between "external negation" and "internal negation" that I now turn; failure to observe this distinction is our second source of confusion.

(23a–d) are not very natural. Much more colloquial versions would be (25a–d):

(25) a. It wasn't John who caught the thief.
      b. John is not aware that Mary is pregnant.
      c. Irv doesn't know that Sam is a Martian.
      d. It isn't significant that Mary is pregnant.

It is easy, when dealing with sentences like (25a–d), to fail to distinguish external from internal negation, and thus to believe that the internal negation of (say) (25a), which we might symbolize as $(\exists x)$ (CAUGHT $(x,$ the thief$)$ & $\sim$(John $= x$)) and which does necessitate

(26) Someone caught the thief,

is the denial of

(27) It was John who caught the thief,

which it is not. (The *denial* of a sentence, logically speaking, is the result of prefixing "It is false that" or an equivalent negation operator to the entire sentence, i.e., the denial is the sentence's external or wide-scope negation. (23a), symbolized as $\sim(\exists x)$ (CAUGHT $(x,$ the thief$)$ & John $= x$), is (27)'s denial.) In general, a sentence's external negation is not only true but mandated to be true when that sentence's alleged "semantic presupposition" fails.

Occasionally in conversation it has been protested to me that external negations like (23a–d) are not good English. E.g.: "No one talks that way except philosophers. In English, when you want to deny

(28) It was Peter who got sand in the parsnips,

you say

(29)   It wasn't Peter who got sand in the parsnips,

and when you want to deny

(30)   The present king of France is ugly,

you say

(31)   The present king of France isn't ugly,

etc. 'External negation' is just logicians' claptrap, and so it isn't recognized by the syntax or semantics of English.''

There are two grains of truth here (but only grains). First, it is
certainly true that some external negations are difficult or impossible
to form in surface structure (e.g., those of sentences involving non-
restrictive relative clauses, as Boër and I discussed in sec. 3.1 of
MSP). But this admission has no effect on antipresupposition arguments of the sort I just gave concerning (23a), (25a), (26), and (27).
The external/internal distinction is forced on us by the assumption
that syntactic transformations operate on fully disambiguated logical
structures. Second, it is also true that unambiguously external negations of complex sentences, uttered without verbal qualification, are
rarely acceptable in everyday English conversation. But why? Partly
because disambiguation renders them grammatically cumbersome;
partly because they are almost always frowned upon by the Maxim of
Strength, as being uncooperatively weak and cautious; not because
there is anything *semantically* wrong with them. Anyone can truly
and felicitously utter

(32)   It wasn't Peter who got sand in the parsnips, if anyone
       at all did

or

(33)   It's false that the present king of France is ugly, because
       France doesn't have a king.

And anyone can *truly* utter

(34)   It's false that it was Peter who got sand in the parsnips

or

(35)   It's false that the present king of France is ugly

in the circumstances envisioned; the deficiencies of (34) and (35) are
stylistic and conversational, not semantic.[10]

As a final way of seeing this, notice that any external negation is
perfectly acceptable in the precise speech of philosophical logi-

cians—the salient characteristic of that patois being that, in it, conversational maxims are ignored in the interest of rigor and precision.

Following Russell, I have assumed here that the distinction between external and internal negation is a scope distinction, a negation being external when it has wide scope, internal when it occurs within the scope of the "presupposition"-generating locution. Martin (1979) evidently does not see the distinction in the same way. He writes:

> A . . . major flaw in Boër and Lycan's definitions of presupposition is the sense of negation they use. For some quixotic reason, they decide that presupposition is supposed to be defined in terms of external negation, whereas in every precise treatment of presupposition I know of, negation is internal. . . . Even Russell's theory of existential presupposition is formulated by negation in secondary occurrence which is the classical version of 3-valued internal negation. (p. 267)

This criticism is very puzzling at first glance. The reason Boër and I concentrated on the external or wide-scope readings of sentences such as (24a–d) is hardly "quixotic": it is simply that the internal readings do not generate the kind of truth-valuelessness that is characteristic (indeed definitive) of semantic presupposition. (27) and (25a) on its internal reading both do necessitate (26), for example, but (27) is not therefore truth-valueless when (26) is false. (If (23a) also necessitated (26), it *would* follow that (27) was neither true nor false when (26) "failed.") If Martin means to introduce a new notion of "presupposition," defined in terms of internal negation in the present sense but not involving truth-valuelessness, I have no objection, but this new notion is semantically unremarkable and is not the one that has figured so long, so ostentatiously, so tenaciously, and so regrettably in linguistics.

Indeed, it is clear that this is not Martin's intention. He does embrace truth-valuelessness (I have quoted him doing so earlier in this section), and he evidently does not understand the "external"/"internal" distinction in terms of scope at all. Indeed, he claims that our fairly standard use of the term "external negation" to mean negation in wide scope or primary occurrence and "internal negation" to mean negation in narrow scope or secondary occurrence is neologistic: ". . . these terms are best reserved for varieties of 3-valued negations that they were originally intended to describe" (p. 252). According to Martin (personal communication), the "external"/"internal" terminology originated with Bochvar (1939) (cf. also Smiley (1960)) and was defined in terms of three-valued truth-tables, without reference to scope.[11] In Bochvar's usage the distinction is a *lexical* ambiguity: crudely, an "external" negation in Bochvar's sense is true when the negation sign's operand is neuter, whereas an "internal" negation is itself neuter in that case.

Plainly, as Martin observes, it is in terms of Bochvar-"internal" negation that semantic presupposition would have to be defined, given just the two senses of negation. Martin concludes (p. 268) that in confusedly understanding "not" in its Bochvar-"external" (i.e., bivalent) sense throughout, Boër and I simply misconceived the presupposition issue, and that "Boër and Lycan in effect argue *for* the existence of presuppositions, once the concept is correctly defined." But the misconception is Martin's. Our concern was, and my concern here is, to defame the idea that English admits a third truth-value of the presuppositional type at all. Of course "semantic presupposition" is correctly defined in terms of Bochvar-"internal" rather than in terms of ordinary bivalent negation; what I question is whether there is any such operator as Bochvar-"internal" negation and hence any such phenomenon as semantic presupposition, in English. The arguments of *MSP* were aimed at showing that no such thing exists, or at least that we have no reason to grant that it does. *This* is the main (and genuine) issue between Martin and ourselves.[12] I shall return to Martin's further arguments in the next section; for now let us turn to our third polluted source of intuitions about "presupposition" and truth-valuelessness.

The third source is the distinction sometimes drawn between what a sentence (or speaker) *asserts* and what that sentence (or speaker) merely *implies*. This distinction appears to be a pragmatic matter of relative emphasis. That is, the utterer of a sentence S_1 is held to have merely implied rather than asserted S_2 generally on the ground that S_2, although entailed by S_1, does not express what was uppermost in the speaker's mind when he uttered S_1. Consider the following example of Boër's:

(36)   a. Peering through the keyhole, I saw my wife *in bed
            with my best friend!*
        b. I saw my wife in bed with my best friend.
        c. I peered through the keyhole.

There is some inclination to say that the utterer of (36a) "asserts" (36b) but only "implies" (36c). The utterer's remark about the keyhole is only incidental; his primary concern is with what he saw (witness the stress contour). So far as I can see, this marginal sort of "implication" has no semantic content over and above that supplied by classical entailment; it merely superadds to entailment a variety of purely pragmatic considerations having to do with the speaker's system of values and interests, viz., involving the relative importance to the speaker of one entailment as opposed to another.

To see how the distinction has figured covertly in discussions of presupposition, consider (11a), "Fred, who was fat, could not run." It is hard for me to think of (11a) as being *truth-valueless* when (11b), "Fred was fat," is false. For, in light of the considerable evidence that sentences like (11a) derive from underlying conjunctions (Thompson (1971)), it seems clear that the *truth*-conditions of such sentences are those of conjunctions. Thus, (11a) has the same truth-condition as

(37) Fred was fat and Fred could not run,

as does

(38) Fred, who could not run, was fat.

Necessarily, therefore, (11a) is false if (11b) is false; (11a) *entails* (11b). The important thing to notice with regard to "asserting" is that a sentence S_1's merely entailing a sentence S_2 in no way guarantees that S_1 asserts S_2, or that one who uttered S_1 would thereby assert S_2, or that S_2 gives any part of the content of "what S_1 says" in any intuitive sense. (11a) clearly does not "assert" (11b). Evidently, relativization is (perhaps among other things) a way of *deemphasizing* certain parts of the total semantic content of a sentence, to such a degree that we want to deny that those parts are asserted by the sentence or by the speaker who utters it; those parts are, if you like, merely taken for granted (it *is* tempting to say "presupposed" here, in a quite nontechnical sense). But all this is perfectly consistent with their being simply entailed by the original sentences. What is not asserted may still be entailed in virtue of logical form. For example, Peano's axioms do not assert the theorems of elementary arithmetic, but they certainly entail them. And

(39) Snow is white

does not assert

(40) Either snow is white or pigs have wings

or

(41) If Lincoln is dead, then Lincoln is dead,

but it entails both. Thus, it is fallacious to suppose that what is not asserted by a sentence is *a fortiori* not entailed by that sentence. The relevance of this point becomes clear when we reflect that historically, the term 'presuppose' has been used in each of two different ways: one as contrasting with 'assert,' and the second as contrasting with 'entail.' The former usage is more natural, the latter technical.

Despite the vagueness of the notion of what a sentence "says" or "asserts," we have some tolerably clear cases (such as those of non-restrictive relative clauses and clefting) in which information that is plainly part of the semantic content of a sentence may have been placed (by one syntactic transformation or another) in so unemphatic a position in the surface structure of that sentence that we are disinclined to admit that that information is part of what that sentence says or asserts. It is natural and harmless to say of this information that it is "presupposed, rather than asserted" by the sentence, i.e., that it is taken for granted, rather than actively put forward or emphatically pushed by the speaker. But this natural notion of "presupposition" is not the one that contrasts with entailment. It is the Strawsonian notion, that of "semantic presupposition," that contrasts with and precludes that of entailment. It is therefore an equivocation to argue (explicitly or implicitly) from purely intuitive data concerning what some sentence asserts or does not assert to positive technical conclusions about semantic presupposition. It is this fallacy that, I think, has in spots misled Keenan (1971), Karttunen (1971, 1973), and other writers on presupposition.

Parallel considerations hold for denying and contradicting. Just as it is fallacious to argue from failure to assert to failure to entail, it is fallacious to infer from the fact that a sentence S_1 (or someone who tokens it) cannot properly be said to have denied or contradicted an utterance of S_2, that S_1 does not entail the falsity of S_2. Not every utterance, or even every assertion, of an S_1 that entails the falsity of S_2 is properly said to contradict S_2, especially if S_2 is (logically) much stronger than the denial of S_1 and if the latter is an unemphasized consequence of S_2. For example, if a speaker were to utter

(42) Hud certainly is a *devious* swinging bachelor,

one who replied by uttering

(43) Hud is not an adult

could not properly be said to have contradicted the first speaker, even though (43) (on the assumption that being a bachelor entails being an adult) entails the falsity of (42). Similarly, if a speaker were to utter

(44) So it was *Moriarty* who killed Holmes,

one who replied by uttering

(45)   Actually, Holmes was only put in suspended animation

would not properly be said to have contradicted the original speaker or to have denied what was asserted. Finally (to take a degenerate but therefore even more obvious example), one who uttered

(46)   The economy will soon take a turn for the better

could not in any nontechnical sense be said to have contradicted a (demented) speaker who had tokened

(47)   Three is both prime and not prime,

though (46)—like any other sentence—entails the falsity of (47). Thus, we must beware of the tendency to confuse the linguistic act of *denying what someone has asserted* with the quite different act of uttering *the denial of* the *sentence* that person has used in making his assertion.

It is this general point that is overlooked by Strawson (1950a) in offering the second of his two arguments against Russell's treatment of nondenoting singular terms:

> Now suppose someone were in fact to say to you with a perfectly serious air: 'The king of France is wise.' . . . when, in response to his statement, we say (as we should) 'There is no king of France', we should certainly not say we were contradicting the statement that the king of France is wise. We are certainly not saying that it is false. (pp. 183–84)

Doubtless Strawson's premise is correct: in general, we would not say that one who uttered

(48)   There is no king of France

in response to

(49)   The king of France is wise

had *contradicted* the utterer of (49) or *said that* (49) was false, at least not without further comment or qualification. But, as our foregoing examples have shown, it does not follow that the utterer of (48) did not token a sentence that in fact entails the falsity of (49); the utterer of (48) has merely attacked (49) at a deemphasized outpost, showing (49) none the less surely to be false. Thus, the fact that we would not ordinarily say of an utterer of (48) that he had denied (49) or contradicted the utterer of (49) is of no consequence.

It is worth remarking that, although I believe the notion of "semantic presupposition" to be empty and uninteresting, the harmless "natural" notion of presupposing in the sense of "taking for granted" deserves thorough investigation—first, because the contrasting notion of "asserting" is intuitively viable but terribly unclear; second, because it may prove illuminating to issues in pragmatics; and, third, because it may well play a role in epistemology and in the theory of dialectic.

6. Martin's Defense: Existential and Sortal Cases

I have said that the main disagreement between the critics of semantic presupposition (at least Boër and me) and its devotees such as Martin concerns the positing of the third truth-value within English in the first place. The type of theory Martin favors inherits the bizarreness that I tried to bring out in section 4. I should emphasize that it also labors under the burden of entailing that the English word "not" is lexically ambiguous (between bivalent and Bochvar-"internal" readings). I find this supposed ambiguity nearly intolerable. Are we really to believe that "not" in (50a) and "not" in (50b) are merely *homonyms?*

> (50)   a. It is not true that the murderer is crazy.
>   b. The murderer is not crazy.

It would require a very powerful argument to convince me, or I hope, to convince anyone, that what difference there may be between (50a) and (50b) is a lexical difference rather than a scope difference of *some* kind. Further, Martin is committed to the *thoroughgoing* ambiguity of "not" in English. If his view is correct, then anyone who ever hears the word "not" used in a sentence, whether or not the sentence contains any "presupposition"-related constructions, must disambiguate "not" in order to understand the sentence. This strikes me as preposterous.[13]

Is there any positive reason, then, to posit both a second lexical entry for "not" and a third truth-value, that does not rest on a confusion of some sort? Martin is mindful of the need for a positive justification, and he offers several considerations: (a) By positing the third truth-value and the second reading for "not," we can represent semantic presupposition in an "appealing" way (pp. 253–254; cf. 267). (b) When "not" is regarded as unambiguously bivalent, unwieldy syntax is required to accommodate "presuppositional" phenomena, e.g., the syntax that would be needed to mediate Russell's theory of descriptions (p. 253). (c) "There is an intuitively recognizable difference that separates at least [two] core cases of presupposition failure, as in existential cases . . . or sortal cases . . . , from other non-truths. . . . Even the critics of presupposition admit this intuitive data for existential and sortal cases" (p. 254).

Those of us who deny the existence of semantic presupposition in English can hardly be impressed by consideration (a). Consideration (b) has some force in some cases, but Martin has not shown how a posited third truth-value and second reading of "not" would help to simplify the syntax of (e.g.) definite descriptions, given that definite descriptions have structure that must be revealed by syntax regardless of the underlying semantic. interpretation. The syntactic superiority of presuppositional theories over their bivalent competitors would have to be exhibited on a case-by-case basis (and would have to prove great enough to offset Martin's repellent proliferation of lexical ambiguities).

Consideration (c) is more interesting. I have argued in section 4 that informants' hesitation in issuing truth-value judgments does not amount to reporting the detection of a third truth-value, and I have pointed out earlier in this section that even theorists' intuitions of the necessitation of sentences' presupposita by the sentences' negations are commonly just wrong. But Martin is correct in claiming that informants' characteristic hesitation over sentences whose existential or sortal implications fail (this being "the intuitive difference in non-truths," I take it) still needs explanation. Martin of course contends that the introduction of a third truth-value offers the *best* explanation of such facts.[14] Boër and I proposed competing explanations that I believe are better ones. But it should be admitted that the cases of existential and sortal "presupposition" in particular encourage talk of truth-valuelessness in a more intimate way than do other reputedly "presuppositional" phenomena. I shall now try to bring out the reason why theorists have been so tempted to judge sentences containing singular terms truth-valueless when the world fails to cooperate in certain ways. Utterances of sentences of this type comprise a centrally important case in point, I think, because they provide the sole legitimate basis for Strawson's original intimations of truth-valuelessness in his attack on Russell.

Most superficially singular terms, in English at any rate, contribute meaning to sentences in which they occur, whether or not they have (existing) denotata. For example, most definite descriptions (though not all) do seem to "disappear on analysis" in Russell's way (witness the difficulty of hearing a noncontradictory reading of

(51)   The man reading *Word and Object* in the corner is not reading *Word and Object*).

On the view of singular terms adumbrated in section 3.7 of *MSP* and in Boër and Lycan (1975), this means that such singular terms as "the man reading *Word and Object* in the corner" are "singular" only superficially, being derived from underlying quantificational constructions; it is in part scope confusion with regard to these quantificational structures that has given rise to some talk of semantic presuppositions of sentences containing the superficial descriptions. Some apparent proper names function in this way as well (Boër (1978)).[15] Thus, we may pick out a large class of "singular" terms or term-occurrences that are attributive (Donnellan (1966)) or nonrigid (Kripke (1972)) and do not force the theoretician to invoke semantic presupposition as opposed to entailment. But what of terms that are *not* semantically structured in this way, i.e., genuine or "logically proper" singular terms? *Pace* Russell (1905), who held that *all* singular terms of natural languages are or abbreviate superficial descriptions used attributively, many philosophers believed that some singular terms, primarily demonstratives and proper names, are semantically fused—that they have no hidden semantic structure, but function solely in such a way as to pick out particular individuals as their referents and have meaning solely in virtue of functioning just in this way. It may be that almost all proper names have this "purely referential" use, and if Donnellan (1966) is right on some well-known further points, definite descriptions sometimes do too.

What, then, about a *nondenoting* name or a description that is not being used attributively, that does not vanish in favor of its hidden structure in Russell's way? That is, suppose a singular term (say, the surface subject of an atomic sentence) has neither a denotation nor any semantic connotation. What I believe is that Russell was exactly right in claiming that "the meaning of a genuine [i.e., purely referential] name is its bearer," or, less metaphysically, that a genuine name has meaning or significance only in that it serves to denote what it denotes. Consequently, a connotationless *and* denotationless "name" is, literally, a meaningless particle—not a word of our language.[16] And a string that contains it is therefore simply *ungrammatical,* ill-formed. Thus, there is at least this case in which reference-failure gives rise to truth-valuelessness. For a string such as

(52)   Kanrog rides poorly,

where "Kanrog" neither carries attributive connotation nor denotes anything, is not a sentence, but merely a surface predicate preceded by a meaningless mark or noise; obviously it is therefore neither true nor false.

However, this is cold comfort for the champion of truth-valueless sentences. For a sentence that semantically presupposes another sentence is at least supposed to be a *sentence*, i.e., a *meaningful* or well-formed string, and (52) fails to satisfy this requirement. More trenchantly, notice that the alleged presuppositum in this case,

(53)   Kanrog exists,

is ill-formed and meaningless just as (52) is, for the same reason. It would be pointless indeed to insist of one string of gibberish that it "semantically presupposed" another string of gibberish.

My thesis concerning nonattributive but nondenoting superficial names may strike some readers as being obviously false. Consider

(54)   John loves Mary.

There is an inclination to say that (54) just is grammatical, whether or not the names "John" and "Mary" are imagined to refer to anything. But we intuitively regard (54) as grammatical only because we know that these expressions are commonly used as names of persons. Compare

(55)   Flork loves glork.[17]

Is (55) grammatical or not? If (55) is considered in isolation from any particular context of utterance, this question cannot be answered. If we are told that "flork" and "glork" are names, on the other hand, then our indecision vanishes: (55) gets treated just like (54). But to be a nonattributive name, an expression must be used by someone as a name *of* something. Names are very special lexical items, as everyone knows; except in a loose way, they do not "belong" to any particular language, but are the transitory contributions of particular speakers to the business of speech. The grammaticality of (55) is relative to an assumption about the semantic status of "flork" and "glork," viz., an assumption to the effect that the real or hypothetical utterer of (55) employs these expressions as names of actual things or people.

As discussed at length in chapter 3, a sentence-type is true, or false, only relative to an assignment of denotata to its indexicals and (genuine) names. A particular token of (55) will be grammatical on its occasion of utterance only if denotata are in fact assigned on that occasion to the ingredient tokens of "flork" and "glork," i.e., only if those tokens are used by the speaker on that occasion to name something; and our token of (55) will (if so) have a definite truth-value determined by the amatory relations of the objects so named. If the utterer—improbably—fails to name anything on that occasion, then his utterance of (55) lacks a truth-value in virtue of being ill-formed. But not even this admitted truth-valuelessness requires the semanticist to forsake the framework of classical two-valued logic in favor of an encumbrance of novel semantical apparatus, since no form of logic need respect strings that are simply nonsensical.

Several recent writers on the theory of reference have argued persuasively that the two types of superficial singular terms I have discussed so far do not exhaust the possibilities, or even the actualities. It seems that some apparent singular terms, particularly some proper names, may neither abbreviate full-blown descriptions in Russell's way nor serve *solely* to denote their bearers. If this is so, the semantics of these recalcitrant singular terms is still a mystery; no acceptable account of them has been found.[18] But it is hard to imagine that any such *tertium quid*, once discovered, will prompt the positing of truth-valuelessness in sentences containing nondenoting names, unless the truth-valuelessness is due either to unfixed parameters or to straightforward meaninglessness.

Let us turn to the case of sortals. Sortal "presupposition" was not discussed as a case study in *MSP*, because it had not figured prominently in the "presupposition" literature prior to that time. But the connection between "sortal incorrectness" and semantic presupposition has since been drawn by Martin (1975, 1979) and by von Stechow (1981), on the basis of data like the following:

(56)   a. S is red.
       b. S is not red.
       c. S is colored.

(57)   a. S drinks Y.
       b. S does not drink Y.
       c. S is animate and Y is a liquid.

(58)   a. S is tuned to G♯.
       b. S is not tuned to G♯.
       c. S is capable of producing a musical tone.

(56a), (57a), and (58a) are held to presuppose (56c), (57c), and (58c), respectively.

Ryle's original doctrine of "sortal incorrectness" or "category mistake" (1938, 1949) was that offending instances of (56a), (57a), and (58a), such as

(59)   Well-played golf is red,

(60)   Quadruplicity drinks procrastination,

and

(61) π is tuned to G♯

are *meaningless*. If they are meaningless, then plainly their "denials" are too; "It is false that three spadlaps sat on a bazzafrazz" is no more meaningful than "Three spadlaps sat on a bazzafrazz." If Ryle's doctrine is right, then the case of "sortal presupposition" is like that of the "existential presupposition" of a sentence containing a non-denoting *and* nonconnoting (hence meaningless) "name": (59), (60), and (61) do lack truth-value when the corresponding instances of (56c), (57c), and (58c) are untrue, but (again) only because they are ungrammatical or ill-formed. Semanticists would not have to introduce novel apparatus in order to respect the semantic status of literally nonsensical strings; such strings have no semantic status.

Of course, the doctrine of the literal meaninglessness of category mistakes is highly suspect (I doubt that even Ryle himself would have assimilated category mistakes strictly to *gibberish* such as "Three spadlaps sat on a bazzafrazz" or "Umph the but g kreesplat blunk"). For one thing, none of (59)–(61) contains either any non-word or any illicit surface-grammatical concatenation. If any of them is marked "ungrammatical" by any theorist's syntax, it is only because the theorist has *stipulated* by means of a "selectional restriction" or a "meaning postulate" that category mistakes like these are not to be counted as well-formed. I think the doctrine is also impugned by the same sort of argument that worked plausibly against verificationism: We have to know what (59)–(61) say in order to tell that they cannot be true. For example, we have to know that (60) ascribes to quadruplicity (an abstract numerical attribute of all manner of things) the property of drinking (hence ingesting) procrastination (a habit indulged in by certain people). Otherwise we would not be able to apply our prior knowledge that such things cannot be (that the items in question are not the kinds of things that can drink each other), in order to judge that (60) cannot be true. If we know what (60) says, then there is something that (60) says. If (60) says something, then (60) is not *meaningless*, even if there is something drastically wrong with (60).

If they are not literally meaningless, what *is* wrong with (59)–(61)? To say that they violate selectional restrictions or the like is no answer, since this is just to repeat that they are category mistakes. Martin's answer is, simply, that their semantic presuppositions fail. If they have semantic presuppositions that fail, of course, they are truth-valueless; that is what is wrong with them. The occurrences of "not" in the corresponding instances of (56b), (57b), and (58b) presumably express Bochvar-"internal" negation again, or some souped-up version of it based on the theory of superlanguages. And again, some informants' intuitions about category-mistaken sentences are noteworthy: many people feel that (59)–(61) are not just false in the ordinary way, but suffer from some more radical deficiency.

I am not sure what solid motivation one might find for accepting Martin's hypothesis. If someone simply announces that what is wrong with (59)–(61) is that they lack truth-value, and lets it go at that, he has raised more questions than he has answered: *Why* do these sentences lack truth-value instead of being false, given that they are not meaningless? Why should truth-valueless (though meaningful) sentences sound any funnier than sentences that are just so absurdly false that no one could possibly believe them? What exactly distinguishes a "sortally incorrect" sentence from an ordinary falsehood, and how might we represent the distinguishing property in our semantics without simply marking certain predicates as "restricted against" or "contraindicated for" other expressions?

Besides these awkward questions, there are the standard difficulties for Ryle's notion of a "category mistake" that do not turn specifically on a strong and literal interpretation of the pejorative "meaningless." First, what is the difference between a "category" or *kind* (as in "X is not the *kind* of thing that could ϕ") and a mere group? Is a "category" simply *larger* or more inclusive than an ordinary collection of things? But size and inclusiveness come in degrees; they do not lend themselves to the absolute distinction one draws when one marks some sentences as merely false but others as neuter. Indeed, intuitions of sortal incorrectness themselves seem to come in degrees—"category mistakes" shade off rather smoothly into ordinary falsehoods ("π weighs twenty pounds"—"Honesty weighs twenty pounds"—"Ali's honesty weighs twenty pounds"—"Ali's left hook weighs twenty pounds"—"The singularity in field F weighs twenty pounds"—"The electron in the chamber weighs twenty pounds"—"Fort Knox weighs twenty pounds"—"Jumbo the elephant weighs twenty pounds"). These facts strongly suggest that the deficiency of (59)–(61), whatever exactly it may be, is itself something that comes in degrees (such as outrageousness or obviousness of falsity), rather than something absolute such as lack of truth-value.

Martin has a more powerful motivation in mind for maintaining the truth-valuelessness of category mistakes (pp. 250, 274). He contends that negations like (56b), (57b), and (58b) "imply" or necessitate the alleged presupposita just as (56a), (57a), and (58a) do. If this is correct, then the truth-valuelessness of (59)–(61) is not a dubious explanatory claim that enlightens less than it mystifies, but an apodeictic consequence of facts of logical necessitation.

My objection to this argument is that Martin's claims of necessitation seem plainly false. I suppose the negations of (59), (60), and (61) respectively suggest (62), (63), and (64) *via* the Maxim of Strength:

(62) Well-played golf is colored.

(63) Quadruplicity is animate and procrastination is a liquid.

(64) π is capable of producing a musical tone.

But these suggestions are easily cancellable:

(65) Well-played golf is not red, or any other color.

(66) It's false that quadruplicity drinks procrastination; quadruplicity isn't even animate, and procrastination is a habit people have, not a liquid.

(67) π is not tuned to G♯ or any other pitch. It's not even capable of producing a musical tone—it's a *number*, for God's sake.

Any strangeness I can hear in (65)–(67) is due entirely to their forehead-smacking obviousness. Certainly they are not contradictions; indeed, I would call them excessively plain truths. Martin may reply (again) that I am hearing the negations as bivalent rather than as Bochvar-"internal" and therefore am missing the point. But, as in the case of (32) and (33), it is precisely this "point" that is in dispute; I see no motive at all for supposing that (65)–(67) *have* Bochvar-"internal" readings. I cannot hear any alternative self-contradictory readings of those sentences at all. Of course, I cannot *prove* to anyone that they have no such readings, any more than I can prove to anyone that "Pigs have wings" has no reading on which it is a contradiction, or on which it entails "John Glenn will win the Democratic nomination," but the facts seem equally plain. If so, (59)–(61) do not semantically presuppose (62)–(64).

There is a further objection that to my knowledge has never been noticed before. What about the alleged presupposita, (62)–(64) themselves? They sound quite odd. In fact, to my ear they sound exactly as peculiar as (59)–(61), and in just the same way. Are we to conclude that they themselves semantically presuppose some still weaker sentences? If so, what could these further, weaker presupposita be? If not, then the oddity of (62)–(64) is not to be explained by reference to semantic presupposition, and so there is no reason to think that the oddity of (59)–(61) is either.

7. Diagnosis

If my skepticism about truth-valuelessness is as well justified as I believe it is, then there ought to be some further diagnosis of the fervor with which philosophers and linguists have embraced the notion. I believe that the correct causal explanation is to be found in Austin's pellucid doctrine of infelicities (1962, lectures XI and XII), though I shall expand somewhat on Austin's remarks in a way of which he might have disapproved.[19]

Austin was concerned to point out that, from the standpoint of speech-act theory taken in the large, a given speech act can be (and is, in particular cases) assessed or evaluated along a number of distinct and independent "dimensions of criticism," or types of satisfactoriness and unsatisfactoriness. This is clearest in the case of "pure" (explicit) performatives; a performative speech act can go wrong in any one of a number of different ways, some more tragic than others depending on context. But the same is true of any other speech act. So far as I can see, there is in nature no such thing as a "pure constative," though (on my view) an SR or logical form is a picture of one, in perhaps the same sense as that in which we can draw a picture of a mass-point or a black box.

The true/false dimension is just one avenue of criticism among others; there are many other ways of being satisfactory or unsatisfactory, felicitous or infelicitous, happy or unhappy. And (here is the key point) the importance of the true/false dimension in fact varies widely from context to context with the passing purposes of speakers, hearers, and assessors. Sometimes we care very much about truth and falsity. At other times we care much more about other sorts of virtues and faults. I think, in fact, that cases of the latter sort predominate rather heavily. Philosophers' treatment (prior to Austin) of English sentences as if all that mattered about them were their truth-values is an occupational disease, and has resulted in "true"'s having come to be, in many philosophers' vocabularies, the only honorific applicable to utterances. This is a crucial point to which I shall return.

Consider a case of Richard Garner's, offered in conversation: A speaker suddenly utters a declarative sentence on a topic that he knows nothing about, say,

> (68)   At this moment there are exactly three customers sitting in the Cantonese restaurant downtown,

in a context in which it is clear that the speaker cannot possibly have any positive evidence for the truth of (68). Something is wrong; the utterance is unhappy in some way yet to be specified. But it certainly need not be denigrated along the true/false dimension; the sentence uttered, (68), may very well be true—or, more likely, false.

Similarly, take Moore's Paradox:

(69)   It's raining, but I don't believe that it is.

In the absence of very special stage-setting, (69) is anomalous. Though much has been written about it, both by "ordinary language" philosophers and by epistemic logicians, no one has ever quite succeeded in showing exactly what is wrong with it.[20] The important thing to see here is that although an utterance of (69) is almost invariably as infelicitous as any utterance could be, (69) might perfectly well be true (of the speaker); this fact, indeed, is essential to setting up the Paradox.

Finally, take a negated factive,

(70)   Herbert doesn't know that June is a go-go dancer,

uttered in a situation in which its complement is false. There is no question but that this utterance, given appropriate stress contour, is infelicitous (in *MSP* Boër and I suggested that the infelicity is partly statistical and partly Gricean). But, as we have seen, that does not affect (70)'s truth-value in the situation envisioned, since (70) is straightforwardly true—for what that is worth!

It is this last phrase that best expresses my view about "presupposition" and truth-value. In each of the foregoing three cases, something has gone badly wrong with the speaker's utterance. But there is no reason at all why this should lead us to judge that the sentence uttered lacks a truth-value.

Now we may proceed to explain philosophers' and linguists' enthusiasm for imputing truth-valuelessness to sentences whose only crime is that their "presuppositions" have failed. As I remarked earlier, philosophers at least have always grotesquely overemphasized the true/false dimension in thinking about language, to the extent that "true" is regarded as a kind of diploma. Once we have decided that a sentence is true, we pat it on the head and pass on to the next sentence we want to evaluate. And, I believe, it is this habit that accounts at least for philosophers' occasional invocations of truth-valuelessness. Faced with a sentence that, although undeniably grammatical, sounds funny when its "presupposition" has failed, a philosopher is extremely reluctant to call it "true," for to do this is to give the sentence a passing grade, to honor it in what seems to the philosopher to be a conclusive way. And yet the philosopher does not want to call the sentence "false," either, for to do that is to fail the sentence, to condemn it in an apparently conclusive way obviously unwarranted by the situation. The philosopher concludes that the sentence is not true, and that it is not false—hence, that it is neither true nor false, and so, truth-valueless.

The mistake is the philosopher's taking "true" and "false" far too seriously in the first place. Why not just admit that the sentence is true (or false, whichever seems dictated by the assumed facts, what we know of its truth-conditions, and considerations of theoretical elegance), for what that is worth (very little), and get on to more important kinds of evaluation of the sentence and hypothetical speech acts in which it occurs? That is, let us give up our excessively honorific use of "true" and recognize that, in the sorts of cases we are talking about, to admit that a sentence is true is no great concession, but is only a prefatory note to getting on with evaluation along dimensions perhaps more pertinent to everyday life.

This same failure to appreciate Austin's vital insight that "true" and "false" comprise only one among many important pairs of terms used for the praise and blame of utterances has, I suspect, misled linguists as well. For example, Karttunen writes (1971, p. 344), "[*John didn't manage to solve the problem*, if John did not even try to solve the problem,] would have to be rejected as an infelicitous utterance to which no truth value could be assigned"—the implication being that the infelicitousness of the utterance in the context envisioned is the *reason why* "no truth value could be assigned" to the sentence uttered; in that context (as I have heard some linguists put it), the sentence is "too infelicitous" to be true or false. But this attitude radically misconceives the status of truth and falsity as evaluative properties of utterances or sentences. The true/false dimension, it will be remembered, is only one avenue of evaluation among others; it is not a final touchstone that an assessor applies only after having run through all the "lesser" infelicities and found the sentence acceptable in all preliminary respects. A sentence or utterance can be infelicitous to an arbitrarily extreme degree in any number of respects and still be true (or false). To say of a sentence that it must lack a truth-value because it "is infelicitous," or that it is "too infelicitous to have a truth-value," is like saying of a dog that is blind and bad at following scents that it is therefore neither loyal nor disloyal, or of a man that he is so bad at his job and so ugly and such a rotten poker player that he is neither kind to his mother nor unkind to her.[21]

8. "The Projection Problem"

A notable quantity of ink has been spilled over what Langendoen and Savin (1971) called "the projection problem" for presupposition, viz., the task of explaining how the (alleged) presuppositions of a complex sentence are determined by those of that sentence's component clauses. Is there a recursive recipe for predicting the presuppositions of a compound sentence given the presupposition set of each of its atomic parts? Langendoen and Savin proposed simply that "[p]resuppositions of a subordinate clause . . . stand as presuppositions of the complex sentence in which they occur" (p. 57). This "cumulative hypothesis" was multiply counterexampled (Morgan (1969), Katz (1972), Karttunen (1973)). Karttunen argued that although some sentence operators are indeed "holes" in that they preserve all the presuppositions of their operands, others are "plugs" and preserve none whatever except under special conditions, and some binary connectives, "filters," block the presuppositions of one of their operands given certain contextual facts about the other. Numerous attempts have since been made to improve on this account (Hausser (1973), Liberman (1973), Reis (1974), Stalnaker (1974), Karttunen (1974), Soames (1979b), Gazdar (1979b), and Karttunen and Peters (1979), among others).

My response to "the projection problem" should already be clear from earlier sections of this chapter (particularly sections 3, 4, 5, and 7). If by 'presupposition' a theorist means genuine semantic presupposition, then even if there is such a thing in English we are in no great difficulty. The notion of semantic presupposition as defined in section 3 is a nice, clear one, requiring only an adequate three-valued logic to display its formal properties. For truth-functional sentence operators, e.g., the three-valued logic will show us at a glance how the semantic presuppositions of a compound sentence depend on those of its atomic constituents.[22] For non-truth-functional operators the logic will have to be extended in a natural way. (Certainly there will be some arbitrariness introduced at one point or another, as there is even for three-valued definitions of the truth-functions; so much the worse for positing a third truth-value.) For constructions so troublesome as to threaten compositionality itself, such as propositional-attitude operators and quotation, semantic presupposition still occasions no *especial* difficulty. Whatever methods are invoked to handle such troublemakers in the normal case will presumably be adaptable to a three-valued system also.[23]

Continuing ardent concern over "the projection problem" seems to me symptomatic of deep confusion, just as was Lakoff's worry about transitivity (see note 4). *If by 'presupposition' a theorist genuinely means semantic presupposition,* he should see no particular problem about projection, but only the usual difficulties of compositionality slightly augmented by occasionally having to settle decisions about the distribution of the third truth-value.

If by 'presupposition' we mean something looser, on the other hand, complications ensue. Suppose we concentrate exclusively on "pragmatic presupposition," i.e., on the seething multiplicity of diverse pragmatic implicative relations that do obtain within natural languages. Then, I submit, there is no *single* "projection problem," and certainly no interesting (and statable) generalizations about projection. The implicative relations over which any such generalizations would be defined are simply too various and rooted in too disparate areas of pragmatics. Of course, each particular relation— conversational implicature, "invited inference," unemphasized entailment, illocutionary felicity-conditions of various kinds, etc., etc. — might be tackled individually if sufficiently amenable to formalization. For example, Gazdar (1979b) formalizes the Maxim of Strength and offers a theory of the projective behavior of implicatures based on it. But a piecemeal approach of this sort is the best and the most interesting that we can hope for. There can be no general solution to "the" projection problem.

Chapter 5
Lexical Presumption

Some linguists[1] have alleged that certain syntactic phenomena require a notion of presupposition, in that one and the same sentence may be *grammatically* deviant or ill-formed relative to some ways the world might be, and yet perfectly acceptable relative to other ways the world might be. (I use "relative to" here as a gloss designed to blur the distinction between the fact of the way the world is, the speaker's or hearer's belief about the way the world is, the speech community's shared background information about the way the world is, etc.[2] I shall speak hereafter simply of "*presumptions.*") Now, if a string S_1 is well-formed only given the truth of a sentence S_2 or in light of the fact S_2 describes, this provides considerable temptation to say that S_1 presumes or "presupposes" S_2 in some sense or other; and in view of the intimate connection between syntactic deep structure and semantic representation or logical form, it suggests that the kind of presumption in question is semantical or at least semantically relevant. In fact, a brief argument suffices to show that if well-formedness is relative in this way to factual presumptions about the world, then a strong form of Strawsonian semantic presupposition is viable after all: if the failure of some (logically contingent) factual presumption S_2 suffices to render an otherwise grammatical string S_1 ungrammatical or ill-formed, and if (as is uncontroversial) a string must at least be well-formed in order to be either true or false, then the failure of S_2 *a fortiori* renders S_1 truth-valueless; thus, if Lakoff (1969) is right about the relativity of grammaticality, S_1(by definition) semantically presupposes S_2.

Notice that the brand of truth-valuelessness appealed to here is far less mysterious (on its face) than that denigrated in section 4 of chapter 4. The latter is the reputed truth-valuelessness of an admittedly well-formed sentence in certain contingent circumstances, requiring bizarre alterations in what we would ordinarily and naturally take to be the truth-condition to be assigned to that sentence (see particularly the cases of nonrestrictive relative clauses and negated factives discussed in sections 3.1 and 3.3 of *MSP*) and seemingly needless complications in our logic. The truth-valuelessness that allegedly arises from presumption failure in a case of "relative grammaticality," however, is nothing so offensively arcane or baroque—it is simply the unexciting truth-valuelessness of an ill-formed string. An ungrammatical sequence of words need not be assigned any unusual truth-condition, since it is assigned no truth-condition at all.

1. Factual Presumptions and Logical Form

Unlike most of the data underlying the claims Boër and I discussed in chapter 3 of *MSP*, some of the phenomena cited as examples of "relative grammaticality" are striking, evidently real, and hard to explain away. I shall take up only a few of the cases that I find the most interesting and troublesome for a semantic purist of my stripe.

A. Laurence Horn (1969) argues that certain sentences containing "only" and "even" are well-formed only in contexts in which certain contingent factual presumptions hold. (Lakoff (1972, pp. 581ff.) gives a useful summary of Horn's data.) For example, a sentence of the form

  (1)   Even A ϕ'd

is deviant, ungrammatical, or at least quite peculiar if it was not expected that A would not ϕ, or if there was no one besides A that ϕ'd. (As always, I leave open the question of who it is that is doing the expecting.) The exact nature of the deviance or peculiarity here is as yet unspecified.[3]

B. Lakoff (1969) argues convincingly that the relative pronoun "who" can be used grammatically only when it is presumed that its subject is regarded for purposes of the discussion as denoting a person, as opposed to a mere thing or lower animal. (Lakoff, citing McCawley, finds it interesting that "semantics" is here invading an area that used to be thought of as "purely syntactic," viz., judgments of deviance or ungrammaticality; since syntax and semantics are no longer regarded as being separate and autonomous areas of inquiry, this invasion is not surprising. What is surprising is that our judgments of syntactic/semantic *deviance* should vary with our background beliefs or presumptions. To a semantic purist like me, what information about a sentence is encapsulated in that sentence's SR *qua* deep structure *or* logical form should not depend on any contingent factual presumptions about the way the nonlinguistic world is; it is a purely formal matter. I shall pursue this below.)

C. Lakoff goes on to show (pp. 109–10) that intonation contour is sometimes dictated by background beliefs. Contrast:

(2)   a. John called Mary a lexicalist and then *she* insulted *him*.
    b. John called Mary a lexicalist and then she *insulted* him.

If we agree that intonation contour is at least sometimes a semantic matter—e.g., that intonation contour sometimes suffices literally to disambiguate an utterance that it characterizes—we can generate more cases in which background beliefs appear to affect syntactic and semantic well-formedness.

    D. "Either," "too," and "instead" carry factual presumptions not unlike those carried by "even" (cf. case A). Lakoff claims, citing (3a) and (3b),

(3)   a.   Jane is a sloppy housekeeper and she doesn't take
       baths either.
    b.   ?*Jane is a neat housekeeper and she doesn't take
       baths either.

that "[t]he construction, *A and not B either,* carries with it the presupposition that one might expect *A* to entail *not B*" (p. 110). Of course, this is wrong as it stands—what speakers expect about entailment is irrelevant. Presumably what Lakoff means is just that one would not expect *A and B,* and in this he seems unmistakably right. Consider also the following contrasts:[4]

(4)   a.   Jane just succeeded in proving Fermat's Last Theorem,
       and her husband is very brilliant $\left\{\begin{array}{l}\text{too}\\\text{as well}\end{array}\right\}$.
    b.   ?*Jane just added 2 and 2 and got 6, and her husband is
       very brilliant $\left\{\begin{array}{l}\text{too}\\\text{as well}\end{array}\right\}$.

(5)   a.   Jane considered going to the dentist, but decided to
       enjoy her day off instead.
    b.   ?*Jane considered taking a pleasant ride through the
       countryside, having a really good dinner, and seeing
       a movie, but decided to enjoy her day off instead.

    Lakoff concludes on the basis of such data[5] that, whereas we may continue to use "deviant," "ill-formed," "ungrammatical," etc., as predicates of utterance(-token)s in context, they and their positive cognates must now be construed as designating relations between string(-type)s and sets of factual judgments; a string is well- or ill-formed only relative to such a set. Thus, we arrive at a strong notion of semantic presupposition by allowing factual presumptions to invade semantics *via* syntax.

Two theoretical arguments are contained here. One, which we may call the Argument from Generative Semantics, is not fully explicit in Lakoff's text, but I think it is one he would accept, since it captures a piece of motivation for the invocation of "presupposition" in semantic theory that is based squarely on the central claim of the semantical program he helped to found: (i) The Lakovian presumptions affect syntactic well-formedness. (ii) SRs or logical forms are the input to syntactic derivations. Therefore, (iii) the Lakovian presumptions are in some way part of semantic content or logical form.

The second theoretical argument (hereafter, the Argument from Meaningfulness) is a more explicitly semantical version of that provided at the beginning of the present section: neglecting well-known cases of "semi-," borderline, or marginal grammaticalness, a string must be well-formed or grammatical in order to be meaningful. Further, a string must be meaningful in order to have any semantic properties at all (save, trivially, that of meaninglessness). Therefore, if the grammaticalness of a string depends on contingent factual presumptions, then so do the string's very meaningfulness and *a fortiori* its other semantic properties.

The moral of each of the two arguments is that factual presumptions ought in some way to be represented in our semantic accounts of the target sentences in question. And, more generally, syntax and semantics ought hereafter to be conceived as being context-relative; they are not the austere, purely formal disciplines they have been supposed to be; one cannot pursue them successfully without taking into account particular utterers in particular situations.

In keeping with the overall thrust of this book, I want to resist these conclusions. I believe there is important theoretical utility to be gained by splitting semiotic study into that which pertains to the formal properties of sentences considered apart from particular contexts, on the one hand, and relations that the same sentences bear to features of particular situations, on the other. In particular, I want to hold to our perfectly natural inclination to say that a sentence simply has a certain meaning or meanings in English, and that it simply has a certain range of possible uses, these being specifiable quite independently of contextual considerations.[6] And certainly we should not want to court the counterintuitiveness and ugly theoretical complications of supposing that the very recursive rules that delineate well-formedness (rules that seem by their very nature to be purely formal) depend in any way on mention of specific possible states of affairs. Intuitively, a sentence is either a well-formed string of English or it is not (again barring borderline cases), regardless of what speakers, hearers, or theorists may happen to believe about nonlinguistic reality.

If we are to resist Lakoff's skeptical conclusions, then, we must turn aside both of the theoretical arguments I have sketched, and find some alternative account of the phenomena; and this will not be entirely easy to do, since the arguments appear to be valid and the data are hard. Let us begin with the Argument from Generative Semantics. (I shall return to the Argument from Meaningfulness considerably later.)

Lakoff has not *shown* that premise (i) is true. In the respective contexts envisioned, it is plain that there is something wrong with tokening the strings in question—"wrong" at least in the general sense of "inappropriate," "illicit," or "nasty." What Lakoff has not demonstrated is that the awfulness is specifically syntactic ill-formedness. It is *possible* in each of the cases I have listed that the penalty of "presupposition" failure is not syntactic defectiveness at all, but infelicitousness of an Austinian sort, Gricean conversational unacceptability, or some other nonsyntactic flaw. (In short, the relation between a string and its associated set of factual presumptions may well be pragmatic, as its essential contextualness naturally leads us to expect.) The problem for us here, which distinguishes Lakoff's phenomena from most alleged cases of semantic presupposition, is that no such pragmatic explanation comes readily to mind—the ugliness of (3b), (4b), and (5b), and the like has no obvious pragmatic source.

Fortunately, we need not await the development of a detailed pragmatics in order to defuse the Argument from Generative Semantics. For we still have the option of denying premise (ii), despite its apparent centrality to the Metatheory. The first thing to notice is that, if the argument is to be regarded as valid, premise (ii) must be interpreted exclusively, i.e., as (ii') SRs or logical forms are the *sole* input to syntactic derivations. Otherwise (ii) would leave it open that the Lakovian presumptions be *nonsemantic* input to the syntactic derivations. And indeed, this latter possibility is precisely what I want to hypothesize as fact. This requires, of course, that we deny (ii'); I hereby do so, for there is independent evidence of its falsity.

For example, there are several convincing reasons to think that syntactic transformations operate in part on underlying performative prefaces that refer to the speech act that the speaker is thereby performing.[7] Thus, for example, a declarative sentence such as

(6)   Fred is fat

has an underlying syntactic structure something like

(7)

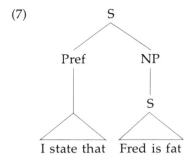

I state that   Fred is fat

Now, contrary to slips or malapropisms on the part of a few linguists, it is plain that this posited performative preface is not part of *logical form* or *semantic content* in acceptably precise senses of those terms. A logical form assigned to a sentence, on the Russellian usage we have pursued so far, determines a fully disambiguated reading of that sentence, along with a truth-condition for that reading, and thereby (in the context of a containing logical theory) codifies all of the sentence's entailment-relations—nothing more. And it is clear that the performative preface displayed in (7) plays no role in determining the conditions under which (6) is true, or what is or is not entailed by (6). Thus, Lakoff himself writes, plausibly,[8]

> Note that in sentences it is the propositional content, not the entire sentence, that will be true or false . . . in sentences where there is an overt performative verb of saying or stating or asserting, the propositional content, which is true or false, is not given by the sentence as a whole, but rather by the object of that performative verb. (1972, p. 560)

The "propositional content" referred to is precisely the scope or complement of the performative operator. The specification of *overt* performative verbs is inessential to the point. Entailment-relations, and truth-conditions generally, are to be read *out from under* the performative preface, and so, consequently, is logical form. Contrary to what Lakoff goes on neologistically to say, a (fully interpreted) logical form does not properly contain propositional content—it *is* propositional content. The semantic content of a sentence is one thing; the illocutionary force of that sentence, or the (pragmatic) use to which it is put on some occasion, is quite another, though both notions are important to the understanding of "meaning" taken diffusely in the large.

The relevance of the underlying performative prefaces to our discussion of "relative grammaticality" is that they provide a counterexample to premise (ii') of the revised Argument from Generative Semantics. Logical form, properly construed, is not the *sole* input to the transformational component, for transformations operate as well on performative material, and performative material is not part of logical form. (Thus, if we take "deep structure" to be, by definition, whatever it is that syntactic transformations take as input, we can no longer accept the suggestion that deep structure may simply be identified with logical form. Deep structure has logical form as a proper part.) Now, what I want to suggest is that there is at least a second sort of input to the transformational component: factual presumptions. That is, I intend to concede that contingent factual presumptions do indeed affect syntactic processes, but deny the alleged implication that these presumptions have semantical repercussions. In this way we may admit their existence and their syntactic relevance without courting the troublesome and counterintuitive claim that a sentence's semantic properties (as codified in the logical form(s) assigned to the sentence) vary with contingent fact.

No one who takes seriously the contention that syntactic processes have "psychological reality" need find this proposal startling. It is not surprising that performative prefaces affect syntactic derivations, since what one wants and intends to *do* with one's words, no less than the thought (so to speak) passing through one's mind, may certainly be expected to affect the causal processes that structure one's actual speech. Likewise, we would expect the background beliefs stored in one's belief-stockpile to affect these processes too. So it is quite natural to suggest that sets of beliefs should serve as input to syntactic transformations just as performative prefaces do, or at least that some transformations should be sensitive to them.

2. Alternative Analyses

I hypothesize that the transformations that are sensitive to contingent factual beliefs are relatively superficial. Consider case C in the previous section, that of presumptive intonation contours. My inclination is to suppose that the relevant stress is functioning only conversationally in such cases; but, rather than put forward a Gricean theory applicable to stress phenomena (cf. Grice (1978)), let us suppose for the sake of argument that stress contour cuts deeper than this, to the extent that a sentence uttered with inappropriate intonation relative to the contextually presumed beliefs is syntactically and not just conversationally unacceptable. If so, I suggest, the beliefs affect the syntactic process somewhere in the relatively superficial subprocess of *lexicalization* (if intonation is taken to be a lexical matter), or even in the phonological component (if we are careful to distinguish a theoretical level of "surface structure" from what is ultimately produced in the form of patterns of noises or marks). It seems clear that the truth-conditions of (2a) and (2b) are precisely the same—though of course this would be denied by someone who held that (2a) is ill-formed and hence has no truth-condition at all in contexts in which it is presumed that it is good to be a lexicalist. Why not adopt the far more natural alternative of saying, not that in such a context (2a) has been produced from no logical form at all, but that it has been produced from a conjunctive logical form (the same one that underlies (2b)) by a syntactic process culminating in a regrettably defective lexicalization?

It is much more obvious that Lakoff's data concerning "who" (case B) are lexical in nature. When a syntactic process requires the insertion of a relative pronoun, the syntactic component waits until almost all its operations have been completed before deciding whether to lexicalize that pronoun as "who" or as "which." The choice, to be sure, is dictated by a nonsemantic factor; but it is quite a superficial choice.

The insertion of "even," "too," and "either" (cf. cases A and D) is nearly as superficial, I should think, triggered rather late in the transformational process by items from whatever set of factual presumptions is in play. Since I want so far as possible to avoid resting my main contentions on substantive and probably controversial syntactic claims (not being in a position to defend such claims in any detail), I shall not try to flesh out an articulated theory of the sources of the Lakovian particles. But if a grammar is to be sensitive enough to factual presumptions to mark the Lakovian target sentences as being ungrammatical relative to the relevant presumptions, then that grammar must have some way of recording that relativity. I suggest that the most natural and appropriate procedure is simply to flag some transformations in such a way as to limit their operation to occasions of favorable conditions in a speaker's (or whoever's) belief-store.[9]

I am a little more troubled by example (5). The presumption of (5a) is evidently that going to the dentist is not enjoyable (that going to the dentist and enjoying oneself tend to preclude one another); and the (true) presumption relative to which (5b) is deviant is that taking a pleasant ride through the countryside, etc., are enjoyable (or at least do not tend to preclude one's enjoying oneself). I am not sure exactly what is going on here, but I shall hazard some cautious preliminary syntactic remarks designed simply to illustrate the pattern of explanation that I find attractive.

It seems clear enough that "instead," at least in sentences like (5a–b), contains a hidden reference back to a previously occurring item; "instead" cannot occur in the absence of any assumed antecedent:

(8)   *The whale is a mammal instead.

(9)   *Two and two is four instead.

Probably there is a deleted redundancy—viz., "instead" in (5) very likely comes from *instead of NP,* where "NP" is replaced by a repetition of the original noun or nominal phrase. Thus, (5a) would come from

(10)   Jane considered going to the dentist, but decided to enjoy her day off instead of going to the dentist,

the "instead of"-clause being inside the scope of "decided."[10]

It is less plausible here to say that "instead" is inserted superficially in response to the presence of a factual belief, if "instead" is indeed not a merely inserted item like "even" or "too." If "instead" derives from an entire underlying clause, then it is less easy to fall back on our practice of saying that it is just kicked in lexically at the eleventh hour by a piece of background information.

What may possibly be happening here is that *instead of* in intermediate structure comes from a sentential connective, and is inserted when the connected sentences are nominalized (if the nominalizations do come from underlying sentences, as they may or may not). The connective in question may well be *and not.* If so, then it is plausible to suggest that "instead of" as a particular lexicalization of & has a contrastive connotation (unlike other lexicalizations such as *and not*), just as "but" is a lexicalization of & that is distinguished from other possible lexicalizations in that it carries the suggestion of contrast. And this brings us to a brief discussion of the nature of "contrastive connotation" itself. (Cf. R. Lakoff (1971).)

A naive theorist might demand that sentences whose main surface connective is "and" and those whose main connective is "but" be assigned different logical forms. For example, since

(11)   George believes in semantic presupposition but he's smart

suggests in whatever sense that we do not expect believers in semantic presupposition to be smart, whereas

(12)   George believes in semantic presupposition and he's smart

carries no such suggestion, it might be said that (11) and (12) have different underlying semantic structures. I believe this would be seriously mistaken. For, considered from the austere standpoint of truth-conditions alone, (11) and (12) would seem to be equivalent. Since (12) is true if George believes in semantic presupposition and George is smart, this commits us to saying that (11) is true in that circumstance as well.

Perhaps the contention that (11) and (12) have the same truth-condition will be seen as simply question-begging. After all, if (11) is ill-formed in a context in which it is not presumed that belief in semantic presupposition tends to preclude being smart, then (11) and (12) can hardly have the same truth-condition, there being at least one possible state of affairs in which (12) is true but (11) is un-true (because ungrammatical). I shall argue against this last claim by considering that possible state of affairs a little more closely. Suppose we are in a seminar room full of semantic presupposition enthusi-asts, and that these worthies have convinced us that the notion of semantic presupposition is not only viable but a sharp and indis-pensable tool for linguistic semantics in this century. No one in the room doubts this for a moment; any one of us, faced with a philos-opher who failed to recognize the prevalence of truth-valuelessness, would conclude either that the philosopher's intuitions and *a priori* assumptions were badly soured or clouded by years of teaching in-troductory logic, or that the philosopher was a jerk. Now suppose that someone in the company asserts (11), referring by his use of "George" to someone who is not present. It seems clear that, al-though the speaker's utterance is deviant in the context, nevertheless what he says has significant implications. For example, he could jus-tifiably be held linguistically responsible for the truth of the claim that George is smart (the speaker did, after all, *say* that George is smart). If George turns out to be stupid despite his belief in semantic presupposition, then, it seems to me, the speaker has *inter alia* asserted something false. Now, if even in a context elaborately safe-guarded against the presumption that believing in semantic presup-position tends to preclude being smart, the speaker's utterance is held to have implications (it entails its conjuncts at least) and to be (even "in part") false, then it has semantic properties and hence is not meaningless or semantically ill-formed in the context.

The case is even clearer if we imagine that the speaker, rather than being one of our own number, has just entered from the outside. He may utter (11), believing that Boër and Lycan were right in *MSP* and that they never should have been persuaded to recant. What are we (the occupants of the seminar room) to say about this utterance of

(11)? Should we say that it is ungrammatical and hence meaningless, though the speaker remains gaily unaware of this? That the speaker's own apparent belief in (11)'s presumption suffices by itself to render his utterance is meaningful "for him" but not meaningful "for us," whatever that might mean? Whatever choice we make here, one thing that seems indisputable is that, as before, the utterance has implications and admits at least of the possibility of being false; and if so, then it is meaningful and hence grammatical in the context, period.

But is there not something wrong with uttering (11) in a context in which no one believes or pretends to believe that believing in semantic presupposition tends to preclude being smart? Certainly there is, but not necessarily falsity, truth-valuelessness, or any other semantic defect. An utterance of (11) would be inappropriate. But why?

3. Lexical Presumption and Conventional Implicature

It would be hard to explain the inappropriateness in terms of conversational implicature, since there is nothing wrong with the literal locutionary content of (11)—it does not appear to violate any conversational maxim, and hence does not give rise to a Gricean argument on the part of the hearer. Nor, though the utterance of (11) in a hostile situation would certainly be infelicitous in some way, would the infelicity be of any characteristic Austinian sort, for nothing would go wrong in any standard way with the speech act performed (*qua* speech act)—there is no temptation to accuse the utterer of having failed to make a statement, or of having violated any of the standard "regulative" conditions on stating.

The problem seems intuitively to reside in the choice of the *word* "but," and thus to be a lexical problem. This brings us back to the pattern of explanation employed in connection with "who," "even," "too," and "either." The lexicalizing transformation that produces English reflections of $\&$ is sensitive to factual presumptions: if it is presumed (by whomever) that the truth of S_1 tends to preclude that of S_2, then the occurrence of $\&$ in $S_1 \& S_2$ will be lexicalized as "but"; otherwise not. And what is wrong with (11) in a context in which no one has the relevant belief is that *But*-Lexicalization has gone off half-cocked. It has operated on its own, without the appropriate trigger. A parallel account may explain the behavior of "instead": I have suggested that "instead" reflects a shallowly underlying *instead of*, and the latter appears to be a specialized lexicalization of $\&\sim$ (waiving questions of how and where in the derivation lexical insertion

occurs), properly triggered only when the speaker's store of presumptions includes the belief that one of the relevant alternatives
excludes the other. The string

> (13)   *Jane thought of going swimming, but decided to go
>   swimming instead

is completely unacceptable because the presumption that going
swimming tends to preclude going swimming is self-contradictory.

A similar if slightly extended strategy may suffice to account for
the presumptive behavior of counterfactuals. Our feelings about
counterfactuals with true antecedents are very strong, and (in my
own case) they bear interesting introspective similarities to my feelings about "even," "but," "instead," etc. It is possible that the deviance of a counterfactual with a true antecedent is, like theirs,
lexical. Notice that the problem arises only in connection with the
superficial subjunctive mood. Even when a conditional expresses a
speculative hypothesis, its antecedent may acceptably be true if it is
couched in the overtly indicative mood, as in

> (14)   If it turns out that Haj comes to the party, there'll be a
>   volleyball game,

which is perfectly acceptable even when it does turn out that Haj
attends. Now it is interesting that the subjunctive mood (excluding
the hortatory subjunctive) is in a way not on a par with the other
moods of a traditional English grammar: indicative, interrogative,
imperative. Each of the latter corresponds to a general type of speech
act (stating, asking, ordering, etc.) and is produced at the surface
presumably by transformations that are triggered by something like
corresponding performative prefaces in syntactic deep structure. The
subjunctive mood, by contrast, corresponds to no familiar general
type of speech act and is presumably not so produced. My suggestion
(only that) is that the superficial subjunctive mood is a lexical item,
introduced by a lexicalizing transformation, and that this lexicalizing
rule is a factually restricted one, like But-Lexicalization. One further
small piece of evidence for this is the fact that, whereas the transformations that produce surface interrogatives and imperatives reorder
structural elements of underlying forms, whatever produces surface
subjunctives changes only individual words. To make a subjunctive,
one need only change "does" to "should," "was" to "were," "will"
to "would," etc.[11] If all this is right, then the deviance of a counterfactual with a true antecedent is of just the same sort as that of (11)
tokened in a hostile context; a sentence of the form "If it were the

case that S_1, then it would be the case that S_2" presumes (let us say, *lexically presumes*) the falsity of S_1.

More generally: if a sentence S lexically presumes a sentence S' and S' is false, then S will be heard as being deviant in a characteristic way, viz., as containing an inappropriately chosen lexical item for which probably there is a more acceptable substitute ("I trust that when you said 'but' you meant 'and' "), though S may still be semantically true. I shall explain the mechanics of lexical presumption more fully in the next section, but for now we may note the following features: (a) Like "semantic presuppositions" but unlike conversational implicatures, lexical presumptions are noncancellable:

(15)   *She was poor but she was honest; being poor makes people honest.

(16)   *Even Grandma gave up cocaine for Lent; she's always into self-denial, and she hardly ever touches cocaine anyway.

(17)   *Who knocked the jam into the catbox? A falling lamp, I assume.

(18)   *Jane works as an accountant, and her husband is very brilliant too; you have to be pretty stupid to be an accountant.

(b) Lexical presumptions are *detachable* in Grice's sense; a sentence S_1 that lexically presumes a sentence S_2 may be logically equivalent to a sentence S_3 that does not lexically presume S_2. This follows from two characteristic features of lexical presumption: that presumptions are generated by particular choices of words, and that a presuming sentence may be true even though its presumption is false. (c) Lexical presumptions are not *calculated* in the sense in which conversational implicatures are calculated. It is simply a lexical convention that "but," for example, carries its contrastive connotation; no one who fails to grasp that connotation knows the conventional meaning of the word "but." No reasoning of the Gricean sort is needed to compute lexical presumptions.

Features (a), (b), and (c) distinguish lexical presumption sharply from conversational implicature; yet lexical presumption also contrasts with entailment and (I should think) with semantic presupposition.[12] Indeed, (a), (b), and (c) taken together are strangely familiar. They bring to mind Grice's cryptic notion of *conventional* implicature. Let us explore the relation between lexical presumption and conventional implicature as Grice characterizes it.

A difficulty here is that Grice's remarks on conventional implicature are scanty at best. I quote them nearly in full:

> In some cases the conventional meaning of the words used will determine what is implicated, besides helping to determine what is said. If I say (smugly), *He is an Englishman; he is, therefore, brave,* I have certainly committed myself, by virtue of the meaning of my words, to its being the case that his being brave is a consequence of (follows from) his being an Englishman. But while I have said that he is an Englishman, and said that he is brave, I do not want to say that I have SAID (in the favored sense) that it follows from his being an Englishman that he is brave, though I have certainly indicated, and so implicated, that this is so. I do not want to say that my utterance of this sentence would be, STRICTLY SPEAKING, false should the consequence in question fail to hold. So SOME implications are conventional, unlike the [conversational] one with which I introduced this discussion of implicature. (1975, pp. 44–45)

Thus: (i) What is conventionally implicated (as opposed to what is conversationally implicated) is determined by "the conventional meaning of the words used." The same is true of lexical presumption. (ii) In uttering a sentence that conventionally implicates that p, I *commit* myself "by virtue of the meaning of my words" to its being the case that p. The same is true of lexical presumption. But (iii) in uttering such a sentence I have not said that p, "in the favored sense." If we plausibly identify the notion of what is said "in the favored sense" with what is entailed (cf. p. 44), the same is true of lexical presumption. (iv) My utterance is not, "STRICTLY SPEAKING, false" if it is not the case that p. The same is true of lexical presumption. Further, again, our features (a), (b), and (c) square well with Grice's characterization of conventional implicature: (ii) implies that conventional implicatures are noncancellable; if a sentence's conventional implicatures outstrip that sentence's entailments but are nevertheless generated by "the conventional meaning of the words used," we would expect the implicatures to be detachable; and a late remark of Grice's seems to indicate that conventional implicatures are not calculated.[13] On the basis of all the foregoing evidence, I propose that what Grice calls "conventional implicature" *is* just lexical presumption in our sense.[14] This identification has the advantage of much potential clarification; let us see in more detail how lexical presumption works.

4. Narrow Grammaticality and Broad Grammaticality

A serious objection comes to mind. I have conceded that the failure of a Lakovian or lexical presumption has syntactic repercussions, insofar as lexicalization is a syntactic matter, and I have suggested that the resulting odd utterance is the product of illicit lexicalization. Now, to say that the lexicalization of "but" in a hostile context is "illicit" is presumably to say that the appearance of "but" at the surface is not the result of a correct application of *But*-Lexicalization. But (so the objection goes) there is no such thing as an *incorrect* application of *But*-Lexicalization—a syntactic rule either applies or does not apply. Consequently, the surfacing of "but" is not the result of an application of *But*-Lexicalization at all. And it certainly is not the result of an application of any other syntactic rule; so it is not generated by the set of syntactic rules taken as a whole, i.e., not generated by the grammar. But a grammar is first and foremost a recursive device that delineates the notion of grammaticality. So our string whose factual presumption has failed is ungrammatical (in the context in which the failure occurs). Moreover, since it is not the output of any syntactic rule(s), and since our syntactic rules (run in reverse) are what assign semantic representations to surface structures, it seems we are forced to the conclusion that our defective string has no semantic interpretation, and hence expresses no logical form, and hence is assigned no truth-condition, and hence cannot be either true or false! In short, in offering the "lexical presumption" account of "but" and other particles, have I not almost explicitly conceded Lakoff's claim in its strongest form, and opened the door to semantic presupposition after all?

This argument is impressive, and though I think it fails because of several crucial oversimplifications, I shall be able here to offer only a rough sketch of a reply. I begin with a datum that is tolerably clear and points toward complexities unrecognized by the argument.

There is a substantial intuitive difference between the sense in which (11) is "ungrammatical" relative to the presumption that believing in semantic presupposition does not tend to preclude being smart—at best a somewhat attenuated sense—and that in which

(19)   *Good of believe off table the the the why

or even

(20)   *Bertrand believes who Gottlob is

is ungrammatical.

What I want to maintain is that (11) is "grammatical" *enough* to have a truth-condition, and indeed to be *true* even when lexically inappropriate. The utterer of (11) (in the hostile circumstances) has violated a rule of grammar, but it is not a rule whose violation produces semantic anomaly. I propose the hypothesis that, even though the rule in this case has not been properly triggered, it can still be run backward as a semantic-interpretation mapping in such a way that (11), even in our hostile context, will be assigned a (truth-conditional) semantic interpretation and hence can be understood in a rather narrow sense (for what that is worth). Thus, to address the formidable objection raised a few paragraphs above, the factual restriction on our *But*-Lexicalization rule does not serve as an impenetrable filter. That is, it is not an absolute restriction that, if violated, prevents the rule from operating at all; rather, it functions (if you like) as a strainer—the product succeeds in coming through, but not in a very appetizing form. It is, I shall argue, grammatical in a broad but useful sense, though deviant in a considerably narrower sense.

If there are (as I contend, contrary at least to the letter of the Metatheory), several disparate sources of input to the transformational component, at least two of which must function jointly to produce a particular string that is grammatical in the context in which it occurs, then it is (though perhaps unfamiliar) not at all surprising that there should be more than one sort of syntactic or quasi-syntactic "deviance," corresponding to failures of various sorts of triggers. The deviance of (11) in our hostile context is due, not to any malfunction or misuse of the rules that rearrange elements of logical form to produce surface form, but to the unlicensed application (nevertheless, an application) of a presumption-sensitive lexicalizing rule that has nothing to do with structuring. The *form* is the same, and it is this form for which truth-conditions are defined. Thus, a sentence uttered in a context may be lexically deviant without being semantically deviant or uninterpretable. In this quaint sense, the sentence may (somewhat paradoxically) be both "ungrammatical" in its context and *true*, unlike (19) or (20), which simply have no semantic interpretation. And *a fortiori*, the sentence can be both "ungrammatical" in this way and meaningful. This suffices to turn aside the Argument from Meaningfulness, since that argument baldly assumed, equivocating on "grammatical," that ungrammaticality entails meaninglessness.

What is to become, then, of Lakoff's claim that "a sentence will be well-formed only with respect to certain presuppositions about the nature of the world"? I have distinguished two notions of "grammaticalness" that might paraphrase "well-formed" here, a broad one and a narrow one. A sentence is "grammatical" in the broad sense if it is assigned a semantic interpretation, whether or not it has been appropriately lexicalized (alternatively, if it is the product of some application of the relevant syntactic rules, even if one or more of the rules has been applied in violation of a "strainer"-style restriction). A sentence is "grammatical" in the narrow sense, however, only if it is not only semantically interpretable but also correctly lexicalized given the factual presumptions that in fact obtain in the context in which it is uttered. Thus, a sentence *in vacuo* is "grammatical" in the broad sense, or else it is not; it is "grammatical" (or "ungrammatical") in the narrow sense only relative to a set of contingent beliefs.

To be semantically interpretable is to have a specific logical form or forms. In view of this, I prefer to reserve the term "well-formed" as a synonym for "grammatical" in the broad sense. (Thus, some well-formed sentences are lexically improper.) We may relate well-formedness in this sense to "grammaticalness" in the narrow sense in the way suggested by Lakoff himself (1969, p. 113): a string S is well-formed (= "grammatical" in the broad sense) if there is at least one set of factual presumptions relative to which S is "grammatical" in the narrow sense. On this usage, the well-formedness of S does not vary with contextually specified sets of beliefs.

Lakoff writes, "However, if a speaker is called upon to make a judgment as to whether or not S is 'deviant', then his extra-linguistic knowledge enters the picture" (1969, p. 115). On our usage, "deviant" is to be read as "not 'grammatical' in the narrow sense"; a sentence's being "deviant" in this sense is (contrary to Lakoff's usage) compatible with that sentence's being well-formed (semantically interpretable).

The contrast between the broad and narrow senses of "grammatical" has so far been highlighted only by the behavior of words of a certain class ("even," "too," "either," "instead," "but," etc.), which (so to speak) themselves carry implicatures of various kinds. If I am right in supposing all this, then possibly other syntactic phenomena will be seen to point toward the distinction as well. And it should be added that there are probably many different senses (or kinds, or grades) of grammaticality besides these two; "grammatical," "deviant," "OK," and other evaluative predicates applied by linguists to strings mask many different kinds of linguistic (and sometimes nonlinguistic) goodness and badness, and someday these must all be straightened out.

Lakoff anticipates and disparages my suggestion of defining "grammaticality" in the broad sense in terms of "grammaticality" in the narrow sense and reserving "well-formedness" as a synonym for the former:

> Such a definition would define a field of presupposition-free syntax. One might ask then what would be the content of this field, what phenomena would it deal with, would it be interesting? Such a field of presupposition-free syntax would deviate from the traditional study of syntax in that it would no longer involve the study of the distribution of all grammatical morphemes. As we have seen, the distribution of grammatical morphemes like *who* versus *which* cannot be stated in terms of presupposition-free syntax. . . . It is not at all clear that very much that is interesting would be part of the study of presupposition-free syntax. It is not even clear that principled grounds could be found for motivating the notion of grammatical transformation within the bounds of such a field. . . . In fact, it may well turn out that such a field would be limited to the study of the well-formedness conditions on possible surface structures of a language. Such a field might well be no more interesting than traditional phrase structure grammar. At present, there is no reason to believe that it would be. (pp. 115–16)

Lakoff seems to concede here that my distinction between well-formedness and "grammaticality" in the narrow sense is tenable; what he doubts is that, as a matter of empirical fact, a "presupposition-free syntax" or recursive characterization of (what I am calling) well-formedness would be able to explain many of what are traditionally taken to be syntactic phenomena—or so I read the quoted remarks.

He points out that "presupposition-free" syntax would fail to account for the distribution of all grammatical morphemes, e.g., for that of "who" and "which." This is correct; on my account, a recursive grammar of (mere) well-formedness would not predict whether "who" or "which" was correct in a given context—obviously, since it would not be context-relative at all. But this consequence is entirely congenial to me. Whether one uses "who" or "which" in a given context is not a matter of form or structure and, so far as I can see, has nothing to do with truth-conditions in the semanticists' sense of the term. It is a matter of the appropriateness of a single word. Possibly appropriateness-conditions should be built into an adequate semantics in the form of nonlogical axioms or "meaning postulates," for those linguists and philosophers who countenance such things (and it seems clear that our syntax will have to countenance them, though philosophers may go on to argue over their logical or epistemic status). But axioms, for those who appeal to them, serve strictly to account for (or "account for") those semantic phenomena that are nonstructural, that turn on particular information about particular morphemes or semantic primes. Thus, it seems to me that a recursive theory of well-*formed*ness *should* fail to predict the behavior of all morphemes.

A more serious question is whether a "presupposition-free" syntax would be interesting or important. Lakoff contents himself with giving a few examples of allegedly interesting phenomena that would fail to be treated by such a syntax. That in itself is unexciting. What makes Lakoff's examples more interesting is that the phenomena in question are ones that have been thought of by linguists specifically *as syntactic* phenomena. And data of this sort drive home my earlier contention that syntactic rules operate on something in addition to SRs.

However (assuming that Lakoff's points concerning selectional restrictions, coreference, and identity, etc., can be dealt with independently), we have found only one class of syntactic phenomena that require us to posit input from the belief-store, and the hypothesized syntactic effect of such beliefs is (so far as has been shown) quite superficial. There seems to be a group of morphemes whose distribution, rather late in the transformational process, is indeed governed by background beliefs. But that in itself hardly warrants Lakoff's grandly skeptical predictions quoted above. He would have to find much more evidence, and many more different kinds of plainly syntactic but equally plainly context-bound data, in order to make a case for doubting the importance or interest of "presupposition-free" syntax.

Two final comments:

1. Lakoff says, "It is not even clear that principled grounds could be found for motivating the notion of grammatical transformation within the bounds of such a field." His reason for this (deleted from the foregoing quotation) is that

> since selectional restrictions in general involve presuppositions, any such restrictions could not be used to motivate transformations. If such grounds for motivating transformations were taken away, it is not clear that very many, if any, of the traditionally assumed transformations could be motivated within a presupposition-free syntax. (p. 116)

Two questionable claims are involved here: that "selectional restrictions in general involve presuppositions" and that most of the "traditionally assumed" transformations are assumed largely on the basis of arguments from selectional restrictions. The first of these claims is entirely unclear as it stands. "Selectional restrictions" do rather obviously depend on the beliefs of speakers or hearers and consequently may be expected to vary considerably with those beliefs (this is one reason for supposing that "selectional restrictions" should play only a minor role in syntax); and our discussion of "sortal presupposition" in section 6 of chapter 4 yields a basis for clarification. But if Lakoff's claim is to be explicated in the latter way and if my arguments in that section were sound, the claim is false.

The second thesis is much more striking. Obviously Lakoff knows far more of the history of syntax than I do, but (i) I have never noticed that appeals to selectional restrictions loomed particularly large in the syntactic argumentation that I have come across, and (ii) we should regard such appeals as argumentatively suspect, since (intuitively speaking) they bear not on formal structure, but on what we say about the meanings of words. Only much further work can settle these issues.

The matter of selectional restrictions aside, it is easy enough to provide "principled grounds" for motivating the notion of a grammatical transformation within the bounds of presupposition-free syntax. The job of a presupposition-free syntax as limned above is, given SRs or logical forms written in a logician's canonical idiom, to map these forms onto well-formed (in Lakoff's phrase, "possible") English surface structures. A syntax of well-formedness is needed (whether or not it is as "important" as some other branches and subbranches of semiotics); and it is hard to see how such a mapping would be able to function in the absence of grammatical transformations—indeed, it seems to require them by definition.

2. Lakoff says, "[Presupposition-free syntax] might well be no more interesting than traditional phrase structure grammar. At present, there is no reason to believe that it would be." If what he is looking for is an *a priori* reason to believe that presupposition-free syntax would be interesting, in addition to the rather obvious fact that both logic and grammar require some notion of abstract structure (however unimportant that structure might turn out to be in comparison to other features of a natural language), he can find that reason in his own remark about "well-formedness conditions on possible surface structures." For we have the notion, marked vividly in intuition, of a possible sentence, a string that has a possible use in English, though of course not every possible sentence is appropriate in every (or even any) context. There is a firm distinction between strings that are possible sentences of English and strings that simply have no semantic interpretation. (I would be the last to rule out the

possibility that this distinction masks further and more refined distinctions as well.) It is precisely the job of "presupposition-free" syntax, as Lakoff sees, to mark this distinction and thereby to delineate the class of strings that are *candidates* for lexically correct, felicitous, and conversationally acceptable utterance. And that is interesting enough for me.

Chapter 6
The Performadox

Context has been seen to affect the interpretation of a sentence in each of four ways: it chooses a single SR from among a set of SRs assigned to the sentence; it provides denotata for the free variables occurring in the designated SR, thus fully determining the proposition expressed by the sentence; the background assumptions it involves generate "secondary meanings," "invited inferences," and some of the implicatures commonly mistaken for semantic presuppositions; and it triggers special transformations that produce unmistakable surface clues to the sentence's lexical presumptions. As yet we have said little about context's determining the sentence's *illocutionary force:* the type of speech act that its utterer is performing in tokening it. Illocutionary force is normally contrasted with propositional content, but we shall see that the two threaten to interact in troublesome ways. Some careful sorting out must be done if our continuing project of distinguishing semantics from pragmatics is to succeed.

1. Performatives in Philosophy and in Linguistics

J. L. Austin, who first called contemporary philosophers' attention to performative verbs and their behavior, originally supposed (1961) that utterances could fairly neatly be divided into two classes: "constative" utterances, whose linguistic function was to describe states of affairs or to state facts, and which were true or false; and "performative" utterances, whose functions were more ceremonial and ritualistic than descriptive, and which were "happy" or "unhappy" (properly or defectively performed) but not either true or false. (1) and (2) are clear examples of the former class.

(1) The cat is on the mat.

(2) There is at least one marble in this box.

(3)–(5) are clear examples of the latter.

(3) I double.

(4) I christen this ship the *Alexius Meinong*.

(5) I pronounce you man and wife.

It is characteristic of these performative sentences that a speaker who utters one in conventionally favorable circumstances is not describing himself as performing a certain linguistic act, but is simply performing it. Accordingly, a decisive test of a performative utterance is whether its verb could appropriately have been modified by the adverb "hereby." Utterances that satisfy the "hereby" criterion continue to be called "pure" or "explicit" performatives.

In (1962) Austin saw that this simple performative/constative distinction would not do, and he expanded and ramified it into his now familiar detailed account of illocutionary force. One of his principal reasons for abandoning the distinction was that verbs of stating or asserting seem to have the defining properties of performative verbs and the defining properties of constative verbs simultaneously. Consider

(6) I state that I have never been a Communist.

A speaker who tokens (6) in appropriate circumstances is simply performing the linguistic act of stating or making a statement, not describing himself as doing some stating. And "state" in (6) is quite naturally modified by "hereby"; so (6) qualifies as a pure performative. At the same time, our speaker would be taken to have said something true or false, and has certainly described himself as never having been a Communist. So it seems that (6) is both performative and constative, or, less anomalously, that (6) has both performative (or illocutionary) properties and constative (or locutionary) properties. And it is important to note that the truth-value of "what the speaker said" in uttering (6) is determined by the speaker's political affiliation alone; the performative preface "I state that" does not figure in this determination. (One would not escape a perjury charge by pointing out that when one tokened (6) while testifying before HUAC one did in fact state something and so was telling the truth.)

Austin was easily able to solve this problem for limited purposes within his ramified theory of illocutionary force. However, Steven Boër has pointed out that an aggravated analogue of the problem arises for the treatment of performatives in truth-conditional semantics.[1] This time the difficulty will not disappear so readily; I shall develop it in due course.

The philosophical literature on performatives and illocutionary force burgeoned in response to Austin's seminal work, to say the least, but only in the late 1960s did linguists begin to study the specifically syntactic properties of explicit performatives and their syntactic relations to ordinary nonperformatives. These investigations led to the so-called "Performative Analysis," mentioned briefly in chapter 5. This theory first appeared in the context of Generative Semantics (McCawley (1968), Ross (1970), Lakoff (1972), Sadock (1975)), but it is no mere artifact of that program; most of the arguments for it could be stated just as convincingly (or unconvincingly) in the framework of any instance of the Metatheory.

According to the Performative Analysis, a sentence's underlying syntactic structure contains not only what would normally have been taken to be that sentence's logical form, but also a governing performative preface that represents the sentence's normal or intended illocutionary force. Thus, the sentence's presumed logical form appears in underlying structure as the complement of a higher performative verb whose subject is *I* and whose indirect object is *you*, as illustrated in (7):

(7)   a. Katie ate an entire outboard motor.
    b.

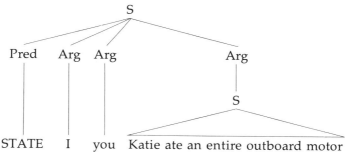

Every sentence, even an apparently nonperformative sentence, is explicitly performative at the level of deep structure; the underlying performative preface normally is deleted, but sometimes is allowed to reach the surface, producing an *overtly* explicit performative.

The arguments for this ambitious syntactic hypothesis have been many, various, and much contested. I shall not recapitulate them here, but only mention a few of the most persuasive: (a) The Performative Analysis enables us to broaden a number of syntactic generalizations, involving the rules of Topicalization, Equi-NP-Deletion, Adverb Fronting, and Pronoun Agreement (Lakoff, pp. 561–68). (b) The Analysis explains the appearance in surface structure of certain otherwise anomalous reflexives (Ross, secs. 2.1 and 2.3). (c) The posited performative verbs serve as the actual operands of super-ficially anchorless adverbial modifiers, such as *literally, frankly,* and the like (Lakoff, pp. 566–67; much more on this below). (d) The Analysis explains the fact that ordinary declaratives, imperatives, and interrogatives are at least loosely paraphrased by explicit per-formatives of the appropriate types. (e) Some underlying markers are needed to account for surface indications of grammatical mood in any case; performative prefaces might as well do that job. (f) Overtly explicit performatives, otherwise something of a curiosity, can be seen as the result of a derivation in which the underlying prefaces have not been optionally deleted.

Suppose the Performative Analysis is correct. Then considerable further modification in our truth-theoretic format will be required: It would seem that on primarily *syntactic* grounds, we will have to in-corporate into the SR of an ordinary declarative a reference to the (or a) speech act in which it is tokened, including mention of a particu-lar speaker and hearer. Since SRs express logical form, this amounts to concluding (as Lakoff (p. 569) and Sadock (p. 17) do conclude) that performative prefaces mentioning speaker, hearer, and type of speech act are part of logical form and so must be represented in "natural logic," the logic of our canonical idiom. What would seem (paradigmatically) to be features of context and hence pragmatic items thus thrust their way into the most abstract and removed reaches of the study of a natural language.

The argument just sketched bears a close similarity to the "Argu-ment from Generative Semantics" discussed in chapter 5. Indeed, I used the example of an underlying performative marker to refute premise (ii') of that argument ("SRs or logical forms are the sole input to syntactic derivations"), and that very premise is plainly at work here as well. My preliminary reason for denying (ii') was that se-mantic properties of sentences seem to be read "out from under" the underlying performance markers; we must therefore bifurcate our notion of underlying syntactic structure, by taking "deep structure" to comprehend both the SR itself *and* representations of whatever other local factors may affect subsequent syntactic manipulation. Here, we see that one such local factor is the illocutionary force to be vested in the surface structure on an occasion of its tokening. Though this pragmatic feature of context seemingly affects syntactic pro-cesses, which is not terribly surprising once we reflect on it, we are able to block the anomalous further conclusion that it is somehow to be accommodated within formal logic and truth theory.

For some years I thought this to be the happy end of the matter. Boër shattered my complacency by propounding the objection I have mentioned earlier in this section. It is the puzzle that in Boër and Lycan (1980) (henceforth, "PTS") we christened "the Performadox." This christening was rhetorically unwise and also substantively harmful, for two reasons: (i) Nothing so firmly recalls the dear (but) dead 1960s as a cute portmanteau. (ii) Besides thereby creating the false impression that the Performative Analysis was an artifact of Generative Semantics (defunct), our label created the more importantly false impression that Boër's problem is an artifact of the Performative Analysis. Alice Davison (1983) points out that even pragmatically rather than syntactically based theories of the relation between linguistic objects and illocutionary forces inevitably raise the same problem (more on this shortly). Prescinding from the foregoing misconceptions, let us now review the Performadox, as I shall resignedly continue to call it, along with revised versions of the two most promising solutions, and then draw what I hope is a well-motivated moral.

2. Genesis of the Performadox

Consider the underlying structure that the Performative Analysis assigns to (6):

(8)   STATE(I, you, I have never been a Communist),

or, in tree form,

(9)

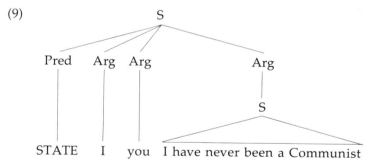

One would naturally be inclined to think that (8) or (9) would be true just in case the speaker was stating to the hearer that the speaker had never been a Communist. But we have seen that this seems wrong as an account of (6)'s truth-conditions. Lakoff's observation that the semantic properties of overt performatives are to be read off the complement of the performative preface seems obviously right, and it is even more compelling when we apply it to the *covert* prefaces posited by the Performative Analysis: the truth-value of an ordinary declarative sentence is determined by the way the world happens to be; a declarative is not made true automatically just because a speaker is saying something in tokening it. As I have suggested, the Performative Analysis bifurcates deep structure into logical form *plus* performative preface. This bifurcation is a justly venerable one, being in effect the distinction between sentence-mood and sentence-radical (Stenius (1967)), neustic and phrastic (Hare (1952)), and force and content (Austin (1962), Searle (1969)). However, its present application to (6) in particular seems quite *ad hoc:* an untutored truth-conditional semanticist who looked at (8) or (9) would take them to underlie an overt sentence that had something to do with the speaker's stating something and that was nonfactive.

To see the *ad-hoc*-ness of the Lakovian treatment of (6) more clearly, consider nondeclarative overt sentential performative prefaces such as those occurring in (10)–(12):

(10)   I promise to return your copy of *Syntactic Structures.*

(11)   I bet you $5 that Meryl Streep wears a toupee.

(12)   I order you to attack and capture the University of Chicago.

These sentences are intuitively truth-valueless; but if we were to take our cue from Lakoff and read truth-conditions out from under performative prefaces, we would mark these sentences as true or false depending on whether (respectively) I do return your copy of *Syntactic Structures,* Meryl Streep does wear a toupee, and you do attack and capture the University of Chicago. Thus, the Performative Analysis, conjoined with Lakoff's claim about truth-conditions and extrapolated to performative verbs other than verbs of assertion, predicts seemingly irrelevant truth-values for sentences that do not seem to have them (not that this is a very serious objection to the Analysis; in fact, I shall tentatively accept this consequence in chapter 8).

David Lewis, though he does not himself accept the Performative Analysis, expresses a view that might help us adjust the situation:

> . . . I propose that there is no difference in kind between the meanings of . . . performatives and non-declaratives and the meanings of . . . ordinary declarative sentences. . . . The only distinction among meanings is the distinction between those sentential meanings that can only be represented by declarative sentences and those that can be represented either by suitable

declarative sentences (performatives) or by non-declarative paraphrases thereof . . .

[This] method of paraphrased performatives . . . call[s] for the
assignment of truth-values to non-declarative sentences. The
truth-value assigned is not that of the embedded sentence (corresponding to the sentence-radical), however, but rather that of
the paraphrased performative. If I say to you, 'Be late!' and you
are not late, the embedded sentence is false, but the paraphrased
performative is true because I *do* command that you be late. I see
no problem in letting non-declaratives have the truth-values of
the performatives they paraphrase; after all, we need not ever
mention their truth-values if we would rather not.

    . . . If someone says, 'I declare that the Earth is flat' (sincerely,
not play-acting, etc.) I claim that he has spoken truly; he does
indeed so declare. I claim this not only for the sake of my theory
but as a point of common sense. (1972, pp. 208–10)

Thus, Lewis rejects Lakoff's maneuver and indeed our intuitions on
the point, choosing to regard the supposed truth-valuelessness of
overt nondeclarative performatives as a "don't-care." His easy as-
surance here is admirable, for (a) as he says, there is no reason why
we should care about or take any further notice of the newly assigned
truth-values, since the interesting features of nondeclaratives and
explicit performatives are their illocutionary and not their locutionary properties (cf. my downplaying of the true/false dimension in
section 7 of chapter 4); (b) we have a strong motive for assigning
truth-*conditions* to nondeclaratives, viz., a desire to preserve universally the idea that sentences have their meanings in virtue of their
syntactic deep structures' being truth-defined in the style of Tarski;
and (c) we can still make the radical/mood distinction, and explicate
the notion of a "common propositional content" between various
nondeclaratives, in terms of sameness of immediately embedded
clause.

But for our purposes, Lewis's proposal will not do. The rub is that,
according to the Performative Analysis, *every* sentence is explicitly
performative at the level of underlying syntactic structure, and this
fact suffices to raise our difficulty even for ordinary declarative sentences that show no performative elements at all in surface structure.
Since every overt declarative is supposed to contain an underlying
performative verb of stating, Lewis's proposal would end up assigning the value True to any declarative sentence whatever, on any
occasion on which that sentence was genuinely being used to make
an assertion and not (e.g.) merely being shouted down an elevator

shaft for echo-testing purposes.[2] This result is no "don't-care." Our intuitions about the truth-values of ordinary declaratives are not so easily sacrificed; it would take a lot to make anyone swallow the conclusion that we can make any declarative sentence true just by asserting it. Ernest LePore points out also (in correspondence) that Lewis's proposal taken together with the Performative Analysis would demolish ordinary sentential embedding.

The universal comprehensiveness of the Performative Analysis has a second ugly consequence for Lewis's proposal as well. Notice that on a semantically interpreted, nonperformative understanding, the operator "X states that" creates referential opacity throughout its complement. (A person can state that Clark Kent works at the *Daily Planet* without stating that Superman works there.) If we are to regard every declarative sentence as reflecting a structure whose main operator is STATE(I, you, ———), then every singular-term position in every declarative sentence must be judged opaque, and the logical rule of substitution of coreferring terms discarded as simply fallacious even in uncontroversially extensional contexts. But this is absurd.

It seems, then, that if we are to continue to accept the Performative Analysis, we must rejoin Lakoff in insisting that a sentence's truth-condition is to be read off the complement of its underlying performative preface, and not off the underlying syntactic structure as a whole. But no sooner have we reaffirmed that truth-conditions are determined by logical form alone than we face Boër's problem specifically: if it does not contribute to the truth-condition of a sentence, what *is* the role of the performative preface? At one level, the answer is obvious. Performative prefaces, we are told, have a purely pragmatic and syntactic function: they provide, *via* a specification of the intended illocutionary force, a means by which pragmatic considerations may have syntactic impact. The identity of the higher illocutionary verb (together with its subject and indirect object) will determine which syntactic transformation may be applied. The higher verb itself, however, is apparently not to be regarded as *semantically* interpreted—at least not in the sense in which elements of logical form are accorded semantic interpretation. The performative preface as a whole seems to be treated as a mere marker, a "flag" with no independent semantic role. (So I assumed in chapter 5.)

Reassuring though it may be, this stock answer will not do at this stage. For representations such as (8) not only contain sentences of a formal language as complements but also appear themselves to *be* sentences of some artificial language, calling for semantic interpretations of their own. This becomes more clearly evident when we re-

mind ourselves that performative prefaces like STATE(I, you, ——)
have *structure*, and that at least two parts of this structure (viz., the
higher subject *I* and the indirect object *you*) must themselves tacitly
be regarded as semantically interpreted (the former denoting the
speaker and the latter denoting the addressee). But how are we to
make sense of a triadic predicate STATE whose arguments are
semantically interpreted but which itself is not a semantically interpreted item? Moreover, notice that the STATE in our performative
preface *is* our word "state" (it has its normal meaning); we could not
have represented the preface as GLOP(I, you, S_1).[3]

Matters reach the crisis stage when we consider that the higher
illocutionary verbs in performative prefaces can be *modified* by semantically interpreted adverbial elements. Consider the following
examples:

(13)   John has left, in case you haven't heard.

(14)   Since you're interested, John is a Catholic.

(15)   Confidentially, the boss is a moron.

(16)   John is undiplomatic, frankly.

In each of these sentences the adverbial element can be regarded only
as modifying the deleted higher verb STATE. Indeed, sentences like
(13)–(16) illustrate one of the chief sources of evidence I have cited on
behalf of the Performative Analysis. (15), for example, might be represented as having the general form

(17)   CONFIDENTIALLY-STATE(I, you, S_1),

where 'S_1' in this case is replaced by the logical form of "The boss is a
moron" and CONFIDENTIALLY is a predicate-modifying adverb.
But unless STATE is regarded as having a semantic interpretation, it
is difficult if not impossible to see what the adverb CONFIDEN-
TIALLY is doing in (15). Presumably the adverb is *capable* of semantic interpretation, since it occurs as part of the logical form of
sentences like "John spoke confidentially." But a predicate-modifying adverb contributes meaning to a sentence in which it occurs only
insofar as there is a meaningful (interpreted) predicate for it to modify; so if STATE has no semantic interpretation, (13)–(16)—along
with infinitely many related sentences—will be uninterpretable.

It is clear in any case that reason-adverbials such as those featured
in (13) and (14) do contribute to the truth-conditions of sentences
containing them. No one could deny that (18) and (19) have different
truth-conditions:

(18)   Since you're interested, and since I'm in an ebullient and obliging and talkative mood because I just picked up my paycheck, the answer to your question is, "The butler did it."

(19)   The answer to your question is, "The butler did it."

Nor would anyone deny that this difference is directly attributable to the presence of the rather elaborate reason-adverbial in (18). Yet the proposed extension of the Performative Analysis involves just such denials *anent* (13) and (14). For example, (14) would turn out to be *logically equivalent* to (20), since by hypothesis the reason-adverbial in (14), like the manner-adverbials in (15) and (16), has been banned from logical form and made part of the preface:

(20)   John is a Catholic.

But it seems that (14) and (20) differ truth-conditionally just as (18) and (19) do. Intuitively, to utter (14) is not only to assert the content of (20) but also to say (however unemphatically) that one has such-and-such reasons for speaking. This tandem feature is even more readily apparent when the sentence embedded in the reason-adverbial is both long and tendentious in content, as in

(21)   Since you are my best friend and there is an all-powerful God who commands that one should always tell the truth to one's best friend and who sends to Hell all those who disobey His wishes, you have bad breath.

Anyone tokening (21) in appropriate circumstances would correctly be understood as saying, indeed asserting, that the addressee is his best friend, that there is an all-powerful God, that God commands certain things, etc.; and the truth-value of (21) as a whole seems to depend as much on the truth of these assertions as it does on whether or not the addressee has bad breath. Moreover, it is plain that (21)'s reason-adverbial has (fairly elaborate) truth-conditional structure *inside* it. These two facts may not prove apodeictically that the reason-adverbial contributes to (21)'s truth-condition, but certainly they create a very strong presumption.[4] It seems clear that adverbial modifiers of performative prefaces contribute somehow to logical form. Yet we have seen that the attempt to incorporate them directly into logical form leads to the assignment of incorrect truth-conditions.

The upshot is that the Performative Analysis enmeshes the truth-conditional semanticist in a nasty and genuine paradox, which we may summarize as follows:

1. If the Performative Analysis is correct, then every complete English sentence contains (at the level of deep structure) a governing performative verb.

2. If any of (13)–(16) contains (at the level of deep structure) a performative verb that is not semantically interpreted, then it itself is uninterpretable.

3. If any of (13)–(16) contains (at the level of deep structure) a performative verb that is semantically interpreted, then it is assigned the wrong truth-condition.

Therefore,

4. If the Performative Analysis is correct, then either (13)–(16) are uninterpretable or they are assigned the wrong truth-conditions.

But

5. Each of these consequences is intolerable.

The implication is that the Performative Analysis is incorrect. But a not insignificant body of *prima facie* plausible evidence has been urged in support of the Analysis or some pragmatic surrogate, and so we have considerable motivation for *not* rejecting it. Yet premises 2 and 3 seem inescapable.

The foregoing way of stating the problem, Davison (1983) points out, pins the blame too squarely on the syntactic Performative Analysis and thereby invites us just to trash the Analysis and explain away the "not insignificant body of *prima facie* plausible evidence" in pragmatic terms of some sort. But—unless we simply deny the well-formedness of sentences like (13)–(16), (18), and (21)—any pragmatically based theory of the relation between force and surface grammar is going to posit semantically interpreted structures that themselves initiate the Performadox (Davison, secs. 2–5).

In "PTS" Boër and I surveyed and criticized an extravagantly broad range of possible solutions.[5] Only three of these have attracted much interest in response to our initial discussion: the appeal to "pragmatic presupposition" that we attributed to George Lakoff and tentatively to Alice Davison ("PTS," secs. 3.3 and 3.4); the approach that we called "Cresswell's Preferred Method" (sec. 3.2); and my paratactic method (sec. 4.2). I have nothing to add to our original criticism of the first of these, so I shall not repeat it. Jerry Sadock has proposed an interesting variation on the second, so I shall pay more attention to it here. This will involve revisiting the third, paratactic method as well, since that method tends to coalesce with Sadock's variant of Cresswell's view.

3. Development of Cresswell's Preferred Method

Cresswell's remarks (1973, chap. 14) on overt performative verbs of stating point toward an approach to the Performadox. Initially he follows Lewis in assigning counterintuitively literal truth-conditions to sentences like (6), and simply swallows the consequence that assertive utterances of such sentences are self-verifying. But he adds a piquant sop to our intuitions: he says that although his sample sentence

(22)   I state that every bird has a beak

is true iff its utterer is in fact stating that every bird has a beak, the utterer's *tokening* (22) in an appropriate context "conventionally counts as" an assertion simply that every bird has a beak. Thus, one who utters (22) can make a false assertion (if there are birds who lack beaks) even though the sentence uttered, (22) itself, is simultaneously and automatically made true.

Thus, we may want to associate a second truth-value with an overt performative statement such as (22), letting this second truth-value be that of the *assertion* or *statement* made on an utterance-occasion, as opposed to that of the sentence tokened on that occasion. Some philosophers have thought that this distinction is independently well-motivated (being closely tied to the fairly straightforward distinction between speaker-meaning and sentence-meaning); by making this move, we may soften the callousness of the Lewis-Cresswell approach. And our notion of the statement made, as distinct from the sentence tokened, might be clarified and elaborated within a general theory of assertion that would, among other things, display the connections between speaker-meaning and the illocutionary properties of assertive utterance. (Even though no such theory has ever been formulated,[6] we know that one exists, since as hearers in ordinary conversation we do correctly process speaker-meaning partly as a function of illocutionary considerations and other pragmatic factors.)[7] One important task of this theory of assertion would then be to make the right plausible predictions, on some principled basis, concerning which among utterances of, say, (14), (15), (21), and (22) assert what.

However, Cresswell follows Lewis in limiting his own account to overt explicit performatives, which limitation, we have seen, encourages the dismissal of such cases as "don't-cares." But the Performadox is raised the most trenchantly by the wildly complex adverbials that seem to modify hidden performative verbs. Not only has Cresswell so far given us no account of these adverbials, but, since he rejects the Performative Analysis, he cannot even admit that they modify our underlying verbs. In light of this, he goes on to suggest that sentences like (13)–(16) are not really grammatical as they stand (on their intended readings), being rather sentence-fragments that are contextually understood as ellipses of related, well-formed sentences. By this he cannot mean that an ellipsis in the ordinary grammatical sense has taken place, for that would be for some deleting transformation to have expunged underlying performative material of the sort in question. He wants to excuse formal grammar from generating such sentences and to maintain that what is needed instead is a *pragmatic* theory of conversational ellipsis. A grammar produces only well-formed sentences; a pragmatic theory of ellipsis would be invoked to *correlate* sentence-fragments with genuine sentences in context, thus indirectly bringing these fragments into sufficiently close contact with our semantics. Bach and Harnish (1979) second this motion with vigor.

Now, normal speakers' reactions to (13)–(16) differ in no way from their reactions to uncontroversially grammatical sentences. (Davison (1983) quotes several nontheoretical sources of our characteristically dangling adverbials.) *Prima facie*, (13)–(16) are syntactically well-formed as they stand. Therefore, *prima facie*, whatever ellipsis figures in their production is ordinary syntactic ellipsis. What evidence (other than a desire to resolve the Performadox by meataxe) do Cresswell, Bach, and Harnish have for supposing that what seems to be the case is in reality not the case? They offer nothing specific. If this were the only unpalatable feature of their account, perhaps it would be tolerable, since we know in advance that no escape from the Performadox is going to be comfortable. But the worst is yet to come: as in Lewis's case, if we extrapolate Cresswell's Preferred Method from overt explicit performatives to the hidden ones posited by the Performative Analysis, our semantics goes wildly wrong. (7a), for example, will be assigned the truth-condition literally associated with (7b); it would follow that (7a) itself was true whenever asserted, that (7a) is referentially opaque, that (7a) entails the existence of its speaker and hearer, and (worst) that (7a) does not entail that Katie ate an entire outboard motor.

It was at this point that Boër and I felt it was time to move on, but it is also here that Sadock stepped in, picking up Cresswell's remark that the uttering of (22) "conventionally counts as" an act of asserting that every bird has a beak. Cresswell points out that if what is asserted in an utterance of (22) is distinct from what is expressed by (22), then two truth-values may be in play as well. Sadock (1979) introduces the notion of "truth$_2$" ("truth$_1$" being standard semantic truth); truth$_2$ is a property of assertions, which Sadock understands as being utterance-act-tokens having assertive force. (Let us add that a *sentence* is "true$_2$" when the assertion that would be made in a normal utterance of that sentence would be true$_2$.)[8] Thus, any discussion of the truth-values of our various performative and nonperformative target sentences runs the risk of equivocation, unless occurrences of "true," "false," and even "entail" are properly subscripted. (22) is true$_1$ whenever asserted, but not necessarily true$_2$ (i.e., the assertion made may not be true); (22) entails$_1$ the existence of its speaker and hearer, but does not entail$_2$ those things (i.e., (22) can be true$_2$ even though they are false); (22) does not entail$_1$ that every bird has a beak, but does entail$_2$ that; and so on.

Sadock believes that the instances of *modus tollens* I have implicitly flung against Cresswell at the end of the last paragraph but one need to be disambiguated in just this way, and that when they are so disambiguated they fail. (7a) *is* true$_1$ whenever asserted, he says, but not true$_2$. (7a)—I assume he would agree—is referentially opaque, but what is asserted in an utterance of (7a) is not. (7a) entails$_1$ the existence of its speaker and hearer, but does not entail$_2$ those things. And, though (7a) does not entail$_1$ that Katie ate an entire outboard motor, (7a) does entail$_1$ itself and does entail$_2$ that she did. Now, how does this disambiguation help? Sadock maintains that our *intuitions* about the "truth"-values of performative and nonperformative sentences alike are intuitions about truth$_2$ rather than about truth$_1$; he shrugs off truth$_1$ as a "theoretical construct" and "true$_1$" as "a technical term without direct empirical content" (p. 3)—"true$_1$" has empirical content at all only in virtue of its theoretical connection with truth$_2$.[9] Thus, the consequences concerning (7a) that I have drawn from Cresswell's semantic theory do not after all offend our intuitions about semantic truth, or truth$_1$, because we have no intuitions about truth$_1$, and the consequences do not offend our intuitions about truth$_2$, because they are not about truth$_2$; my criticisms go wide of Cresswell's Preferred Method when it is elaborated in Sadock's way.

Sadock is at pains to insist that his notion of "truth$_2$" is not stipulated *ad hoc* (cf. the "Method of Stipulation" disparaged in "PTS," sec. 3.1), but is an intuitive notion entrenched in everyday language, better known, indeed, to the ordinary person than is that of truth$_1$. Now, I very much doubt this. First, the notion of "truth$_1$" or semantic truth has been very intuitively introduced by Tarski and by Davidson, by Austin in the ordinary-language tradition (1950), by thousands of introductory logic teachers, and by great dead philosophers long before. Further, it has been introduced directly, without the aid of any bridge laws or correspondence rules to connect it to any "more empirical" notion of truth. Audiences have not responded with bafflement or with demands for stronger empirical connections. Indeed, I cannot think that anyone would ever imagine a distinction between semantic truth and "truth$_2$" unless trick sentences such as (6) or (22) were (much) later called to his attention. So far as I can see, it is just false to deny that we have sharp and clear intuitions about truth$_1$; further, these intuitions shape up uncommonly well into formal theories of truth.[10]

Second, we must grant Sadock his contention that the notion of "truth$_2$" captures our everyday intuitions about overtly performative sentences like (6) and (22). To this extent, "true$_2$" is entrenched in ordinary language and is not stipulated *ad hoc*; but, I think, only to this extent and no further.[11] For it is hard to get any *general* handle on the notion of "what is asserted" in an utterance of S, as opposed to what is entailed$_{(1)}$ by S itself, that will fit Sadock's intentions exactly. In my discussion of Cresswell I mentioned that "what is asserted" might coincide with *speaker-meaning* (as opposed to sentence-meaning), but Sadock's notion of "what is asserted" is much narrower than that of speaker-meaning as it is given by Grice (1957, 1975). Conversational implicatures can convey speaker-meaning, but I doubt Sadock would want to say that they are "asserted" or that a sentence that generates a conversational implicature is true$_2$ when what is implicated is true (a truth can be implicated when what is uttered is intuitively false—indeed, sometimes *because* what is uttered is intuitively false, as in a case of irony). Likewise, an overt performative assertion can be false$_2$ in Sadock's sense even though the utterer's own meaning is true ("I tell you, this is a fine kettle of fish").

Further, granting that the complement of an overt *or* hidden performative verb of stating does express what is asserted, we would like to know the ground of this connection; *why* does that particular rule hold? Cresswell maintains that it is a brute convention—that that is simply what it is for something to be a performative verb of stating. But then what makes it true that "state," "assert," and their ilk *are* performative verbs of stating in this sense? Sadock offers (p. 9) a sufficient condition in general for someone's asserting P by uttering S, but if I understand it correctly it is tautologous and "S" appears only eliminably in the definiens.[12] The best account I know of the relation between performative verbs of stating and "what is asserted" that fits well with Sadock's program appears in Ginet (1979). Perhaps it can answer the present question for us.

Even if Sadock is eventually successful in characterizing and grounding a notion of "what is asserted" that will back his claims about $truth_2$, he will not have exonerated Cresswell from the charge of trampling our intuitions at least in the case of ordinary (superficially nonperformative) declaratives. First, if I am right in insisting *contra* Sadock that $truth_1$ is at least as intuitive a notion as $truth_2$, then the consequences of Cresswell's Preferred Method that I have mentioned are still very nasty even after they have been disambiguated in terms of $truth_1$: Every ordinary declarative is $true_1$ whenever asserted. Every ordinary declarative is referentially opaque at every singular-term position (I am not sure exactly how Sadock would have explained away the absurdity of this particular consequence even with the aid of $truth_2$, unless by defining "$opacity_2$" in terms of "$truth_2$"). Every ordinary declarative $entails_1$ the existence of its speaker and hearer. No instance of " 'S' $entails_1$ that S" is true. Sadock can receive these blows without a whimper only because he has protected himself by anaesthetizing his intuitions about $truth_1$ and $entailment_1$. But on those of us who have not, the blows fall hard. If "Jones is fat" is not semantically true iff Jones if fat, then it is not clear that we have any "semantic" notion of truth at all in whatever sense is intended.

Sadock might reply that indeed we do not. Perhaps "$truth_1$" is even less robust than a "theoretical construct," and is only the abstract shadow that $truth_2$ casts from inside the pale of performative prefaces. After all, $truth_2$ itself behaves rather nicely in the case of ordinary declaratives *if* the Performative Analysis is correct (cf. note 11). Perhaps, when we construct truth-tables and offer truth definitions for quantificational and other, more complex languages, we are always really abstracting away from literal content to "what would normally be asserted" and talking about $truth_2$. Certainly this does not *seem* to be what we are doing, but no obvious harm comes from saying that it is what we are doing nevertheless, particularly since we have independent evidence for the truth of the Performative Analysis.

As yet I see no clear difference between making this move and merely reverting to Lakoff's original proposal. That is, I see no difference between calling $truth_1$ an "abstract shadow" that does not really figure in textbook semantics and simply dispensing with $truth_1$ for practical purposes *in favor of* $truth_2$; only one notion of truth is on line after all, and this notion and its dependents are read systematically out from under performative prefaces. This suspicion is reinforced by two further observations: (i) On Sadock's proposal, a

T-sentence will be *false* when its truth predicate is read as "true$_1$"; it will be true only when its truth predicate is read as "true$_2$." Notice also that "truth$_2$" does not even support the truth-functions. For example, that $S_1 \lor S_2$ is true$_2$ does not guarantee that either S_1 is true$_2$ or S_2 is true$_2$ (cf. Geach (1965, pp. 252–53)). (ii) "Entailment$_1$" no longer obeys the standard laws of entailment. For example, a sentence S_1 can fail to entail$_1$ a logically weaker sentence; if the Performative Analysis is right, (7a) does not entail$_1$

(23)   There is no greatest prime,

even though (23) is a logical truth and is logically implied by any sentence whatever. By the same token, a sentence does not even entail$_1$ all its own provable logical equivalents, since I can assert S_1 without thereby asserting every sentence S_2 that is distantly equivalent to S_1. Facts (i) and (ii) show fairly conclusively, I think, that truth$_1$ is not semantical truth as we know it and entailment$_1$ is not entailment. Since "true$_1$" and "entail$_1$" were introduced by Sadock as expressing precisely our semantic notions as opposed to his illocutionary notions, this constitutes a *reductio* of the semantic notions *tout court;* the only truth is truth$_2$, and the only "semantics" is semantics$_2$.

Finally, let us test Sadock's proposal against our nemeses, the long and tendentious reason-adverbials modifying hidden performative prefaces. Consider (18) and (21). On Sadock's view, those sentences assert but do not entail$_1$ that the answer to your question is "The butler did it" and that you have bad breath, respectively, thanks to a proviso he adds (p. 9) allowing adverbially modified verbs of stating to count as verbs of stating *simpliciter* in the definition of "true$_2$." But we have seen that (18) and (21) make a number of other assertions as well, viz., they assert each of the conjuncts impacted into the adverbial modifiers themselves. Sadock has provided no way of bringing this out. He would have to ramify his theory of "assertion" in such a way as to count these assertions as "assertions" in his sense (then, since "true$_2$" is defined in terms of "assertion," the truth$_2$-value of (18) and (21) would be affected by the truth$_2$-values of the adverbial conjuncts, as they should be). This ramification would have to proceed on some principled basis, not merely *ad hoc* (cf. the objection put in section 3.1 of "PTS" to the "Method of Stipulation"). It is here that the "Paratactic Method" may help, as a way of implementing the Cresswell-Sadock approach.

4. The Paratactic Method

To begin with, notice the close paraphrase relations between pairs such as (24a–b) and (25a–b):

(24)   a. Just between ourselves, Idi makes me sick.
       b. Idi makes me sick—that's just between ourselves.

(25)   a. Just so I'll be able to tell my mother if she asks, what is this stuff we're smoking?
       b. What is this stuff we're smoking? I ask that just so I'll be able to tell my mother if she asks.

In (24b) and (25b), primary locutions are expressed and then followed by assertions that make reference to these locutions and characterize their tokenings in certain ways. It may be fruitful to hypothesize that some such duple constructions actually underlie (24a) and (25a). Thus, let us explore the suggestion that (a) such sentences (including (13)–(16), (18), and (21)) make implicit demonstrative reference, on occasions of their utterance, to the very act(-token)s of uttering them on those occasions, and (b) the overt adverbial modifiers reflect structured predicates that apply to those underlying demonstratives.

According to the Paratactic Method, a performative preface's complement is introduced simply as an example or token of the kind of thing the speaker is referring to by means of his demonstrative. Thus, (15) would be regarded as deriving from

(26)   ⌐ The boss is a moron. ⤺ I state that confidentially. ⌐

Here "The boss is a moron" is produced as a specimen or example of what it is that is being stated confidentially; it is not itself being tokened assertively. Likewise, given the Performative Analysis, a straightforward declarative such as

(27)   The boss is a moron

would be said to derive from

(28)   ⌐The boss is a moron. ⤺ I state that. ⌐

The main virtues of the Paratactic Method are (a) that it explains paraphrase relations such as those noted in (24) and (25), (b) that it does not require any special convention or meaning rule to predict that a normal utterance of (15) is an assertion that the boss is a moron (the demonstrative takes care of that), (c) that it interprets the performative preface without requiring an utterer to assert that he is asserting (an advantage shared by Sadock's version of Cresswell's

Preferred Method), and (d) that it avoids an objection—"(B)"—that Boër and I raised against the very similar account that we called "Cresswell's Tolerated Method" ("PTS," sec. 4.1). Now, in "PTS" we claimed that the Paratactic Method avoids the objection (B) only by trading it off for a further problem:

> (C) If (what is intuitively) the complement of our performative preface is produced merely as a specimen and is not asserted, then what are we to say about sentences governed by performative verbs of stating? On the Paratactic Method, a speaker who utters [(27)] with assertive intent asserts or implies that he or she is stating something, but does *not* assert [(27)] itself! The Paratactic Method, then, seems to prevent speakers from asserting just the sorts of things they want to assert in tokening ordinary declaratives. (p. 93)

In light of Sadock's discussion of assertion, I now think this objection is confused. The confusion is indicated already by a felt tension between two of my earlier remarks: that "The boss is a moron" "is not itself being tokened assertively," and that the Paratactic Method "predict[s] the fact that a normal utterance of (15) is an assertion that the boss is a moron." Is "The boss is a moron" being asserted, or not?

In making the first of the two remarks just cited, I meant that in tokening "The boss is a moron" while writing out (26) (or while generating (15) in one's mind), one is not asserting that the boss is a moron; if one got only that far and stopped before adding "I state that confidentially" or some other explicitly performative tag, one would not have performed any illocutionary act at all (any more than one would have if one merely wrote (27) on a blackboard outside any appropriate context and then left the room). But it does not follow, as argument (C) tacitly assumes it does, that an utterer of (15) does not assert that the boss is a moron. For such a speaker does not express merely (26)'s contained token of "The boss is a moron," but all of (26), including the performative tag. *Via* its demonstrative, that performative tag is what accomplishes the assertion of what is expressed by the demonstrative's referent. This is why the second of my two cited remarks is true, i.e., why an utterer of (15) does assert that the boss is a moron, contrary to argument (C).[13] Now, the performative tag itself is part of logical form, and so (15) is interpreted as entailing that its utterer states something, but this entailment is not asserted by an utterer of (15) (in order for it to be asserted, a second performative tag would have to be appended that demonstrated *it*); the latter feature softens the possible counterintuitiveness of including the performative preface in logical form, and accommodates our intuition that an utterer of (15) does not assert *that* his utterance is confidential.

Some theorists may take umbrage at the idea that (15) even entails the speaker's stating something confidentially. I believe the presence of the surface adverb and the paraphrastic evidence for the underlying demonstrative suffice to motivate this idea. The intuitive datum that gets in the way here is the fact that people would not ordinarily call a token of (15) false merely because they believed that the utterer was not making an assertion or that the utterer was not in fact speaking confidentially. No doubt they would feel that something had gone wrong, but they would probably find it difficult to pinpoint the problem. But this datum is not decisive, for it admits of alternative explanations—explanations that are plausible and that preserve the disputed entailments. Boër and I offered such an explanation in section 4.2 of "PTS," based on considerations of implicature and relative emphasis now familiar from chapter 4.

Once the mixup concerning objection (C) has been straightened out, the Paratactic Method begins closely to resemble the Sadock variant of Cresswell's Preferred Method. In fact, suppose we agree to treat (15) in Cresswell's way (thus representing it as taking the interpreted form (17)), and then ask ourselves how its shallowly underlying "that"-clause itself ought to be analyzed at a somewhat deeper level of structure. Suppose we also adopt an analysis of "that"-clauses, such as Davidson's or Sellars's (tentatively advocated in the Appendix), according to which such clauses display and demonstrate (but do not *themselves* assert) interpreted object-language sentence-tokens. The result will be virtually indistinguishable from the Paratactic treatment of (15) as presented here. And as we have seen, the underlying demonstrative helps to dispel our earlier worry about the "ground" of the connection between the complement of a performative verb of stating and "what is asserted": that ground is the demonstrative connection itself.[14] Thus, our development of Cresswell's Preferred Method and our revised understanding of the Paratactic Method have converged on what is probably the most plausible resolution of the Performadox (given the truth of the Performative Analysis) to date. Let us take this resolution as our leading contender and press on to a final adjudication.

We have seen in the previous section that "truth$_1$" on Sadock's account does not obey the standard laws of truth, nor "entailment$_1$" the standard laws of entailment. I concluded on Sadock's behalf that the only truth is truth$_2$, and likewise for all semantical notions defined in terms of truth. This result leaves us with two difficulties for the covert performative prefaces posited by the Performative Analysis. The first difficulty is that we seem to be back where we started, with Boër's original question: If we are in effect reading semantical properties out from under performative prefaces (by understanding them all as being semantical$_2$ properties), are we not just leaving the prefaces themselves semantically uninterpreted?

It may be replied that the whole SRs underlying ordinary declaratives still *have* truth-conditional interpretations *qua* logical formulas, even if those interpretations do not predict the felt (truth$_2$)-values of the surface declaratives and even if the semantic properties conferred by those interpretations are ignored by the generating transformations. (Transformations now must be construed as preserving truth$_2$ and meaning$_2$, not "truth$_1$" and "meaning$_1$." This is an interesting dislocation in the role of transformations, since they operate on performative prefaces as well as on the asserted complements of those prefaces; for example, they will ignore the truth-conditional contribution of the alleged higher *I* and *you*, while nevertheless allowing those elements to trigger reflexivization even though this operation requires that *I* and *you* have their normal semantic interpretations.) Let us say, not that performative prefaces are uninterpreted, but just that interpretations do not affect the semantic$_{(2)}$ properties of the resulting surface forms.

I do not see that this proposal improves overall on the Method of Stipulation, criticized in "PTS." That method posits two truth-conditions for each ordinary declarative—a "narrow" truth-condition determined in Lakoff's way, and a "wide" truth-condition determined in Lewis's way. A practitioner of the Method simply stipulates that only the narrow truth-condition counts in predicting perceived semantic properties of the sentence among ordinary speakers; this corresponds to Sadock's claim that these properties are a function of truth$_2$. Now, Sadock's theory replaces the latter stipulation with a (potential) theory of asserting, and so cannot be accused of the raw *ac-hoc*-ness of the original Method in that respect. But it is *ad hoc* in a second way. His notion of "truth$_1$" corresponds to "wide" truth. Truth of whatever stripe is a semantical notion, but we have seen that "truth$_1$" *qua* property of English sentences is nothing of the kind, since it neither obeys truth-tables nor supports Convention T nor yields a recognizable notion of entailment. Insofar as "truth$_1$" is a semantical property at all, it is merely the shadow of the Lewisian semantical truth of the posited underlying explicit performative, and does not attach to target sentences themselves even on an attenuated understanding. It is a semantical posit that does no explanatory work except to lend legitimacy to the Performative Analysis.

This much *ad-hoc*-ness in aid of syntactically desirable theory is not conclusively vicious, but its degrading effect is reinforced by the second difficulty mentioned above, viz., an apparent circularity in Sadock's scheme of notions. He proposes to explain perceived implications and other semantical properties in terms of $truth_2$. "$Truth_2$" is defined as the truth of what is asserted. But what is *assertion?* Normally, to assert that p is to utter, in appropriate circumstances and in an appropriate tone, a declarative sentence which entails that p (where the sentence replacing "p" is an *emphasized* entailment of the sentence uttered); thus, "assertion" is defined in terms of entailment. But "entailment" here cannot be $entailment_1$, for (a) "$entailment_1$" is not any species of entailment, and (b) what is asserted is not in any case $entailed_1$ by the sentence uttered. Thus, either Sadock's notion of "assertion" is nonstandard and unexplicated (and so totally *ad hoc*), or it is defined in terms of $entailment_2$; but $entailment_2$ is defined in terms of $truth_2$, which is defined in terms of assertion. . . .

The two difficulties I have outlined are not fatal, or at least would not be considered so by one firmly determined to preserve the Performative Analysis. But, given that our fusion of the Cresswell-Sadock approach with the old Paratactic Method is the Analysis's last stand, it is surely time to reassess the evidence in favor of the Analysis. Some of this reassessment has already been carried out, and much of the more theory-laden syntactic argumentation has been questioned;[15] I think it is fair to say that the Analysis now seems much less firmly supported than it may have at the time it was proposed. On the whole I now think it easier to jettison the Analysis than to work at shoring up the still problematic Cresswell-Sadock semantics, and that is the policy I shall pursue here. That is, I shall drop the Analysis in its full-blown form; we shall see that a much weaker related claim must still be maintained and will still require interaction between pragmatic factors and syntactic processes—but this time, as in the case of lexical presumption, the interaction will be able to bypass semantics entirely.

5. An Eviscerated "Performative Hypothesis"

A few of the data listed in section 1 of this chapter as lending support to the Performative Analysis continue to demand accommodation even if we reject the claim that every ordinary declarative is performative at an underlying level of syntactic structure: the superficially anchorless adverbial modifiers (c), the paraphrase relations between overtly nonperformative sentences and explicit performatives (d), the prevalence of grammatical mood (e), and the existence of overtly explicit performatives (f). Let us begin with (c).

For all our difficulties over the Performative Analysis, and contrary to what Cresswell says in defense of his Preferred Method, the presence in surface structure of a "dangling" adverbial is a nearly infallible indication of an underlying verb. It does not follow that ordinary declarative sentences that contain no apparently metalinguistic adverbial modifiers have performative prefaces in *their* underlying structures.[16] But what about the sentences in which the dangling adverbials do appear? It seems they, at least, must be construed as incorporating performative prefaces within their SRs, and so the Performadox arises at least in their case. The same is true of overtly explicit performatives (datum (f)).

Here I think the Paratactic version of the Cresswell-Sadock approach can be of use. In fact, let us simply help ourselves to it, for cases of (c) and (f) in particular. Target sentences of these two types will receive the Lewisian or "wide" truth-value assignments, then, and will not be understood as entailing what they assert. The asserting will be accomplished instead by the performative prefaces acting through Sellars- or Davidson-style demonstratives that indicate displayed sentence-tokens.

The suggestion that one who utters a sentence of type (c) or (f) may assert that p even though the sentence itself does not entail that p may seem incongruous, perhaps incompatible, with the criticisms I raised in the previous section against the Cresswell-Sadock attempt at saving the Performative Analysis: it may seem to conflict with the rough definition I offered of assertion in terms of entailment, and it may raise the suspicion of the very circularity with which I have charged Sadock. But neither danger is real. A sentence of the form "I state that p" does not entail its complement, to be sure, but according to its paratactic analyis a speaker who tokens it does in the process utter a token of the complement sentence, and *that* sentence, assuming now the falsity of the Performative Analysis, does entail what is asserted (viz., itself); we may suppose the tokening is done in appropriate circumstances and in an appropriate tone. Thus, sentences of types (c) and (f) can be used to assert their complements consistently with the rough definition of assertion. Nor does any circle of technical terms materialize; now that we have eschewed the distinction between entailment$_{(1)}$ and "entailment$_2$," only the standard sense of "entail" is in play, and it is defined in terms of the standard (Tarskian) notion of truth, so "assertion" may noncircularly be defined in terms of entailment.

My remaining charge against the Cresswell-Sadock interpretation of the Performative Analysis was that "truth₁" would be a semantical property of ordinary declaratives only by aggravated courtesy and would do no theoretical work whatever except to save the Performative Analysis from semantic speechlessness concerning performative prefaces. This charge does not apply against our treatment of data (c) and (f), since our Cresswell-Sadock-Paratactic approach to those data in particular appeals only to the standard notion of truth defined in Tarski's way, both in predicating it of whole sentences and in predicating it of their complements.

Thus, I think, we can fairly plausibly adopt the Cresswell-Sadock-Paratactic approach to data (c) and (f), without committing ourselves to the full-blown Performative Analysis. What now of (d)?

The paraphrase relation that holds between an ordinary declarative sentence S and the explicit performative ⌜I state that S⌝ is very loose. Certainly either sentence could do duty for the other in most conversational situations, but this hardly shows that they are synonymous or even logically equivalent (compare "That's right" and "I agree"; "Ouch" and "That hurts"; "I disapprove of you" and "You bastard"). In fact, the account I have just offered of overtly explicit performatives predicts the paraphrase relation anyway, without positing logical equivalence. An utterer of such a performative asserts the complement even though the (whole) performative sentence does not entail the complement sentence; a person who merely asserts the complement sentence itself as an ordinary declarative makes just the same assertion, and this accounts for the feeling of paraphrase.[17]

This leaves us with (e). Our Cresswell-Sadock approach to (c), (d), and (f) will not help us here, since (e) concerns ordinary declaratives, interrogatives, and imperatives rather than puzzle sentences of types (c) or (f). If no performative prefaces underlie ordinary sentences, then what accounts for their respective moods?

I propose for this purpose to reintroduce semantically uninterpreted mood markers. Each SR will be marked for declarative, interrogative, or imperative (or whatever) force, and the markers will trigger the characteristic transformations that produce declarative, interrogative, and imperative surface forms, respectively. It may be felt that an element of underlying structure that has no semantic interpretation is as oddly dislocated as is Sadock's semantic₍₁₎ interpretation that has no syntactic effects (cf. section 4), but at least there is precedent for the former "dislocation": in adopting our theory of lexical presumption in chapter 5, we have already given up the assumption that *only* logical structure determines surface form; factual presumptions may affect surface form even after logical structure has made its contribution. And if one sort of element over and above logical form can affect syntax, then there may be other elements that do so as well. Let me expand on this a bit.

Reversion to semantically negligible mood triggers may seem paradigmatically *ad hoc* (cf. the troubles of the old "Q" morpheme).[18] We are to "explain" the surface marks of declarative mood by positing a little letter "D" in underlying structure, and then "explain" the surface marks of interrogative mood by positing a little letter "I" (or "Q") in underlying structure, and so on; it seems not unlike "explaining" observed perturbations in the orbit of a planet by positing a little letter "P" in the planet's center of gravity. But there is an important reason why positing uninterpreted mood markers is not, after all, *ad hoc* or vacuous. Just as it is unsurprising that a speaker's beliefs or contextual presumptions can affect syntactic processes, as we supposed in chapter 5, it should be no more surprising that the speaker's desires and intentions, particularly intentions to achieve certain goals by or in uttering his words, can affect syntactic processes also. Thus, although our mood markers are *semantically* uninterpreted, they are not *flatus vocis*. We should regard them, not as otherwise meaningless "letters" whose only function is to trigger the transformations that will make our surface forms come out right, but as signals entering a speaker's grammar through an *input gate*, whose function is to allow syntax to be affected by conative states in a way that bypasses logical form. Since it is independently reasonable to suppose that conative states do affect syntactic processes in this way, it is independently reasonable and so not *ad hoc* to posit the input gates and the traffic that enters through them.

In the next chapter we shall see that this account of mood needs to be complicated a bit. But if something like it is correct, then surface marks of mood have much in common with the lexical elements investigated in chapter 5. Just as those elements' appearance at the surface is a distinctive indication that a particular kind of transformation has been triggered independently of logical structure, the appearance of the surface marks of mood indicates that certain other types of transformations have been triggered just as independently. Mood is very like lexical presumption.

Though we have abandoned the Performative Analysis in its fullblown form, we have retained what may be regarded as a very weak version of it. The version is weak because it eschews the key claim that a declarative's SR contains *I*, STATE, and *you* occurring in a higher clause with their normal meanings. It is a *version* (at all) because it retains the idea that formal syntax is affected by messy, informal illocutionary and perhaps perlocutionary factors. It is harmless for my purposes because it requires no erosion of the semantics/pragmatics distinction and no consequent sullying of semantics.

Chapter 7
Indirect Force

Our "weak version" of the Performative Analysis, amounting just to the claim that surface mood features result from the operation of special transformations triggered by conative input of certain sorts, preserves the idea that mood is a function of illocutionary force. It is tempting to think of the three principal English moods as simply coinciding with three broad illocutionary genera of which individual types of speech act are species: the normal use of a declarative is to make a statement, that of an interrogative to ask a question, and that of an imperative to issue a directive of some kind. But an important class of data, called to our attention by Searle (1969), Sadock (1970), and others, indicates that the correspondence cannot be so straightforward. For a sentence of such-and-such a mood may sometimes, in entirely normal circumstances, be used with other than the "corresponding" illocutionary force. Consider:

(1) I want you to take out the garbage.

(2) Can you take out the garbage?

(3) Believe me when I say I hate broccoli.

(4) Tell me what has become of my children three.

(1), grammatically a declarative, can be used instead to issue a directive, typically a request that the hearer take out the garbage. More to the point, (1) would *normally* be used with directive force. Though it could be used as a bona fide description of one's state of mind (e.g., in answer to a psychiatrist's question, "Just for my notes, what is your strongest occurrent desire at this moment?"), this use is uncommon and needs a bit of stage-setting. Similarly, (2), an interrogative, is normally also used with directive force; the imperatives (3) and (4) may well be used to make a statement and to ask a question, respectively. (We shall see that some related data are even more dramatic than these.) The problem that would result for the Performative Analysis is plain: If (1), for example, reflects an SR governed by the performative preface STATE(I, you, . . .), where the elements of this preface are understood as having their normal meanings, then we would surely expect an utterer of (1) to be making a statement rather than issuing a request. Likewise, if (1)'s *normal* force really is directive (specifically, requestive) in character, we would expect the underlying preface to be REQUEST(I, you, . . .) or at least IMPERE(I, you, . . :); but according to the Performative Analysis it is not, and besides, if it were, we would expect it to trigger imperative rather than declarative surface mood features.

Since we have (provisionally) abandoned the Performative Analysis, this apparent conflict does not affect us directly. But surely some principled correspondence must be established between illocutionary force and mood-plus-locutionary-content. And my tentative account of our underlying mood markers as being signals accessed by a speaker's grammar from that speaker's conative components still presupposes as it stands that force or intended force determines mood, which presupposition is also impugned by the foregoing data. Let us call these data "indirect-force phenomena," and see what can be done about them.

1. The Conservative Approach

In keeping with the conservative attitude toward semantics that I have maintained so far in this book, it is attractive to think that our indirect-force phenomena can somehow be handled using existing apparatus. We may attempt to rely just on rules and principles that are already entrenched in our pragmatics and independently motivated. And it is initially attractive to suppose that indirect-force phenomena result from the application of purely pragmatic principles and contextual information to logical-forms-plus-mood-markers determined in the standard way. This conservative approach would resist the positing of novel or exotic semantic or syntactic machinery that serves no independent purpose. A number of theorists have taken this line, including Searle (1975), Fraser (1975), and Stampe (1975). David Gordon and George Lakoff (1975) too take the conservative line at the outset, but in the middle of their paper they execute a sudden swerve toward the exotic, for impressive reasons that I shall examine below. For now I shall discuss just the first, conservative half of their important article (the first half is almost completely independent of the second half, though this is unremarked by Gordon and Lakoff themselves) and compare it briefly to Searle's treatment.

Gordon and Lakoff's opening discussion focusses or indirectly performed requests. Their main syntactic contention, in virtue of which I have classified their initial approach as conservative, is that normally requestive sentences such as (1) and (2) have SRs that nevertheless correspond to the sentences' original or literal meanings and forces. The sentences' requestive force is therefore *not* literal, Gordon and Lakoff maintain, but rather is conveyed by means of "conversational postulates" that both speaker and hearer tacitly assume to be operating as background principles in context. (The sense of "literal" here is not as opposed to "metaphorical" or "figurative," but is much the same as that in which conversational implicatures are not parts of the literal meanings of the sentences that carry them: "literal" means roughly "a function of the sentence's SR." I do not think this use is pickwickian; a smart-alecky hearer who upon hearing (1) replied "Do you? What an interesting fact about you" would rightly be accused of excessive literalness.)

According to Gordon and Lakoff, the application of their "conversational postulates" is mediated by certain sorts of felicity-conditions on the speech acts indirectly performed (here, requesting), dubiously recast in the form of meaning postulates governing these terms of the object language[1] that express illocutionary virtues such as sincerity and reasonableness. Suppose, for example, that a speaker utters (2) with its requestive connotation. As a meaning postulate governing "sincere" as it applies to requests, Gordon and Lakoff say, we have

(5)   SINCERE(a,REQUEST(a,b,Q) $\rightarrow$ ASSUME(a,CAN(b,Q)),

which they call a "hearer-based sincerity-condition" on requests. They also put forward the following principle (defended on several grounds):

(GL-1)   One can convey a request by (a) asserting a speaker-based sincerity-condition or (b) questioning a hearer-based sincerity-condition. (p. 86)

From (GL-1) and (5) Gordon and Lakoff infer

(6)   ASK(a,b,CAN(b,Q))* $\rightarrow$ REQUEST(a,b,Q),

a conversational postulate. (The asterisk indicates that "the literal meaning . . . is not intended to be conveyed and . . . the hearer assumes that it is not"[2] (p. 87).) (6) explains why an utterance of (2) can be a request.

Gordon and Lakoff begin their paper by citing Grice's principles of conversation and declaring an intention "to outline a way in which conversational principles can begin to be formalized and incorporated into the theory of generative semantics," by which I assume they here mean, to use Gricean principles in accounting for indirect-force phenomena in particular. However, it should be noted that their explanation by appeal to (6) is not Gricean in any very clear sense; it does not appeal even tacitly to Grice's Cooperative Principle or invoke any other principle designed to expedite communication of information, and it depends essentially on a premise dragged out of speech-act theory. (I shall expand on this point shortly.) But this does not affect the account's status as an instance of the conservative approach. It explains our ability to grasp the normal but nonliteral requestive force of (2) by applying already motivated pragmatic principles to (2)'s ostensibly literal SR.

Gordon and Lakoff go on to indicate a number of directions in which their account may be extended in order to illuminate otherwise unexplained phenomena outside their immediate concern. For example, *via* the commonly posited decomposition of the underlying performance verb ASK into the structure REQUEST(TELL), Gordon and Lakoff are able to predict the ability of such sentences as (7a–d) to convey questions corresponding to their complements (pp. 87–88).

(7) a. I want you to tell me whether Harry left.
   b. Can you tell me where the bus stops?
   c. Would you be willing to tell me why you left your wife?
   d. Will you tell me how to adjust the TV?

They also point out that by formulating sincerity-conditions on speech acts other than requesting, their opening strategy can be brought to bear on those other speech acts as well (pp. 88, 88n, 89). And they use their conservative strategy to predict that what would literally be bland factual questions, such as (8), or factual reports, such as (9), can function as *challenges* to requests, in virtue of reasonableness-conditions on felicitous requesting (p. 91; these felicity-conditions are taken to be meaning postulates).

(8) Why do you want me to do that?

(9) I was going to do that anyway.

(The motivating generalization here is roughly "if you cast doubt on one of the reasonableness conditions, you cast doubt on the reasonableness of the act itself" (p. 91), which is of course less surprising than (GL-1).)

Perhaps I have been overhasty in crediting Gordon and Lakoff with having *explained* their indirect-request phenomena. In fact, their account falls far short of being a genuine explanation in each of several related ways:

(i) The principles, such as (GL-1), that yield Gordon and Lakoff's individual "conversational postulates" are (so far) not genuinely *theoretical* principles and probably should not strictly be called "principles" at all; they are, rather, empirical generalizations mechanically culled from Gordon and Lakoff's data and are themselves just as badly in need of explanation as are those data taken individually. For example, why does (GL-1) itself hold? Gordon and Lakoff have left this general fact just as preanalytically mysterious as is each of the singular facts that it subsumes. (ii) To put much the same point somewhat more sharply: Though they invoke the name of Grice and though they speak throughout of "conversational" considerations and of felicity-conditions on speech acts, Gordon and Lakoff make no attempt actually to justify such findings as (GL-1) on the basis of pragmatic principles *already understood.* (GL-1) and its ilk are not shown to follow from Grice's Cooperative Principle, from independently motivated principles of speech-act theory, from pragmatic rules for the use of context-supplied background information, from any combination of the foregoing, or from any other body of principles for which pragmatics has antecedently found use. Thus, Gordon and Lakoff have failed to explain their data at least in the sense of deriving the relevant empirical generalizations from independently justified laws; they have not economized the unexpected by reducing it to the familiar. (iii) (GL-1) in any case is a very weak generalization, in that it asserts merely the *possibility* of performing a certain speech act in a certain way. Even if (as is belied by (i) and (ii)) Gordon and Lakoff had explained how it is that such performances are possible, they would not have explained why (2) is *normally* used as a request. Nor would they even have begun to answer more substantive questions such as what determines when an indirect request *has been* performed in this way, how a hearer *tells* that the intended force is nonliteral or indirect, and how the hearer tells *which* of the (usually) several possible nonliteral forces is intended. (This is not to intimate that Gordon and Lakoff claim to have explained these more substantive things; they candidly duck such questions on p. 87 (cf. the asterisk they insert into (6)).)

Searle (1975) addresses these more substantive questions squarely and makes a creditable start at answering them. He proposes to explain how a speaker can succeed in performing an "indirect" speech act and how a hearer can achieve uptake, despite the disparity between the indirect act and the literal content-plus-mood-marker of the sentence uttered. Moreover, he proposes to do this by conservative means. He begins with considerations of speaker-meaning. The speaker in such a case means what he literally says (including its mood), but also has an ulterior, nonliteral illocutionary motive. Therefore, the speaker must provide the hearer with materials for recognizing this motive over and above logical form and literal mood, and the hearer must exploit these added materials in order to secure uptake. In a case of indirect requesting, the speaker's nonliteral meaning is that the hearer should do A, and, Searle says (p. 72), "the following generalizations naturally emerge" from his taxonomy and his list of "putative facts":

> Generalization 1: *S can make an indirect request (or other directive) by either asking whether or stating that a preparatory condition concerning H's ability to do A obtains.*
> Generalization 2: *S can make an indirect directive by either asking whether or stating that the propositional content condition obtains.*
> Generalization 3: *S can make an indirect directive by stating that the sincerity condition obtains, but not by asking whether it obtains.*
> Generalization 4: *S can make an indirect directive by either stating that or asking whether there are good or overriding reasons for doing A, except where the reason is that H wants or wishes, etc., to do A, in which case he can only ask whether H wants, wishes, etc., to do A.* (p. 72)

These strategies are cognate with and roughly subsume the "principles" that (together with felicity-conditions) yield Gordon and Lakoff's "conversational postulates." Accordingly, Generalizations 1–4 too have only the status of empirical generalizations still in need of principled explanation in turn. And, given Searle's heralded conservative program, it remains to be shown in particular that the generalizations' truth can be explained solely in conservative terms. Searle displays the kind of reasoning that is needed, by deriving an instance of Generalization 1 using only lemmas from speech-act theory and the theory of conversation, supplemented by ordinary background information. The details are somewhat lengthy, but the idea is that the hearer uses Gricean principles and background information to infer that there *is* an ulterior illocutionary intention, and then uses speech-act theory and more background information to determine what that ulterior intention is. Thus, in Searle's example (the use of "Can you pass the salt?" to make a request (pp. 73–74)), the hearer first infers on the basis of straightforward Gricean maxims and specific points of factual information (such as the speaker's obvious lack of *theoretical* interest in the hearer's salt-passing ability) that the speaker intends to convey something nonliterally, and then cleverly notes both that the speaker has "alluded to the satisfaction of a preparatory condition for a request" and that the request in question is one "whose obedience conditions it is quite likely (the speaker) wants (the hearer) to bring about." The hearer concludes that "in the absence of any other plausible illocutionary point," the speaker is probably asking for the salt.

As I have observed, Searle's proposed format is an advance over Gordon and Lakoff's, but let us note that it is still not as tight an explanation as would be required of an adequate pragmatics. Though the (Gricean) first half of the hearer's reasoning is straightforward, the second is thin. Even granting that the hearer would notice that in querying his *ability* to pass the salt the speaker has "alluded to the satisfaction of a preparatory condition for a request," why would the hearer automatically notice *this* meta-illocutionary fact in particular, and why would he focus on the act of *requesting* rather than on any of the other speech acts to which hearers' abilities are relevant (commands, suggestions, offers of help,[3] challenges, etc.)? Naturally, Searle intends "context" to help the hearer make this selection, but that is a vacuous truism, and pointing it out contributes nothing to our still superficial account of the hearer's reasoning. Perhaps Searle supposes that the hearer will invoke further factual assumptions, such as that the speaker is known to like heavily salted okra but has not yet gained access to any of the seasonings. Or the hearer might rely on more facts about particular speech acts, such as that the speaker has no particular socially determined authority with which to back up a command directed to the hearer; or both. Possibly Searle would like simply to posit a *convention* to the effect that the indisputably nonliteral querying of the hearer's ability to ϕ counts as a request that the hearer ϕ; he remarks on p. 75 that the *form of words* "Can you ϕ?" is more closely associated with the making of indirect requests than is its semantical equivalent "Are you able to ϕ?" and explains this fact by saying that the former has "become conventionally established" as a "standard idiomatic form" for making requests (p. 76). Presumably the convention Searle has in mind would fix a range of locutions that *could* be used to make requests as opposed to equivalent locutions that normally are not so used, and this convention would heighten the salience of *requesting* as a possible intention of our speaker. But notice that appeal to such a convention seems essential to our hearer's reasoning in the case of "Can you pass the salt?," since otherwise "Are you able to pass the salt?" would have just the same indirect act-potential. (And let us remember that the brute positing of specific conventions is usually *ad hoc*.)[4]

Despite these difficulties, Searle's line is attractive and his program is promising. He admits he cannot "prove" that all indirect-force phenomena can be explained by a set of conservatively defended generalizations of the sort exemplified by Generalizations 1–4, but his embryonic success with requestives, and later with commissives, gives cause for hope. It is tempting to stop with this promissory note and turn it unobtrusively into methodological dogma, but this, though relaxing, would be premature, for we have not yet taken account of the second half of Gordon and Lakoff's paper, in which (without apparently realizing that they are spiking the promise of their opening half) they present very convincing evidence for thinking that the business of indirect speech acts simply cannot be settled by purely conservative means.

2. Indirect Force and Syntax

Gordon and Lakoff begin by turning to the case of "why"-questions. After noting that (10) can be understood either literally or as suggesting that the hearer should not be painting his house purple, they point out the surprising fact that a superficial syntactic change can serve to remove the literal understanding, as in (11).

   (10)   Why are you painting your house purple?

   (11)   Why paint your house purple?

(11) cannot be understood as an ingenuous *or* disingenuous request for information about the hearer's state of mind. Gordon and Lakoff draw the moral that "the rule that deletes *you* + tense can apply only if [the suggestion that the hearer should not be painting his house purple] is conveyed. . . . it follows that the conditions for the correct application of *you* + tense deletion are dependent on context and on conversational implication" (p. 96). They go on to mention several other cases in which the applicability of syntactic rules seems to be constrained by prior considerations of what is conversationally to be conveyed, involving the distribution of "please," the distribution of "here," and verb-subject inversion in questions. After examining these data and posing some interesting unsolved problems, Gordon and Lakoff conclude that "grammar requires . . . a set of transderivational rules" (p. 104), rules of *grammar* (in that they determine the distribution of morphemes) "that depend on the conveyed, not the literal, meaning of sentences" (p. 101). Thus, according to Gordon and Lakoff, the completion of some straightforward syntactic processes is conditional upon the existence of certain specific material in SRs that are only contextually *associated* with the sentences produced in part by those processes. And this is certainly novel apparatus, at

least relative to the Metatheory and to the idea that syntax and pragmatics are for the most part separate enterprises, though it is important to note that Gordon and Lakoff never abandon the conservative
practice of insisting that the sentences that are used in performing
indirect speech acts nevertheless retain their original, literal SRs. I
shall follow Sadock (1975) in calling this method of transderivational
constraints the "logicogrammatical" account.

A number of linguists have criticized Gordon and Lakoff's theory
(Sadock (1974, 1975), Cole (1975), Ross (1975), Green (1975), Davison
(1975), Morgan (1977), and others). I cannot survey even all the
plausible criticisms here; a number of them fail, I think, by ignoring
the conventional speech-act-theoretic elements that figure in Gordon
and Lakoff's (and Searle's) conservative lines of reasoning.[5] Instead I
shall raise two objections of my own. The first is only cautionary, the
second more serious.

Gordon and Lakoff's transderivational rules may be prohibitively
hard to state, for the hypothesized literal SRs are rather severely
constrained. Notice that each of the SRs assigned to (11) and to the
following sentences called to our attention by Green

(12)   Why don't you be quiet?

(13)   Why don't you be nice to your brother for a change?

(14)   Would you get me a glass of water?

(15)   Would you be so kind as to let me through?

would have to meet each of two entirely nonnegotiable conditions:
(i) Serving as a representation of the euphemistic literal content of
what the speaker says, it must be a structure that initiates a specifiable chain of Gricean-*cum*-speechacty reasoning on the hearer's
part—specifically, a chain that terminates in the hearer's believing
that the speaker is trying to convey such-and-such an imperative.
(And we must be able to reconstruct this chain.) (ii) The hypothetical
literal structure must also originate a real transformational history
(punctuated, of course, by the operation of a fairly unusual transderivational constraint) that terminates in a surface representation of
the actual string uttered by the speaker. (And we must have independent syntactic evidence of the existence and nature of this derivation.) These two requirements may be hard to fulfill jointly. In the
case of their proposed treatment of (13), for example, Gordon and
Lakoff would have to show both that a structure that would ordinarily surface as "Why aren't you being nice to your brother for a
change?" yields an imperative implicature (by specifying a Gricean

chain of reasoning) and that it is plausible to think that the latter sentence normally is derived from an underlying structure that contains DO+BE and that in this particular context has given rise in virtue of the implicature and our transderivational constraint to the otherwise ungrammatical (13).

Of course, the very positing of the constraint itself must also not be *ad hoc*. This raises my second and more general problem for Gordon and Lakoff's strategy. Remember that we must examine the proposed semantactic process both from the speaker's and from the hearer's points of view, i.e., both with an eye to the production of a sentence and with an eye to the recognition of the indirect speech act thus produced.

The goings-on in the speaker are not too hard to sketch. Very crudely: A desire occurs in me to convey to my hearer that he should ϕ. For reasons of politeness or caution, the censor-homunculus within me takes the imperative thought that has formed itself in my mind and censors it by replacing it with a "softer" or less blunt thought that, when somehow expressed, will nevertheless get the hearer to recognize my desire that he ϕ and my intention to convey this desire; that is, I (or my homuncular deputy) predict that the hearer will engage in Gricean and/or speechacty reasoning based on the literal realization of the literal, euphemistic thought, which will enable the hearer to work out my desires, intentions, metadesires, and meta-intentions. The literal thought is then fed to my syntactic component, which begins to restructure and remold it ultimately into a set of phonological instructions in the familiar way. However, although I want to be polite, I also want my intention to be unmistakable and hence unambiguous. So I (in the person of my syntactic deputy) take the option of kicking in the appropriate transderivational rule, i.e., the rule that produces a surface form that can have come *only* from a process that was triggered by an intention on my part to implicate the relevant imperative, and I assume that the hearer has the tacit knowledge and linguistic competence to draw the intended conclusions.

So far, so good. But notice (and view with caution) the fact that in this last sketch of the paramechanics of whimperative[6] production I have located the transderivational constraint psychologically as being activated *by an intention* on the part of the speaker *to convey* a nonliteral message. This is a substantive piece of psycholinguistic interpretation, and may well be fraught with (perhaps prohibitive) psychological difficulties. In stating their thesis concerning the need for positing transderivational rules of grammar, Gordon and Lakoff express the dependence of these rules on conversational considerations by saying that a rule "can apply only if" such-and-such a sentence "is conveyed" (p. 96); "the conditions for the correct application of" the rule "are dependent on context and on conversational implication" (p. 96); "the environment for the application or nonapplication of" the rule "mentions not the literal content of the sentence but the conversationally implied content" (p. 100); the rule "depend(s) on the conveyed, not the literal, meaning of sentences" (p. 101); etc. Gordon and Lakoff's deliberate caution here marks a commendable unwillingness to commit themselves prematurely regarding the semiotic details of the alleged dependence. But such commitment must eventually be made, and we need to peer ahead at least a little. My reason for casting the dependence in terms of a conative state of the speaker is that conversational implicature and speech-act-theoretic felicity-relations are explicated precisely in terms of the speaker's and hearer's actual or hypothetical psychological states, and no very different alternative occurs to me offhand. But the issue is one that must be kept in mind.

One immediately pressing reason why it must be kept in mind is that our formulation of our speaker's propaedeutic predictive reasoning raises a *prima facie* problem of circularity. Roughly: A hearer is given only the speaker's utterance, which we may represent simply as a *string* together with whatever intonation and whatever contextual factors may be present, and must draw conclusions about the speaker's illocutionary act or intent based solely on those things. Now it seems that, in order to know that a string such as (11) is grammatical in the context, the hearer would antecedently have to know that the string was the product of a transderivational constraint of the appropriate type, since it is Gordon and Lakoff's essential thesis that strings of this sort are deviant on any but their indirect imperative understandings. In order to know that the string was the product of the transderivational constraint in question, the hearer would antecedently have to know that the whimperative implicature was present or intended, since to understand the transderivational rule would require knowing its characteristic condition of application. But if the hearer already knows that the whimperative implicature is present or intended (on whatever grounds), then all the foregoing reasoning ascribed to the hearer is superfluous, and would contribute nothing to the hearer's uptake. This leaves us with the question of how the hearer does achieve conversational/speechacty uptake, and, in the case of our characteristic strings, Gordon and Lakoff leave this entirely unanswered. We cannot just suppose that the hearer runs syntactic transformations backward (exploiting them in their obverse guise as rules of semantic interpretation), because unless we accept *and make use of* Gordon and Lakoff's special trans-derivational rules, we cannot recover a legitimate transformational history for the string in question (this being the salient feature of the kind of case we are considering), and if we do make use of Gordon-Lakovian constraints, we will (as argued just now) presuppose prior knowledge of the implicature whose very uptake we are trying to explain.[7]

This apparent circularity poses a serious problem for the logico-grammatical account. For I find it hard even to begin a gloss of the hearer's recognition or uptake reasoning of the sort I offered for the speaker's propadeutic or production reasoning. It would begin: I hear the speaker utter a string s with intonation i. I know that s is grammatical (that s is the product of a series of correct applications of extant syntactic transformations) only if s has been produced by a series of transformations one member of which is a Gordon-La-kovian transderivational constraint of type t, where t subsumes the transderivational rules that are triggered just by the presence of an imperative implicature, in this case the implicature that I should ϕ. Therefore, the speaker has implicated that I am to ϕ.

The trouble is that the hearer's reasoning can stop here; it has reached the intended conclusion—*without any Gricean or speechacty reasoning having taken place on the hearer's part.* But, by definition, this cannot happen; for an implicature (even in Gordon and Lakoff's neologistically broad sense of that term) to be grasped as such by a hearer just *is* for that hearer to perform the characteristic conversa-tional reasoning. This result seems to constitute an effective *reductio* of the logicogrammatical account as Gordon and Lakoff have pre-sented it, or at least as I have interpreted it here. I see no obvious way out of this difficulty, though perhaps some break in the circle will be found.

Since indirect force has been shown to be marked in syntax, one might naturally turn to seeking a syntactic explanation. Proponents of the Performative Analysis are in the best position to attempt this, since they claim already to have established a lawlike connection between illocutionary force and syntactic structure. As a first pass we might simply suppose that a sentence such as (11) that grammatically must have indirect force reflects a performative preface correspond-ing directly to that force; (11) would reflect SUGGEST(I, you, . . .) *rather than* ASK(I, you, . . .), or REQUEST(I, you, . . .) (or RE-QUEST(I, you(TELL(you, me . . .))) (cf. Heringer (1972), Davison (1973a, 1973b)). Likewise, a sentence that normally has, or can have, indirect force but in some circumstances can also have literal force is syntactically ambiguous; on the former occasions it reflects a performative preface corresponding to its indirect force, and on the latter it reflects that which corresponds to its literal force. The trouble with this simple proposal is twofold. First, it fails to explain why sentences that grammatically must have indirect force bear the grammatical surface marks of their literal force that they do; for example, why does (11) display the question-forming particle *wh* . . . and the verb-subject inversion characteristic of questions, if it is really a suggestion rather than a question at the level of deep structure? Second, in the case of the allegedly ambiguous sentences that can have either indirect or literal force depending on context, the simple proposal belies a great many facts that point similarly toward the simultaneous presence of distinct illocutionary influences (see Searle, pp. 67–71). In sum, as Davison (1975) puts it (p. 145), the proposal "fails to note or predict the . . . differences between indirect speech acts and corresponding direct ones . . ."; if the proposal were true, there would be no serious problem of indirect force to begin with.

More complex and responsive syntactic solutions have been offered, exploiting the Performative Analysis as before but attempting to capture the elusive dual nature of indirect speech acts as the simple proposal does not. Most of these take the form of combining a performative preface representing indirect force *with* a preface representing literal force: Sadock (1970) conjoins them; Green (1975) sketches a view of whimperatives in particular, according to which they reflect requestive prefaces operating on disjunctions roughly of the form "you do X or tell me why not" (the combination of REQUEST with lower TELL presumably explains the surface marks of interrogativity in a whimperative). Each such proposal faces syntactic difficulties because of its complexity (e.g., some of the problems incurred by Sadock's proposal are pointed out by Green), and each looks somewhat contrived. However, the main objection to the combined-preface approach from my point of view is that I have rejected the Performative Analysis, and so I do not believe in even one of the posited underlying prefaces in the first place, much less two occurring in conspiracy. (Notice particularly that any combined-preface approach would occasion an aggravated instance of the Performadox.) So we shall have to look elsewhere for a solution to the problem of indirect force, though obviously our pale shadow of the Performative Analysis, viz., our system of posited unstructured mood markers, will play a key role.

3. Almost a Solution

Let us begin by stating the problem more sharply than we have done so far. (Van der Auwera (1980) points out correctly that the notion of "indirect force" or of an "indirect speech act" has never been precisely defined, and that unrecognized differences in conception have influenced discussion.) The principal unclarities to date are these: (i) If "indirect" is supposed to mean "not direct," what exactly is "direct" force or a "direct" speech act? (Note that these notions cannot properly be defined in terms of the underlying prefaces posited by the Performative Analysis, both because this would be tendentious in general and because it would beg the question in favor of some specific proposed solutions and against others.) (ii) If a "direct" speech act is supposed to be one in which are conveyed both the "literal" force and the literal propositional content of the sentence uttered, and nothing else, then many types of utterance fall neither within this category nor within that of the utterances generally lumped together under the label of "indirect-force phenomena": instances of irony, insinuation, metaphor, and good old conversational implicature and conventional implicature of any of a number of kinds. (As van der Auwera puts it (sec. 3.1), some speech acts are neither direct nor indirect.) (iii) Ought use of the term "indirect force" to require without exception that a *switch* of illocutionary subtype has occurred? Or might one indirectly perform an act of subtype T by literally performing another act of subtype T that differs from it not in type of force but only in locutionary content?[8]

Let us tackle these questions in reverse order. The answer to (iii) should be "no," I believe, though some writers on the topic of indirect force have unreflectively supposed otherwise in characterizing the phenomenon that concerned them. Consider the following:

(16)   I must tell you that your cat has been arrested.

(17)   May I ask you why you salt your milkshakes so heavily?

(18)   Don't let me catch you scarfing the parsnip pudding.

Each of (16)–(18) has the unmistakable ring of indirect act-potential. (16), literally a modal statement that entails nothing expressed in the complement of "tell," nevertheless normally has the force of a statement that the hearer's cat has been arrested. (17) literally inquires about permission, but normally functions as a query about the hearer's culinary preferences. (18) is normally an order not to scarf the parsnip pudding. Each of the speech acts that would be performed in typical utterances of (16)–(18) is nonliteral and to some extent conventional in a way that is characteristic though yet to be explained; each admits a literal reply that would be received as cheaply smart-alecky. Yet none shows a switch of illocutionary subtype. (16) is a statement on both its literal and its usual understanding; (17) is uniformly a question, (18) an order. What is "switched" in each case is merely the locutionary content. The mechanisms— whatever they are—that mediate indirect speech acts can affect the overall speech act performed without actually switching force; thus, the term "indirect force" is a bit of a misnomer, though I shall continue to use it for convenience.

This answer to question (iii) forces us to consider the relation between indirect speech acts and conversational implicatures (cf. Matthews (1975); van der Auwera (1980, secs. 4.1, 5)). For if an indirect speech act can be performed without a switch of illocutionary subtype, then a literal *statement* that typically would convey nonliteral locutionary content may be counted as an indirect speech act, and this raises the possibility that conversational implicature is merely a special case of indirect force or vice versa. (Insofar as indirect speech acts involve conventional elements, the distinction between indirect force and conventional implicature may blur as well; but let us neglect this for now, since we have already adopted a rather specific and technical analysis of "conventional implicature" in terms of lexical presumption (chapter 5), and we should leave open the question of whether the latter device is incorporated in whatever mechanisms underlie indirect force.)

Matthews inclines toward subsuming conversational implicature under indirect force; van der Auwera proposes to extend the former notion to encompass the latter. Neither of these strategies appeals to me, first, because I think it is a bad idea to conflate notions from speech-act theory with notions from the *prima facie* distinct branch of pragmatics concerned with the efficient communication of information,[9] and second, because most conversational implicatures do not in fact satisfy even the looser requirement that indirect force be expressible in the form of a "pure performative" as defined by the "hereby" criterion. Suppose a speaker states literally that p, deliberately implicating that q. Virtually never will such a speaker have *stated* that q. If in response to a query about chess I tell you that Jones is great at ping-pong, thereby implicating that Jones's ability at chess is negligible, I have not stated that his ability is negligible. *Au contraire*; I have gone out of my way *not* to state that but to convey it more gently by stating something else that is more complimentary. In a standard case of implicature, literal sentence-meaning is what is stated, even though it would be a bit misleading to report the speaker's having stated it and let it go at that. (Such a report made by one who was privy to the implicature would be misleading because it would wantonly omit a more important piece of information, viz., information regarding the contents of what the speaker primarily meant to convey.) As a final indication that conversational implicature is not a subspecies of indirect force, note that an implicative utterance tolerates overliteral rejoinder in a way that an indirect speech act does not. A hearer might respond to my remark about Jones by saying "Oh, is he?", "No, he isn't," "I play ping-pong too," or whatever, without branding himself a smart-aleck.

Turning back to question (ii), we find that the same considerations hold for irony, hinting, and insinuation, at least. Practitioners of these usages state (or ask, or command, etc.) the literal meanings of their sentences, and only secondarily achieve other illocutionary and perlocutionary goals. An utterance of

(19)   Buddy, do you think if you sit at the stoplight long enough it will turn some color besides red, yellow, and green?

serves as an urging, but only derivatively so; the speaker urges *by* literally asking the hearer whether he thinks such-and-such. An utterance of

(20)   Have you noticed that the boss and his secretary have been leaving together every day at 3:30?

hints or insinuates that the boss and his secretary are having an affair, but cannot be used to perform any illocutionary act having that locutionary content. Literally it is just a question.

The case of metaphor is a bit trickier. One who utters a sentence using some of its terms metaphorically is not comfortably reported as having stated the literal content of that sentence, since by hypothesis such a person is not speaking literally. Insofar as metaphoricalness is a feature that comes in degrees, we find that the appropriateness of such a report varies inversely with the "liveness" or freshness of the metaphor; (21)–(24) are decreasingly happy reports:

(21)   She stated that her vocal technique had reached a new plateau.

(22)   She stated that her ex-husband was a real bastard.

(23)   She stated that her blood had sung when Errol kissed her.

(24)   She stated that she had rolled a gutter ball on life's bowling alley.

Nor, however, are we comfortable with reports that cash the fresher metaphors too explicitly:

(21a)   She stated that she had completed an incremental improvement in her vocal technique.

(22a)   She stated that her ex-husband was mean and unscrupulous.

(23a)   She stated that she had become vibrantly excited when Errol kissed her.

(24a)   She stated that some enterprise of hers had been a dismal failure.

There does not seem to be any perfectly straightforward way of reporting a freshly metaphorical speech act. Many metaphorical utterances do not even lend themselves to literal translation at all.

In any case, metaphor differs in each of several ways from our paradigm cases of indirect force: (a) The locus of metaphor is the individual term or phrase, not the entire sentence; a sentence is used metaphorically only in virtue of one or more of its component expressions' being used metaphorically. The indirectness of a paradigmatically indirect speech act does not share this dependent character. (b) In a typical case of indirect force, the conveyed locutionary content is embedded within the more elaborate literal content (cf. (1)–(4), (12)–(15), and especially (16)–(18)). It is as if the speaker had constructed his sentence by taking what he meant to convey and modifying it by adding prefatory material. Typical metaphor shows no such structure. (c) As has been remarked, the prefatory material that normally makes for indirect force tends to have a conventional ring. Forms of words such as "I must tell you that . . . ," "May I ask you to . . . ," and the like are "conventional phrases" in the layman's sense of that term. Live metaphors are just the opposite. (d) Metaphors figure in no true empirical generalizations of Gordon and Lakoff's type. (e) It seems clear that metaphor has essentially to do with locutionary meaning or content and its manipulation rather than with force or with mood *per se*. Metaphor is just not an illocutionary phenomenon, and so it seems unnatural to classify it as a subspecies of derived force.

Of course, we could not reach a truly reliable taxonomic conclusion unless we had delved deeper into the positive nature of metaphor itself; but I think it is fair to judge tentatively at this point that metaphorical utterances are not *per se* instances of indirect force. This leaves the way clear for us to answer our original question above by defining "direct" in such a way as to render "indirect" equivalent to "not direct": a direct speech act will be one in which there occurs neither a switch of illocutionary subtype nor a switch of propositional content under the subtype in question. I take conversational implicature, irony, insinuation, and (for now) metaphor all to satisfy that definition.

A second refinement in our statement of the problem should make a solution easier to come by. Notice that sentences differ systematically in their grades of indirect-force potential. Some sentences merely *can* be used with indirect force (call this category "Type 1"); some *normally* have indirect force and can be used with direct force only in contrived circumstances (Type 2); and some can be used *only* with indirect force owing to the presence of some syntactic peculiarity of the sort discussed by Gordon and Lakoff (Type 3). Theorists have tended to overlook these distinctions, or at least to suppose that a single unified theory will handle all three types of sentence. It would be nice to have a single unified theory that did, but I see no reason for optimism on this point, given that the differences between the three types are fairly striking. So I shall offer a tripartite treatment of indirect speech acts.

Let us begin with our first category, Type 1, some members of which are:

(25)   It's cold in here.

(26)   Are you tall enough to reach the top shelf?

(27)   I wonder what time it is.

When uttered in appropriate circumstances, as by Lord Peter Wimsey to his man Bunter, (25) can be used to command (not just to hint); (26) can be used to request; and (27) can be used to ask a question. But all three sentences have perfectly straightforward literal uses that require no stage-setting, and when they are used with indirect force, we feel the conveyed force depends pretty squarely on the literal content. By the same token, hearers do not compute these sentences' indirect forces conventionally or automatically; multiple contextual factors are needed in the determination. These facts suggest that what we have called the conservative approach will be able to explain the Type-1 mode(s) of conveyance. Simple Gricean reasoning will not suffice, of course, since a hearer's uptake in these cases will consist in part of knowing what illocutionary act was indirectly performed, over and above the locutionary content that may have been conveyed by Gricean means. Fortunately, the annals of speech-act theory furnish a way of connecting Gricean conversational considerations with illocutionary matters.

First, Strawson (1964) has argued convincingly that illocutionary acts lie along a "scale" or continuum, at one end of which we find acts that are almost completely determined or constituted by institutional convention virtually regardless of the private beliefs and intentions of individual participants, and at the other end of which we find acts that are not really conventional at all in the relevant sense, but are almost completely constituted by the attendant beliefs, intentions, and meta-intentions of the speakers, much in the manner of Grice's theory of speaker-meaning (1957, 1969). What is common to all illocutionary acts, Strawson says, is that ". . . the understanding of the force of an utterance . . . involves recognizing what may be called broadly an audience-directed intention and recognizing it as wholly overt, as intended to be recognized" (p. 613). Where acts differ is in the hearers' mode or intended mode of recognition; sometimes it involves highly specific and stylized institutional or linguistic conventions, sometimes it involves no conventions in particular but only conversational and factual reasoning, and sometimes, in an intermediate case, it involves some mixture of convention and reasoning. In commenting on Strawson, Stephen Schiffer (1972) argues that

> . . . such speech acts as belong to highly conventionalized institutions are, from the point of view of the theory of language and communication, of marginal interest only. The primary and important case is that of the kind of illocutionary act which is not essentially conventional . . . (pp. 93–94)

Schiffer goes on to propose his own analysis, in Gricean terms, of what it is for an utterance to have illocutionary force in the "not essentially conventional" way.

Second, Searle (1969) has suggested that most (though perhaps not all) individual illocutionary notions can be analyzed in terms of intended perlocutionary effects; in chapter 3 he offers a few sample analyses of promising, requesting, asserting, warning, and the like in terms of "essential," "sincerity," and "preparatory" conditions whose satisfaction makes those acts respectively what they are. Schiffer too essays a specific analysis of particular types of speech act (pp. 99ff.). This implementation of the connection Strawson has drawn between illocutionary force and the ingredients that figure in the Gricean analysis of speaker-meaning allows us to build our bridge between the literal and the indirect uses of Type-1 sentences such as (25)–(27). Our strategy, and presumably a hearer's strategy, will be roughly this: Using conversational reasoning based on the literal content of the speaker's utterance, we will determine that such-and-such a further content is being implicated or conversationally conveyed. Using our knowledge of contextual facts and perhaps further conversational reasoning, we will also come to suppose that the speaker has certain beliefs and intentions, particularly intentions to produce in us as hearers responses of such-and-such a kind by means of our recognition of those very intentions. We will then note that a combination of contextual facts with our speaker-hypothesized beliefs and intentions satisfies the *analysans* of a plausible Searle- or Schiffer-style explication of what it is for an utterance to count as an illocutionary act of such-and-such a type, and straightaway deduce that the speaker has performed an act of that type having the relevant propositional content.

Let us take just one example, (27). (27) could have a perfectly literal use, or it could have a direct use in which it also served as a hint; the clearest case in which it has a full-fledged indirect requestive use is one in which the speaker is not wearing a watch but can see that the hearer is wearing one, and indeed looks pointedly at the hearer's watch as he speaks. In such a case the hearer's reasoning might go something like this: "He has said that he wonders what time it is. He knows, and knows that I know that he knows, that I have no particular interest in the minutiae of his passing mental conditions *per se*, and he is also constrained by the Maxim of Relevance, so I must assume there is a special reason why he wants me to know that he is currently in a state of wonderment concerning the time. In general, people who wonder concerning X also desire to come to know concerning X. Further, the speaker knows, and knows that I know that he knows, that he is currently powerless to satisfy his presumed desire but that I have the capacity to satisfy it with only a very minimal expenditure of effort; we both also know that a conversationally cooperative person does not hesitate to supply information that someone else wants if it costs him nothing, and, more generally, that a decent and civil person does not hesitate to satisfy someone else's desire if it costs him nothing. Finally, the speaker has both motive and opportunity for making his desire known to me, and so, other things being equal, has formed the intention to do so and to get me to satisfy the desire by telling him the time. That he is looking pointedly at my watch further suggests that he intends me to be reasoning in the very way I am reasoning now, and that recognition of that very intention (not just generalized benevolence alone) will motivate me to tell him the time. But to *request* of a person that he do φ just is (roughly) to make an utterance with the intention of getting that person to do φ by means of causing the person to recognize that very intention. Therefore, the speaker has requested of me that I tell him the time." Lengthy as it is in the telling, this reasoning is both plausible and natural. If similar glosses can be produced for (25), (26), and other Type-1 sentences, as I think they can, we should conclude that for the members of Type 1 something like Searle's original (1975) conservative approach will work.

This hypothesis makes two predictions, both of which seem to me to be confirmed. The first is that no special conventions figure in hearers' uptake regarding sentences of Type 1. This seems right, since if there were special conventions associated with such sentences we would expect those sentences to have *normally* or even invariably indirect uses, in which case they would no longer count as being of Type 1. Second, we would expect to find no particular syntactic marks of indirect force in these cases, and indeed we do not. In fact, if we try to impose syntactic marks of indirect force we find Type-1 sentences inhospitable:

(25a)　*Wimsey:* It's cold in here.
　　　　Bunter: ??At once, my lord. [Failure of normal reply to command]

(26a)　*Are you tall enough to please reach the top shelf? [Failure of preverbal "please" characteristic of conventional requests]

(27a)　*I wonder what time it is, just because I like to hear the sound of your voice when you answer questions. [Failure of reason-adverbial test for questionhood; cf. Davison (1975, pp. 162–64)]

What this suggests is that although Type-1 sentences can be used to perform speech acts indirectly, the burden of effort lies with the speaker; there is no preestablished or conventional setting already in place to facilitate such usage. This is what Type-1 sentences have in common with mere hints, insinuations, and other nonillocutionary implicatures. But they differ from such implicatures in that when they are being used with indirect force they satisfy Strawson's and Schiffer's Gricean recognition-of-intention criterion for having illocutionary forces of the relevant sorts.

Where does this leave our weak version of the Performative Analysis? Our problem was the apparent disparity between underlying conative input to a sentence's underlying mood-marking gate and the surface mood features actually triggered by that input. On the present proposal for handling Type-1 sentences, there is no such disparity, since the proposal attributes literal force to such sentences and recognizes that one and the same utterance can have more than one illocutionary point at the same time.[10] In the circumstances imagined, (27) has, primarily, the force of a statement; secondarily and derivatively, it also has the force of a question. Its primary force determines its underlying mood marker, and that is why it has declarative surface features. Its interrogative force is a creature of extraneous psychological conditions and other contextual factors.

Sentences of our second category, Type 2, are by far the most commonly discussed in the literature on derived force, and the job of explaining their behavior is more demanding; the problem is not to show merely why they can have indirect force but why they *normally do* even in the face of their contrasting literal meanings and grammatical moods. In this case it seems the purely conservative approach will not do, since (a) as we have observed (note 5), the felt indirect force of a sentence of this type is typically not preserved under substitution of synonyms, and (b) when one hears such a sentence uttered, one gets the indirect point more immediately than one does in the case of a Type-1 sentence; although the derived force seems to be calculable in principle, it is not calculated, but grasped directly. The trick, then, is to account for these features of Type-2 sentences without sacrificing our original intuition that derived force is *derived*— that a sentence has the indirect act-potential it does only in virtue of having the literal meaning it does. For this purpose I think we cannot do better than to follow Morgan (1978) in appealing to a type of linguistic convention that has gone generally unnoticed.

Morgan calls our attention to what he terms "conventions of usage," which are conventions to the effect that on an occasion of such-and-such a type, we are to achieve a certain purpose by certain locutionary means (pp. 269–72). For example:

(C1) Upon parting, one expresses one's regard for the other person, by. . . .

A given linguistic community may "specify" (C1) as to means in any of a number of conventional ways:

. . . expressing concern for the other person's welfare.

. . . expressing a desire or intention to see the other person again, etc.

Still more detailed conventions may specify these means even further; "expressing concern for the other person's welfare" could be further specified theologically, for example:

> . . . by asking God to watch over the other person or expressing the hope that God will accompany the other person.

Morgan points out that different societies do have different "specifying" conventions of this type. What is most important to notice is that such conventions do not transform the expressions they govern into idioms. If a member of our theologically-minded community habitually says "May God be with you" upon parting, this need not be understood as a fused idiom; it still has its literal meaning and hortatory force, even though this meaning and force are subordinated in the context to its conventional force as a parting salutation. (Atheists cannot use it comfortably, in the way that they can use the genuine idioms "for Christ's sake" or "god-damned.")

Morgan points out a diachronic tendency of what were first mere habits to turn into "conventions of usage" of this sort (and then over the years to lose their historical associations and ultimately *become* idioms; "for Christ's sake" is perhaps an example, as is "Break a leg" used in its theatrical sense). Morgan now proposes, plausibly, that sentences of our second type are examples of the first half of this process. The "indirect" uses of phrases like "I must tell you that . . . ," "Could you . . . ," "May I ask you to . . . ," and "Believe me when I say . . . ," began as straightforward implicatures or implicatures-*cum*-speech-act-reasoning, of the sort I have associated with sentences of Type 1, but these phrases have for whatever reason "short-circuited" and become conventional signals of indirect force in a way that even some of their synonyms have not. In calling them "conventional," however, Morgan emphatically does not mean that they are now idioms or that they have lost their literal meanings. If it seems puzzling that an expression should have come to have a normally conventional indirect force without losing its original literal force or becoming semantically ambiguous, there are further examples of phrases that are "conventional" in just the same weak sense:

(28) This is William Lycan. [Said when identifying myself on the telephone.]

(29) If you've seen one, you've seen them all.

(30) You can say that again.

(31) How many times have I told you not to do that?

(32) It takes one to know one.

(33) Where's the fire, buddy? [Said by traffic cop.]

(34) Your place or mine?

(35) Is the Pope Catholic? [Said in answer to an obvious question.]

(36) Am I my brother's keeper?

All these have become "conventional phrases" in the layman's sense, but none has lost its literal meaning either. Let us introduce the term "semiconvention" to designate locutions of this sort.

In some cases, it has become conventional in this sense to perform a certain speech act by offering, not a specific phrase, but any instance of a type of expression. Morgan (pp. 277–78) offers the example of its being

> more or less conventional to challenge the wisdom of a suggested course of action by questioning the mental health of the suggestor, by *any* appropriate linguistic means, as in

> [37] Are you crazy?

> [38] Have you lost your mind?

> [39] Are you out of your gourd?

Though Morgan himself does not remark on it, this very example is a case of indirect force, and can serve as a paradigm of a (presumably) former implicature that has become a general "convention of usage" in Morgan's sense. With this sort of example in mind, we may now see Type-2 sentences as instances of the same phenomenon. Phrases like "I must tell you that . . . ," "Could you . . . ," and the like, originally used (we may suppose) to implicate their conveyed contents, have "short-circuited" and become analogous to (28)–(39); the reason they *normally* have their indirect use is that "conventions of usage" have arisen to that effect.[11] (Notice that (28)–(39) also have the property of admitting literal readings under contrived circumstances.) And Morgan's account promises to explain why it is that indirect force of our second type is not felt by hearers to be calculated by conversational reasoning, but seems to be grasped more or less immediately.

I say only "promises to explain" because, although the foregoing sketch has the ring of truth, it gives no account of any mechanism by which our posited semiconventions or "conventions of usage" are computed; we are told only that conversational reasoning does *not* occur and that somehow a convention is applied. But the psychological nature of this "short-circuited" mechanism is left mysterious. It is like nothing we have had occasion to posit so far. One would expect that if a convention were in play that overrode normal semantactic processing, it would work brutely, at one stroke; the homunculus in charge of proprieties would simply impose his conventional interpretation upon receiving the appropriate triggering formula as input. But if this were so, the triggering formula (here, our Type-2-style preface) would be a genuine idiom, with none but etymological vestiges of its original meaning, and we have agreed that Type-2-style phrases are not idioms in that sense. Semiconventions do not blot out normal word-meaning or normal grammatical structure; as Morgan says, they only govern the conveyance of a nonstandard illocutionary force and a nonliteral locutionary content that is typically but not invariably recoverable from the literal content itself.

So far as I can see at this point, we must leave our homunculus undischarged. That is, until someone thinks of a way in which the function of interpreting semiconventions could be performed by antecedently recognized apparatus, we must suppose that it is a special and autonomous function in the sense of having no familiar *linguistic* mechanisms as subcomponents. (This is not to say that the computation of Type-2 indirect force *per se* is special and autonomous; Type-2 expressions still comprise only one subcategory of the important kind of semiconvention to which Morgan has called our attention.) Presumably our mechanism will involve the storage in some form of rules such as (C1) along with their relevant "specifications," but the storage cannot be such as to require explicit calculation every time the rules are to be mobilized. It is still more than a bit mysterious how a locution can be an apparently "canned" or stock response to a particular type of speech-occasion and still be uttered with its literal meaning (which requires computation of *some* kind) rather than as an idiom. But that appears to be what—somehow—happens.

What about syntax, then? Our assumption that Type-2 expressions are used with their literal meanings and forces even though these are overridden by a "convention of usage" implies that their underlying mood markers and logical forms are literal. So, as in the case of Type 1, there is no problem of mismatch between force and surface mood features. The only genuine problem that remains is that of discovering the details of the process by which a semiconvention can actually override the normal literal pragmatics that interprets surface structure.

On to Type 3. It is sentences of this category that cause us the most trouble, as I have remarked, because such sentences force us to admit that syntax itself is after all affected by diffuse and obscure pragmatic factors, and thereby obligate us to discover how this works. Unlike sentences of Types 1 or 2, sentences of Type 3 cannot be supposed to have completely normal underlying structures.[12] (However, notice that typical sentences of Type 3 can be produced by taking sentences of Type 2 and adding one or more of the telltale surface features discovered by Gordon and Lakoff and discussed by Davison.) (11) is an example; here are a few more:

(40)   Can you please be a little quieter?

(41)   Here, I need that wrench. [Gordon and Lakoff, p. 99]

(42)   Can you reach the Granola jar?—because I'm desperate for some Granola and my arm is broken.

(43)   Unfortunately, let me tell you that our agent has been arrested. [Cf. Davison, p. 161]

(44)   The soufflé is delicious, may I say. [Davison, p. 171]

If anything seems obvious about (40)–(44), it is that the beliefs, desires, and intentions of a speaker that are associated with his performing the relevant indirect speech acts have directly affected syntactic processes in the production of these Type-3 sentences, inserting "please" in (40) and "here" in (41), allowing the reason-adverbial in (42), fronting "unfortunately" in (43), and slifting (44)'s complement. Costa (1979) takes this to suggest the presence of something very like lexical presumption in the sense of chapter 5, since in these cases too we see conative input apparently bypassing logical form and nevertheless contriving to affect the surface distribution of morphemes. But what keeps us from simply writing off Type-3 sentences as being cases of lexical presumption is that the telltale surface properties we have just remarked on do not mix with the sentences' equally overt mood features; the telltale properties tell us to look for an underlying marker or input corresponding to the relevant indirect force, whereas the mood features tell us to look for the underlying mood marker appropriate to them instead. We might irenically hypothesize that underlying structure simply contains both kinds of marker; but we have already supposed in chapter 5 that mood markers are precisely the gates that admit conative input corresponding to the force intended by the utterer, and this thesis is impugned by sentences of Type 3.

A clue to the mystery is provided, I think, by my earlier parenthetical observation that sentences of Type 3 can be viewed as if they were the results of adding telltale surface properties to sentences of Type 2. This generalization holds for (40)–(44), which are related in that way to (40a)–(44a), respectively:

(40a)   Can you be a little quieter?

(41a)   I need that wrench.

(42a)   Can you reach the Granola jar?[13]

(43a)   Let me tell you that our agent has unfortunately been arrested.

(44a)   May I say the soufflé is delicious?

And I can think of no clear counterexamples. Notice too that the "telltale" properties absent from (40a)–(44a) are precisely those that are most at home in sentences having the literal mood and locutionary contents that (40)–(44) have indirectly:

(40b)   Please be a little quieter.

(41b)   Here, give me that wrench.

(42b)   Pass me the Granola jar, because I'm desperate for some Granola and my arm is broken.

(43b)   Unfortunately, our agent has been arrested.

(44b)   The soufflé is delicious, I tell you.[14]

Now, it seems to me possible to apply some of Morgan's insights concerning Type-2 sentences to the present problem; in fact, we can adopt Morgan's speculative-historical approach and extend it from Type-2 to Type-3 sentences just as Morgan used it to connect Type 2 to Type 1. Suppose that after Morgan's "conventions of usage" became established in our speech population and their conventional force intuitively felt by normal English speakers, they came to be *heard as* having their indirect forces except in unusual discourse settings. (Indeed, English speakers do not normally hear Type-2 sentences' literal understandings at all; a hearer who makes a smart-alecky literal reply to an indirect speech act is indulging in a very low form of wit, but at least is being far more observant than the average person.) In this way it came to feel natural to apply to them the surface elements such as "please" and "here" and grammatical maneuvers such as sentence-adverb fronting, precisely because their perceived forces were conferred by (semi-)convention and to that extent officially enshrined in English in a way that the occasional indirect forces of Type-1 sentences were not. (Compare the use, in some semiliterate dialects, of "RSVP" as a fused intransitive verb; as soon as this usage became conventional in those dialects, the startling bilingual redundancy "Please RSVP" automatically became grammatical in them as well.)

Now I shall argue that *if* our sketch of a solution to the problem of Type-2 sentences is correct as far as it goes, then Type-3 sentences can be handled with no new apparatus save the homunculus we have already posited that forms and/or interprets semiconventional utterances. If what might originally have been conversational implicatures "short-circuited" and became available for grasping without calculation, then we may after all regard Type-3 phenomena as analogous to instances of lexical presumption. Certain transformations simply are sensitive to the speaker's illocutionary intentions, just as in the case of lexical presumption or conventional implicature certain transformations are sensitive to the speaker's (or whoever's) beliefs; and, as in the latter case, it is not particularly surprising on reflection that this should be so.[15] So there is no great mystery with regard to how the "telltale" surface properties in Type-3 sentences come to be as they are.

But what about our original objection to assimilating Type-3 indirectness to lexical presumption? It was that this assimilation seemingly deprives Type-3 sentences' underlying (literal) mood markers of *their* supposed function as illocutionary input gates. But on my account of Type-2 indirectness, this function has been largely usurped by Morgan's semiconventions in any case. In some way yet to be discovered, a speaker's production and his hearer's interpretation of an utterance having indirect force of Type 2 bypasses computation on the uttered sentence's literal logical form and mood marker, without thereby depriving the sentence's components of their literal meanings in the way that mobilization of a full-fledged idiom would. And if so, then it is unsurprising that the mood marker is not performing its normal function as a conative input gate. It remains only to answer the question of why, then, the mood marker still does perform its syntactic function of distributing surface morphemes associated with the appropriate literal force. And this answer must lie in the nature of the vestigial computation on the sentence's literal structure that our consideration of Type-2 sentences assures us must somehow go on. Given that this vestigial computation does for some reason go on, it is fairly unsurprising that the literal mood marker exhibits perseveration in distributing morphemes at the surface in its characteristic way.[16]

We may want to ask whether the utterer of a Type-3 sentence is (like the utterer of a Type-2 sentence) performing two or more different speech acts simultaneously. Is an utterer of (41), for example, making a statement as well as a demand? Is the utterer of (44) asking for permission, in addition to making a statement and offering a compliment? The connection I have drawn between Type-3 sentences and Type-2 sentences suggests that distinct speech acts are being performed simultaneously, as is the case for Type 2; the only relevant special feature of Type-3 sentences is that their "telltale" properties apodeictically ensure that their literal forces are understood solely as vehicles for the conveyance of their more important indirect forces. It might be objected that utterers of (41) could not comfortably be reported as having made a statement, nor utterers of (44) as having asked their hearers' permission for anything, but it seems clear that the discomfort can be written off as occasioned by the Rule of Strength.

It is worth recapitulating in outline the strategy I have employed in dealing with sentences of Type 3, since that strategy is neither common nor wholly satisfactory. When we considered cases of Type 2, I argued that if all our intuitions are right, then a certain mysterious thing must be happening even though we cannot say how it happens or even perhaps how it is possible. Tentatively we (well, I) concluded that our speech centers contain black boxes in which that thing happens. Then I argued that if there are such black boxes, phenomena of Type 3 can be explained without the positing of any *further* novel mechanisms save a natural illocutionary counterpart to lexical presumption. It is already evident that if our account of Type-2 sentences is true as far as it goes (even if inadequate as a genuine explanation), there *exists* an explanation; now we see that if there exists an explanation of cases of Type 2, then there also exists an explanation of cases of Type 3. The modest gain made here is just that we can now cease to regard Type-3 sentences as a *particularly* daunting, aggravated, maddening case of the problem of indirect force.

It may be wondered whether the distinctions between our three types are as sharp and clear as I have made them sound. Surely they are not; the border between Type 1 and Type 2 is certainly vague and relative to idiolect, and even the border between Type 2 and Type 3 is subject to disagreement. But on the speculative-historical account of "conventions of usage" that I have gleaned from Morgan, this is just what we should expect. Whether some form of words has become semiconventional is vague and relative to idiolect, and speakers may differ with regard to whether a particular "convention of usage" has become firmly enough entrenched as to warrant the deployment of "telltale" features. Border troubles confirm rather than embarrass the present prototheory.[17]

Chapter 8

Truth and the *Lebenswelt*

The semantical program I have been defending and developing presupposes what is sometimes called the "computational paradigm," or sounds for all the world as though it does. Syntactic rules are conceived as being algorithmic; a complete and finished *grammar* for a language, in Chomsky's original sense at least, is a machine program. Speakers are thought of as computing truth-conditions using a Tarskian truth theory. Even the pragmatic operations limned in the earlier chapters of this Part, involving contextual determination of reference, nondeductive implicature, illocutionary force, and so on, are intended to be rule-governed in a very strong sense of that term. An ultimate (though entirely visionary) aim of the Metatheory as I construe it is the construction of a huge flowchart or functional diagram that would model a normal English speaker's linguistic competence perfectly and serve as a blueprint for building a machine that speaks English (see chapter 11).

The computational paradigm is currently being resisted by any number of philosophers, who want to deny that human beings are computing machines and that distinctively human capacities are computational capacities. In particular, some philosophers and even a few linguists find it bizarre to think of human languages as big, complex, crystalline, and eternal *sets*, rather than as the sweaty, grittily concrete practices of groups of socialized organisms. Much of this opposition comes from neo-Wittgensteinians, who feel about computationalism just as Wittgenstein came to feel about logical atomism, and for most of the same reasons; some comes from the not unrelated phenomenological tradition, as represented by Heidegger and Merleau-Ponty, with its holism regarding persons and action; and some, based on the inextricably context-bound nature of truth and falsity, comes from Austinian skepticism concerning the positivistic regimentation of natural languages.[1] I cannot hope to address each of the relevant camps in turn and allay all their fears and hostility at once. Rather, in this chapter I shall single out what I take to be a few representative objections to truth-theoretic semantics and give what I hope are both representative and satisfactory replies.

1. Truth and Linguistic Acts

Let us begin with the concern expressed in the previous paragraph over the apparent incongruity between the logician's or semanticist's picture and the anthropologist's picture of "a language." Speaking a language is first and foremost our leading form of *social behavior.* Insofar as a "theory of meaning" for a language is supposed to be a key component in socio-psychological explanations of such behavior, then, we would expect such a theory to be a story about flesh-and-blood people and their interactions, their lives and loves. Yet if we ask a truth-theoretic semanticist to exhibit his finished theory of meaning for English, he will point to a single, Platonic abstract object, albeit a fantastically complex one.[2] (The ostension is deferred.)

The worry here is aggravated by such remarks as the following:

> Literal meaning and truth conditions can be assigned to words and sentences apart from particular contexts of use. (Davidson (1978b, p. 33))

> I regard the construction of a theory of truth—or rather, of the more general notion of truth under an arbitrary interpretation—as the basic goal of a serious syntax and semantics. (Montague (1970, p. 188))

> My proposals will . . . not conform to the expectations of those who, in analyzing meaning, turn immediately to the psychology and sociology of language users: to intentions, sense-experience, and mental ideas, or to social rules, conventions, and regularities. I distinguish . . . the description of possible languages or grammars as abstract semantic systems whereby symbols are associated with aspects of the world . . . [from] the description of the psychological and sociological facts whereby a particular one of these abstract semantical systems is the one used by a person or population. (Lewis (1972, p. 170))

Lakoff and Johnson (1980b) take these passages to entail that

> . . . objective meaning is not meaning *to* anyone. Expressions in a natural language can be said to have objective meaning only if that meaning is independent of anything human beings do, either in speaking or in acting. That is, meaning must be disembodied. (p. 199)

Put in this way, the alleged consequence of formalist or computationalist approaches to semantics seems damning. But the rap is bum, for several reasons. First, no semanticist takes sentences to express determinate propositions out of context; that is why Kaplan, Lewis, *et al.* have provided the elaborate treatment of deixis that we have surveyed in chapter 3. What is portrayed as the "objective meaning" of a sentence is not a proposition but a (partial) function from contexts to propositions, the point of which function is precisely to represent the dependence of the proposition expressed on the complex ways in which particular human speakers are embedded in their respective speech situations.[3] Second, it should surprise no one that "a language" such as English is an abstract object rather than a physical bevy of bustling human activity, for that has been the categorical status of natural as well as artificial languages all along. *English* is a thing that Davidson, Lakoff, Johnson, the reader, and I all have in common; it is also what countless speech acts scattered wildly throughout the recent history of this planet have in common, and what any number of speech communities have in common. Thus, *of course* "English" is an abstract entity and not something more sweatily physical. Third, Lewis has provided an elaborate and plausible account of the *connection between* a "language" in the standard abstract sense and the "psychological and sociological facts whereby [that language] is the one used by a person or population." The language's being *used by*, or being *the language of*, the population is explicated in terms of Lewis's elegant theory of tacit convention (1969), and such an explication is just what is needed to make the connection between a big set and a bevy of bustling activity. The perceived incongruity evaporates.[4]

But let us consider a more sustained and less short-sighted criticism, indeed the classic objection made by a philosopher whose eye is on linguistic activity as a whole against a vendor of logical form in the truth-conditional sense: Strawson against Russell on referring. As I have noted in chapter 4, Strawson's claim about the truth-valuelessness of sentences containing nondenoting singular terms was not (in "On Referring," anyway) a plug for many-valued logic; his claim was not that such sentences differed in truth-value from true sentences and from false sentences, but rather that *sentences* are not the bearers of truth-value at all. The "statements made" when people *use* sentences are what are true or false, and what statement is made by the user of a given sentence on a particular occasion depends very much on features of context. Russell seems to think that sentences have meanings entirely on their own and in the abstract, independently of real flesh-and-blood human activity, etc.

There are two issues here: the classic question of the bearers of truth, and the context-dependence of the "statement made." Let us take these in reverse order.

Strawson's best example of the context-dependence in question (and to my mind his only telling criticism of Russell) is that of imperfectly definite descriptions. Consider "The table is covered with books" (1950a, p. 185). If the Theory of Descriptions were true as it stands, the latter sentence would entail that there is exactly one table in the entire universe. But that is silly. The sentence does not have the truth-value False, for that or any other reason; rather, it is used from occasion to occasion to refer to some contextually picked-out table and to predicate being-covered-with-books of that table, truly or falsely.

The objection is sound, but the moral Strawson draws from it is far too drastic; for our semantactic format can handle imperfectly definite descriptions with ease. David Lewis offers a subtle treatment based on his semantics for subjunctive conditionals (1973, sec. 5.3). For those who disdain possible worlds, Alan Brinton (1977) has constructed a nice theory of imperfectly definite descriptions, according to which "the" is actually a demonstrative etymologically akin to "that"; on this view Strawson's sentence would be equivalent to "*That* table is covered with books," and the referent of the demonstrative would be computed by speaker and hearer in the normal way, using the apparatus described in chapter 3. A third alternative, closer to Russell's in spirit,[5] is suggested by the fact (remarked on in note 4 of chapter 3) that virtually no quantification in English is unrestricted. It is entirely plausible to suppose that some of the quantifiers occurring in Russellian analyses of definite descriptions are restricted quantifiers also. Thus, we can form the notion of a "restricted definite description." Such a description is derived from restricted quantifiers in just the way that perfectly definite descriptions—if any[6]—are derived from unrestricted quantifiers. It is a little messy to try to specify the relevant restriction class, of course, but that problem haunts all of conversational English quantification anyway. In Strawson's example, there is one and only one table *in this room,* or perhaps only one *perceptually salient* table, or only one table *expected to be clear.* Which of these delineations is correct could be revealed by behavioral tests. (Note that I am not suggesting that Strawson's sentence is elliptical, or contains hidden predicates of the sort I have just italicized. Rather, its underlying quantifiers are flagged by a standard restriction parameter; α determines what restriction class is denoted by the parameter.)

The moral is that imperfectly definite descriptions cause the truth-theoretic semanticist no embarrassment; they lie easily within the range of existing weaponry. Let us therefore turn to the larger question of truth-bearers.

Philosophers used to bicker over whether it was sentence-tokens, sentence-types, "statements," propositions, utterances, locutionary acts, or illocutionary acts that are the primary subjects of "true" and "false." Strawson maintained that "The present king of France is bald" cannot be used to make a true or false assertion because one who tokens it does not succeed in referring to anything;[7] for him, then, "assertions" are the bearers of truth, and he thought Russell had lost sight of this and fallen into the error of thinking that sentences are. (Cf. "Guns don't kill people; people kill people.")[8] I am unsure whether there is a real issue here about which someone might be correct or mistaken, let alone whether Strawson was correct and Russell mistaken. Let me at the outset disclaim any binding interest in the strictly colloquial use of the words "true" and "false"; I am concerned instead with their role in explanatory philosophical theories, and their everyday conversational uses are probably neither consistent nor fully determinate anyway.

If the interesting dispute is not over nuances of ordinary usage, what is it? Presumably the question is one of *dependency;* among all the different sorts of entity that can without genuinely vicious oddity be called "true," some depend for their truth on that of others. It used to be thought that *propositions* were the basic truth-bearers, in that an utterance, a sentence-token, a sentence-type, or even a belief is true only in virtue of expressing a proposition that is true; enemies of propositions would try to substitute some competing candidate, such as eternal sentences.

According to the Metatheory, a sentence-token or even a sentence-type has its truth-condition only in virtue of being transformationally derived from an SR having that truth-condition, and either a sentence-token or a sentence-type may lack a truth-value. SRs themselves are true or false only relative to assignments. But by definition of "assignment," an SR-on-an-assignment has a determinate truth-value, and it is an SR-type together with an assignment that I would uphold as the primary truth-bearer, again in the sense that the truth-valuedness of such less exotic items as sentence-types and sentence-tokens depends on that of SRs-on-assignments but not vice versa.[9]

What other linguistic entities can be true or false? *Statements* in the illocutionary sense, presumably—either utterance-act-types or (in view of explicit performatives) utterance-act-tokens. Here too, the truth-value of such a thing will depend on that of the sentence uttered.[10] What in chapter 4 I called "secondary meanings" are truth-valued also; a speaker can say something true while by some implicative means conveying something false, or (less commonly) vice versa, this amounting in some quarters to a fine art. Here I think we would have to identify the SR representing the conveyed meaning—the input to the speaker's implicator—as the ground of the truth-value of what the speaker meant to convey.

One further candidate for primary truth-bearer has achieved considerable popularity but seems to me very dubious. It is Strawson's: the "assertion made" by a speaker in using a sentence, where an "assertion" is not a speech act but the "object" or "product" of one. (The term "statement" displays the same process/product ambiguity.) Now, these "assertion-products" are supposed to differ from the objects or products of utterances *qua* utterances, which products are merely sentence-tokens. What, then, are they? Austin (using the term "statement") called them "logical constructions" out of statings, but this does not help, for he did not go on to say what method of logical construction he had in mind. (It was not his intention simply to identify them with traditional propositions; nor did he join Strawson in dubbing them the primary truth-bearers. Perhaps he thought of them as fictions.) Richard Cartwright (1966) has examined many proposed reductions of "what is asserted" to more familiar entities, and found each wanting; he scorns even to identify "what is asserted" with sentence-meaning. He concludes that even though the "statement made" is a leading truth-bearer (this he considers "obvious"), "[t]here is . . . an important sense in which it remains to be said *what* it is that is susceptible of truth and falsity" (p. 103). Unless the "assertion-product" or "statement made" is simply identified with a proposition in the traditional sense, then, it remains a will-o'-the-wisp. My own bet is that the everyday notion of "what is asserted" is simply garbled, just as the notion of "what is believed" has recently been shown to be.[11]

What about propositions? The Metatheory as I have developed it is committed to something proposition-like, viz., to SR-types or in any case (barring nominalist scruples) to equivalence-classes of sentences having the same SR. (Sentences that are never tokened may be regarded as morpheme sequences; all morphemes are tokened.) Propositions in this sense are harmless, provided sets are, and I have already designated SR-types together with assignments as being the primary truth-bearers. Whether this should motivate us to designate these items also as being the "meanings" of sentences, and whether they might also serve as the objects of propositional attitudes, I leave open.[12]

Not only declarative sentences have SRs. If SRs-on-assignments are the primary truth-bearers, then it would seem that interrogative and imperative sentences have truth-values in just the same sense as

declaratives do, since they differ only in their underlying unstructured mood markers and not semantically. I am not at all unhappy
with this. There are obvious reasons why we do not ordinarily think
of questions and commands as being true or false, such as the fact
that truth is a leading felicity-condition on the use of declaratives but
figures not at all in the felicity-conditions for interrogatives and imperatives. Yet some readers may find this ubiquity of truth-value
counterintuitive. Such readers are free simply to stipulate that nondeclaratives lack truth-values, though this stipulation seems pointless to me.

2. Truth and Purpose-Relativity

Austin and his followers have maintained that "true" and "false" are
often inappropriate to apply even to declaratives used assertively.[13]

> Is the constative, then, always true or false? When a constative is
> confronted with the facts, we in fact appraise it in ways involv-
> ing the employment of a vast array of terms which overlap with
> those we use in the appraisal of performatives. In real life, as
> opposed to the simple situations envisaged in logical theory, one
> cannot always answer in a simple manner whether it is true or
> false. (Austin (1962, pp. 141–42))

Austin gives several examples, in lecture XI:

(1)   France is hexagonal.

(1), Austin says, "is a rough description; it is not a true or a false
one" (p. 142).

(2)   Lord Raglan won the battle of Alma.

(2) is merely "exaggerated and suitable to some contexts and not to
others; it would be pointless to insist on its truth or falsity" (p. 143).

(3)   All snow geese migrate to Labrador.

". . . perhaps one maimed one sometimes fails when migrating to
get quite the whole way. . . . [We] cannot quite make the simple
statement that the truth of statements depends on facts as distinct
from knowledge of facts" (p. 143).

(4)   All swans are white.

"If you later find a black swan in Australia, is [(4)] refuted? . . . Not
necessarily. . . . " (p. 143).

I believe that (1)–(4) *are* true or false, for what that is worth. Let us briefly take up each in turn.

(1) leaves us with several options. First, we might plausibly hold that "hexagonal," like most other predicates, is purpose-relative; one and the same thing can be hexagonal for some purposes but not for others. If so, then the relativity in (1) lies inside the predicate, not in the attribution of truth. Second, we might simply insist, with some justice, that France is just *not* hexagonal, and that (1) is false. That would leave us with the task of explaining why Austin's general gets away with describing France as being hexagonal. But recall Austin's own derogatory remarks about the "true"/"false" fetish, which I have already reviewed in section 7 of chapter 4. For many purposes we do not *care* whether what is said (better, the sentence uttered) is true or false. Literal truth-value just is not important to the particular kind of speech act being performed. In the case of the general it just does not matter that France is not in fact hexagonal; the general is not playing the Cartesian coordinates game, but rather the game of Strategic Approximations or some such; his speech act is not a case of describing-precisely, but of estimating, assimilating, or approximating.

Third, we might simply throw (1) back onto our Lakovian theory of vagueness, treating "hexagonal" simply as a vague predicate. (Notice, by the way, that Austin's term "rough" is not as it stands a term of determinate appraisal, for it has neither positive nor negative connotation on its own. "Rough" used as a term of approval has to mean "roughly *true*.") I daresay this option is the best of the three, since Lakoff's theory already gives us the means of saying that "hexagonal" is true of France to a certain degree relative to a teleologically determined standard of strictness. In any case (1) is no threat to truth-theoretic semantics.

(2) is an interesting example. Suppose we agree that Lord Raglan's command of the British army in the Crimea was the main cause of the victory (such as it was) at the Alma. We still may be reluctant to call (2) true, just like that, for it may be unfair to the British troopers to speak as if Raglan's own behavior sufficed for winning the battle quite apart from their contributions. And certainly, as Austin says, it would be pointless to *insist* on its truth or falsity, if by this Austin means that it is pointless to take an insistent stand on the issue.

Alternatively, as is more likely, (2) may be heard as figurative—as metonymy or *pars pro toto*. On this understanding (2) would be literally false, just as is "She hit me with the milk" if what she threw was a sealed milk bottle. This falsity does not matter, since much if not most of colloquial speech is nonliteral. I would say that either (2) is false but acceptable as a figure of speech explicable in Gricean terms, or "won" is paronymously ambiguous between its ordinary sense and "commanded a force that won"; I prefer the former option.

(3) is puzzling. Note that (3) differs from the more casual *prima facie* generalization, "Snow geese migrate to Labrador," which is not falsified by the existence of one snow goose that has manacled itself to a fire hydrant in Princeton. It seems to me that (3) taken at face value *is* falsified by the existence of even one nonmigrating snow goose. (Notice that it would be very unusual for a zoologist to announce (3) to a class.)

There are at least two ways in which (3) might be used and regarded as true despite the uncooperative nonmigrator. It might be elliptical for "All *varieties* of snow goose migrate to Labrador," a universally quantified *prima facie* generalization. Or the "all" in (3) might be a restricted quantifier, the reference-class being understood *via* α, if the context supplies a motive for the restriction. In any case, (3) leaves truth-theoretic semantics unscathed.

Austin's remarks on (4) are puzzling also. It seems quite clear that (4) means what it says, and that (4) certainly is falsified by the existence of a black or other nonwhite swan. If in some contexts (4) is not so falsified, then in those contexts "all" is again a restricted quantifier. "All swans" might mean "all swans in any geographical area with which any pommy bastard concerns himself," just as when we say "All students think they are ethical relativists" we do not mean to include a 45-year-old policeman who is taking an evening course in criminal justice to fulfill the requirements for his Sergeant's exam.

Garner (1975) draws the following moral from Austin's examples:

> Truth [is] correspondence to the facts, but the situation determines how much correspondence is required. . . . Suppose that meaning is analyzed in terms of truth-conditions. Austin would reply to this that 'truth or falsity of a statement depends not merely on the meanings of words but on what act you were performing in what circumstances'. . . . We might render this, paradoxically, as: Truth or falsity of a statement depends not merely on the truth-conditions of that statement but on what act you were performing in what circumstances. (p. 5)

Garner says this in criticism of truth-theoretic semantics, but it is not obviously an objection. Context-dependence that is controlled by conversational purposes is a fact of semantic theory as well as a fact of life; α and fuzzy logic between them are there to accommodate it. Indeed, we know *a priori* that no form of contextual *relativity*, whether relativity of a target-language predicate or relativity of truth itself, can embarrass the Metatheory, for any that exists can be formally reflected on the spot by an appropriate parameter. Moreover, we must remind ourselves that a speaker often does not mean what (literally and structurally speaking) his sentence means. In chapter 4 I have already indicated my relative unconcern (in most contexts) with literal truth-value as opposed to other Austinian dimensions of criticism. Truth and falsity in the strict sense play only a very small role in everyday conversation (and an even smaller one in physics). They loom large only in a fairly recondite area that engages the attention of only a few mildly crazed theorists—formal semantics.

With this in mind, note how odd Strawson's view really is. Strawson holds that truth-value is generated at all only by speech acts of asserting. We must agree that if no such act occurs, then no true or false statement has been made. But why should the latter tautology be taken even to suggest that sentences do not have truth-values of their own while they are unemployed? If I enter a classroom and find "Lord Cardigan misunderstood Airey's order at Balaclava" written on the blackboard, surely I have found a true sentence, quite regardless of the illocutionary force, if any, that its author imparted to it, and if I find "Lord Lucan was a splendid tactician" I have found a hilarious falsehood. There is nothing strange in the idea that one can take a sentence that has certain semantic properties and go on to use that sentence in a way that exploits few or even none of those semantic properties, for some purpose on a particular occasion. If I shout "Chapel Hill is west of Raleigh" over and over down an elevator shaft, just to hear the echo and with no thought of what those words mean, the sentence I shout is true (is a true sentence of English). For what that is worth.

3. Holism

Hilary Putnam once wrote that "language skills are the only skills that cannot be modelled without modelling a whole human being" (1966, p. 235). This advice has been taken to heart by critics of truth-theoretic semantics who deny the existence of an autonomous language faculty and the possibility of building a computing machine that speaks English. Syntactic and semantic processing are held to interpenetrate so thoroughly with background knowledge, with motor skills, and with the perspective determined by the way in which our speaker is embedded within his life-world, that the idea of flow-diagramming someone's "speech center" or of writing a "language-understanding" program is a pipe dream. In this section I shall review and comment on a few of the arguments and examples that have been urged in support of this darkling skepticism.

Lakoff, a comparatively recent convert to the sort of holism I have sketched (Lakoff (1982), Lakoff and Johnson (1980b)), now stresses the context-dependence of truth in the way I have discussed in section 1 of this chapter, and gestures anew toward problems of vagueness and hedging. That there are problems and complexities here no one would deny, but it has been my purpose in the earlier chapters of this Part precisely to show how the Metatheory can attack such difficulties; so Lakoff's recent writings cause us no new worries on that score. However, he has offered further examples. I shall discuss those that I take to have the greatest force.

(i) Cases in which syntax or semantics is affected in mid-utterance by online processing up to that point. The best examples are the correction and editing devices studied (Lakoff reports) by Monica Mac-Caulay and J. DuBois. (5) is syntactic, (6) and (7) semantic:

(5) a. I looked up her dress—I mean, her address.
    b. *I looked up her dress—I mean, up her address.

(6) I bought five—no, six—bottles of cream soda.

(7) I've known thousands of people like that—well, hundreds.

The correction in (5a) is sensitive to previous grammatical structure. ("Looked up" is a separated transitive verb; "up her dress" is not an adverbial modifier of "looked.") "No" and "well" in (6) and (7) are used to cancel either semantical content or conversational assumptions established earlier in the utterance. Lakoff denies that correcting and editing of this sort is a matter of simply "erasing a tape and saying what you really meant." But his positive point is inexplicit, to say the least, and I do not see the force of his appeal to these phenomena against truth-theoretic semantics. We may certainly grant that in such cases the tape is not erased, since the speaker starts to say something false before correcting it and the hearer apprehends the false start as well as the corrected version. But we have been shown no reason to doubt that false-start-followed-by-immediate-correction is not precisely what is going on semantically. Indeed, (5a), (6), and (7) are respectively well paraphrased by

(5a') I looked up her dress. I mean, I looked up her address.

(6') I bought five bottles of cream soda. No, I bought six bottles of cream soda.

(7') I've known thousands of people like that. Well, I've known hundreds of people like that.

(5) and (7) each make two assertions, the second of which contradicts and cancels the first; that is unproblematic. (6) is less straightforward, since the correction occurs before a hearer can apprehend a full assertion; it is not an assertion followed by a cancelling assertion. But it is a sentence *fragment*, an uncompleted assertion, followed by an assertion that makes it clear what the completion would have been and cancels it at the same time. I do not in this book provide an account of fragmentary utterances, but I see no great obstacle to constructing one once we have a psychological picture of how whole sentences are produced, and so I do not doubt that (6) can be assimilated to (5) and (7).

(ii) Lakoff offers a counterexample to the schema "If A, then C and if B, then C / ∴ If A and B, then C" and contends that the failure of this inference is due to a difference in the "scenarios" associated with the substituends for "A" and "B" as between premise and conclusion. When I say, "If we go to Florence tomorrow, we'll have a good time, and if we go to Siena tomorrow, we'll have a good time," my Florence scenario does not include a trip on the same day to Siena, and vice versa, but when I say "If we go to Florence and Siena tomorrow, we'll have a good time," a new scenario is forced that does include the cramping of two trips into the same day, and the shift of scenario is what invalidates the inference.[14]

I am convinced that Lakoff is right about this, but, to put it bluntly, so is everyone else. The invalidity of the foregoing schema is a simple and familiar case of failure of Antecedent Strengthening, respected by almost any of the going theories of conditionals. Most theories capture Lakoff's notion of a "scenario" by implementing the idea that a conditional's antecedent takes us to a different possible world (and noting that context may determine different sets of antecedent worlds from occasion to occasion). My own theory of conditionals (1984b) is even closer to the spirit of Lakoff's notion, in that it appeals to nonactual but envisioned "events" or states of affairs. Indeed, it is a commonplace of possible-worlds semantics that context associates "scenarios" with certain sorts of clauses on particular speech-occasions. However deep our metaphysical and psychological reservations about possible-worlds semantics may run, it cannot be said that Lakoff's notion has been neglected by truth-theoretic semanticists or that it poses a global threat to the Metatheory.

(iii) There are also "regularities involving complementizers that have to do with the internal structures of scenarios" (p. 152). Lakoff points to a difference between infinitival complements and gerunds, as in (8) and (9):

(8) I like to jog, because it keeps me fit, but I hate jogging itself.

(9) a. I enjoy jogging.
    b. *I enjoy to jog.

But the difference between the complements "jogging" and "to jog" is easily explained within our existing framework. "Jogging" is merely an abstract NP, whereas "to jog" is the result of Equi-NP-Deletion or some such transformation that requires not only an underlying subject of "jog" but also a strong reflexive identity of that subject with the higher sentence subject:

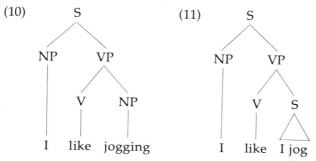

(10)   (11)

"Jogging" is used in (10) as it is in "Jogging gives you shin splints." As Lakoff says, the reason (9b) is bad is that " 'enjoy' must focus on the central part of the activity" (p. 153) rather than the activity's subject. However the details may go, there is no reason to fear that such differences between complements are not ordinary syntactic and semantic differences.

Lakoff concludes that "scenarios provide a way of structuring your experience, and the structure of scenarios is reflected in the structure of language" (p. 154). I think we can accept this, without tears.

(iv) Lakoff and Johnson have argued persuasively (1980a, 1980b) that semanticists' notorious habit of concentrating on literal usage and ignoring metaphor is even more reprehensible than it is conventionally conceded to be. Philosophers have uniformly talked as if literal speech were the standard case and metaphorical utterances were merely occasional aberrations from normal linguistic practice, although it is granted that among the literal expressions there are "dead" metaphors, i.e., phrases that were once novel metaphors but have turned into cliches and changed their literal meanings. Lakoff and Johnson point out (a) that the distinction between novel metaphor and "dead" metaphor is no more than a difference of degree, with terms like "entirely novel" and "stone dead" marking the extreme ends of what is really a smooth continuum, and (b) that almost none of ordinary English is *purely* literal in the sense of having no metaphorical antecedents at all.[15] Thus, the naive notion of "literal" speech presupposed by semanticists is bankrupt.

I am convinced by Lakoff and Johnson's arguments, and if I were a decent and honest person I would not essay to publish a book on natural-language semantics without offering a theory of metaphor to handle this tail that wags its dog. Fortunately I am no more decent and honest than most philosophers of language, and unfortunately I have no better theory of metaphor than do most people who have written on that topic, so, with regret, I pass.[16] However, I do have one suggestion to make about the idea of a continuum of metaphor-icalness. Suppose that in a certain context two utterances are made: U_1 contains what we would ordinarily consider a "dead" metaphor and counts as literally and not just figuratively true, and U_2 contains a novel and self-consciously poetic metaphor and counts as figuratively true at best. If U_1 and U_2 do not really differ in kind but merely lie toward the opposite ends of a continuum, then perhaps what we should say is that U_1's metaphor is literal *enough* for U_1 to be counted as literally true to some degree, whereas U_2's metaphor is too novel for U_2 to be counted as more than figuratively true. If literalness is a matter of degree in this way, we are encouraged to break up literal truth into degrees as well, particularly since we have already admitted degrees of truth in chapter 3. It is not unnatural to say that some utterances are less literally true than others, and that seems to amount to saying that the former are less *true* than the latter. If so, then the question arises of how the scale of degrees generated here is to be mixed together combinatorially with the scale generated by vagueness, the readjustments imposed by hedges, and so on. The problems of such mixing are already severe, as we have seen, but are not made much more so by the addition of one more variable.

(v) Lakoff and Johnson, and Dreyfus (1979) before them, stress the conceptual impact of our body-image and of the ways we are physi-cally embedded in a world of objects that we perceive and conceive in terms of their relation to our needs and purposes. Lakoff and Johnson trace our homeliest and most ubiquitous "literal metaphors" to the orientation of the human body in relation to the physical ob-jects that matter most to the body's owner.

> . . . a universe of discourse . . . is taken to be a set of *entities*. Relative to this set of entities, we can define world states, in which all the properties that the entities have and all the rela-tions among them are specified. It is assumed that this concept

of a world state is sufficiently general to apply to any conceivable situation, including the real world. In such a system, sentences like 'The fog is in front of the mountain' would present no problem, since there would be an entity corresponding to *the fog*, an entity corresponding to *the mountain*, and a relation *in front of*, relating the two entities. But such models do not correspond to the world in itself, free of human understanding, since there are in the world no well-defined entities corresponding to *the mountain* and *the fog* and there is no inherent *front* to the mountain. The entity structure and the front-back orientation are imposed by virtue of human understanding. (1982b, pp. 182–83)

I cannot think that Davidson, Montague, Lewis, or any other semanticist would doubt this for a second. Lakoff and Johnson seem to me to be confusing the technical problem of writing T-sentences for deictic constructions with the metaphysical issue of natural kinds, in each of two ways. (a) That a lexical item has its meaning only in virtue of human concerns and not because it picks out a God-given natural kind as its extension has nothing to do with its ability to be assigned a base clause in a truth theory for its containing language; all that is required is that it *have* an extension that is determined in some way or other. (b) That a lexical item's extension is context-dependent in a way that subtly but strikingly reflects basic human needs and purposes does not bar us from handling its context-dependence in the same sort of way we have handled more humdrum context-dependence. Primitive though they are, the methods of chapter 3 will, when adequately refined, apply just as readily to context-dependence that arises from our orientation in the *Lebenswelt* as they will to the less glamorous cases of deixis that they were originally designed to accommodate.

(vi) Finally, there is the notorious problem of disambiguation in parsing, first called to our attention in modern times by Bar-Hillel (1964). Since until recently linguists have concentrated their thinking far more heavily on models of speech production than on reception and parsing, the disambiguation problem has been for the most part shrugged aside. But if one does turn to face it squarely, one sees that the disambiguation even of a simple and apparently straightforward utterance exploits and depends on a sizeable chunk of background information, empirical knowledge of the world. Bar-Hillel's example was

(12)   The box was in the pen.

Bar-Hillel contended that "no existing or imaginable program will enable an electronic computer to determine that the word *pen* in [(12)] within the given context [means an enclosure rather than a writing utensil], whereas every reader with a sufficient knowledge of English will do this 'automatically'" (pp. 158–59). The English speaker exploits his general knowledge of the relative sizes of ordinary boxes with respect to writing implements and playpens, and this knowledge is not something that a computer chosen at random would be likely to have stored either explicitly or implicitly. Dreyfus (1979) adds (p. 216) that even if a computer did have that general knowledge stored somehow, the knowledge would mislead the machine if the machine heard (12) whispered in a James Bond movie or in some other unusual context involving a very small box and a motive for concealment. More elaborate examples of the dependence of disambiguation on background knowledge include:

(13)   I left my raincoat in the bathtub because it was still wet. [Haugeland (1979, p. 621)]

(14)   Though her blouse draped stylishly, her pants seemed painted on. [Haugeland, *ibid.*]

(15)   Don't stand in my *way!* [Uttered by John in the course of an argument with Mary over his desire to shoot Peter; Ringle (1982, p. 57)]

The reader may initially not hear such sentences as ambiguous and have to strain to come up with alternative readings.[17] This underscores Dreyfus's point: that what human hearers do completely automatically, a machine program would have to be elaborately prepared for in ways that lie far beyond anything like our present technical competence.

I do not wish to underestimate the gravity of this disambiguation problem. Although progress is being made from a syntactic point of view (e.g., by Frazier and Fodor (1978), Frazier (1979), and J. D. Fodor (1982)), the basic difficulty of representing implicit background knowledge is a special case of the vexing and vicious "frame problem" in Artificial Intelligence.[18] But it is, I think, *just* a special case of the frame problem and not an especially aggravated instance of it. Somehow Mother Nature has solved the frame problem for human beings, and in particular has bestowed on us a way of storing the background knowledge needed for disambiguating. Perhaps current digital machine models of this storage are all wrong (actually there seems to be no "perhaps" about it), but there must be some correct theory, for we do succeed in disambiguating—indeed, as

Dreyfus emphasizes, that success is breathtaking—and we do not do this by magic, nor is it done for us by individual specialist neurons that might be described purely neuroanatomically. The complete mysteriousness of Mother Nature's method is no proof of its nonexistence.

The disambiguation problem underscores Lakoff's earlier point about the interpenetration of speech processing with more general features of a speaker's current psychological profile—with beliefs, memories, desires, and intentions. That such interpenetration is prevalent cannot be denied. Nor is it particularly surprising, and it certainly does not entail (as Lakoff hints) that there is no such human organ as the speech center. All it entails is that the speech center constantly and simultaneously accepts input from a number of diverse extraneous sources—which, given the ways in which we have had to ramify our theory earlier in this Part, we knew anyway. I will try to respect this fact when I begin to construct my preliminary flowchart, in chapter 11.

III
Psychology

Chapter 9
Semantics and Indeterminacy

I now turn to a more general issue: that of a semantic theory's status as a theory face to face with the world—as a theory of a wedge of reality, psychological or otherwise.

1. The Problem of Indeterminacy

For the most part, semanticists conceive of themselves as scientists attempting to discover real empirical facts about particular natural languages. Their theories are intended to be rigorously tested against unquestionably empirical data (instances of Convention T; native speakers' intuitions about grammaticality, synonymy, etc.; native speakers' actual unreflective usage; the inferences they intuitively recognize as being valid; and more). The theories are also constrained by something relevantly like Harman's five principles, and those principles appear to be corollaries of the same general rules of empirical method that govern any scientific enterprise in psychology, biology, and even physics.[1] If a semantic theory of a particular natural language or fragment of one is adequate to the phenomena and is rated higher than any other extant theory by our canons of theory-preference, then it would be natural to conclude, however tentatively, that this "best" available theory is *correct*—that the SRs it assigns to English sentences are in fact the deep structures and contain the logical forms of those sentences. A linguist's coming to this conclusion would be no more presumptuous or arrogant than is a chemist's coming to believe that a substance such as water in fact has the chemical structure assigned to it by the best available theory of atomic and molecular structure. And in fact linguists have always taken themselves (or at least talked as if they were taking themselves) to be trying to discover *the truth about*, or at least *facts* about, sentences of English.

Now at least one prominent and distinguished contemporary philosopher holds that this picture of the semanticist as scientist is entirely and perniciously wrong. W. V. Quine has argued at length (a) that the various methods that underpin the Metatheory are *not* empirical methods, and (b) that the linguists' "hypotheses" are not genuine hypotheses and their "results" are not genuine results, there being no linguistic fact of the matter for semanticists to be right or wrong about. Moreover, Quine has made many converts over the last twenty years, and raised serious doubts in the minds of still others. What is remarkable is that both Davidson and Harman themselves have at one time or another seemed to accept the arguments that lead Quine to his metaphysically skeptical position,[2] and neither to my knowledge has explicitly criticized or publicly doubted that position. There is, then, a sharp and dramatic tension between two major trends or outlooks in current philosophy of language concerning the relation of language and the study of language to reality or to "facts in the world."

Quine's arguments for his skeptical view are recondite and controversial. Before trying to address them, we should take on the comparatively much easier task of looking for a way in which his position and the Metatheory can be reconciled, since neither Davidson nor Harman seems to feel the tension very keenly. I have characterized the two views in such a way as to make them as sharply opposed as possible; so we should not expect that each view will survive reconciliation in full detail. The most we should demand is that a mutual reconstruction preserve the least expendable tenets of both.

In two well-known papers on linguistics (1970b, 1972), Quine makes (or reiterates) the following claims:

> (A) Translation is indeterminate: there is no correct (or incorrect) answer to the question of whether a sentence S_1 is an accurate translation of another sentence S_2, except (trivially) relative to some prechosen translation manual.
>
> (B) Syntax is likewise indeterminate. There is no "fact of the matter" involved in a choice between two extensionally equivalent grammars. "If . . . we held every grammar to be as authentic as every extensionally equivalent grammar, and to be preferred only for its simplicity and convenience, then deep structure loses its objectivity but need not lose its place" (1972, p. 395); though syntacticians' assignments of "deep structure" or other grammatical properties are neither true nor false, neither correct nor incorrect, they are still *useful* in the demarcation of the class of well-formed strings (just as what Quine calls "paraphrase" can be useful to philosophers and to linguists even though translation is indeterminate).

Quine gives little argument for (B), a relatively recent claim. Presumably his reasons for holding (B) are analogous to his familiar reasons for holding (A): the linguist is a behaviorist *ex officio,* and no behaviorist can distinguish between the native's being guided by grammar G_1 and his being guided by grammar G_2 if G_1 and G_2 are extensionally equivalent.[3]

> (C) "I find the phrase 'logical analysis' misleading, in its suggestion that we are exposing a logical structure that lay hidden in the sentence all along. This conception I find both obscure and idle. When we move from verbal sentence to logical formulas we are merely retreating to a notation that has certain technical advantages, algorithmic and conceptual . . . No one wants to say that the binominals of Linnaeus or the fourth dimension of Einstein or the binary code of the computer were somehow implicit in ordinary language; and I have seen no more reason to so regard the quantifiers and truth functions" ((1972, p. 395); see also (1960, pp. 260–62)). Thus, a natural sentence has no one *real* "logical form"; to assign a "logical form" to a sentence is just to paraphrase that sentence into some (presumably more formal) idiom for one or more of various possible purposes (disambiguation; deductive inference within a context; the avoidance of paradox; the sidestepping of philosophical puzzles; the facilitation of computation; etc.). But such paraphrases are just that—they make no claim to uniqueness, no claim to objective correctness, and no claim to necessary *equivalence* of any sort.[4]
>
> (D) Even granting (B) and (C), it might still be said that the "most useful" deep structure and the "most useful" canonical paraphrase will probably coincide (perhaps for reasons such as those given by Harman (1972a)). But this is not so. "These different purposes, the grammarian's and the logician's, are not in general best served by the same paraphrases; and for this reason the grammarian's deep structure is not to be identified with logical structure, suggestive though the one may be for the other" (1972, p. 396).

Quine argues for (D) by adducing two examples of logical paraphrases that, he says, would be useless to grammarians even though they are (at present anyway) indispensable for philosophical logicians: his own way of eliminating singular terms, and the use of tenseless predication in connection with the treatment of objects in one's domain as four-dimensional. A second, more general argument is suggested by Quine's view that there *is* no single "most useful" way of paraphrasing English sentences into logical structures (except relative to rather narrow theoretical purposes and in some cases not even that), in conjunction with the parallel view that perhaps there is not even one single "most useful" deep structure (he concludes his (1972) with a "plea against absolutism" in syntax, though he does not spell out any considerations that tend to support such a plea). If there is neither a single most useful logical paraphrase nor a single most useful deep structure, then *a fortiori* (D) is true.

Each of the theses (A)–(D) is at first blush incompatible with the Metatheory. As I have said, what is odd is that the two progenitors of the Metatheory nevertheless have taken at least (A)–(C) very seriously indeed. This suggests that, unbeknownst to me and presumably to Quine, the apparent incompatibility of the Metatheory with (A)–(D) is illusory. I shall now set out the reasons why the incompatibilities *seem* to obtain, and then go on to see whether they might plausibly be resolved.

(A) seems to conflict with the Metatheory in that the latter, if correct, would provide a determinate basis for translation between speakers of the same natural language if not interlinguistically. A sentence S_1 would be a correct (though of course not unique) translation of a second sentence S_2 just in case S_1 and S_2 share (on whatever readings are in question) the same SR.

It might be replied that S_1 and S_2 would be so related only relative to a particular theory of logical form. That is true; but it appears that (according to the Metatheory) one theory of logical form for a language is *correct,* to the exclusion of its competitors. So the relativity of the mutual-translation relation between S_1 and S_2 to a background theory of logical form does not deprive the relation of its objectivity. Therefore, if our Metatheory is right, (A) is false.

(B): A generative grammar, of whatever type, is supposed to be part of a psychological theory (see, e.g., Harman (1973b, chaps. 5 and 6)), whether that theory is spelled out in Chomsky's occult vernacular of "innate ideas," "implicit guidance," and "competence," or in terms of functionally characterized brain apparatus. And surely, even Quine would admit, such theories are either true or false; either the brain contains some physical realization of a set of syntactic transformations (such sets of transformations can be written as Turing machine programs) or it does not.

It is hard to dispute this last claim. But Quine's psychological methodology does not allow him to admit that a generative grammar is really a bona fide piece of psychology, since he appears to believe that the only genuine psychological theory of verbal behavior is a weak behavioristic theory, rather than a neurological, computational, information-theoretic, or other functionalist theory.[5]

In any case, most linguists of my acquaintance believe that they are discovering something about the empirical nature of reality, when they hit upon what they take to be the best hypothesis concerning the transformational history of some English sentence. Accordingly, since the Metatheory seems to encapsulate the linguists' view and methods, it appears to be incompatible with (B).

The case of (C) is similar. The Metatheory speaks of "the" logical form of an English sentence, and urges us to go about *uncovering* logical forms in a respectably and relentlessly empirical manner. And the criteria that we use to test proposed assignments of SRs (such as Harman's five principles, in conjunction with more general considerations of simplicity, elegance, and convenience) look like the same sorts of criteria that we use to test any empirical theory of anything.

(D) is self-evidently incompatible with the view that logical form and deep structure are one and the same, which view or our slightly weaker version of it is crucial to the Metatheory.

Although we shall turn only later in this chapter to the merits of (A)–(D) themselves, a few brief comments on their current plausibility are in order.

(A), a central thesis of Quine's philosophical position as a whole, is very much up in the air, particularly since it is generally not well enough understood to have been decided one way or the other. On the one hand, Quine's arguments in its favor are by no means fully convincing; on the other, certain widely conceded facts, such as our inability to make sense of the analytic-synthetic distinction and the well-known trade-off in radical translation between ascription of the meaning and ascription of belief, strongly suggest its truth.

(B) opposes itself to the view, held by many linguists and tentatively subscribed to here, that a grammar is a functional description of a machine that models an ideal speaker of a natural language. On this view, a grammar is a piece of functionalist psychology, a preliminary hypothesis about the organization of the relevant part of a speaker's nervous system, just as other potential machine programs serve cognitive psychologists as models of other human mental capacities. Therefore, if syntax is indeterminate (if (B) is correct), then either (a) functional descriptions of human mental apparatus are indeterminate as well, or (b) ascriptions of mental capacities and states to humans are indeterminate as well, or (c) functionalist psychology is totally wrongheaded for some other reason. (c) is unlikely. However, (a) has been suggested,[6] and Quine himself holds (b) (see (1960, sec. 54)). Quine's arguments against the determinacy of the mental turn either on his indeterminacy doctrine (A) or on what he calls the inscrutability of reference, which stands or falls with (A). So the question of (B) is open, just the same extent.

(C) can claim a fair amount of antecedent plausibility. Had we been offered no grandiose and technical method of assigning logical forms to natural sentences that enabled us to "tamp down" theories of logical form in a much more practical way than any proposed by Russell, (C) might seem truistic. (C) seems particularly obvious to those who have been taught (not inaccurately) in their elementary logic classes that translation of English sentences into first-order quantification theory is only a convenient device for predicting inferences of an elementary sort. So the apparent conflict between (C) and the Metatheory is vexing.

(D) is an empirical thesis, and will be decided empirically. Quine (1972) was written in advance of the linguists' sudden and intense fascination with logic in general and with philosophical logic in particular. Issues concerning tense, to take Quine's own example, are still very much unresolved; but it seems certain that whatever analysis of tense emerges victorious in any useful study of natural language will be one that is acceptable both to logicians and to linguists.[7] Similar considerations apply in the case of singular terms: the treatment of expressions of the form "$=a$" as unstructured predicates has (to date) been of little use to theorists concerned with *natural* language; Quine himself, when he originally eliminated singular terms, meant to suggest only that the ideal (regimented) language of science would contain no singular terms, not that English (in the mouths of speakers) contained none. If Quine's device should gain interest among investigators of natural language, it will be because it begins to show promise of illuminating English speakers' actual use of names.[8] And to do that, presumably, it must figure in some way in syntax as well as in logical explication.

More generally, it is difficult to imagine that the actual logical form of a sentence (presuming there is one) should have nothing to do with the procedures by which that sentence is produced in speech (cf. chapter 1, note 16). The Metatheorist hypothesizes, plausibly, that the relation is intimate: that logical form is itself the immediate input to syntactic operations. This hypothesis is appealing; one who would refute it faces the task of finding solid logical and syntactic evidence against it. On the other hand, as we have seen, it is still quite problematic and requires further confirmation in the form of impressive results gained by practitioners of the method; and there have been few such results.

It seems, then, that (A)–(D) must be taken seriously. Let us now ask how much (if any) of the Metatheory can be salvaged, on the hypothesis that (A)–(D), at least, are true. In other words, could Davidson admit (A)–(D) explicitly and still carry out more than a pastiche of his semantical program?

2. A First Reinterpretation of the Metatheory

We might cease to regard a theory of logical form for a language as revealing the "hidden" semantic and syntactic structures of the sentences of that language, and say only that the canonical formula (SR) assigned by a theory to a given sentence is the most useful all-purpose paraphrase of that sentence into the canonical idiom in question. It may be desirable to have one preferred canonical language if we can devise one, so that our regimentation or "rational reconstruction" of ordinary language will be as general as possible, and so that we will be able to interconnect locutions of many different kinds and thus to solve or sidestep philosophical problems that arise when two or more problematic natural expressions are mixed. (Quine appears to hold something like this view apropos first-order quantification theory.) On this first reinterpretation of the Metatheory, what a semantics gives us is a set of formally related *paraphrases* of natural sentences, which respectively bear no interesting equivalence-relations to those sentences—they merely match them in general purport, clean them up, perform some of their central (mostly cognitive) functions, etc. The paraphrases are picked out uniquely by our theory of logical form just because it is nice to have a single canonical language in which to write paraphrases, and each proposed "logical form" happens to be better suited to replace its associated English sentence than is any of its fellows.

One of the tasks of a theory of logical form for a language, according to the Metatheorists, is to yield a set of logical truths. An English sentence will be marked as logically true if the SR assigned to it by our theory of logical form is ruled tautologous by the semantics of our formal canonical idiom. It is worth noting that, in light of the linguists' penchant for positing more and more abstract and complicated truth-conditional structures, some baroque and unlikely English sentences will end up being marked as logical (not merely obvious or even "conceptual") truths ("If the stew is cooking slowly, then the rate of change of degree of doneness of the stew with respect to time is slow" is a logical truth according to Lakoff's theory of adverbs in (1973b), and see our possible-worlds treatment of BELIEVE in the Appendix). On our present reinterpretation, what will be the force or purport of a theory's marking a natural sentence as a logical truth?

It would seem that for the reconstructed Metatheorist to label a sentence logically true is for him to claim that we could better accomplish the theoretical goals that seem important to us for the purpose of solving philosophical and scientific problems (etc.) if we were to replace that sentence by a tautology of our canonical idiom (in just the same spirit as that in which we sometimes replace English "or" with "$\vee$" or "If . . . then . . ." with "$\supset$"). This does not imply that the English sentence bears any determinate metaphysical relation to the canonical tautology. Nor does it mean that the English sentence has any special status *vis-à-vis* the remainder of the class of English sentences—viz., any status such as that of being knowable by reason alone, being true *by virtue of* meaning, being unable to be false, or anything of the sort.

In sum, on the reinterpretation we are considering, a theory of logical form is a handy tool for some technical and philosophical purposes, but no more than that. It is certainly not a "theory of *meaning*" in any accepted traditional sense of that expression.

Several objections may be brought against the Metatheory thus reconstrued.

(i) If the relation between a sentence and its SR is as loose as has been suggested, the value of generality is being considerably overestimated. As Quine says, there is no reason to give any one paraphrase or system of paraphrases (not even first-order logic) permanent preeminence of any kind. Canonical idioms should be encouraged to proliferate and flourish, so that we may have more and more linguistic and conceptual resources at our disposal in order to meet all the various needs that paraphrases serve. On the present reinterpretation of the Metatheory, there would be no need for all the constraints, adequacy-conditions, preference principles, or other metatheoretical trappings, designed to enable us to pick the "best" theory of logical form from among a range of alternatives. For it is an earmark of a Quinean paraphrase that it is used purely at one's convenience; paraphrases and paraphrase programs may be assumed and discarded as often as one likes, depending on common and straightforward changes in one's purposes of the moment (cf. Quine on number theory and set theory in (1960, secs. 53–54)).

In fact, Harman's vaunted five principles would be entirely inappropriate. They are introduced with an eye to making the semanticist's job difficult. Since their function is to "tamp down" theories of logical form for the purpose of making evaluative comparisons, they comprise, by design, a very strong (and conservative) set of demands. But such demands are appropriate to the task of choosing among a range of theories all of which are adequate to the phenomena, in order to determine which is most likely to be *true*; it is not appropriate to an enterprise as carefree as that of simply picking a paraphrase that will be useful to us in connection with certain limited, topical goals. As is suggested by Quine's thesis (D), Harman's principles (1)–(5) hamper the *paraphrastic* process intolerably: sometimes syntactic considerations are quite irrelevant to the purposes of the moment; at other times the capturing of felt implications may be negligible. If all we are after is a general program for effecting enlightening paraphrases, principles (1)–(5) are just too strict.

(ii) A theory of logical form, on the Metatheory as presently reconstrued, would give us no real account of felt implications and synonymies. For example, we could not *show* that a (natural) sentence S_1 entails a sentence S_2, in the way that Davidson evidently wants to do. For in order to show something of that sort, we would have to assume that there was some strong (presumably intensional) special relation between S_2 and its "paraphrase." And of course on Quine's usage no such guarantee is forthcoming. We are already stretching Quine's notion of paraphrase even in assuming (as we must do even on our weakened reconstruction of the Metatheory) that a sentence and its SR have the same truth-condition—this is a constraint on paraphrase that Quine explicitly disavows (1960, pp. 159, 160, 176ff.).

On our first reinterpretation, then, to say that S_1 entails S_2 is to say that S_1 and S_2 could be dispensed with, for all practical purposes or at least for those of the moment, by canonical formulas L_1 and L_2, which are neater, more easily systematizable, and more useful for certain theoretical purposes, and which are such that L_2 is a deductive consequence of L_1 according to the semantical rules of the formal language that contains them. (This is roughly what Quine means, with respect to first-order logic as a canonical idiom, when he occasionally says of an English sentence that it "entails" a second.) But so far as I can see, Davidson is not content to make claims merely about what our S_1 and S_2 could be *replaced by* without detriment to our theoretical enterprise, etc.; the point of resting a theory of logical form in large part on a (fragmentary) grammar is to guarantee that theory's saying something interesting and important about actual features of S_1 and S_2 in and of themselves.

(iii) It is hard to see how our reconstructed Metatheory could be taken to portray linguistics as being a branch of psychology. How, on our reinterpretation, could a theory of logical form help to explain verbal behavior or facts about communication, if deep structures are not to be construed as being real theoretical terms? So long as neither a logical "paraphrase" nor a proposed deep structure is regarded as being a genuine hypothesis (cf. Quine's (B) and (C)), an SR *a fortiori* cannot be regarded as having direct explanatory value.

For the same reason, it is hard to see how a theory of logical form on our reinterpretation could be said to explain our having the *intuitions* that we report concerning natural sentences. For unless there is alleged to be a determinate connection between an English sentence and its SR, the formation-rules and the truth definition that underlie the canonical language can in no way be extended to apply to natural sentences in such a way as to account for our intuitions concerning natural-language grammaticality, ambiguity, implication, synonymy, and the rest.

On our proposed reconstruction, then, a Davidsonian theory could accomplish neither of the two main tasks it was designed to perform. This becomes especially clear when we consider what Davidson at least in the 1960s took to be the metaphysical and epistemological implications of theories of logical form. For example, he argued that, since his theory of logical form for English action sentences and causal sentences assigns to those sentences SRs that contain quantification over events, and since we surely want to hold that at least one action sentence or causal sentence is true, we ought to accept the metaphysical view that there are events in addition to physical objects, sets, etc. (His article (1967a) is as much a defense of this ontological thesis as it is a proposal about semantic structure.) What would become of this sort of argument on the reinterpreted Metatheory? If we are no longer authorized to suppose, on the strength of our linguistic evidence, that such-and-such an event-mentioning formula of our canonical language is *the correct* logical form of an action sentence, ontological consequences are blocked. (Quine would welcome this result, because of his belief in the inscrutability of reference (1968), but it defuses a substantial piece of motivation for the Metatheory.)[9]

Our reconstructed Metatheory is one that neither Quine nor the semantical enthusiast could be happy with. Let us see if a second reinterpretation fares any better.

3. A Second Reinterpretation

Suppose we construe the Metatheory as an *eliminative* theory of meaning. A theory of logical form, on this "eliminative" interpretation, is an elaborate theory of *truth* for a natural language. It is admitted that, insofar as truth-conditions may fail to exhaust meaning, a theory of logical form is not a theory of meaning. It is pointed out (following Davidson in (1967b) and (1970)) that a theory of truth for a language serves many, most, or all of the important functions that we commonly ascribe to a theory of meaning for that language. It is then claimed that, although a theory of truth does not perhaps catch all the intuitions that a proper theory of meaning would, it catches all those that are worth catching, the remainder being either "don't-cares" or positively spurious (due to failure to perceive indeterminacy and the like). So we should rest content with theories of truth for natural languages; theories of meaning (over and above theories of truth) are otiose, since (i) they make use of obscure intensional notions, (ii) the indeterminacy of translation (cf. (A)) vitiates talk of meaning at the outset, and (iii) all the proper explanatory functions of theories of meaning are served by theories of truth anyway. On this view, the Metatheory is not, after all, a theory of meaning. It is purely a theory of truth and truth-conditions, and *replaces* theories of meaning, which are useless and possibly vicious; henceforth, we shall esteem *no* theory of meaning as true.[10]

This second reinterpretation of the Metatheory is certainly compatible with Quine's (A), if (as is normal) we take the alleged indeterminacy of translation to be the indeterminacy of synonymy. On this interpretation, all the Metatheory authorizes is determinate theories of truth-conditions, not determinate theories of meaning and of meaning-preserving translation. But is even a Tarskian theory of truth for a language acceptable as determinate to Quine? The following account, gleaned from early writings and lectures of Davidson,[11] suggests that it is:

On the present proposal, to learn a foreigner's language is to learn the truth-conditions of his sentences, which is simply to be able to construct a theory of logical form for his language using a regimented cognate of our own language as a metalanguage. We begin by learning his acceptance-pattern (the set of stimulus-meanings of his words), on the basis of normal inductive inferences (say, by Mill's Methods) from his behavior under controlled questioning. After investigating some simple sentences of his language, along with what we take to be projective devices such as truth-functional connectives, we arrive at a set of instances of Convention T, the left-hand structural description naming sentences of the foreigner's language and the right-hand sides of the biconditionals consisting of correlated sentences of our own. Each such T-sentence is for us a *hypothesis*, a hypothesized universal law, subject to further confirmation or refutation. And, just as before, these T-sentences will serve as crucial data for our theory of logical form—we will demand that our truth definition for the foreigner's language entail them. Consider the foreigner's sentence, "Stefan schläft." We would, after a brief period of ostensive teaching, naturally form the hypothesis that this sentence is true just in case Stefan is asleep. In any situation, we can learn the truth-value of " 'Stefan schläft' is true" by taking the foreigner's assent-behavior toward "Stefan schläft" at its face value and assuming that the foreigner is accepting the sentence because it *is* true. (This involves assuming as well that we can antecedently recognize assent- and dissent-behavior on the foreigner's part.)[12] To verify or falsify "Stefan is asleep," we go through our standard epistemic procedures. Thus, every occasion on which our foreigner assents to "Stefan schläft" and on which we believe that Stefan is asleep confirms our hypothesized T-sentence (" 'Stefan schläft' is true iff Stefan is asleep"). There is room for empirical error here, of course, but that possibility is, at least in the initial stages of radical translation, only the possibility of a perturbation. (On such "perturbations," more in chapter 10.)

Notice that theorizing along these lines begs no questions concerning what the foreigner's sentence *means* or what he means by it—it trades only in more or less straightforward decisions concerning which sentences he *accepts* or *believes-true*. His assent to a token of "Stefan schläft" is good evidence for our belief that he accepts that sentence. Once we have inductively confirmed a good-sized stock of T-sentences, we may proceed to construct a truth definition that entails them and a grammar that accounts for the well-formedness of the foreigner's sentences, thus arriving at a theory of logical form for the portion of his language that is accessible to us. This theory will provide a meaning-free basis for translation between his language and ours: since our statement of truth-conditions for his sentences will be written in the same (meta-)language as our statement of truth-conditions for our own, we can pair his sentences with ours according to sameness of truth-conditions, and regard equivalence of the latter sort as being a necessary and sufficient condition for minimal accuracy of translation.

This new interpretation of the theorist's procedure does not succumb to the second and third objections I raised against our first reconstruction. Since on our second reconstruction, the semanticist still purports to be discovering real information about intrinsic features of English sentences (viz., their truth-conditions), the reconstruction offers a weak sense in which the many sentences that will be marked as "logical truths" are true "in virtue of their form": to say that a sentence is a logical truth would be just to say (following Quine) that its SR is true on any uniform reinterpretation of its nonlogical elements. But the phrase "in virtue of" here does not carry its usually explanatory connotation; the possibility is left open that our "logical truths" are contingent, for in calling them "logical truths" all we have said is that all sentences like them in certain ways are also true. And this last generalization is established, not by pure reason or by attending to stipulative definitions or what have you, but rather by empirical inquiry into conditions under which (in fact) certain sentences of our language *are* true. The "logical truths" may be awarded the status of our most fundamental hypotheses, if you like; but it does not follow that they *could not* turn out to be false in any stronger sense of "could not" than that of incompatibility with a well-established science.

And a theory of logical form, on our second reinterpretation of the Metatheory, does have explanatory force, as it did not on the first reinterpretation. Our intuitions about ambiguity, synonymy, etc., are explained in what promises to be a very elegant way, as being intuitions about truth-conditions. Moreover, the explanations will, it is hoped, connect up nicely with similar explanations of verbal behavior and behavioral regularities; the production of English sentences will be accounted for by the positing of SRs occurring somehow in the brain, along with the encapsulating functionalist psychology.

Does the account of radical translation given above evade Quine's objections to more ambitious semantic programs? We have made no explicit appeal to any notions or methods that are impugned by (A)–(D).

Alas, I believe we must nevertheless conclude that Quine would reject the Metatheory even on its promising second reinterpretation. Consider the stage of radical translation at which we have just finished compiling a stock of simple T-sentences (or, more likely, a stock of pairs of foreign predicates and their hypothesized extensions). On the account sketched above, our tasks are now (a) to construct a Tarski-style truth definition that entails these data, and (b) to construct a grammar that projects the SRs occurring in this truth definition onto actual sentences of the foreigner's language and that characterizes the class of grammatical strings in that language. But on reflection it seems clear that (A)–(D) guarantee the impossibility of (determinately) performing either of these tasks.

In order to construct a Tarski-style truth definition for the foreigner's language, we would have to choose some of that language's predicates as primitives, in order to form the base of the recursion. We would then have to pick out some reiterable constructions (truth-functional connectives, etc.) to figure in the recursive rules. But to do these things is to *regiment* the foreigner's language, to assign it a structure that is not behaviorally discernible. In fact, since the construction of a truth definition is a formal operation, we can regard the translator on this model as simply constructing a formal language that apes the foreigner's language in certain ways, and then giving that formal idiom a semantical foundation. Of course that can be done. But it follows from (A) that the formal idiom thus constructed would bear no determinate relation to the foreigner's language itself. To regiment is simply to replace one language by another, not to make any statement about the language that is replaced.

Nor does the translator's remaining enterprise fare any better. He is portrayed as constructing a grammar that maps SRs onto the foreign sentences. But (B) guarantees the indeterminacy of that performance as well. Once the linguist has finished the job of recording the foreigner's stimulus-meanings, he has reached the limit of the genuine theorizing that is open to him—the rest is only the manufacture of tools for certain projects, not the gathering of further truths.[13]

Now that our second reinterpretation has come to grief as well, there seems to be little hope of reconciling even the essentials of the Metatheory with Quine's view on linguistics. If the Metatheorist takes his semanticist to be discovering *facts,* even facts about so limited a subject-matter as truth-conditions weakly construed, he must flatly reject Quine's view on translation and on grammar, and thus must reject much of Quine's philosophy taken as a whole. If, on the other hand, we take the relaxed, nonempirical view of semantics that would be congenial to Quine, then the Metatheory ought itself to be relaxed, and rewritten in a far less grandiose and misleading way.[14] Since I favor the Metatheory in its original form, then, I am obliged to address Quine's arguments after all, to which duty I now turn. (So much has been written on those arguments in the past twenty years that there cannot be very much left to say, so I shall try to be succinct. Any reader who shrieks with exasperation at the thought of plowing through this issue still another time is serenely invited to skip the rest of this chapter. In chapter 10 I shall take up the related but clearer and more recent issue of the impact of "methodological solipsism" on semantics.)

In the enormous secondary literature on Quine's indeterminacy thesis there is a good deal of confusion over what the thesis comes to, and frequent conflation of its claims with others. In the next two sections of this chapter I shall trace Quine's doctrine, from its origins in the crude context of "radical" translation to its final flowering as a striking general thesis that effects what Harman (1967) has called "the death of meaning."[15]

4. Indeterminacy and Underdetermination

As is well known, Quine begins with the rare case of the translator who is correlating expressions of a hitherto unspoiled tribe's language with those of his own, aided by a willing native or two and by the familiar practice of ostension (which, we assume for the sake of argument, the native antecedently understands). Quine's conclusions about this radical translator, which he takes to be fairly obvious, will be handily generalized to cover all translation of any kind—in which generalized form they are not at all obvious.

In trying to write his Native-English dictionary, the "field linguist" arrives at his conclusions about what the natives' words and sentences "mean" by framing preliminary hypotheses based on the natives' random speech, and then firming these up by asking the native calculated experimental questions on later occasions and tabulating their patterns of assent and dissent. In this way, supplemented by judicious application of Mill's Methods, the linguist gets a clear idea of the stimulus meanings (1960, pp. 32–36) of the natives' expressions. Having filtered out "unidentified interferences" (p. 40) and made various other legitimate idealizations, he pairs Native expressions with English ones and extends his list of pairs or "analytical hypotheses" by more sophisticated querying and extrapolation, eventually constructing a full-fledged manual or "general scheme" for translating Native into English and vice versa. A translation manual thus expresses a mapping of the set of known Native expressions onto English ones.

Certain obvious constraints are placed on the linguist's choice of analytical hypotheses at the outset: "observation sentences" of Native (see (1960, sec. 10)) are to be taken onto English sentences having more or less the same stimulus-meaning; apparent truth-functional particles of Native are to be taken onto those of English (1960, sec. 13); and stimulus-analyticity and stimulus-synonymy are to be preserved. These constraints are presented as being purely practical rules of thumb for the linguist, which get him started in a natural way. They reflect his uncritical tendency to assume that his native informant perceives things in more or less the way that he (the linguist) does, that the native is not a logical idiot, that the native shares pretty much the same general background beliefs, etc. But Quine does not award the constraints the status of sound inductive rules or guides toward the truth; they have little if any epistemological force (though it is not always easy to tell just how much weight Quine is willing to put on them, as will be considered below).

Quine's maddeningly familiar point concerning this procedure is that the linguist's data, all his tabulated facts about the natives' assent-dissent patterns under various complicated and controlled stimuli, do not uniquely determine any one particular translation manual. This is unsurprising, since the stock of data is small, relative to the infinite corpus of expressions that the typical native has at his command, infinitely many of which will never even be uttered. But further, Quine says,

> (I) ". . . manuals for translating one language into another can be set up in divergent ways, all compatible with the totality of speech dispositions, yet incompatible with one another. In countless places they will diverge in giving, as their respective translations of a sentence of the one language, sentences of the other language which stand to each other in no plausible sort of equivalence however loose." (1960, p. 27)

Let us express (I) by saying that the linguist's translation manual is underdetermined not only by his actual data but also by all the verbal *dispositions* anyone could discover by ordinary field methods. (I shall also refer to (I) as "the underdetermination thesis.")

(I) tells us, in effect, that a translation manual is at best only an (inductive) hypothesis, not a direct transcription of observed facts. This notoriously invites us to respond that *of course* our views about the meanings in English of the natives' expressions are underdetermined inductive hypotheses; so are practically all our views about anything. We simply construct a bona fide, well-supported theory of what the native means, extrapolating from the data on the basis of Mill's Methods and more sophisticated empirical considerations of simplicity and elegance. If the theory that results is demonstrably the best one that we have come up with, and if it is as firmly established, inductively speaking, as any other everyday theory that we accept, then we will of course be justified in accepting the theory and claiming to know that the translation manual it provides is the correct one.

But (I), the underdetermination thesis, is far from all that Quine has to say on the matter:

> Most of the semantic correlation is supported only by analytical hypotheses, in their extension beyond the zone where independent evidence for translation is possible. That those unverifiable translations proceed without mishap must not be taken as pragmatic evidence of good lexicography, for mishap is impossible. (1960, p. 71)

May we conclude that translational synonymy at its worst is no worse off than truth in physics? To be thus reassured is to misjudge the parallel. In being able to speak of the truth of a sentence only within a more inclusive theory, one is not much hampered; for one is always working within some comfortably inclusive theory, however tentative. Truth is even overtly relative to language, in that e.g., the form of words 'Brutus killed Caesar' could by coincidence have unrelated uses in two languages; yet this again little hampers one's talk of truth, for one works within some language. In short, the parameters of truth stay conveniently fixed most of the time. Not so the analytical hypotheses that constitute the parameter of translation. . . . (1960, pp. 75–76)

. . . it would be forever impossible to know of one of these translations that it was the right one, and the other wrong. Still, *if* the museum myth were true, there would be a right and wrong of the matter; it is just that we would never know, not having access to the museum. See language naturalistically, on the other hand, and you have to see the notion of likeness of meaning in such a case simply as nonsense. (1968, pp. 29–30)

The point about indeterminacy of translation is that it withstands even all this truth, the whole truth about nature. (1969a, p. 303)

Obviously a number of nonequivalent views may be extracted from the foregoing passages.[16] I shall isolate two of these, each of which may safely be attributed to Quine and is interestingly stronger than (I):

(II) The linguist's translation manual is underdetermined, not just by his actual data and generalizations based on them, but on all *possible* data.[17]

(III) No translation manual is ever *true* or *correct* or right, *simpliciter*. A single translation is "correct" only relative to some antecedently constructed and chosen translation manual.

(The relative "correctness" mentioned in (III) is trivial, amounting just to the fact that the single translation *appears in* the manual in question.) It is important to see what a strong thesis (III) is. (III) sweepingly forestalls our patronizing response to (I). If (III) is true, our well-intentioned theory-constructing enterprise would be idle, because there is literally "no fact of the matter" to be right or wrong about. No sentence of the form "x means y" or "y is the correct translation of x'' is true, or false, *in vacuo*. (I believe this lack of truth-conditions is what prompts Quine to use the term "nonsense" in the third quotation above.) To those who would protest that, even if we cannot be terribly precise about these things, we can still come close with some translation T_1 while seeing that some other translation T_2 is flatly incorrect, Quine says in effect, "You only have those feelings because you recognize implicitly that T_2 would be inconvenient to use in practice. But this inconvenience or practical clumsiness is *all* that is the matter with T_2. It's not *wrong* to translate 'Der Schnee ist weiss' by 'Pigs have wings'—only useless, ungainly, and aesthetically unpleasing."

I believe Quine thinks that (II) and (III) come to much the same thing (he sometimes appears to be using them interchangeably). But they are not equivalent.[18] Here is a counterexample that I think would appeal to Quine: The existence of *classes* is underdetermined by all possible observations in space-time (since classes cannot be observed at all). Yet there is a "fact of the matter" about the existence of classes; it is that they do exist. The same goes for numbers and perhaps even for some of the more recondite objects that are actually in space and time, such as quarks. So something's being underdetermined even by all possible observations in space-time does not guarantee its nonfactuality or indeterminacy in the sense of (III).[19] (II) is thus a weaker thesis than (III), though it is stronger than (I).

But let us get on to the exposition and evaluation of Quine's arguments for indeterminacy. (I shall leave open for now the question of which argument is designed to support which indeterminacy thesis.)

5. Quine's Arguments

The arguments are of two kinds: "from below" and "from above" (1970a, p. 183). The former are plausibility arguments based on particular examples:

(i) "Gavagai." The translation of "gavagai" is indeterminate mostly because of our uncertainty about the native's way of individuating rabbit-stuff. "Gavagai" could, for all we know, mean any philosopher's-eye-view of undifferentiated rabbit-stuff, because we can "compensatorily juggle the translation of numerical identity and associated particles," without sacrifice of "conformity to stimulus meanings of occasion sentences" ((1960, pp. 52–54); the point is familiar).

(ii) The Japanese classifiers (1968, pp. 35–37). The three-word Japanese expression can safely be translated as "five oxen," but one can regard its middle word alternatively as constituting part of or being fused with the numeral, or as a mass-term individuator such as "bucket of," "stick of," "chunk of," or (in this case) "head of." There is "no question of right and wrong" between these two accounts. "The one . . . makes for more efficient translation into idiomatic English; the other makes for more of a feeling for the Japanese idiom." Nothing can be said about which interpretation of the third Japanese word is *correct*.

(iii) "Ne . . . rien." "We can represent 'rien' as 'anything' or as 'nothing,' by compensatorily taking 'ne' as negative or vacuous" (1968, p. 30). Similarly, there are at least three behaviorally indistinguishable ways of interpreting "ne" and "pas" in the French idiom, "ne . . . pas": (a) Let "ne" mean "not" and translate "pas" simply as a null particle; (b) let "pas" mean "not" and construe "ne" as being pleonastic; (c) treat the two words as being the halves of one separable term "nepas." Surely, Quine would say, there is no fact of the matter distinguishing (a), (b), and (c).

(iv) Number theory and set theory. In a way this is Quine's most formidable example. We cannot at first blush imagine what would count as a "fact of the matter" in a dispute between someone who wanted to translate number theory into set theory following von Neumann and one who wanted to do it in the manner of Zermelo.[20] The choice does seem to be merely one of convenience relative to certain purposes (as Quine says *all* translation is) and nothing more, though I shall argue that this intuition can be questioned. The strength of the example lies in the fact that the "purposes" Quine is talking about (the operative notion here, as one can see by looking at his notion of "paraphrase" (1960, chaps. V, VII) can be quite precisely spelled out, as our "purposes" in using and translating natural languages typically cannot be.

Quine generalizes on these cases in a way I shall discuss presently.

The argument "from above" (1970a, pp. 179–80), which depends to some extent on a rough distinction between theoretical and observational sentences,[21] goes approximately as follows:

1. "In order . . . to construe the foreigner's theoretical sentences we have to project analytical hypotheses, whose ultimate justification is substantially just that the implied observation sentences match up."

But

2. "[T]he truth of a physical theory is underdetermined by observables."
3. We could attribute different theories to the foreigner, each of which would imply the same set of observation sentences. (2)

So

> 4. "[O]ur translation of his physical theory can vary though our translations of all possible observation reports on his part be fixed." (3)
> 5. (suppressed) If our ultimate justification for choosing an analytical hypothesis *anent* a theoretical sentence is "substantially just that the implied observation sentences match up," then, given two proffered translations of some theoretical sentence of the foreigner's language that imply the *same* set of observation sentences, any choice of one of the two over the other must be governed only by practical expedience (and is to that extent arbitrary).
> 6. Our choice of what theory to attribute to the foreigner (over and above his observation sentences) must in this way be arbitrary. (1,4,5)
> 7. There is no fact of the matter with regard to what language-independent beliefs or *meanings* stand behind the theoretical sentences he accepts. (6)
> 8. All ordinary sentences in any language are theoretical sentences. (Quinean tenet, acknowledged as being controversial on p. 181)
> 9. There is no fact of the matter with regard to what language-independent meanings stand behind any of the sentences the foreigner accepts. (7,8)
> 10. Radical translation is indeterminate (claim (III) is correct). (9)

Now we are ready to generalize[22] on the case of radical translation. Quine claims, simply, that *all* translation is radical translation.

> . . . radical translation begins at home. Must we equate our neighbor's English words with the same strings of phonemes in our own mouths? Certainly not; for sometimes we do not thus equate them. Sometimes we find it to be in the interests of communication to recognize that our neighbor's use of some word, such as 'cool' or 'square' or 'hopefully,' differs from ours, and so we translate that word of his into a different string of phonemes in our idiolect. Our usual domestic rule of translation is indeed the homophonic one, which simply carries each string of phonemes into itself; but . . . we will construe a neighbor's word heterophonically now and again if we thereby see our way to making his message less absurd. (1968, p. 46)

If we do not always translate our friends' words homophonically, then it is false that we must do so. If it is false that we must do so, then we have a choice. If we have a choice and if we are to translate, then we must make a choice. But to make such a choice is just to frame an analytical hypothesis just like those framed in the Native-English case. And all the same considerations, of course, apply to these analytical hypotheses.

We could, given any sentence that our neighbor utters, always make it natural to translate that sentence heterophonically if we attributed certain wildly deviant constructions and/or beliefs to our neighbor. The main reason we typically do translate his sentences homophonically as a matter of course is that we usually operate on the "principle of charity": our general neighborliness prevents us from insulting our friend if we have no particular reason to think he does hold the relevant odd beliefs; and so we assume him innocent of them unless extralinguistic evidence proves him guilty.

Finally:

> . . . the inscrutability of reference can be brought even closer to home than the neighbor's case; we can apply it to ourselves. If it is to make sense to say even of oneself that one is referring to rabbits and formulas and not to rabbit states and Gödel numbers, then it should make sense to say it of someone else. (1968, p. 47)

If there were a fact of the matter, scrutable to me, as to what my words mean or refer to, then obviously there would be a "fact of the matter" *tout court*, even if no one but me could know it. (Either there is a fact of the matter or there is not; the notion is not relative to persons.) So, if (III) is correct, there is no right answer to the question, asked by me of myself, of what I mean by some expression, or of what my singular terms (objectively speaking, not relative to a translation manual) refer to.[23]

I accept these last two arguments, and thus that their sweepingly skeptical conclusions do follow from (III), perhaps with the aid of some uncontroversial assumptions. So it seems that, if Quine has adequately demonstrated (III), he has effected "the death of meaning," the expulsion of any traditional notion of meaning from serious philosophy or linguistics. And this would be quite an achievement.

6. Assessment

We are now ready to assess the arguments presented in section 5. I shall first look at the arguments "from below," adverting to a much more recent and compelling related point raised by Hartry Field and Stephen Leeds, then look at the argument "from above," and then move on to some general considerations that seem to count against all of the arguments equally.

I think it is relatively uncontroversial that Quine's four examples support (I), the underdetermination thesis, and that (I) is true. In the interest of brevity I shall pass over (II), since (II)'s consequences are less drastic for our project than are those of the indeterminacy thesis, (III). Do the four examples support (III)?

"Gavagai" is mildly troublesome. Sometimes Quine seems to say that since the stimulus-meanings of "gavagai" and "rabbit" are so close, and since the stimulus-meaning of "rabbit" is pretty much the same for all speakers of English, the "gavagai"/"rabbit" situation is "the normal inductive one" (1960, p. 68) and the translation "a genuine hypothesis from sample observations, though possibly wrong" (p. 73). Yet he also gives an argument (p. 72) that shows, if any of the arguments for (III) show anything successfully, that the translation of "gavagai" is as indeterminate as anything else, and he says (1968, p. 34) of the "gavagai" translator's maxim that it is no universal inductive rule of translation but "his own imposition, toward settling what is objectively indeterminate." What is going on?

Two distinctions should be observed. One is between terms ("gavagai") and one-word occasion sentences ("Gavagai").[24] One-word occasion sentences need no parsing and hence no analytical hypotheses directed upon component terms, and we have just the "normal inductive" problem of determining their stimulus-meanings; terms' stimulus-meanings are presumed to be settled in the course of parsing.[25] But this difference alone does not alleviate our difficulty, since for each possible English correlate of the term "gavagai" there is a corresponding possible translation of "Gavagai"—"Lo, a rabbit-stage," "Lo, a part of the Great Rabbit," etc.—and these translations compete in the way Quine considers indeterminate. (Boorse (1975) also calls attention to this.) The answer lies with our second distinction: between stimulus-meaning and meaning. What Quine says is genuinely factual is sameness of the former only. If "translation" either of occasion sentences or of observation terms requires only preservation of stimulus-meaning, then it is determinate (provided counterfactuals are determinate). But to preserve stimulus-meaning is not *eo ipso* to preserve meaning, as Quine's examples are designed precisely to show.[26] Insofar as the standard of translation is preservation of meaning *simpliciter*, translation either of "gavagai" or of "Gavagai" is indeterminate just as is any other translation.[27]

The "gavagai" example does not seem convincing when it stands alone. We would normally regard all the considerations that Quine cites in favor of the linguist's translating "gavagai" as "rabbit" as being exactly the sorts of considerations that would indeed show that "gavagai" *means* "rabbit" rather than "rabbit-stage" or what have you. We need a farther-reaching theoretical argument to impugn determinacy in the "gavagai" case. Such an argument has been provided by Hartry Field (1975) (cf. Leeds (1978), Wallace (1979), and Davidson (1977)).[28] Field points out that besides the valuation function that assigns the intuitively correct extensions to our singular terms and predicates, there are countless other functions from expressions to items in the world that would preserve the same distribution of truth-values over sentences; the intuitively correct extensions can be systematically permuted. For example, let V be a function that maps each physical object onto the space-time chunk that lies exactly one mile in such-and-such a direction from the object itself, and let a predicate be "V-satisfied" by an object x just in case it is satisfied by $V(x)$. Then in our truth theory for English we can replace the denotata of all the singular terms by their images under V and compensate by mobilizing V-satisfaction instead of "real" satisfaction. Nothing else in the truth theory will be affected. Now, why are what we think of as "genuine" reference and satisfaction to be thus distinguished from among all the other "schemes of reference" we could devise in this arbitrary way? Not for any reason depending solely on the Metatheory. A truth theory for Native will not care whether "gavagai" genuinely refers to rabbits or to rabbit-shaped space-time chunks over in the next county, so long as a compensating pseudosatisfaction relation makes the truth-values of sentences come out right.

This last observation itself tips us off that the Metatheory is in no immediate trouble. Logical form is invariant under all the different reference schemes; from the viewpoint of the truth theory, they are notational variants of each other. And it is still a determinate fact (so far as has been shown) that the truth-condition of a Native sentence containing "gavagai" is something involving rabbits, even if it is also a fact that the "V-truth"-condition of the same sentence is something about oddly distributed rabbit-shaped space-time chunks. (I shall say more in chapter 10 on the question of why reference and truth are more important and interesting to us than are imposters such as V-reference and V-truth.)

Yet, as Field argues (pp. 399–400), we cannot answer Quine just by making these points and adding that we have a splendid causal theory of "genuine" reference. For although the causal theory (say, as in Devitt (1981)) or some teleologically tricked-out variant of it may rule out most of the phony reference-schemes, it does not obviously rule out Quine's own alternative schemes, which assign to "gavagai" this-or-that *individuative resection* of a rabbit. Where there is a rabbit, there are also collections of undetached rabbit parts, rabbity time-slices, and the like, and all of these could equally be said to be involved in the etiologies of utterances of "gavagai." So long as causal theories of reference do not discriminate among all the individuative resections, they will not help in restoring determinacy.

My initial inclination is to suppose that a correct theory of causality itself will tell us what ontological categories figure directly in causal relations (my own preference is for *events* rather than individuals or states or properties); if a theory of causality thus distinguishes an ontological category, then a causal theory of reference will after all distinguish a particular mode of rabbit individuation. But, as Field points out (pp. 383–84), this strategy merely shifts Quine's skeptical question to that of why the authors of the relevant theory of reference chose to invoke causality proper rather than "slice-causality" or "state-causality" or some other easily definable variant. It is somewhat tempting to respond that causality proper simply is and ought to be our criterion of what is real and fundamental (cf. Armstrong (1980, 1983)), but this puts too much weight on the hope that there is a factual answer to the question of which ontological categories do figure directly in causal relations, which hope may well be vain.

Fortunately, any remaining indeterminacy is unoppressive. Brian Loar has argued convincingly (1981, pp. 234–37) that precisely because causality (putatively) does not discriminate between individuative resections of things, the "arbitrariness" of our causal ascriptions between resections holds throughout our theory of nature and is hardly specific to semantics. To use Loar's own example, where there is a heart pumping blood, there are also collections of undetached heart parts, cardiac time-slices, Hearthood instances, and so on. Insofar as it is "indeterminate" or relative to a scheme of interpretation which of these things is really doing the pumping, the indeterminacy is of little interest in general and of no interest in particular to the semanticist. So far, then, the Metatheory remains unthreatened. Let us move on to Quine's further examples.

"Ne rien" and "ne pas" serve merely to pave the way for the Japanese classifiers. One's natural response to "ne rien" is to say that the expression should be treated as a whole, that its two parts are too small to be units of empirical significance in themselves. One is then trapped by Quine into saying the same thing of the third Japanese word and of the classifier itself. But, Quine says,

> . . . you cannot take this line unless you are prepared to call a word too short for significant translation even when it is long

enough to be a term and carry denotation. For the third Japanese word is, on either approach, a term; on one approach a term of divided reference, and on the other a mass term. If you are indeed prepared thus to call a word too short for significant translation even when it is a denoting term, then in a back-handed way you are granting what I wanted to prove: the inscrutability of reference. (1968, p. 37)

This is a modest piece of therapy. We are supposed to get the idea that the "units of empirical significance" are *longer* chunks of language than we thought—they are plainly longer than single words; now it appears that they are even longer than *terms*. Now we are invited to entertain the possibility that they may be longer yet— longer even than sentences and paragraphs.

Most people would agree that there is no fact of the matter in the "ne rien" and Japanese classifier cases. But have we been given any conclusive reason to accept Quine's invitation to extend this intuition to predicates, whole sentences, and more? It is well that we should entertain the possibility that Quine offers, for he may be right, and his being right would have the grave philosophical consequences mentioned in section 5. But we naturally resist extending our "too short for a significant translation" intuition very far, even if this is only because we resist the view that such extension will quickly land us in; and still, so far, Quine has provided no real argument with which to weaken this resistance.

What about number theory and set theory? The example does seem a clear case of the indeterminacy of translation of an entire language (though this can be disputed). The problem here is that, for that very reason, most people do not preanalytically regard the case as being analogous to that of "real" translation (between natural languages) anyway. Besides, the "languages" in question are formal systems; and no philosopher of mathematics ever claimed that "meaning was preserved" by such a "translation." Translation between natural languages is supposed to preserve meaning; theoretical identification in mathematics is not. It is of course this distinction that Quine wants to erode in sections 53–55 of (1960), but I think the views he expresses there rest on the indeterminacy doctrine and thus cannot be used as support for the analogy here. So I do not believe that the number-theory/set-theory case, by itself, is convincing in support of (III) either, though for a different reason.

If Quine has given us any good reason to accept (III), then, it must be codified in the argument "from above."[29] I shall, then, present a criticism of that argument as I have reconstructed it.

It would seem at the outset that premise 1 is not strictly true. Presumably the matching up of implied observation sentences is not the only desideratum; considerations of simplicity and elegance (or, not to prejudge an issue that will come up later, convenience and manageability and aesthetic appeal) surely play just as large a role. This is taken account of by the qualification at the end of premise 5, ". . . governed only by expedience."

Therefore, we have to interpret the intermediate conclusion 6 in a very special way. A choice between theories attributed to the foreigner is "arbitrary," apparently, just when the observation sentences implied by each of the two are the same and no desiderata save the quasi-aesthetic ones mentioned are available. But now, when "arbitrary" is given this (I think attenuated) sense, does 7 follow from 6?

To hold that 6 (on our special sense of "arbitrary") entails 7 is simply to hold that considerations of elegance, simplicity, practical convenience, theoretical power, etc., are not desiderata in the translator's enterprise, at least not desiderata in the sense of *guides toward the truth*. Some philosophers would not find this surprising, since there are still some who believe that considerations of elegance have nothing to do with the truth in philosophy. But (i) Quine, of all people, is not one of these—he has done more than any other recent philosopher to show that these considerations have more to do with philosophy than any others do. And worse, (ii) the business of translation, insofar as it can preanalytically be said to aim toward the truth at all, does so in an empirical manner; linguistics is an empirical business. Even those who believe that elegance, etc., have nothing to do with philosophy believe so, presumably, only because they believe that philosophy is not an empirical discipline; most would not deny that considerations of elegance are guides toward the truth in science. (For explicit defense of the latter thesis, see Lycan (in press).)

The question is, then, if elegance counts toward the truth in science, as most scientific realists will admit, why does it not count toward the truth in translation, which seems to be every bit the empirical discipline that psychology and biology are? (If linguistics, including semantics, *is* just a branch of psychology, and if what linguists are investigating is ultimately the functional architecture of the brain and the mechanics of communication, then presumably there is a fact of the matter about that.) This question is fundamental because it motivates most of our intuitive dissatisfaction with the substance of (III): that translation is "worse off than physics." *Why* is translation worse off than physics, when we seem to have just the same sort of evidence for a translation manual that we have for a physical theory (even though semantics and psychology generally investigate a higher level of nature)?[30]

Several possible answers suggest themselves, but each would take us deeper into the labyrinth of Quine's philosophy as a whole, so I shall spare the reader at this point.[31] However, before concluding I would like to explore one alternative account of Quine's program, for we shall return to it in chapter 10.

7. Translation and the Inverted Spectrum

I have taken Quine to be inferring his conclusion (III) from the underdetermination thesis (I) and the premise that the native's speech dispositions are all we have to go on in constructing our translation manual for his language (which is certainly true). Accordingly, I have doubted the validity of the inference. But suppose that we attribute a stronger thesis about speech dispositions to Quine: that speech dispositions do not merely provide our only point of evidential *access* to the native's language, but rather *exhaust* the native's language itself. If a person's language is nothing but the totality of his speech dispositions, then (III) becomes much more plausible, indeed obvious. For "translation" would then be nothing but the correlation of the native's individual dispositions to assent or dissent with the linguist's individual dispositions; and, as (I) asserts, of course there are many different ways of doing this, each of which may be codified in a translation manual and none of which has any better claim to "correctness" than any other. If these dispositions are all there is to a person's language, then (trivially) there are no further facts about a person's language that are pointed to by a convenient translation manual.[32]

Of course, the behavioristic premise that we are considering is much stronger than our original epistemological one. We must therefore ask whether it is plausible. In light of our discussion in section 6, I think we must conclude that it is question-begging at best: a linguist proceeding along the lines I have outlined would reject it as a matter of course, for he believes that different neural structures (or different functional states of the same neural system), corresponding to systematically different parsings of the same sort of sentence, may be behaviorally indistinguishable (presuming he accepts the underdetermination thesis). Consequently, he would be the last to admit that a person's language is exhausted by the totality of that person's speech *dispositions*, if "dispositions" are understood (following Ryle) purely in counterfactual terms. And insofar as one has a feel for the empiricalness of the linguist's enterprise, one must share this un-willingness to accept the strong premise without new evidence. It amounts, after all, to Turing-Test-ism applied to linguistics, and Turing-Test-ism is no more plausible here than it is for psychology in general (Block (1981)).

To reinforce this assimilation of Quine to Turing, note his comparison (1968, p. 49) of his opponent to a defender of the "inverted spectrum" hypothesis. Presumably Quine holds that "inner visual experience" is exhausted by the totality of one's color-relevant behavioral dispositions, and that the supposition of behaviorally undetectable variation in color sensations between individuals makes no sense either. But the inverted spectrum hypothesis *does* make sense, or so I have argued in (1973b), and more refined materialist theories of the mind than Behaviorism can accommodate that fact (see Lycan (1981a)). I see no reason why meaning is any worse off, provided that the encapsulating psychology is satisfactorily materialist also. Behaviorists used to brand opposition to Behaviorism as *per se* tantamount to Cartesian dualism and belief in spookstuff; there is more than a hint of this in Quine's labelling of his own opponents as purveyors of the "museum myth." Why should our minds not contain museums, so long as the museums are made of good palpable neural hardware?[33]

Yet a legitimate worry is left over. Talk of *neural hardware* in this connection suggests that meaning and semantic competence are located (entirely) within speakers' heads, and that suggestion has been forcefully challenged in recent years. I believe that "methodological solipsism" and the skepticism it tends to engender regarding truth-conditional semantics are the contemporary legacy of Quine's argument and capture at least an important core of Quine's (and Michael Dummett's) intuitions. It is now time for more careful discussion of the "psychological reality" of semantics and, in particular, about the sense in which a truth-theoretic semantics for someone's language is part of a psychological theory of that person, and the sense in which it is not.

Chapter 10
Psychological Reality

In chapter 1 I attempted to draw a contrast between the psychological role of a grammar and the psychological role of a semantics. Although we have no good reason to think that an ordinary speaker even tacitly knows *that* such-and-such grammatical rules hold, a grammar being merely part of a functional analysis of part of the speaker's speech center, there is at least some reason to think that speakers tacitly know that "Snow is white" is true iff snow is white, or can be brought to know this explicitly with a minimum of effort, and that this bit of knowledge plays a causal role in their behavioral economies. But Hilary Putnam and Jerry Fodor have raised an issue that casts some doubt.

1. Semantics and Methodological Solipsism

The issue turns on the key distinction between what is "in the head" and what is not.[1] For example, the "content" or propositional object of a propositional attitude is not in the head, surprising as that may seem. Two subjects can be molecule-for-molecule alike inside their heads and still have intuitively different beliefs. My belief that water is wet is about H_2O, while my Twin Earth doppelgänger's belief "that water is wet" is about XYZ, and their truth-conditions differ accordingly; likewise, my belief that I am lucky clearly differs in truth-condition from Twin Bill's belief that he is lucky. Such examples are now commonplace, and what they show is that the "contents" of beliefs in the propositional or truth-conditional sense do not *per se* figure in the explanation of behavior, so long as "behavior" is understood as brute physical motion of bodily parts, since people who are molecule-for-molecule alike will behave alike regardless of their belief contents, and people who believe the same proposition (people whose beliefs have the same truth-condition) may behave entirely differently depending on how that proposition is represented inside their heads.

Now, I have been going on for chapter after chapter about semantics' being part of an *explanation of verbal behavior,* part of psychology. But this sort of claim is just what Putnam and Fodor have taught us to beware. If not even the propositional content of a belief figures in the explanation of behavior, why should we think that knowledge of truth-conditions does? For that matter, why should we think that *English sentences' having the truth-conditions that they do* is a key element of any behavioral explanation? If the reference of a physical or mental symbol is not in its user's head, then neither is the truth-condition of any sentence or other representation containing that symbol, and what is not in the head cannot affect behavior.

This worry seems to be part of what bothers Putnam and Michael Dummett[2] regarding truth-theoretic semantics, and it figures as an important subissue in the current debate between "realists" and "antirealists" as Putnam and Dummett use those unhappy terms. It is also (I believe) what has motivated some recent work in "conceptual-role" semantics, a purported competitor of the Metatheory. I shall return later in this chapter to "antirealist" criticisms of truth-theoretic semantics, but let us now consider whether "methodological solipsism"—reliance in explaining behavior only on what is "in the head"—embarrasses our program.

It must be conceded at once that if we take a relentlessly narrow view of our explanandum, knowledge of truth-conditions will not figure *per se* in our explanans—for just the usual Fodorean reasons (this point is also made by Scott Soames (1984); cf. McGinn (1982)). Neither a sentence's having a particular truth-condition nor a speaker's knowing that the sentence has that truth-condition, nor typically even just the speaker's *believing* that the sentence has that truth-condition, is (entirely) in the speaker's head, and what is not in the head does not *in propria persona* produce behavior conceived as physical motion of the body. My belief that "Snow is white" is true iff *snow* is white is indistinguishable in causal role from Twin Bill's belief that "Snow is white" is true iff Twin snow (i.e., frosty crystalline XYZ) is white; the difference in propositional content between our beliefs about truth-conditions is irrelevant to our matching behavior, and so plays no direct role in explaining it.[3] If semantics helps to "explain behavior," then, "behavior" must be understood more broadly than in the sense of particular physical motions of individual bodies.

I believe the answer lies in the fact that what a linguist studies is the structure of a *public* language, the language of some speech community. Suppose our target language is English (let us prescind for now from our scruples in section 4 of chapter 3 about the individuation of "languages"). Then we would expect our explananda to be, not individuals' verbal act-tokens, but rather sociologically interesting regularities obtaining among these, as well as other facts about the community of English speakers. Linguistics is the study of what the members of a speech community have in common.

To see the explanatory needs for truth theory in this regard, consider its solipsistically motivated rival, "conceptual-role" semantics (CRS).[4] According to CRS, the meaning of a sentence is a matter, not of its truth-condition, but of its conventional association with the belief or other propositional attitude that it would normally be used to express. Sentence-meaning thus derives from attitude content. Attitude content is determined in turn by conceptual role, i.e., by the attitude's

> . . . role in a system of states that are modified by sensory input, inference, and reasoning, and that have an influence on action. To specify a thought is to specify its role in such a conceptual system. To specify the meaning of a sentence of the relevant sort is to specify a thought, so to specify its meaning is to specify a role in a conceptual scheme. (Harman (1974, p. 11))

Harman gives a fairly persuasive *ad hominem* argument for his view (1975a, p. 286): the Metatheory would have it that speakers understand English in virtue of knowing the truth-conditions of English sentences. Donald understands "Snow is white" in virtue of knowing *via* his finite truth theory that that sentence is true iff snow is white. In order to accomplish the latter epistemic achievement, Donald must have (somehow) represented to himself *that* "Snow is white" is true iff snow is white. But this requires an internal system of representation, say a "language of thought," capable of expressing the proposition that snow is white; and so the problem of meaning has only been put off. To suggest that a truth-theoretic semantics now be provided for the Mentalese language launches an obviously vicious regress, cognate with what Dennett (1978a) calls "Hume's Problem" of self-understanding representations.

The solution is to think of the "language of thought" as hardwired, as a language that we are simply *built* to use correctly. (Think of an output cell that is built to fire just in case each of two input cells fire; this is a hard-wired "and"-gate.) I do not "understand" my own language of thought in the same sense as that in which I understand a natural language. To understand a natural language is (Harman says) to be able to translate it into one's language of thought, whereas to "understand" one's language of thought—so far as this locution makes sense at all—is simply to use it correctly, where correctness is determined not by a convention or practice of any sort but by one's own functional design. Neither sort of understanding needs be explicated in terms of a truth theory, though (Harman adds) a truth theory figures peripherally as exhibiting the respective conceptual roles of the logical connectives.

We must agree that subjects do not "understand" their own languages of thought in virtue of representing to themselves truth theories directed upon those languages of thought. But it does not follow that a truth definition has no role to play. Recall my objection (chapter 2, note 8) to Edwin Martin's attempt to trivialize the Davidsonian program. If a machine or a human hearer understands by translating, how does the translating proceed? Presumably a recursion is required, for all the familiar Chomskyan and Davidsonian reasons. And what property is the translation required to preserve? *Truth together with its syntactic determination* is the obvious candidate. Thus, even if one understands in virtue of translating, one translates in virtue of constructing a recursive truth theory for the target language.[5]

Perhaps it is question-begging to insist that the translation preserve truth. The CRS theorist (appropriately) may want to demand only that the translation preserve conceptual role. This suggestion requires that we make sense of the idea of a *public sentence's* having a "conceptual role." But as Wilfrid Sellars has emphasized, the network of inferential relations holding between sentences of a public language comes close to mirroring the inner network of functional relations holding between thoughts, and vice versa (cf. Harman (1973b), Loar (1981)); we might simply extend our use of the term "conceptual role" to cover what corresponding nodes of the two networks have in common.

The idea that the translation involved in natural-language understanding need not preserve truth is an odd one. To see this, note again the lesson of methodological solipsism, that functional roles and truth-conditions are not correlated one-to-one. "I am lucky" plays the same functional role in Twin Bill as it plays in me, but one may be true and the other false; similarly for "Water is H_2O." Conversely, my utterance of "Twin Bill is lucky" and Twin Bill's utterance of "I am lucky" have the same truth-condition and necessarily the same truth-value but entirely different respective conceptual roles. Thus, the requirement that the translation involved in understanding preserve just conceptual role seems both too weak and too strong. If my wife tokens "Water is H_2O" and I translate this into the Mentalese sentence "Water is H_2O," I have preserved conceptual role but I have done nothing to distinguish the meaning of my wife's utterance from that of the corresponding one made by Twin Mary—yet the two still differ in truth-value. If Mary tokens "I am lucky" and I translate this into the sentence that plays the same functional role in *my* inner system of representation, I will take her to have said that I am lucky rather than that she is. Sameness of conceptual role alone does not adequately anchor communication.

Let us reconsider the idea that the meaning of a sentence is a matter of its conventional association with the belief or other attitude that it would normally be used to express, in light of the fact that propositional attitudes themselves can be individuated either "narrowly," according to their causal roles, or "widely," according to their truth-conditions. Whether a particular sentence is normally used to express the thought *that P* depends on which scheme of individuation we have in mind.[6] It is entirely natural to think that sentences simply express attitude content, so long as attitude content is itself widely individuated. But the CRS theorist's aims are solipsistic; the "thoughts" he traffics in are behavior-explanatory items, and so much be individuated narrowly. The thesis that sentences simply express attitude content *narrowly individuated,* once we have made Fodor's distinction, is as peculiar as the idea that the translation involved in natural-language translation need not preserve truth, and for just the same reasons as those I have set out in the previous paragraph.

I conclude that Harman's argument fails.[7] But the onus is still on me to show in more detail why the notion of truth is needed in linguistics. As the foregoing remarks imply, I believe that the leading explanatory advantages of truth-theoretic semantics for public languages stem from the fact that whereas an internal language is employed in thinking, a public language is a vehicle of communication.

(i) As has been observed by Hartry Field and many others,[8] we seem to mobilize T-sentences in forming beliefs on the basis of authority; we often gain knowledge of the world by taking another person's word for something and, having taken it, disquoting it. Ernest LePore and Barry Loewer offer this example:

> Arabella, Barbarella, and Esa are in a room with Arabella looking out the window. Arabella and Barbarella understand German but Esa does not. Arabella turns from the window to Barbarella and Esa and utters the words 'Es schneit.' On the basis of this utterance Barbarella comes to believe that it's snowing . . . while Esa comes to believe only that Arabella said something which is probably true. (Loewer (1982, p. 306); cf. LePore and Loewer (1981, 1983a); LePore (1982, 1983))

What would Esa need to have known in order to have gleaned the same information Barbarella did? The obvious candidate is the

T-sentence " 'Es schneit' is true iff it is snowing." The assignment of truth-conditions to sentences allows us to exploit the general reliability of other speakers' beliefs. Nor is this practice casual or only occasionally handy; most of what we know we know by authority. Moreover, the truth-condition of "Es schneit" in the example is not a feature that that sentence just fortunately happens to have in addition to its actual meaning. Intuitively, Esa fails to learn from Arabella's utterance precisely because he does not know what it means.

Informing as well as learning makes use of T-sentences, as Devitt (forthcoming, sec. 6.8) points out. Ubiquitously we pursue our own purposes by implanting beliefs in others (whether sincerely or mendaciously). We implant beliefs in others by uttering sentences having the corresponding truth-conditions; our hearers disquote them and form beliefs as Barbarella did.

More generally, the assignment of full-fledged truth-conditions to sentences of a natural language helps to explain why a population's having that language confers a selectional advantage over otherwise comparable populations that have none (this point is due to Dowty (1979, pp. 379–80): the ability to token and respond appropriately to such noteworthy sentences as "There is a good water source behind those rocks," "There is a freshly killed antelope over here," and "There is a sabre-toothed cat just behind you" just when those sentences' respective truth-conditions actually obtain is obviously of some assistance to individuals who were by chance genetically disposed to acquire that ability. A solipsistic semantics—a semantics designed precisely to establish no connection between a speaker's mind and the external world—makes no such explanatory contribution, though it might display selectional advantages of some other kind.

CRS has a possible competing explanation of learning and informing. When Barbarella hears Arabella's utterance, she has a good enough grasp of Arabella's functional organization to recognize the tokening of "Es schneit" as the typical effect of an inner state of Arabella that is itself typically caused by perceptual registration of nearby snowfall. Since Barbarella has no reason to suspect abnormal circumstances, she infers the best causal explanation of Arabella's tokening, according to which explanation it is indeed snowing. Truth has nothing to do with it.

The trouble with this account of Barbarella's reasoning is that it does not readily generalize.[9] Suppose we try to state a general principle that licenses the inference

(P) (S)(*t*)(If *t* is a token of S, then *t* is the typical effect of an inner state of *t*'s utterer, which is itself normally caused by perceptual registration of its being the case that S).

(Let us restrict our discussion to observation sentences.) But (P) as stated is ill-formed, since 'S' appears both as a variable ranging over sentences and as a schematic letter having sentences as substituends. Is there a way of repairing this use/mention flaw? The obvious suggestion is to understand (P)'s first quantifier substitutionally. This would make (P) effectively equivalent to the infinite conjunction of all its instances. How could Barbarella have learned such a conjunction? Only if S's substituends were composed of elements over which a recursion was defined. The CRS theorist must maintain that these elements are atomic conceptual roles rather naming relations and satisfaction-conditions. And here again we seem to get the wrong predictions about what hearers would learn from typical utterances involving Twin Earth designators and/or indexicals. In LePore and Loewer's example, if Barbarella reasons by way of a recursion on atomic conceptual roles rather than by way of a T-sentence, she will not learn that it is snowing as opposed to XYZing, for the inner state of Arabella's that has been caused by perceptual registration of snow would just as easily (and just as normally) have been caused by registration of crystalline XYZ. Similarly, had Arabella said (pointing to Esa) "He drank a Malaga cooler this morning," Barbarella would not have learned that Esa as opposed to Twin Esa had drunk the Malaga cooler, for the relevant inner state of Arabella would be the same whether it had been produced by a glimpse of the still shuddering Esa or a similar glimpse of Twin Esa. What is needed to distinguish the two is the fact that it really was Esa rather than Twin Esa who figured appropriately in the etiology of Arabella's inner state. And that is as near as matters to saying that the truth-condition rather than the "narrow" conceptual role is the vehicle of learning.

Notice, incidentally, that the schema (P) is not fully solipsistic as stated. What replaces the phrase "its being the case that S" will normally describe a state of affairs in the utterer's external environment, not something in the utterer's head. If Barbarella were to give a *genuinely* "narrow" explanation of Arabella's tokening, she would have to specify the input condition for Arabella's inner state in terms of surface receptors, not in terms of an extrinsic state of affairs. And this, I think, destroys the plausibility of the suggestion that Barbarella learns that it is snowing by constructing a "narrow" causal explanation of Arabella's tokening, for in order to construct such an explanation she would have to have fairly detailed knowledge of the structure of Arabella's retina (in order to cite a retinal event as the typical cause of the relevant inner state), as well as the knowledge that the occurrence of that retinal event is best explained by the local presence of snow. Surely no such thing is needed for learning by authority.

(ii) Speakers' *reporting* of the sayings and beliefs of other speakers presupposes that utterance-meaning is tied to truth-condition rather than to conceptual role (cf. Platts (1980, p. 11), McDowell (1981, pp. 229–30)). If Arabella says, "I am hungry," we report her as having said *that she was* hungry; in constructing our own complement clause we modify the person of Arabella's pronoun and the tense of her verb in order to preserve truth-condition. (If we wanted to preserve conceptual role, we could simply use her own words, which would result in a wildly inaccurate report.) Note too that we often make *de re* reports of sayings. When I hear the police sergeant say, "The criminal must have dropped these anchovies as she ran," I can report to my daughter (who did the deed), "They said you must have dropped the anchovies as you ran" (cf. Sosa (1970, pp. 890ff.)). If utterance-meaning were determined by the contents of the utterer's head, such *de re* locutions would make no sense; the *res de* which an utterer has said something is extracalvarian.

(iii) Public linguistic meaning is what is shared by all or most speakers of a given language. But conceptual role is notoriously not widely shared; it varies idiosyncratically from speaker to speaker. If we think of a sentence's conceptual role as represented by the various subjective conditional probabilities assigned by a speaker to that sentence, then it plainly will vary across speakers, since subjective probabilities do. Even on a nonprobabilistic (perhaps more purely functional) account such as Harman's, names and other designators whose reference is constant in the public language have different "narrow" conceptual roles for different speakers. This is what gives rise to Fregean puzzles about coreferring but otherwise independent names such as "Hesperus" and "Phosphorus" (cf. Field (1977, pp. 390ff.), Lycan (1984a)): whatever the details of one's way of handling such puzzles, one thing that is indisputable is that "Hesperus" and "Phosphorus" play different roles in the victim's behavioral economy. (A more obvious example is that of "Clark Kent" and "Superman.") Natural-kind terms provide another example, if Putnam (1975) is right about the "division of linguistic labor" and the determination of such terms' extensions by appeal to the relevant experts: "elm," "beech," "gold," "molybdenum," *et al.* are unambiguous (so far as I am aware) in English, yet different speakers associate different "stereotypes" with them and draw different inferences from sentences containing them. Conceptual roles, then, are commonly not shared by speakers of the same language. What do the speakers share? Reference and truth-conditions. And a good thing, too; otherwise we would be forever doomed to talk past each other.

I shall close this discussion of CRS by offering three further arguments (only the third of which is original) for denying that CRS can capture key aspects of locutionary meaning. The first (cf. Field (1977, p. 379)) is that meaning *determines* truth-conditions whereas conceptual role notoriously does not. If a person knows the meaning of a sentence and is omniscient regarding fact, then that person knows whether or not the sentence is true. Twin Earth cases show that conceptual role does not satisfy this same condition. I can know the conceptual role that is common to tokens of "This is water" and also know just what things are H_2O and which are XYZ, without thereby knowing whether "This is water" is true (in English) at a given spot, because the conceptual role does nothing to distinguish water from XYZ; similarly, as Putnam says, my stereotype for "elm" does not distinguish genuine elms from trees of countless other species. What does determine truth-value given a totality of facts is, precisely, a truth-condition.[10]

Robert Brandom (1976), following Michael Dummett (1973, p. 451), has pointed out a second reason why CRS alone cannot tell the whole story about locutionary meaning, at least if a sentence's "conceptual role" is to be expressed in the form of an assertibility condition. In a language containing common sorts of sentential embedding devices, such as conditional antecedent places, the assertibility-values of compound sentences are not determined by the assertibility-values of those sentences' components. Brandom considers the first-person future-tensed sentence, "I will marry Jane." For most people,[11] "I will marry Jane" is assertible just when "I foresee that I will marry Jane" is, yet those two sentences are not intersubstitutable *salva* assertibility in the context, "If —— , then I will no longer be a bachelor." Similarly, a disjunction may be assertible to such-and-such a degree even though neither of its disjuncts is assertible at all. Thus, truth-conditions, or something that plays the role of truth-conditions,[12] are needed even by a theorist whose main concern is assertibility, for the job of projecting assertibility-conditions through operations of sentential compounding.

I think similar considerations would apply to varieties of CRS that allude just to causal/functional roles rather than assigning assertibility-*values* to sentences. Truth-conditions will be needed for the task of projecting the functional roles of compound sentences from those of their parts, even if for purposes of dealing with individual behavior one cares more about the functional roles than one does about the truth-conditions. Indeed, it seems reasonable to say the same about theories of *understanding* generally (cf. Dowty (1979, p. 383)): a hearer understands a compound sentence only by decomposing it and exploiting his more basic understanding of the sentence's parts; so he will require the services of a recursion on truth or some truth-like notion for accomplishing the projection.

My third argument is a *reductio*. Let us try to construct a language from which reference and truth-conditions are absent—a purely formal calculus the use of which is governed by purely syntactic "assertion"-conditions. ("Assertions" of sign-designs belonging to the calculus are just acts of tokening; imagine that the "speakers"—or better, the players—hold up placards with the sign-designs printed on them.) We may make the set of "assertion"-conditions fairly large and have its members interlock in various complex ways. Now we can shepherd a group of speakers or players into a room and have them begin following the "assertion" rules. Some of their tokenings will be triggered by the appearance of external objects at the door or windows, others will be tokened in response to previous tokenings by other players or of one's own; some tokenings will themselves trigger various nonlinguistic acts (cf. Sellars (1963)). After the players have had some practice, the game can be played at tournament speed and everyone will have a good time. The placards might be painted in different colors, in such a way as to form pretty patterns that will make the game pleasing for spectators to watch.

I have attempted to describe a paradigmatic "conceptual-role language." Each placard has a role in the players' respective behavioral economies, and what determines tokening at any point is something directly accessible to the players. Nothing is presumed about external things or events not directly visible at doors or windows, and nothing is known to the players about the ultimate external effects of the nonlinguistic acts that are prompted by "command" tokenings. The players' "verbal" behavior is simply determined by the directly visible events and the machine program constituted by the (made-up) rules of the game. If CRS is correct (and perhaps if our game is complex enough), then our players are speakers of a language—it might even be, unbeknownst to them, a notational variant of some fragment of English under some disguising transformation.

My question is, in what sense if any *is* the game a language? In particular, have we succeeded in excluding reference and truth? Not obviously so; it may be that reference and truth have crept in unannounced. For we have sign-designs that are (by rule) tokened only in response to certain sorts of appearances at windows or door, and that lead in turn to other sorts of tokening and ultimately to action that may include behaving discriminatively toward the objects so appearing. If so, is it not natural to speak of the sign-designs as *referring* to individuals and to kinds? And if there is reference and predication, there is truth; there is also assertion in the full-blooded sense.[13]

On this construal we may see the players as constituting a speech community, united by their mutual use of the common formal calculus. Their use of it is public. But insofar as their terms have reference, the language is no longer solipsistic, because the assertion rules key on features of objects that are external to the individual speakers. A player would not succeed in obeying a rule that said, "If a red cylinder appears at the south window, hold up the placard that says 'SQUIGGLE'," unless what was in fact a red cylinder has appeared at what was in fact the south window, however scrupulously he may have tried to obey the rule from his own end. This makes the rule in effect into a truth-condition.

Suppose we tried more carefully to couch our input rules in solipsistic terms: "If you are appeared to red-cylindrically in the south-windowish sector of your visual field, ..." Then, assuming a story similar to the foregoing one of how reference and truth might creep in unannounced, the players' sign-designs would now refer to internal appearings of various qualitative sorts and to phenomenal properties; they would still have truth-conditions, but these new truth-conditions would be solipsistic in the older sense of that term. Each speaker would be able to talk only about his own mental life. So long as it is coherent to suppose that what looks to spectators like a group of people speaking a communal and unambiguous public language is actually a collocation of individuals each of whom speaks his own solipsistic language and thereby talks past all his fellows, the meanings of an individual speaker's tokenings will still be given by a truth definition idiosyncratically tailored to that speaker's private referents. (Given an incorrigibility assumption of the sort that naturally attends the idea of a solipsistic language, the truth-condition of a sentence of the language would coincide with its assertion- or verification-condition.)

However, suppose we ruthlessly refuse to let reference and truth creep as we have suspected back into our "conceptual-role language," either in its public or in its genuinely solipsistic and private form. That is, suppose the sign-designs' significance, in a broader use of that term is exhausted by their conceptual roles *exclusive* of reference and truth, as is the intent of CRS. (I have dwelt on reference-infiltrated versions of our game only to distinguish a genuinely solipsistic version from them; I suspect that some people may find CRS attractive only because they *are* tacitly infusing reference of some sort.) Then, it seems to me, there is nothing to mark the speakers' activity as *linguistic* activity *per se*. For all we know about it on the present construal is that it is rule-governed, and not every rule-governed activity is linguistic in any full-blooded sense. Consider chess, or musical performance, or improvisation within a severely constrained musical form. We sometimes use linguistic metaphors in describing instances of these activities, as when chess gambits are said to be "declined" or a musical "phrase" is said to take the form of "question and answer," but these cases contrast with ones in which chess moves or musical phrases *might literally be used as code symbols*, say as conveying secret messages between spies. Chess moves and musical phrases have no intrinsic locutionary meanings; they are not assertions *that* anything. Nor, I suggest, has a merely syntactically defined "move" in a conceptual-role game an intrinsic meaning (unless it is connected, however indirectly, to an input rule of the sort that would serve to establish either external or solipsistic reference). A move in a conceptual-role game is not an assertion *that* anything either. What is missing? Reference and truth.[14]

As has been foreshadowed in section 6 of chapter 9, we must distinguish two questions: (i) Why need we advert to any wide semantical notion rather than sticking entirely to narrow or solipsistic features of human speakers, and (ii) why do we fasten on *reference* and *truth* in particular as against some other wide notions such as those I called "V-reference" and "V-truth"? An answer to (i) does not *per se* determine an answer to (ii); yet my arguments so far in this chapter have been directed only against pure methodological solipsism in semantics, not specifically toward my advertised question of why the notion of *truth* (in particular) is needed in linguistics, which question incorporates (ii) as well as (i).

The imposter notions generated by Field's permutations of extension are public and common to speakers of the same natural language. If "elm" is satisfied for all English speakers just by genuine elms, then it is V-satisfied for all English speakers by elm-shaped chunks of space located one mile in direction so-and-so from genuine elms. Thus, my general run of objections to pure methodological solipsism does not distinguish satisfaction from V-satisfaction, and so does not show why the latter is only an "imposter." This omission alone would be no great crime, since (as I have noted) the compensatory shift from reference to V-reference would leave the theorems of our truth definition untouched. But why fasten upon a *truth* definition rather than on a *V-truth* definition?[15] Even though the class of true sentences and that of V-true sentences overlap hardly at all, V-truth is as public as truth and is "shared" as widely in any linguistic community, so my objections to CRS do not apply.

Two cases must be distinguished: (a) Field's permutations range freely; any that allows a suitable recursion is allowed. (b) The permutations are restricted to what I called "individuative resections" of normal extensions. Let us begin with (a), the more drastic. Why is it more interesting or important to linguistics that "Mose Allison is white" is true iff Mose Allison is white, than that "Mose Allison is white" is V-true iff Mose Allison is a chunk of space located one mile west of a similarly shaped white object?

A first answer is that the argument from learning and informing still has some force here. The story of Arabella and her listeners gives epistemic and thereby linguistic significance to the fact that "Es schneit" is true iff it is snowing, but I cannot think of a similar story that would give comparable significance to the fact that "Es schneit" is V-true iff we are one mile west of a region in which it is snowing. Barbarella normally would have no reason to think that Arabella's beliefs (of the relevant kind) were almost invariably V-true. V-truth *could* figure in an argument from authority, I suppose, in a world whose inhabitants were V-reliable rather than reliable, but such a world would be an uncanny, magical world, causally very different from ours. In our own world a V-reliable person would be a freak, a weirdo, and as reproductively fit as a lighter-than-air python.

Such practical matters aside, a legitimate metaphysical concern also favors truth over V-truth. If causality, and in particular nondeviant causal chains, serve as our benchmark of reality, then whatever "truthlike" notion best reflects a unified assembly of causal relations in nature will rightly be awarded preeminent ontological status as well as epistemic significance. The connection between "Snow is white" and snow's being white is causally tight, owing to the undoubted connections between utterances of "snow" and snow, and between utterances of "white" and whiteness-instances. But there is no even faintly nondeviant connection between utterances of "snow" and items one mile to the west of quantities of snow, nor between utterances of "white" and chunks of space located one mile to the west of similarly shaped white objects. This seems sufficient to condemn V-truth to a very low ontological caste, at least in our current incarnation.

The more conservative case (b) eludes both these arguments. For an individuative resection of a state of affairs leaves that state of affairs' causal properties unchanged. Let V_c be a Field-style permutation that works by individuative resection alone. Then any speaker who is reliable is also V_c-reliable, and vice versa, the two notions being at least nomologically equivalent; and V_c-truth is causally as top-drawer as truth, so long as we are unjustified in favoring any particular candidate for "causality proper," such as event-causality, over its competitors (state- or object- or slice-causality or whatever).

Here, as in the indeterminacy of translation issue, I believe we should grant some arbitrariness, pending the isolation of a truly basic unit of causality. That "Lo, a rabbit" is true iff the speaker ostends a rabbit has no more intrinsic linquistic significance than that "Lo, a rabbit" is V_c-true iff the speaker ostends a rabbit-stage. Here our choice of a "scheme of reference" is only a matter of convenience, naturalness, and so on. And why not? As Loar observed in connection with the indeterminacy of translation, every science makes similar choices of what to take as the metaphysical unit of causality; semantics is not singled out for embarrassment. Once the truly vicious imposters have been ruled out, then (case (a)), only convenience and naturalness are needed either to explain or to justify our appeal to truth rather than to V-truth in linguistics.

2. Dummett against Davidson

In numerous writings, Michael Dummett has attacked what he calls the "realist" notion of truth and defended what has come to be known as "antirealism." One prong of his attack is aimed against Davidson's semantical program (see particularly (1973, 1975, 1976)) and seems to me to be based in spirit on methodological solipsism. I decline with thanks (but firmly) to enter the metaphysical and meta-metaphysical fray, or to engage in exegesis of Dummett's works. However, I shall set out the most impressive anti-Davidsonian arguments that Dummett's writings suggest to me, and assess them, beginning with a brief, informal one culled from (1978a) and moving on to two more complicated lines of reasoning.

Davidson contends that we have tacit knowledge of English sentences' truth-conditions. If he is right, and if we can have any evidence for attributing such knowledge to speakers on particular occasions, then those speakers' truth-conditional knowledge must somehow be manifested in their behavior—not in the form of semantical *remarks*, since the knowledge is tacit, but presumably in their everyday use of the natural language in question. As is well known, Dummett interprets "use" epistemologically, identifying a speaker's tacit knowledge of the meaning of a sentence with the speaker's recognitional capacity to verify or falsify that sentence. But some sentences' truth-conditions are "recognition-transcendent," in that speakers have no effective procedures for determining those sentences' truth-values. Thus, if Davidson's view were correct, a speaker would have no way of manifesting his understanding of such a sentence, contrary to our requirement that tacit knowledge be manifestable. Therefore, Davidson's view is not correct; knowledge of the meaning of an "effectively undecidable" sentence does not consist in knowledge of its truth-condition.

Any number of hostile questions can be raised concerning this line of reasoning, stated as sketchily as it is. Why interpret "use" epistemologically at all? (I suppose, because Dummett wants to concede that meaning has *something* to do with truth.) What (outside mathematics) is an "effective procedure"? Are any sentences "effectively undecidable" in a sense of "decide" that is weak enough for Dummett's brand of verificationism to be plausible? And why must tacit knowledge be manifested in behavioral dispositions? Is Dummett not just joining Quine by the side of Turing?

The second and third questions would require a very lengthy discussion, careening through epistemology. I do not think the results would prove favorable to Dummett's extrapolation of the mathematical idea of effective decidability into everyday life, but I cannot make such a digression here.[16] Instead I shall briefly address the fourth question on Dummett's behalf. A clue is provided on p. 190 of (1978b) (cf. 1978a, pp. 217–18)):

> A meaning, not reducible to use, which I attach to a word . . . is something which I can recognize only in myself: I cannot recognize it in you, and I cannot tell you how to recognize it in yourself. I may indeed take it for granted that, by saying certain things to you, I can induce you to attach the same meaning to the word as I do, but I can have no evidence that my hypothesis is correct; I must rely on blind faith. Such a concept of meaning has lost all its explanatory power: since everything would be the same if there were no meanings in this sense, the hypothesis of their existence is empty.

Shades of the inverted spectrum. Dummett fears that mental differences unreflected in actual or counterfactual behavior are undetectable and explanatorily idle. But as I said in response to Quine (section 7 of chapter 9), post-Behaviorist theories of the mind have no difficulty with inverted mental entities; there is neither a problem of intelligibility nor a threat of occult Cartesian substance or spookstuff. Distinct and competing functional hypotheses may be offered in explanation of one and the same set of behavioral dispositions, and one may be correct as against the other. Indeed, one may be correct for one subject and the other correct for a different subject. So we should not be intimidated into agreeing with Dummett that meaning hypotheses are "empty."

However, the informal argument stated above does remind us of our methodological solipsist scruples. It is perfectly reasonable to demand that knowledge of meaning be reflected in detectable *functional* differences, whether or not these issues in distinct behavioral dispositions, if one's sole object is to explain individuals' behavior narrowly construed. This is the worry with which we began this chapter, and as I said, I suspect it lies behind the apparent crude behaviorism of Dummett's argument. It is a legitimate and important worry, but I have already tried to lay it to rest in section 1.

Let us turn to two more elaborate anti-Davidsonian arguments. The first I reconstruct from Dummett's well-known article, "Truth" (1959), replacing his term 'statement' with the more Davidsonian 'sentence.'

Let P be any sentence.

> 1. "Realism" is true of P iff P is true, or false, in virtue of some fact "in the world." (Definition, p. 14)
> 2. P is "effectively decidable" iff "we could in a finite time bring ourselves into a position in which we were justified either in asserting or in denying P." (Definition, pp. 16–17)
> 3. If P is true, or false, in virtue of some fact that is not "the sort of fact we have been taught to regard as justifying us in asserting" P, then P does not "have the meaning that *we* have given it." (By a lemma to be given below; p. 16)
> 4. P has the meaning that "we" have given it. (Assumed; p. 16)

Therefore,

> 5. Either P is true, or false, in virtue of the sort of fact we have been taught to regard as justifying us in asserting or denying it, or P is not true or false, in virtue of any fact at all. (3,4)
> 6. If P is true, or false, in virtue of the sort of fact we have been taught to regard as justifying us in asserting or denying it, then we could in a finite time bring ourselves into a position in which we were justified either in asserting or in denying P. (Suppressed assumption)

Therefore,

> 7. If "realism" is true of P, then P is effectively decidable. (1,2,5,6)

8. If truth and falsity play an essential role in the meaning of P, then "realism" is true of P. (Premise, p. 14)

Therefore,

9. If truth and falsity play an essential role in the meaning of P, then P is effectively decidable. (7,8)

But

10. Some sentences are meaningful and yet effectively undecidable. (Dummett offers the examples of "Jones was brave" and "A city will never be built here")

Therefore,

11. Some sentences are such that truth and falsity play no essential role in their meanings. (9,10)

If meaning is not always to be explained in terms of truth-conditions (assuming as Dummett does that natural languages contain *significantly many* "undecidable" sentences), then presumably in its essence meaning is not to be explained in terms of truth-conditions at all.

Premises 1 and 2 are definitions, and 4 and 6 seem reasonable enough. Since the argument is valid, then, a Davidsonian must attack 3, 8, and 10. Let us consider 8 first.

Dummett does not make clear in "Truth" (cf. (1973, p. 464)) why he espouses 8, and 8 is a rather strange claim. Suppose one is *not* a realist about truth. Suppose one holds that truth is not a relation between a sentence and the world, but is a relation (say, of "coherence") between the sentence and other sentences; or suppose one understands truth in epistemic terms, as "warranted assertibility" or the like. Why should accepting either of these proposed philosophical explications or theories of what truth *is* prevent a theorist from basing his theory of meaning for some language on a truth theory for that language? Perhaps Dummett thinks that there cannot be an adequate nonrealistic theory of truth that would support a Tarskian truth theory for a language, because of the prevalence of meaningful but undecidable sentences, but that would take more arguing.

Later he seems to address this worry, and says the real focus of his attack was bivalence rather than truth *tout court*.

I should now be inclined to say that, under any theory of meaning whatever . . . we can represent the meaning (sense) of a sentence as given by the condition for it to be true, on some

> appropriate way of construing 'true': the problem is not whether meaning is to be explained in terms of truth-conditions, but of what notion of truth is admissible. (1978c, pp. xxii–xxiii)

However, he adds that to reject bivalence is to deprive truth of its status as *fundamental* in a theory of meaning, since (he says) in a many-valued logic 'true' and 'false' would have to be defined terms.

Now, with regard to 3: 3 is an overtly verificationist assumption, in that it connects linguistic meaning with epistemic justification-conditions. As such it is suspect, for two obvious reasons: (i) If unsupported, 3 comes infinitely close to begging the question, since Dummett's overall concern is to motivate rejecting a Fregean/Davidsonian truth-based semantics in favor of a highly nonstandard verificationist one. Besides, there is no *prima facie* ground for thinking that any semantical notion has anything to do with any epistemic notion; the thesis that semantical notions are somehow to be analyzed in epistemic terms is a highly substantive theoretical claim and would have to be justified by a well-motivated explanatory theory. Further, (ii) the sorts of verificationist theories that the positivists used to invoke in this connection have been thoroughly discredited, or at least are no longer widely accepted. In particular, Quine has done much to scuttle the idea that *individual* sentences have verification- or justification-conditions at all; Putnam has pointed out (1965) that only when we have independent grounds for thinking that a string of words is meaningless can we have justified confidence that the string is unverifiable; and verificationism is impugned, I think, by its consequences in particular areas of metaphysics, such as behaviorism in the philosophy of mind, phenomenalism regarding the external world, and instrumentalism in the philosophy of science.

Dummett obviously knows these things and is undaunted by them.[17] I suspect he intends a defense of 3 that can be reconstructed from pp. 17–18. Lemma:

> 2a. In a language-teaching situation, we reward a child for asserting a sentence P when his environment warrants him in asserting P, and punish him when his environment does not warrant him in asserting P, regardless of P's actual truth-value. (Premise)
> 2b. If in a language-teaching situation we reward the child for asserting P when his environment warrants him in asserting P and punish him for asserting P when his environment does not warrant him in doing so, regardless of P's actual truth-value, then what the child learns in the situation is P's assertibility- or

justification-condition, and not necessarily P's truth-condition. (Premise)

2c. P's meaning is what the child learns in a language-teaching situation. (Premise)

Therefore,

2d. P's meaning is P's assertibility- or justification-condition. (2a,2b,2c)

2e. P has the meaning that we have given it. (Assumption for later conditionalization)

Therefore,

2f. The meaning we have given P is P's assertibility- or justification-condition. (2d,2e)

2g. If the meaning we have given P is P's assertibility- or justification-condition, then any fact in virtue of which P is true, or false, is the sort of fact we have been taught to regard as justifying us in asserting P. (Premise)

Therefore,

2h. Any fact in virtue of which P is true, or false, is the sort of fact we have been taught to regard as justifying us in asserting P. (2f,2g)

Therefore,

2i. If P has the meaning we have given it, then any fact in virtue of which P is true, or false, is the sort of fact we have been taught to regard as justifying us in asserting P. (2e,2h; conditionalization)

Therefore,

3. If P is true, or false, in virtue of some fact that is *not* the sort of fact we have been taught to regard as justifying us in asserting P, then P does not have the meaning that we have given it. (2i; contraposition)

Premise 2a seems true enough,[18] so the assumptions to examine closely are 2b, 2c, and 2g.

Premise 2g is not obvious. Why should we suppose that verificationism concerning meaning commits us to any particular view about what a sentence's truth consists in? Perhaps what Dummett, or a hypothetical proponent of 2g, has in mind is that meaning *determines* truth-condition. But if justification-conditions determine meaning and meaning determines truth-conditions, then justification-conditions determine truth-conditions, and this last does not seem to be true; the fact in virtue of which we know P (say, our observing someone wincing) may be quite a different fact from the fact in virtue of which P is true (say, the wincing person's feeling pain). Therefore, someone who holds that meaning consists in justification-conditions ought to presume at least for the time being that meaning does *not* determine truth-conditions.[19]

Premises 2b and 2c are a bit unclear, because of the awkwardness of the expression "what the child learns." Let us understand 2c in such a way, though, as to make it uncontroversially true (I believe this is Dummett's intention). Now, 2a and 2b together comprise a form of argument familiar since Wittgenstein.[20] It is flawed, I think, by an ambiguity in 2b. The clause "the child learns P's assertibility- or justification-conditions" could mean either that the child learns *what P's justification-condition is,* or that he learns *that P's justification-condition is satisfied.* Suppose it means the former. Then 2b is by no means obvious. For consider an alternative account of what happens in the teaching situation: as teachers, we reward a child for asserting P when his environmental circumstances warrant it because we assume in such circumstances that the child *believes* P. To see this, suppose that although the child is in a P-warranting environment, we know independently that for whatever reason, the child does *not* believe P. Then, it seems to me, we would *not* reward him for asserting P. This suggests that P's truth-condition is, after all, what we as language teachers are aiming at. In any case we should not accept 2b on its present reading without much further examination.

What about 2b's second reading? Thus interpreted, 2b is compatible with the alternative account of the teacher's aim that I have just sketched, and so is not threatened by the foregoing argument. But if my alternative account is correct, then the child learns that P's justification-condition is satisfied, on an individual teaching occasion, only as a means of learning what P's truth-condition is; the latter information is the main target of the teaching process, and so is what should be identified (if anything should be) with P's meaning. Therefore, if 2c is understood as saying that P's meaning is what the child learns *as the main object of* the teaching procedure, then 2b is too weak to yield 2d when conjoined with 2c.

The upshot is that either 2b is highly dubious or the argument is invalid. Thus, we have failed to obtain the lemma we needed to justify 3; the argument is at best inconclusive.[21] And finally, we may challenge premise 10. As I mentioned earlier, Dummett's notion of

"decidability" must be a fairly weak one if his verificationist ideas
are to be at all plausible. (In his earlier writings Dummett was prone
to speak of "conclusive" justification, his paradigm as always being
mathematical proof, but in the preface to (1978c) (p. xxxviii) he backs
off this requirement, admitting that mathematical proof is often not
to be had in the real world.) Presumably a sentence is meaningful
and capable of affecting our behavioral dispositions if there are ways
in which we could assign it a higher or lower likelihood. And it is not
obvious, at least to me, that any grammatical sentence of English
does not have at least this weak epistemic property. Certainly Dummett's own examples are unconvincing. Far from being undecidable
and indeterminate, "Jones was brave" is true if the relevant counterfactuals hold regarding Jones's behavior in the appropriate nonactual situations, and those counterfactuals could (in principle) be
conclusively verified if we knew enough about Jones's insides. And
even though "A city will never be built here" is a universal statement
and hence (according to Dummett) not *conclusively* verifiable due to
its infinite domain, it is certainly the sort of statement that can be
made very probable, depending, of course, on where it is tokened.

Let us move on to our remaining argument, which is suggested
primarily by Dummett (1973, 1975, 1976).

> 1. If understanding "Snow is white" is knowing what must be
> the case in order for "Snow is white" to be true, then anyone
> who understands "Snow is white" must know at least tacitly that
> "Snow is white" is true iff snow is white. [(1973, pp. 460–61;
> 1975, p. 107)]
> 2. To date, we have only one "general independent character-
> ization" of what one must know in order to know that "Snow is
> white" is true iff snow is white, viz., that based on the ability to
> produce and/or assent to the T-sentence " 'Snow is white' is true
> iff snow is white."

But

> 3. A characterization based on the ability to produce and/or as-
> sent to the T-sentence " 'Snow is white' is true iff snow is white"
> is (by itself) inadequate (since a speaker might easily be able to
> produce or assent to that T-sentence without knowing *that*
> "Snow is white" is true iff snow is white).

Therefore,

> 4. To date, we have no adequate "general independent charac-
> terization" of what one must know in order to know that "Snow

is white" is true iff snow is white. [= We have no adequate "model of" what the latter knowing "consists in"; (1975, pp. 108, 112, 114)]

5. Speakers and hearers of English are not infallible in recognizing from occasion to occasion exactly when a sentence's truth-condition is or is not satisfied.

6. If speakers and hearers of English are not infallible in recognizing from occasion to occasion exactly when a sentence's truth-condition is or is not satisfied, then the testing procedure for a proposed truth theory for English cannot consist in the unmediated and conclusive verification of each T-sentence in succession, but must be formulated in terms of merely the "best possible fit" between proffered truth-conditions and English speakers' actual judgments of truth and falsity. [(1975, pp. 116–17)]

7. If the testing procedure for a proposed truth theory for English must be formulated in terms of merely the "best possible fit" between proffered truth-conditions and English speakers' actual judgments of truth and falsity, then "a speaker's understanding of a sentence cannot be judged [by the truth theorist] save in relation to [the speaker's] employment of the entire language," unless we have a "general independent characterization" of what one must know in order to know that (say) "Snow is white" is true iff snow is white.

Therefore,

8. The truth theorist cannot judge a speaker's understanding of a sentence such as "Snow is white" save in relation to the speaker's employment of the entire language. (4,5,6,7)

9. If the truth theorist cannot judge a speaker's understanding of a sentence save in relation to the speaker's employment of the entire language, then the truth theorist is in principle incapable of allowing for any distinction between a disagreement of substance and a disagreement over meaning. [(1975, p. 119)]

10. Any acceptable theory of meaning must allow for a distinction between a disagreement of substance and a disagreement over meaning (since otherwise it would be committed to the indeterminacy of meaning and hence be a non- or antitheory of meaning).

Therefore,

11. The truth theorist has no acceptable theory of meaning. (8,9,10)

This argument is impressive. It does seem that the fact recorded in 5 is troublesome.[22] Notice, however, that the derivation of 8 is not strictly valid. Because of the qualification "to date," 4 is not quite the same sentence as the "unless"-clause in 7 and does not entail it. That is, there is still the possibility that we might come up with a new and adequate "general independent characterization" of the sort Dummett requires. Since the notion of a *mistake* is the problem, a way out for Davidson would presumably consist in providing a theory of mistakes to supplement the methodology of radical interpretation as it currently stands. Perhaps Dummett suspects that a theory of mistakes (having to do with *beliefs* and their relation to assent- and dissent-behavior and so on) would, when complete, be found already to contain enough apparatus to yield a theory of meaning by itself, thereby rendering truth theory superfluous. (CRS and/or Gricean speaker-semantics come to mind here.) But this would remain to be shown.

I find neither 7 nor 9 obvious either. That my analytical hypothesis regarding "gavagai" or "schläft" is mediated by charity (or by what Grandy (1973) calls a "principle of humanity") as well as by a substantial body of theory—including particular suppositions about the native's beliefs—does not *entail* the whole-hog sort of holism that Dummett darkly forecasts, though no one denies that radical interpretation is a tricky and puzzling business. And even if a dramatic holism does ensue, I do not see that it in turn entails the flat impossibility of distinguishing denying-the-doctrine from changing-the-subject. For one thing, even if our interpretation of one type of verbal utterance on the native's part depends on our respective interpretations of every other type of behavior in the native's repertoire, the dependencies differ greatly in strength and in degree of intimacy. My translation of a Frenchman's "ne" depends entirely on my translation of his "pas" (and vice versa); it depends hardly at all on my translation of his "enseignement" or his "caneton de caoutchouc." Differences of this sort may well help us make the distinction Dummett rightly demands.

Our third argument poses a useful challenge to our methods of radical interpretation; it does not refute truth-theoretic semantics.

3. Empirical Questions

If syntax is psychologically real and semantics is at least partially reflected in mental processing (certainly the logical connectives, sentence compounding, and inference are real), then psychological data must bear on syntactic and semantic theories. And so they have been taken to do, in psycholinguists' reaction-time studies and the like. Indeed, such studies have tended to yield apparently obdurate disconfirmations of several favorite semantic hypotheses. (For example, see Kintsch (1974) and Fodor, Fodor, and Garrett (1975) against certain lexical decomposition theories, and Martin (1978) against the positing of complex first-order quantificational structures. See also the literature reviewed by Fodor, Bever, and Garrett (1974).) Of course, not all psycholinguistic data are germane to syntax or semantics (cf. Soames (1979a, 1979c)); error rates, most developmental facts, and idiosyncratic performance characteristics are irrelevant. The data with which linguistic theory begins come already abstracted drastically away from individuals' actual behavior in real speech situations. This is just what we should expect in light of my earlier contention that linguistics studies what the members of a speech community have in common and not (primarily) the behavior of particular individuals from occasion to occasion. It does not follow, of course, that psycholinguistic data are *never* relevant, as witness the examples mentioned above.[23]

However, it has been argued (as by Soames and particularly Katz (1981)) that we have *a priori* reason to doubt the convergence of linguistic theories based on syntactic and semantic data with the results of psychological investigation. A simple version of one argument is based on the key role of simplicity considerations in linguistics: Linguists aim at capturing as broad generalizations as they can with as few posited rules and constraints as possible; they aim at the overall simplest grammars they can devise that are adequate to the data. Yet psycholinguistic investigations reveal computational complexities that a pure linguist would find gratuitous—and so we should expect, unless we join Dr. Pangloss in believing that Mother Nature has graciously (and miraculously) endowed us with the simplest, neatest, and most efficient speech centers possible. Indeed, if Mother Nature has done roughly as well on speech centers as She has on the various other human organs (particularly the psychological ones), they will not much resemble the classically elegant mathematical structure that would be fashioned by the ideal linguist.[24]

Of course not. We could have arrived at this same conclusion by performing an induction over all of systems theory. Virtually nothing in nature, and certainly not in biology or psychology, works as simply as our ideally simplest theory would portray it as doing. Simplicity is of paramount value and importance to the linguist in particular because we are largely innocent of hard data that bear on processing; the speech center is still an almost entirely closed book to us, and so the linguist has little to go on besides his original syntactic and semantic data plus general epistemic values such as simplicity and conservatism. It is fair to say, upon looking at an actual semantic theory or even at a linguistically ideal theory, "Reality can't be as simple as that." But it does not follow that linguistics is not a branch of psychology or that it has a wholly distinct subject-matter. For the linguist may hold himself responsible to whatever psycholinguistic data do come in. The simplest theory that is adequate to the syntactic and semantic data may still be proved wrong.[25]

Linguistics is so hard. Even after thirty years of exhausting work by scores of brilliant theorists, virtually no actual syntactic or semantic result has been established, has become uncontroversial and counted by the professional community as *known*. At present there is not even a single dominant semantactic format. And the few psycholinguistic data that have presented themselves have borne negatively rather than positively on existing theories. It would be unreasonable to suppose that an adequate theory of English could be completed in time for the heat-death of the universe; certainly the deadline for building a Vietnamese-speaking machine is long past. The daunting enormity of the task is enough to make some theorists doubt its conceptual probity.[26] Yet we can rebut the suggestion that for this reason the semantic enterprise is misconceived. Human beings do in fact produce linguistic output in response to linguistic input, and striking social regularities do obtain across speech communities. Therefore, there must be some actual, psychologically real way in which these things happen. And there must be some description of this processing that yields the right predictions without descending all the way to the neuron-by-neuron level.[27] Thus, if a semantactic theory of English should, through investigative skill on the theorist's part or just through freakish luck, match the processing that actually does occur, then that theory is *a* (if not *the*) *correct* linguistic theory *qua* piece of psychology, to the exclusion of other, perhaps extensionally equivalent accounts; so there is a fact of the matter of assigning logical forms after all, and it is not pointless to have stated the constraints that a psychologically real account ought to satisfy, even if we currently have no theories that offer much hope of satisfying them.

Chapter 11
"Meaning"

In part II I have tried to sketch the complex and various ways in which semantic and pragmatic factors interact. Since I propose to understand the factors, and the interaction, as being psychologically real, and since I favor a "homuncular functionalist" format for psychology (Lycan (1981a, 1981b)), I should expect more detailed research based on the sorts of reasoning employed in part II to issue in a flow diagram, representing a human speech center and its functional connections to its owner's other psychological subagencies. I present a simpleminded and vulgar sample diagram in figure 1. Let me offer a few comments on it, and then turn to a natural botanizing of linguistic theory and the philosophy of language.

1. The Total Study of a Natural Language

I list the following notes, comments, and questions about my simpleminded model in no particular order.

(i) The model represents only a "speaker's" *producing* or tokening mechanism. It says nothing about my organism's capacity to *receive* and interpret or understand speech. So I have modelled only a part or subroutine of a whole human being's linguistic competence. (This is in no way disrespectful of the fact that people could not produce speech unless they also understood speech.) A few methodological points are in order. Following Artificial Intelligence research and recent philosophical accounts thereof,[1] I recommend we go about studying a complex ability by breaking it down into obvious or useful sub-abilities that may be construed as its parts. Of each sub-ability I would ask what subcomponents of the subject organism seem to be needed in order to accomplish the set of distinct tasks that comprise that sub-ability. Having represented each of these subcomponents by a black box,[2] I would then ask which of them need to access which others if all of the constitutive tasks are successfully to be carried out, and represent each needed access relation by an arrow, sometimes interrupted by an output- or input-label if the particular output or input in question is salient for existing theory.

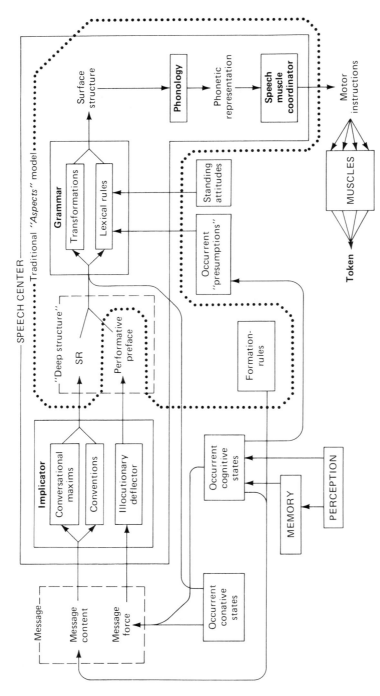

Figure 1

Now, in working on a single sub-ability, I put in only those components and access relations that are needed for representing that sub-ability itself; there is no implication that some or all of the subcomponents do not also figure in the mechanics of a closely related (though distinct) sub-ability, and do not accordingly bear any other access relations to each other than I am troubling to represent for the purposes of the moment. (Similarly, I do not represent access relations that obviously do hold between the peripheral psychological agencies but are not needed (so far as I know) for speech production itself, such as the access that various perceptual mechanisms must have to memory.)

What might a separate model of an *understander* look like? Plainly it would have much in common with our model of a producer, and involve at least the same components, because of the inextricable connection between our ability to speak English and our ability to understand it. It is natural and attractive to suggest that an understander simply runs our whole productive process in reverse, beginning with the noises, marks, or whatever token it receives as input and ending up with a "message" as the output of our (reversed) speech center, which "message" would feed our various cognitive and conative mechanisms. But there are well-known reasons why this cannot be so, the foremost being that a number of the mappings contained in the grammar, the implicator, and elsewhere are not one-to-one. As we have noted in chapter 8, in particular, a parser is a far more difficult thing to design than is a set of transformations that run only in forward gear. Still, something like running-in-reverse must happen.

It should be recalled that one thing an understander does is to compute our valuation function α, i.e., it identifies which things a speaker is talking about. Given what the understander's formation rules have antecedently interpreted as being a singular term, the understander must assign an object to that singular term as its referent. We humans normally have no trouble with this and do not even think about it, but that makes the task of explaining how we do it all the more daunting.

(ii) Of course, a speaker must have internalized α or its inverse as well. I have left α so far unrepresented on our flowchart, because I am unsure whether to place its corresponding mechanism prior or posterior to the implicator. It is natural to assume that since the speaker's job with regard to α is to take an individual that he "has in mind" and lexicalize the NP node corresponding to that individual, thereby producing an expression m such that $\alpha(m) =$ that individual, α ought to be represented by an appropriate component standing between the implicator and the grammar; thus, α would be run in reverse by the speaker's lexical mechanism. But we have seen in section 2 of chapter 3 that α takes elements of SRs, not surface elements, as arguments. This argues for depicting α's inverse as operating prior to the production of the SR, rather than within the lexical subcomponent. Notice, though, that the lexical rules still have to be able to "see" α's inverse operating; otherwise they will not be able to lexicalize a free variable appropriately as "I," as "you," or whatever. I shall not try to settle this question here.

(iii) In the present flow diagram I have shown the formation rules of the canonical idiom as operating jointly with our speaker's occurrent cognitive states to produce the "message content." This is peculiar, at least historically speaking, since the phrase structure component and the transformational component have always been conceived as the two halves of a single grammar. I am not happy about it either, but let me explain why I have done it *faute de mieux*.

The formation-rules are just phrase structure rules for the canonical idiom in which our SRs are written. But they differ from Chomsky's original phrase structure rules in that they play no mechanical role in the production of the SR that is fed into our transformational component. Notice that we have been dealing with two projects that are related but distinct: (a) the task of axiomatizing the predicate "grammatical string," i.e., of drawing up a set of rules that will generate all and only the well-formed sentences of our target language (a mathematical job), and (b) the task of constructing a functional model of a human speaker of the target language. Unlike some syntacticians, I have been thinking of (a) as a direct means to (b), but a difference between the two is pointed up by this issue concerning the formation-rules: the formation-rules are indispensable to task (a), since we need a phrase structure component to tell us what formulas serve as input to our transformations, but the formation-rules seem superfluous to task (b), since every input or output item on our diagram is (already) a structured item and does not depend on any actual mechanical instantiation of the formation-rules in order to be so. It may be that the formation-rules have a purely mathematical and descriptive function and do not belong in a paramechanical representation of speech abilities at all. (Recall that in *Syntactic Structures* (1957), the *locus classicus* of the phrase structure component, Chomsky was bent on task (a) and not on (b). In *Aspects* (1965), Chomsky carried the component over into the new grammar that he put forward in aid of (b), seeing no incongruity in that new setting.)

Note that if the formation-rules function mechanically (in actual human psychology) to produce SRs, then by their nature they do so without benefit of any controlling input. Therefore, there is nothing to impel them to generate any one particular SR rather than another (the ubiquitous "S" being entirely impartial). Consider also that all of our structured items do in any case come from other structured items: SRs emerge from the implicator, which device trades in already interpreted logical structures. The implicator has taken in a structured "message," which came from structured cognitive and conative items such as beliefs and desires, and the latter came ultimately from structured perceptions. It looks as though our English-speaking mechanism is transformational throughout: mechanically speaking, all it does is change structures into other structures.

It is therefore tempting to suppose that the formation-rules play no psychological role and so do not belong anywhere on our flowchart. But this cannot be the whole story either, for only in virtue of the formation-rules (in some way) can we compute the truth-condition of a complex formula, and (according to the Metatheory) it is only in virtue of such computation that we understand sentences or produce them appropriately. So it is not right to deny that the formation-rules play any psychological role either. I shall draw the discreet veil of cowardice over the issue at this point, but it is a matter that needs clearing up.

(iv) The task of connecting up a model of a speaker with a model of an inferrer or reasoner will be a difficult piece of psychology. Even though we have rejected CRS, the requirement that a theory of natural language explain inferential habits is a cornerstone of truth-theoretic semantics in *any* larger methodological setting. Somehow the structure of our linguistic capacity causally affects our belief-stores in response either to externally induced changes in their contents or just to private reflection.

(v) We have said nothing specific about the location of *occurrent thoughts* in our model. Several different cases come under this heading: thinking a sentence consciously to oneself word by word; thinking a complete propositional thought that one has at a particular time, more or less consciously but not painstakingly word by word; thinking quite unconsciously. Thoughts of any of these sorts can issue in speech, so eventually they must be located on our diagram. It seems natural to identify a thought of the word-by-word sort with a surface structure; since it occurs in (mental) English words already arranged according to English surface grammar, it must already have passed through the stage of transformational derivation; but since it is still merely a thought and has not been physically realized in any particular way, it appears not yet to have entered the phonology.

A thought of the still conscious but less articulate sort may be simply a "message" itself, though I have said nothing about what sort of representation a "message" is. I think of messages as being structured and contentful intermediaries between propositional attitudes or congeries of them and the speech center, but certainly introspection affords none of the fine distinctions that will be needed here. Unconscious thoughts presumably affect the speech center in whatever way(s) conscious ones do, only without simultaneously announcing their activities to executive control. It is comparatively rare that we become conscious of our own surface structures or (if at all) of our messages; we can attend to them or not, as we choose or as other psychological factors choose for us.

In any case, it looks as though we will have to allow that speakers often carry out two derivational processes simultaneously. For example, suppose I occurrently think, and implicate, that P, uttering a sentence that means literally that not-P (say, a case of sarcasm). One straightforward derivational process must be producing my occurrent thought (if it is the word-by-word kind) from the SR directly correlated with the message that P. Another must be producing my *utterance* from the SR correlated with the message that not-P, which has been spit out by my implicator upon that organ's having been fed the original message. If I am thinking that P in word-by-word fashion, I may have to restrain myself consciously or unconsciously from physically tokening my actual occurrent thought. In such a case, what I have glibly called my "speech muscle coordinator" will receive some input from my stock of occurrent states, which will suppress the directions that would ordinarily be given by my phonology in response to being fed the occurrent thought as a surface structure.

(vi) Sufficiently ramified, our model will help to distinguish and diagnose various sorts of speech disorders (kinds and grades of aphasia, dyslexia, hyperlexia, dysgraphia, etc.), in terms of which particular access relations in our model are being interrupted by damage. Some kinds of disorder are relatively superficial, being only muscular. Others are more abstract—for example, some aphasics have perfectly sound transformations but defective lexical components. Still less fortunate victims have problems more deeply hidden in the brain, affecting their abilities to form coherent thoughts or "messages" at all. And so on.[3]

It is important to note that the enormously rich variety of speech disorders is a vital source of hard data for elaboration of our model. Each disorder we can isolate and distinguish from others points toward more distinct functional architecture, and toward more complexity and sophistication in our understanding of the organization of the speech center and its neighbors.

(vii) It is useful, especially in relating our programmatic linguistic theory to other issues in psychology and/or to more traditional problems in metaphysics and the philosophy of mind, to think not only of functional *systems* but of functional *hierarchies* as well.[4] A *message* is a very abstractly individuated item. One and the same message-type may be realized by any one of a number of SRs, we may suppose, depending on circumstances. An SR is perhaps a slightly less abstract item, realized by any one of a number of grammatical trees. A tree is realized by any one of a number of surface structures; a surface structure may be realized in any one of a number of different ways by the phonology; and, finally for our purposes, a phonetic representation may be realized by any one of a vast number of physical tokens.

Now that we have sketched a model of a speaker, we may say which branch of linguistics or of philosophy is responsible for studying each distinct aspect of our target language. Let me offer a quick and preliminary breakdown of the academic areas concerned with the theoretical study of natural languages, distinguishing a few subdisciplines within these, and briefly characterize each subdiscipline in terms of the kind of theory it generates and the range of phenomena it comprehends. My purpose in undertaking this modest bit of mock university administration is to underscore my contention that traditional "theories of meaning" that have been treated as competing explanations of the same range of phenomena are in fact mutually compatible and complementary theories of interlocking but different subject-matters; more on this contention in section 2.

Here is my outline:

Linguistic semiotics

A. *Syntax/semantics ("semantax")*
   The study of *logical form* in the traditional Russellian sense and of how logical form is related to surface structure. Given an SR that expresses a logical form directly by wearing its truth-condition on its sleeve, a semantactic theory will tell us exactly which surface structures can grammatically express this truth-condition; and given a surface structure, the theory will tell us exactly which logical forms the structure might have underneath.

B. *Pragmatics*
   1. The pragmatics of reference.
      The study of what Kaplan calls "character," i.e., of how we determine the fully explicit truth-condition of a context-

bound utterance-token embedded in its "total speech situation." This is largely a study of how we compute α, which is primarily but perhaps not entirely a matter of convention. (Recall from chapter 3 that much more is comprehended here than would at first appear.) This is what Cresswell (1973) calls "semantic pragmatics" as opposed to "pragmatic pragmatics."

2. Speech-act theory.
The study of types of speech acts and their respective felicity-conditions. Given a single context, occasion, or "total speech situation," a speech-act theory yields (a) a performative preface for use in syntax, and (b) a more refined description of the utterance's illocutionary properties. It also explains many perceived defects in an utterance, presumably even those that fall under the theory of implicature (since they will be subsumed into the felicity-conditions on asserting, remarking, requesting, and other such acts). Speech-act theory thus would explain all unacceptability that is neither semantical nor merely social.[5]

3. The theory of implicature.
The study of how a speaker, wishing to communicate the content that P with force F, does so by producing a sentence whose literal locutionary content is not the content that P, and/or whose literal illocutionary force is other than F. Given a message, along with some beliefs and desires and so on, a theory of implicature will specify a "censored" or edited SR. Conversely, given a literal SR and some propositional attitudes, the theory will specify one or more possible presumed messages.[6] A theory of implicature is a theory of the structure of someone's implicator.

Phonology

The study of the physical realization of surface structures. Given a surface structure, the theory tells us which patterns of physical tokens count as instances of that structure, and vice versa. (Perhaps it would be well to reserve the term "phonology" for oral speech, using "graphology" for written speech, since the two are so entirely different (and on etymological grounds also).)

Speech anatomy

The physiological study of the body's reaction to its speech center's output: a detailing of the instructions sent to various muscles and the consequent interaction of those muscles to produce acoustical effects.

Psycholinguistics

Narrowly, the neurophysiological study of the way(s) in which the functionally characterized components of the speech center are realized in brain matter. More broadly, the general study of the immensely complex ways in which conscious and subconscious psychological states of all sorts interact with the various components of the speech center, either functionally or neuroanatomically conceived.

Sociolinguistics

The sociological study of the (primarily causal) relations between a natural language, at a time or over a period of time, and the social structures and conditions obtaining within the society that the speakers of the language comprise. Given a particular language, the theory will tell us the various social effects of the various relevant features of that language. Given a social context, conversely, the theory will tell us how it shapes features of the language itself (presumably by providing content for the "standing attitudes" component). A common special case of causal interaction involving a language is interaction with another language or with another dialect of the same language.

Philosophical psychology of language

A. *The theory of thought*

What Harman (1968) calls "Level 1" theory, the study of the representational content of thoughts and messages. The theory will tell us what makes a thought the thought that it is, outlining the way in which it has its truth-condition and the relation it bears to the subject's evidence-base and inferential habits.

B. *The theory of inference*

So far as it is distinct from semantics and from the theory of thought, this is the normative science of valid inference and presumably of correct ampliative inference as well. Its relation to cognitive psychology is extremely unclear.[7]

Philosophy of language

A. *Methodology*

(Of course.)

B. *The theory of speaker-meaning*

The study of what speaker-meaning is (once called "Grice-theorie" by Harman). This tells us what it is for a speaker to mean something in producing a token. Presumably the theory of implicature would tell us how in a practical way to determine what it is that the speaker means in producing that token.

C. *The philosophical theory of reference*

1. The theory of denotation for singular terms.

   The analytical study of what it is, in general, for a singular term to denote an object on an occasion. (This will probably presuppose an answer, vouchsafed by the theory of thought, to the question of what it is for a speaker to have a particular object "in mind.")

2. The theory of lexical meaning and denotation for predicates.

   The study of what it is for a predicate to have a particular class of things as its extension and/or to have a "meaning" of its own.

   (Of course, conclusions in the philosophical theory of reference will have repercussions for the pragmatics of referring, and vice versa.)

D. The study, whatever it may be called, of the implications of linguistic theory and philosophy of language for other branches of philosophy, particularly metaphysics, epistemology, and ethics—and vice versa. These interconnections are complex and very important to clarify.

Doubtless I have left some things out. But I do not think I have left anything superfluous in. All the disciplines and subdisciplines I have listed are worthwhile and important. Some, of course, are more central than others to what philosophers and linguists have traditionally called "meaning." But philosophers, at least, have bickered over which one area is *the* closest, which one contains the *core* notion that all talk of meaning has ultimately been aiming at. In this book, of course, I have made sentences' truth-conditions the centerpiece, and if I had to choose, I would identify truth-conditions as the elusive core notion. But I do not have to choose, and, I shall argue, neither does anyone else.

2. "Meaning"

An argument-form, popular at least since Wittgenstein abandoned logical atomism, runs as follows: "*Meaning*, surely, involves X. No theory that tells us nothing about X could be called a theory of *meaning*. But a truth theory for a language L, a mere Tarskian assignment of truth-conditions to the sentences of L, doesn't tell us anything about X! Therefore, a se*man*tical theory should be based instead on [whatever is taken to be the core notion in a theory of X]!" More often than not, the plaintiff goes on explicitly or subconsciously to add, "And once we've got that kind of theory, we can forget all about truth theories and Tarski and syntax and all those awful things." Substituends for 'X' have historically included "use" in the Wittgensteinian ("Slab!") sense, illocutionary force, speaker's intentions to express thoughts, inferential role, communication, verification-conditions, and more.

There are two fallacies here. First, the word "meaning" is used so multifariously in English, and philosophers' and linguists' ears and intuitions have been knocked about so vigorously by the past eighty years' feverish work in the theory of meaning, that surely there can be nothing obvious about any instance of the foregoing argument-form's first premise. Alternatively, we could agree to use "meaning" as the broadest conceivable cover term for anything about language or thought that anyone found worth studying, thereby making the first premise true, but then the conclusion (and the usual corollary) would plainly not follow. The word "meaning" simply has no established use that would support a crisply factual claim of the sort required for the success of any instance of our argument-form.[8]

Second, even if we stipulate (either in the literal or in the legal sense) the truth of our plaintiff's first premise, and give him the word "semantic" and all its kind, we will still have to investigate aspects of language other than his vaunted X under another name, for they are all interesting and important in their own right. In particular, we will still have to construct truth theories for natural languages, or broader theories that yield truth theories. One reason for this I have tried to bring out in section 1 of chapter 10, arguing that a "semantics" innocent of truth and reference would leave us unable to study key public facts about natural languages. Another reason is that the main competing "theories of meaning" that we have seen since the 1940s have lacked the *recursive* feature that is provided by a truth theory, and this is damning, since one of the few things we can be sure of about meaning is that it is determined recursively. Indeed, some venerable "theories of meaning" have broken down on just this point: Wittgenstein had nothing useful to say about how it is possible for us to understand long, complex, novel sentences at first hearing; speech-act theories such as William Alston's were plagued by circularity (what is it for two sentences to have the same "linguistic act potential"?); Grice had to import his unexplicated relation "R" to accommodate novel sentences; as Brandom reminded us (section 1 of chapter 10), an assertibility semanticist must invoke truth or a truth-like notion to project assertibility-conditions through sentential compounding; etc.

Let me offer my own "theory of meaning" now, of a different kind. Not as a competitor of any of the foregoing theories or of the Metatheory, but as an account of the term "meaning" as it is used in the everyday speech of professional philosophers and linguists embroiled in dispute. I call it the "Double Indexical Theory of Meaning," and it has the virtue of explaining why most disputes over the nature of meaning have seemed so intractable. Here it is:

MEANING $=_{\text{def}}$ Whatever aspect of linguistic activity happens to interest *me now*.

And . . . oh, yes:

UNDERSTANDING $=_{\text{def}}$ Grasp of meaning.[9]

On my view, virtually every theorist who has proposed to identify "meaning" with a favored instance of "X" has simply been making a disguised value judgment, to the effect that X is now worthwhile and important to study, whereas what we were studying before has become dull. Wittgenstein (understandably) lost interest in "objects" and became fascinated by football matches and vulgar Neopolitan gestures. Followers of Austin revelled in the discovery of illocutionary force, and coined the term "descriptive fallacy" for use against opponents who still sought the truth-makers of certain troublesome sorts of statements. Grice persisted in reminding us that sentences express thoughts, and this reminder coupled with a functionalist theory of thoughts becomes CRS with its pooh-poohing of truth theory.

Now, all the discoveries I have just mentioned, and more, were important, perhaps almost as important as they seemed at the time. (Where would either linguistics or philosophy be without speech-act theory?) An innovative theorist may be perfectly justified in shouting, "Meaning is X!!—not that other boring old stuff!," *if* he is using the word "meaning" in the sense codified by the Double Indexical Theory. The error, and the wrong, come when the theorist goes on to infer, from the fact that X is important and has little to do with truth-conditions *per se*, the conclusion that truth-conditions are negligible and have no serious role to play in linguistic theory. And this fallacious inference is precisely what is facilitated by the very dangerous word "meaning." It would be a good thing, I believe, if the word "meaning" were simply banned for the foreseeable future. Theorists could talk usefully about any aspect of language use they pleased—truth-conditions, verification-conditions, illocutionary force, speaker-meaning, implicature, and more, but using those more specific and relatively precise terms. "Meaning" would not be missed.

Appendix:

Non-Truth-Functional Sentence Operators

Non-truth-functional sentence operators pose a special problem for the writing of truth definitions for natural languages. In this appendix I offer an overview of possible approaches to that problem and of some advantages and disadvantages of appeal to possible worlds.

1. Wallace's Problem

Tarski's paradigm is the truth definition one would give for an object language written in first-order quantification theory, making use of the notion of satisfaction. The base clauses of such a theory assign denotations to names and satisfaction-conditions to primitive predicates of the object language, one after the other; the recursive clauses assign distinctive compositional roles to truth-functions and quantifiers. So much is familiar.

Now, consider non-truth-functional operators in English such as "It is necessary that" and "S believes that." On their face, such operators seem to operate on sentences, with or without an additional argument place. Each (primitive) sentence operator ought to receive its own clause in a truth definition for English. But what would such a clause look like? A natural suggestion in the case of a belief-sentence would be

(1) ⌜N believes that S⌝ is true iff BELIEVE (Den(N),S),

where 'N' and 'S' are functioning within the Quine-quotes as metalinguistic variables ranging over object-language names and sentences, respectively. But this is to imply that the English expression "believes that" is, at the level of logical (and hence ultimate syntactic) form a two-place predicate that relates a person simply to a sentence of the target language; to write our recursive clause for "believe" in this way is to embrace a crude form of inscriptionalism concerning belief-sentences. We should not want our mere choice of a *format* for writing recursive clauses to commit us to a substantive decision concerning the logical form of belief-sentences, and particularly not to one so implausible as crude inscriptionalism.

The problem is that Tarski himself simply did not give us any format in which to treat non-truth-functional sentence operators of natural *or* of formal languages; if we want to extend his methods to cover such items, we shall have to devise a workable way of elaborating his apparatus ourselves. John Wallace (1975) has brought out this difficulty very clearly, and has distinguished a number of options for dealing with nonextensional object languages that may help us in this task.[1] In what follows I shall take my cue from his discussion and expand on it.

In keeping with Davidson's conservative preference for extensional metalanguages, let us begin by trying to write a belief clause extensionally. Since "S believes that" is not a truth-function, it cannot be represented as a genuine *and* extensional sentence operator; the truth-value of "S believes that p" is underdetermined by the propositional content of its complement. There seem to be only two other potential ways of keeping our belief clause extensional.

(A) It seems reasonable to suppose that "believes that" reflects a relational predicate. The most obvious candidate for such a predicate would be one that (as above) applies to the name of a person and the name of a sentence; but that would bring us back to crude inscriptionalism again. A more popular suggestion is that the underlying predicate BELIEVE relates a person to a proposition, where the surface "that"-clause functions as a name of the proposition. But now we must ask whether the "that"-clause is supposed to be a primitive, unstructured name of the proposition or a structured singular term that denotes it, and at this point Wallace poses a dilemma: If "that"-clauses are fused or primitive names, like "Fred" or "Jane," then there must be a nonfinite stock of them (since "S believes that" can operate on any of a nonfinite stock of complement sentences), and that violates Davidson's finiteness constraint. But if a "that"-clause is a semantically articulated singular term, like "The proposition that Jimmy Carter won the election," it is not an extensional construction; *that Ronald Reagan won the election* and *that the winner won the election* are distinct propositions and can differ in truth-value. Thus, if our "that"-clause is a structured singular term, we have not succeeded in writing our belief clause in an extensional metalanguage.

Actually, there is a third possibility that Wallace does not consider. We need not assume that if a "that"-clause is a structured name of a proposition at all, then it is the sort of expression that articulates the proposition's content in the standard way. The "that"-clause might be a structured singular term of some other sort. Suppose we read "S believes that p" as "S believes the proposition expressed by 'p'."

Although these two schemata are not logically equivalent, the latter points toward a way of writing an extensional recursive clause for the former, namely, as

(2) ⌜N believes that S⌝ is true iff BELIEVE (Den(N),(ıP)Exp (S,P)),[2]

an instance of which would be

(3) "Albert believes that there are mammals that have webbed feet" is true iff BELIEVE (Den("Albert"),(ıP)Exp ("There are mammals that have webbed feet", P)).

(For simplicity, let us ignore the possibility of an ambiguous complement.)

I have noted that the right-hand side of the foregoing belief clause is not logically equivalent to the target sentence mentioned on the left-hand side. There is nothing untoward in the fact that the right-hand side could be true even though the left-hand side itself is false, since Tarski's and Davidson's biconditionals are truth-functional; what is objectionable is that the right-hand side is not even a plausible philosophical analysis of the mentioned target sentence (however "impure"), much less a metaphrase translation. (Disturbing too is the closely related fact that the right-hand side of our illustrative instance does not tell us *what* Albert believes; one would expect the statement of a truth-condition for "Albert believes that there are mammals that have webbed feet" to do that.) Nor is there any way of deriving an actual pure or impure T-sentence from our biconditional plus other clauses of our truth definition; we can substitute "Albert" for "Den('Albert')" on the basis of our (presumed) clause "Den('Albert') = Albert," but nothing else in the truth definition will help us obtain a statement of what Albert believes. For these reasons, our third possibility seems useless; let us move on to our second approach.

(B) Following modal logicians, we may represent the truth-condition of "S believes that *p*" extensionally by introducing quantification over a domain of possible worlds: roughly,

(4) ⌜N believes that S⌝ is true iff (w)(DOX(w,Den(N), @) ⊃ TRUE-IN(S,w)),

where the right-hand side may be read as "S is true in each world that is one of Den(N)'s doxastic alternatives to this world."[3] The utility of possible-worlds treatments of the propositional attitudes and modalities generally has been amply demonstrated by Hintikka and others (see particularly Hintikka (1969b, 1969c, 1975b)). Wallace (p.

54) brings out a further, interesting motivation for writing truth-conditions in terms of worlds that is specific to the Tarskian program: In writing recursive clauses for the truth-functions, we can get by with only one standard semantical term, "true" itself. But these recursions do not yet allow a finite truth theory for English, since there are still nonfinitely many truth-functionally simple operands for the truth-functions. In order to break into the structures of such operands, Tarski had to introduce a second semantical term, "satisfies." Since (as Wallace puts it) truth-functionally simple sentences are still satisfaction-functionally complex, we are able to obtain a recursion on "satisfies" that will yield a finite theory of truth even for the closed atomic sentences of a first-order language. Now, Wallace points out, the introduction of "satisfies" amounts to a relativization of our original semantical term "true"; its converse, "is satisfied by," is equivalent to "is true *of*," and "truth" *simpliciter* may now be defined in terms of this binary predicate. Wallace sees the introduction of possible worlds as a *second* relativization of this kind, performed for exactly similar reasons:

> [Tarski's] move, in a nutshell, was to relativize the concept of truth. Now, on adding a necessity operator [or other non-truth-functional sentence operator] to the object language, we find that there are [still] an infinite number of closed sentences whose complexity is not [even] satisfaction-functional. . . . It is natural to try to overcome this problem with more of the same relativizing medicine, applied this time to the two argument concept of satisfaction, yielding a three argument one. (p. 54)

Thus, instead of "F is satisfied by x," we shall have "F is satisfied by x at world w." "Truth at" a world may be defined in terms of this ternary predicate, and our belief clause may suitably be written in terms of that notion, as above.[4] (Likewise, "satisfaction" *simpliciter* may be defined if desired.) Thus, the truth-condition as assigned to "S believes that p" may be expressed extensionally, as we had hoped.

But there are obstacles to this third approach as well. First, we must decide whether the SRs underlying belief-sentences are themselves supposed to be complex quantificational formulas containing such predicates as "w_1 is a doxastic alternative to w_2 for S." To suppose this would be quixotic, I think, since it is hard to imagine an independently motivatable sequence of syntactic transformations that would take such a formula *qua* deep structure and realize it at the surface as "S believes that." (I believe George Lakoff did at one point suggest the existence within Generative Semantics of a transformation he called "Possible Worlds Deletion," but I think we may dismiss this as fanciful.) Clearly the possible-worlds theorist would do better to keep syntax simple, by positing only a standard sentence operator in the actual SR and then turning to quantification over worlds only when stating the recursive clause for that operator in the truth definition for our formal canonical idiom (indeed, this is standard practice among Montague Grammarians and other possible-worlds semanticists). Thus, "S believes that p" would be derived straightforwardly from underlying BELIEVE(S,p) and would inherit its assigned truth-condition from that which we have previously assigned in our metalanguage to the latter formula *via* a recursive rule such as the one displayed above.

This procedure is not entirely suited to our purposes. For one thing, as I remarked in our discussion of "empirical bite" in chapter 2, the T-sentences it generates are foully impure. Their right-hand sides are entirely unlike their target sentences in surface grammar and in vocabulary; ordinary English speakers would not even understand them, much less believe them to be true (though in my reply to Stich I have tried to downplay the importance of this). Even among initiates it will frequently not be obvious that the truth-condition assigned is materially adequate.[5] A T-sentence on this approach will be a highly theoretical claim that must be justified along with its containing theory, not an empirical point of contact with the world. This alone is no great sacrifice to make, in view of possible-worlds semantics' compensating achievements, but further difficulties ensue.

A related problem is expressed by Harman (1972b):

> What I find objectionable about these ["shallow SR"] approaches is that the logical forms assigned to sentences are not taken seriously. They are not treated as semantically basic, since they are not used—only referred to—in giving the truth . . . conditions of sentences. Two different logical forms can be associated with an object language sentence, the form it is officially assigned by the theory as well as the form of its translation into the metalanguage. There is unnecessary duplication. Principle (1) functions to avoid that sort of duplication and confine discussion to semantically basic analyses of logical form. (p. 301)

This is obscure, since Harman has not explained his term "semantically basic," but let us try to see what he is getting at. First, what are the "[t]wo different logical forms" he talks about? In the case of "S believes that p," presumably one is the very shallow SR BELIEVE (S,p), and the other is the metalinguistic statement (provable in our formal truth definition for our intensional canonical idiom), "S is true in each world that is one of Den(N)'s doxastic alternatives to this world," which gives the truth-condition for the former and which would count as the former's "translation into the metalanguage." Our truth theory for English would contain the latter but only a name of the former; I assume this is what Harman means in saying that the former (= the first of the two logical forms) is "not used" but "only referred to." And it is the second of the two logical forms that is doing all the work: BELIEVE(S,p) is only a shadow of our target sentence and is truth-conditionally as problematic as that target sentence itself; only our second logical form does anything at all to illuminate the semantics of the target sentence. Thus, it is the second logical form that we are "taking seriously"; the first "logical form" is semantically negligible and hence not really a *logical form* at all. But this puts us back into Russell's position (cf. chapter 1, section 2): a certain formula may "look right" to us as the proposed logical form of a certain target sentence and indeed help in predicting semantical intuitions, but we have no idea what determinate relation it is that makes that formula belong to that target sentence as *its* logical form, and to this extent there is a mystery at the heart of our semantical explanations. According to the Metatheory, the requisite relations are provided by a defensible syntax that connects logical form to surface structure; but here—in the absence of "Possible Worlds Deletion" *et al.*—there is no motivated (or, I suspect, tenable) syntactic derivation of "S believes that p" from "(w)(DOX(w,S,@ $\supset$ TRUE-IN(w,'p'))." In general, when a theory generates T-sentences as impure as those that are characteristically offered by possible-worlds semantics on our present interpretation, we will have no reason to think that any independently defensible syntax connects their right-hand sides (= the logical forms that are *really* being assigned to the target sentences) to the target sentences themselves. This diminishes the robustness of the posited logical forms and also reawakens the suspicion that we are no longer doing linguistic science of any sort, but merely good old analytic philosophy.

I think this complaint can be answered in an interesting way, but the answer I have in mind will take us into matters of psychological reality, so I shall postpone examining it until the next section, and turn instead to a third difficulty for our third approach. It is that few possible-worlds theorists (David Lewis being a beaming exception) take talk of "possible worlds distinct from our own" at face value; usually they regard it as a *façon de parler* for some more cumbersome literal usage, or as a convenient fiction that will someday be replaced by a more literal account.[6] To this extent, possible-worlds accounts of non-truth-functional operators are heuristics rather than finished theories. To put the point in a less pejorative way: what we are offered by a possible-worlds theorist is a "pure" semantics rather than an "applied" semantics; the theorist may succeed in throwing the right target sentences into the intuitively right barrels, but will not even try to tell us, given a particular target sentence, what fact it is in *reality* that would make that sentence true.[7] I shall expand this point, and raise further methodological problems for the practice of stating truth-conditions in terms of possible worlds, in the next section.

Perhaps in light of all the foregoing difficulties it is time to relax our extensionality constraint and consider writing our belief clause in a *non*extensional metalanguage. We could easily translate SRs such as BELIEVE(S,p) into that metalanguage homophonically, just as we translate "p & q" into our usual metalanguage using "&" itself. The latter would be tantamount to accepting Martin's suggestion that we understand troublesome constructions of the target language by translating them into parallel, very similar (and hence equally troublesome) constructions of our metalanguage that we already understand.

We have already seen in chapter 1 that no translational exercise of this sort is likely to secure for us the kind of theoretical understanding of semantical structure that we are seeking; but let us consider the general question of explicating nonextensional operators into nonextensional metalanguages, supposing for example that the surface locution "believes that" does reflect an intensional sentence operator BELIEVES-THAT. Now, how to write a belief clause? We cannot simply ape our original attempt, since the result,

(5)   ⌜N believes that S⌝ is true iff BELIEVES-THAT(Den(N),S),

is ill-formed so long as "S" is a variable ranging over sentences. We might reinterpret "S" here as a schematic letter instead, but this would sacrifice finiteness, since there would be no limit to the stock of possible substituends. Wallace suggests following the standard format for the truth-functions and invoking the truth predicate, as in "⌜~S⌝ is true iff it is not the case that S is true":

(6)   ⌜N believes that S⌝ is true iff BELIEVES-THAT(Den(N),
      S is true).

("S is true" here occupies a sentential complement position.) No other candidate suggests itself.

Wallace offers two objections to this treatment (p. 57). The first is that some instances of the proposed belief clause are false. Some non-English-speakers doubtless believe that truffles are good to eat,

even though these speakers have no beliefs at all about the English
sentence "Truffles are good to eat" because they have never heard
that sentence. The second objection is similar to the one with which I
concluded my case against our final instance of approach (A). I shall
discuss it at a bit more length in hope of making both clearer. Wallace
writes:

> . . . Proofs of T-sentences from a recursive theory of truth . . .
> proceed by repeated replacements, justified by the biconditional
> 'if and only if', within the scope of operators which are intro-
> duced by the recursive clauses. The biconditional of our meta-
> language, as we have understood it so far, is truth-functional,
> and thus does not support replacements within the scope of
> 'Jones believes that'. (p. 57)

Given the already derived T-sentences

(T_1) "Fa" is true iff a is F

and

(T_2) "Ga" is true iff a is G,

along with the ampersand clause

$(\&)$ $\ulcorner S_1 \& S_2 \urcorner$ is true iff S_1 is true and S_2 is true,

we may derive the pure T-sentence

(T_3) "Fa & Ga" is true iff a is F and a is G.

But given just (T_1) and the analogous belief clause

(B) $\ulcorner$N believes that S$\urcorner$ is true iff BELIEVES-THAT(Den(N),
     S is true),

where Den(N) = Jones, we cannot derive

(T_4) "Jones believes that Fa" is true iff Jones believes that
     a is F,

since we cannot substitute on the basis of (T_1) into the right-hand
side of " 'Jones believes that Fa' is true iff Jones believes that 'Fa' is
true," which is the only T-sentence that (B) directly vouchsafes us.[8]

It may sound as though Wallace is just insisting dogmatically that
our truth theory yield pure T-sentences—that (T_4) be derivable or
else any truth-conditional account of "N believes that S" is hopeless.
But we have seen in chapter 2 that no respectable truth theory yields
pure T-sentences in any case; so this demand would be arbitrary and

unreasonable. (The same reply might be made to my concluding objection to the final instance of approach (A).) Once we have accordingly given up the demand, why may we not simply stick with what does follow from belief clause (B) and "Den(N) = Jones" if we charitably construe "S" as occupying a transparent position, viz.,

(T₅)   "Jones believes that Fa" is true iff BELIEVES-THAT (Jones, "Fa" is true),

impure though (T₅) is?

It is important to see that Wallace is not just holding out for purity. (Nor was I.) There are three objections to letting (T₅) stand. First, (T₅)'s right-hand side contains "true" itself. There is no real circularity in that, so long as one is prepared to assume that "true" is there because the concept of truth (*qua* property of sentences) is somehow covertly involved in target-language belief-ascriptions, but that assumption seems dubious at best. The second and more serious objection is that (T₅)'s right-hand side is (as in the case of Albert above) not even a plausible equivalent of the target sentence mentioned on (T₅)'s left-hand side, much less a metaphrase translation of it. Earlier I have accused very impure T-sentences of verging on "good old philosophical analysis"; (T₅) does not meet the demands even of that freewheeling enterprise. Third, as Anil Gupta has suggested to me, it is plausible to require that purity be achieved at least at the level of logical form, i.e., that the result of replacing the target sentence mentioned on the left-hand side of a T-sentence by its SR be provable; and I do not see how " 'BELIEVES-THAT(Jones, "Fa" is true)' is true iff BELIEVES-THAT(Jones, "Fa" is true)" could be derived by Tarskian means.

It may seem that the recursive clauses we write for unproblematic truth-functional connectives do no better. Take (&) above. (&)'s right-hand side is not equivalent to (&)'s target sentence(-schema) either, and for just the same reason: trade-off between material and formal mode. We tolerate inequivalence here; why not in the case of "believes that"?

The answer is that the inequivalence involved in (&) and in (&)'s instances is tolerated because it is only temporary. An instance such as

(7)   "Betty is a philospher and Carl drives a garbage truck" is true iff "Betty is a philosopher" is true and "Carl drives a garbage truck" is true

easily and soon gives way to a proper (if impure) T-sentence, by substitution of "Betty is a philospher" and "Carl drives a garbage truck" into its conjunctive right-hand side on the basis of the already proven T-sentences directed upon those substituends. (&)'s instances are not themselves T-sentences, but only help in the derivation of T-sentences. Likewise, (T_5) is not a T-sentence, and admittedly for a similar reason. The difference is that (T_5) does not even help in the derivation of T-sentences, none being derivable at all; this is what is crucial, and this is what is shown by Wallace's argument.

It seems to me there is a third problem for the attempt to write truth-conditions in nonextensional metalanguages, as well. To say that a T-sentence for a belief-ascription or for any other construction is *nonextensional* is to say that not every term occurring in that T-sentence allows substitution of a coreferring term; in particular, any singular-term position within the scope of the intensional belief operator that will occur on the right-hand side will be referentially opaque. But, I contend, referential opacity must be taken as a sign of hidden semantical structure. As is well known and much agonized over, if an apparent singular term were really a genuine or logically proper name, functioning *solely* to denote what it denotes, then any other genuine name of the same denotatum could be substituted for it *salva veritate* and indeed *salva propositione*; the position it occupies would be referentially transparent. Therefore, when an apparent singular term occupies a position that is not transparent but opaque, that term is making some semantical contribution to the truth-condition of its containing sentence over and above merely denoting what it denotes, and this contribution distinguishes it from other apparent singular terms that have the same denotatum. A T-sentence that contains an opaque position, then, is not fully explicit; its right-hand side does not wear its truth-conditional structure on its sleeve, but admits of and demands further analysis that would reveal the exact semantical contribution that is being made by an apparent singular term occurring opaquely.[9] The moral is that a theory that assigns nonextensional truth-conditions to belief-sentences does not, in Harman's phrase, take those truth-conditions seriously as final, full, and explicit analyses of the target sentences to which they have been assigned.

I think this objection provides sufficient motivation to make us turn back to our search for an adequate extensional way of writing our belief clause. But our only promising extensional candidate so far has been our explicit possible-worlds approach, (B), and that approach was seen to be problematic (more difficulties will be brought to light in the next section). Let us make one further try, and explore a suggestion based on Wilfrid Sellars's theory of indirect discourse.

Sellars treats the non-truth-functional sentence operators such as "x means that" and "S believes that" as metalinguistic;[10] thus, he is an inscriptionalist of sorts, but not a crude one. For S to believe that broccoli is awful, according to Sellars, is for S to believe-true or accept some ·Broccoli is awful· or other. The dot quotes in this last phrase are NP-forming operators that can apply to any linguistic expression, the result being a common noun whose extension includes the expression quoted and any other expression that plays the same linguistic role. (Thus, "Broccoli is awful" is a ·Broccoli is awful·; "Der Spargelkohl ist schrecklich" is also a ·Broccoli is awful·, as is "Le brocoli est terrible." Of course, one needs an account of the conditions under which an expression "plays the same linguistic role as" another: Sellars has his own theory of this; others may prefer a different one. My own view, defended in a series of papers on belief (chiefly (1981b, 1981c)), is that at least two quite distinct individuative schemes are used in English to classify content clauses, and that belief-ascriptions are for that reason pragmatically ambiguous, in a way that is (I contend) responsible for such anomalies as "Kripke's puzzle."

The sentence that appears between the dot quotes (and hence, on Sellars's view, the complement of our original target belief-sentence) is not being used assertively or even with its usual semantic content, but functions solely as a displayed example of the linguistic role in question; thus, Sellars's theory avoids the most obvious objection to crude inscriptionalism—it does not entail that one who believes that broccoli is awful must be acquainted with the English sentence "Broccoli is awful." Such a believer may be related to *any* sentence that plays the same role, even a sentence of his own "language of thought."

Since "believe" on this view is an extensional two-place predicate, we obtain the following extensional belief clause:

(8)   ⌜N believes that S⌝ is true iff $(\exists x)(\text{BELIEVE}(\text{Den}(N),x)\ \&\ \text{Sat}(\ulcorner \cdot S \cdot \urcorner, x))$.

The occurrence of a metalinguistic variable between dot quotes is entirely proper; "⌜·S·⌝" in our belief clause may be read as "the result of concatenating a dot open-quote with S and then concatenating the whole with a dot close-quote." ("Sat," of course, is read as "is satisfied by.")

So far we have provided only for belief-ascriptions *de dicto*. In order to handle belief *de re* we should provide transparent argument-places for possible objects of "relational" belief:

(9) $\ulcorner$N believes that F$(\ldots s\ldots)$$\urcorner$ is true iff $(\exists x)$(BELIEVE(Den(N),
      x,s) & Sat($\ulcorner$·F·$\urcorner$,x)).

BELIEVE now expresses a relation between a person, a predicate, and a sequence, and the dot quotes now apply to the predicate rather than necessarily to the target complement sentence as a whole. Belief *de dicto* may now be construed as the limiting case in which the sequence *s* is null and the "predicate" F is 0-adic, i.e., a closed sentence.

There is no threat of nonfiniteness, since the displayed sentences or predicates that occur inside our dot quotes are built up compositionally out of the standard vocabulary of our object language, even though they do not have their usual semantical functions. We also bypass Wallace's second objection concerning the derivation of non-metalinguistic T-sentences; we obtain " 'Jones believes that Fa' is true iff Jones believes some ·*a* is F·" without having to pass through a step whose right-hand side contains an occurrence of " '*a* is F' is true."[11] And the T-sentences that emerge are relatively pure, since the vocabulary in which they are stated is quite close to that which figures in the target sentences; it will be fairly easy to find a syntactic history that turns dot quotes, which are themselves a kind of demonstrative, into the surface *that*. No doubt there are plenty of bugs in this Sellarsian approach; but for now it seems to have overcome all the obstacles that faced previous approaches to the problem of writing our belief clause, and thus to be the strongest contender for our purposes to date.[12]

Before concluding, I want to expand a little on the reason why I think it unwise to rest content with stating truth-conditions in terms of possible worlds.

2. Possible Worlds and Psychological Reality

Consider a simple possible-worlds analysis of (appropriately enough) a statement of possibility. Let us take the following impure T-sentence as a test case:

(J)   "It is possible that John's cat is a Martian" is true iff there is a world *w* [accessible in such-and-such a way from @] such that "John's cat is a Martian" is true in [or "at"] *w*.

The first thing to note about (J) is that (J) cannot very well be interpreted literally—or at least, the quantifier-like phrase "there is" cannot be understood as being a genuine objectual existential quantifier. For if "there is" were interpreted in this way, (J)'s right-hand side would be understood as asserting that there *really exists* a world in which John's cat is a Martian; and since only one world (ours, @) really exists, this would be tantamount to asserting that John's cat really is a Martian, which is plainly not an implication of (J)'s target sentence. This point is just a special case of a simpler and more general one: that when I say "There are possible worlds that are not actual," or "There are things that don't exist," my phrase "there are" would produce an explicit self-contradiction—$(\exists x)\sim(\exists y)(y = x)$—if it were interpreted as being a genuine standard existential quantifier. So the first point to be made about (J) is that we do not know what it means; we have not yet been told how the phrase "there is" is being used, though we know it cannot be being used in its standard sense.

Many philosophers have suggested ways of reinterpreting the Meinongian quantifier; recently, in fact, dozens of interestingly distinct proposals have been offered, of surprisingly various types. I have surveyed them and discussed them at length in Lycan (1979b).

Each type of proposal is subject to its own highly distinctive set of limitations and drawbacks. Typically these limitations are not fatal, but they put definite and strong constraints on what kind(s) of modal or intensional apparatus one's system of "possible worlds," on the proposed interpretation, will support.

Let me give just one example. Some philosophers, including Saul Kripke himself (1971, pp. 147–48), suggest that "possible-worlds" talk is just a fancy form of *counterfactual* talk. That is, they say, (J)'s right-hand side should be understood as being a mere *façon de parler* for something like, "If things had been otherwise, John's cat might have been a Martian." In itself, this proposal is plausible enough, but it would be entirely inadequate for our purposes, for four reasons: (a) On this view, our semanticist who writes T-sentences such as (J) would be vindicating Harman's contention that possible-worlds theorists do not take their own analyses seriously. For (J)'s right-hand side would not be treated as giving the basic or fundamental truth-condition of its target sentence, but would *ex hypothesi* be subject to further analysis (in terms of counterfactuals). (b) Kripke's proposal would prevent us from using possible worlds to formulate an analysis or explication of counterfactuals themselves, since an analysis of counterfactuals in terms of counterfactuals would be circular. And this is a serious limitation, since the only type of analysis of counterfactuals that has ever provided much illumination is a possible-worlds analysis. (c) Even if quantification over possible worlds could be paraphrased away in counterfactual terms, *set ab-*

straction on worlds would be left intuitively undefined—no counterfactual paraphrase suggests itself. And it is hard to imagine a rigorous formal semantics' proceeding without set abstraction or something relevantly similar. (d) Counterfactuals are referentially opaque. Even if the possible-worlds theorist were to restate the right-hand sides of his T-sentences counterfactually, they would still demand further analysis to account for the opacity.

In choosing a particular understanding of the Meinongian quantifier as applied to worlds, we weave a tangled web. When we accept a semantical program whose goal is to generate T-sentences like (J), we buy into unknown drawbacks and constraints of the sort just illustrated. This is not to say that some explication of the Meinongian quantifier may not be devised that affords a relatively unproblematic interpretation of (J);[13] it is only to point out that there is nothing *obviously* unproblematic about truth-conditions written in terms of possible worlds. But more specific difficulties await us.

Our original exposition in chapter 1 of the relation between meaning and truth would lead us to expect that the truth-condition assigned to a target sentence by an adequate semantics will usually (though not invariably) coincide with what D. M. Armstrong calls the sentence's truth-*maker*.[14] As we have noted, it is natural to think that, for any true sentence, there is a fact in the world, involving constituents of any of a number of general types, *in virtue of which* the sentence is true. Thus, "There is a typewriter in front of me" is true in virtue of there (actually) being a typewriter in front of me; that fact is its truth-maker, and we may reasonably expect a semantics also to predict that that fact is its truth-condition—i.e., that it is the fact we should use, following Tarski, in computing that sentence's pattern of implications and other semantical properties. To take a slightly more interesting example, "John buttered the toast in the bathroom with a knife" is assigned (by Davidson (1967a)) the usual sort of truth-condition having to do with the occurrence of a certain kind of event, and the occurrence of that kind of event is presumably also the foregoing sentence's truth-maker.

The problem this creates for possible-worlds semantics is that such semantics cannot very often allow truth-conditions to coincide with truth-makers. Any sentence containing any nonextensional element whatever will be assigned a truth-condition that mentions "nonactual" objects or worlds, and such a truth-condition will not be a fact of *this* world and hence cannot be whatever it is in this world that makes the target sentence true. Take "John believes that his cat is a Martian." The possible-worlds-style truth-condition for this will be stated as something like, "For any world w that is a doxastic alternative of John's to @, in *w* John's cat is a Martian." By contrast, the truth-*maker* will be John's being in some psychologically characterized inner state in whose etiology his cat distinctively figures. Or take "If I were to hit this vase with a hammer, it would break." The truth-condition assigned to that sentence by a possible-worlds theorist such as Lewis (1973) goes, "Some world in which I hit this vase with a hammer and it breaks is 'closer to' @ than is any world in which I hit this vase with a hammer and it does not break." But the sentence's truth-*maker* is the vase's having, in this world, a brittle sort of structure.

I am not sure how serious a criticism this is. One might reply that there is no particular reason to expect that truth-conditions will normally coincide with truth-makers; perhaps the two notions are simply distinct, and not even very closely related. (Anyone who has paid close critical attention to "The Philosophy of Logical Atomism" knows how to distinguish the *ordo essendi* from the *ordo veritatis*.) It might also be pointed out that once we have separated the two notions in this way, the notion of a "truth-maker" is seen to be quite unclear, since it is a crude intuitive notion and has no established home in any developed and articulate theory.

Actually, I think the separation impugns the notion of a truth-condition about as badly as it does that of a truth-maker, though in a different respect. Our original intuitive motivation for the Davidsonian idea that a truth definition captures at least what philosophers have called "cognitive" or locutionary content was based on the suggestion that sentences are true in virtue of facts in the world to which they combinatorially correspond. But this suggestion assimilates Davidsonian truth-conditions to truth-makers, and assumes that the two are more or less one. If we give up the latter assumption and allow truth-conditions to diverge wildly from truth-makers, we will have lost at least this original motivation for thinking that truth-conditions have something closely to do with meaning and other semantic phenomena, though of course we will still have truth-conditions' connection with inference-patterns as a motivation for thinking that.

Whether or not the separation of truth-conditions from truth-makers is felt to be a serious objection to possible-worlds semantics, I think the general thrust of the criticism is important. This general thrust is that appeal to "nonactual worlds" is *antinaturalistic*. Let me explain this a bit more.

It is attractive to think (and many philosophers simply, if uncritically, assume) that the universe consists of a single, unified, and connected causal and spatiotemporal order—"the natural order," as it is sometimes called. At the very least, if a putative thing had no causal powers of any kind, we could never have any reason for thinking that the thing existed, for it would not then be able to bring itself to our attention in any even indirect way. On this ground, it is plausible to insist that no genuine *explanation* of a natural phenomenon need involve the positing of entities that cannot in principle be connected to us by some causal chains (however irregular) or other.[15] This is not to say that causally ineffectual "things" cannot be introduced into discourse for some purposes—they may be useful fictions that facilitate calculation, for example. If the possible-worlds semanticist is interested only in calculation, I have no quarrel with him; my point here is only that if the naturalistic picture of the universe is the right picture, then no one who claims to explain natural phenomena, such as people's verbal behavior, can make essential and unreduced or unexplicated appeal to "nonactual worlds," for mere possibilia have no causal powers *vis-à-vis* our world and are not part of the natural order.[16]

A reply is available to the possible-worlds enthusiast, one that deserves thorough methodological examination. Naturalism in the form I have stated it is a very strong constraint on ontology, truistic as it may seem to Quine, Sellars, Smart, Armstrong, and others. For example, we make ineliminable use in the "hard" sciences of such things as numbers and sets, which are not, or not ostensibly, part of the natural order and do not seem to have any casual powers. So it seems physicists and chemists are just as "antinaturalistic" as are possible-worlds semanticists, and we do not even think of holding that against them.

I have just one rejoinder to make against this argument, not a conclusive one. A linguist who views semantics not as a branch of mathematics but as a branch of psychology understands his semantical theory of a natural language as being a (perhaps the) crucial component of an explanation of speakers' verbal behavior. (And the ordinary notion of "meaning," for what that is worth, is certainly a psychological notion.) On this view, a semantics for Johann's language explains (in part) why and how Johann produces the utterances he does in situations of various kinds. If we make such a claim to "psychological reality," we presumably are thinking of our semantics as a functional diagram of a *mechanism* functioning within Johann; our explanations are functional explanations, and functional explanations presuppose a causal underpinning. So it is not just naturalistic prejudice that should make us view unexplicated use of "possible worlds" with suspicion. The semanticist *qua* psychologist owes us an account of how *merely possible worlds* considered as entities could figure in a mechanical or functional explanation of a living, breathing human's flesh-and-blood actions—of how mere possibilia that are causally unconnected to a real person can play a role in moving that person's mouth and hand. Because it seems that they could not. That is, it seems that the semanticist's "worlds" must be a *façon de parler* or a metaphor of some kind, used perhaps heuristically to "index" belief states, not components of an actual psychological mechanism; this is suggested by Stalnaker (1979b) (and cf. Lewis (1983, n.2)). (Remember that whether *the speaker*—or any person that the speaker is speaking about—envisions or believes in possible worlds as entities is not relevant and not in question. Perhaps the speaker does, and this fact will enter into a genuine psychological account of his behavior. But the possible-worlds talk that interests us here is in *the theorist's* mouth.)

There is a further naturalistic point to be made. One crucial advantage of working within a totally extensional metalanguage is that the semantical primitives associated with Tarskian truth theory (viz., "denotes" and "satisfies") can fairly easily be accommodated within the natural order, thanks to causal and/or teleological theories of referring; such theories have made it possible to view denoting and satisfaction as real relations *in nature,* namely, causal chains of certain complex kinds.[17] This in turn makes it possible to see semantical theories as genuine theories of certain chunks of nature (those chunks that look and act like human beings). Now, (J) and its fellows refer or "refer" to mere possibilia. But it is not possible, even in principle, to view *this* semantical relation as a real relation in nature, for mere possibilia are not part of nature and cannot interact causally with us at all. Thus, the possible-worlds semanticist's theoretical primitives remain forever cut off from the natural order, and this makes it doubly hard to see how possible-worlds theory can be part of real psychology.

None of the foregoing is meant to suggest that linguists should stop doing possible-worlds semantics, or that possible-worlds semantics is not enormously useful and suggestive, or that a possible-worlds theory may not achieve mathematical adequacy as a "pure" semantics in the way that Montague and others have intended. What I do mean to contend is that anyone who states truth-conditions in terms of possible worlds must be very cautious in characterizing that enterprise, particularly as it relates to the explanation of verbal behavior.

Let us finally return to the problem raised in the previous section concerning the nature of the relation between an English sentence and "its" logical form.[18] Having observed that the T-sentences generated by a possible-worlds semantics are very far from pure, I concluded that it is unreasonable to expect there to be a plausible syntactic history connecting an SR written in possible-worlds jargon to the English target sentence to which it is being assigned. This was felt to leave a gap or a mystery in the semantical explanations thus obtained.

Some possible-worlds theorists offering semantics for (parts of) English have not claimed or intended to display syntax at all.[19] But it should be noted that Montague Grammarians, at least, do interest themselves in syntax and do foresee a characterization of well-formedness along the lines of Montague's "PTQ" (1973) or some extension of it. Montague's phrase structure grammar for English is augmented by a set of translation rules that map English sentences into formulas of an intensional logic; the grammatical structure of the latter formulas is of course given by the logic's own formation-rules. The semantics assigns a possible-worlds-style interpretation to each syntactically primitive lexical item in the intensional logic; truth-conditions for complex formulae are determined compositionally within the logic and then (as usual) forced up through the translation rules and the English grammar to the English surface structures that are translated. So it would be false to suggest that the method of "PTQ" leaves target sentences totally unconnected to the possible-worlds-theoretic formulas that ultimately state their truth-conditions.

But one need not make that suggestion in pressing our difficulty, for the difficulty can be (and was) raised at the level of lexical primitives. Consider again "S believes that p," and suppose that this sentence translates into a very similar formula of the underlying intensional logic, such as "BELIEVE(S,p)," BELIEVE here being a lexical primitive of such-and-such a grammatical category. If BELIEVE is lexically primitive, then a sentence of the form "BELIEVE(S,p)" does not undergo syntactic decomposition (except within its complement); therefore, the relevant base clause for BELIEVE in our possible-worlds-style truth definition assigns a truth-condition to "BELIEVE(S,p)" directly, without any syntactic mediation. Let us suppose the truth-condition is, as before, "(w)(DOX(w,S,@) $\supset$ TRUE-IN(w,$'p'$))."[20] The syntax of "PTQ" is mute on the question of the relation between "BELIEVE(S,p)" and the formula that is "its" (real) logical form. Our Russellian gap remains.[21]

But is there any reason, other than doctrinaire adherence to the letter of the Metatheory, for demanding that the "determinate relation" between target sentence and logical form be one of syntactic derivation? It is open to the possible-worlds theorist to maintain that the relation is instead semantic. In fact, the theorist might say, the relation is simply and precisely that the logical form *is an explicit statement of the target sentence's truth-condition;* is that not "determinate relation" enough? The *evidence* that "(w)(DOX(w,S,@) ⊃ TRUE-IN(w,'*p*')) states "BELIEVES(S,*p*)" 's truth-condition is that by assuming so in the context of our semantics overall, we are able to predict semantical intuitions accurately and by finite means. Now, further, in assigning that truth-condition to "BELIEVE(S,*p*)," the theorist is doing *lexical* semantics, i.e., investigating word meaning. Therefore, if we or the Metatheorist should press further and demand to know why, or in virtue of what, "BELIEVE(S,*p*)" has that truth-condition, we would be asking in effect why or in virtue of what a word means what (by hypothesis) it does mean, and the answer to *that* question can only be an appeal to convention. "BELIEVE(S,*p*)" has that truth-condition, the theorist can say, because that is the meaning our forebears have given "BELIEVE"; that is all there is to it.

Notice that in taking this line the possible-worlds theorist has given up the Metatheorist's idea that a target sentence can be connected *via* syntax to the formula (of a logically perfect language) that precisely expresses that sentence's truth-condition. But the failure of Generative Semantics and subsequent programs to establish any such connections encourages the suspicion that that ambitious idea cannot be fulfilled in any case. Waving this question, I see nothing particularly wrong with the response I have sketched. But at this point psychology rears its head once more.

If "(w)(DOX(w,S,@) ⊃ TRUE-IN(w,'*p*'))" states "BELIEVE(S,*p*)" 's truth-condition in the *ultimate* way I have described (and if "BELIEVE(S,*p*)" is the intensional formula that translates the English "*S* believes that *p*"), then presumably that truth-condition is all there is to the locutionary meaning or propositional content of "*S* believes that *p*"; a token of "*S* believes that *p*" merely serves to express that very content, nothing more. But then in order for an English speaker to come to *know* that an instance of "*S* believes that *p*" is true, the speaker must compute and verify that instance's truth-condition, for by hypothesis there is nothing to its propositional content over and above its expressing that truth-condition. Now, we English speakers frequently know things about other people's beliefs, and so we frequently know instances of "*S* believes that *p*" to be true. Do we in fact do this by verifying formulas of the form "(w)(DOX(w,S,@) ⊃ TRUE-IN(w,'*p*'))"? How could this be? We cannot survey and examine each of nondenumerably many worlds (the cardinalities involved here being beyond even the mathematician's imagination), even if clear sense had been given to the notion of a human being's "examining" a world distinct from that which he inhabits. We cannot even survey and examine all the worlds that are S's doxastic alternatives to this world @, since this subclass is nondenumerable also.

By themselves these observations are not particularly damaging, for our knowledge of mathematical generalizations is almost equally puzzling; how does a human being "survey and examine" all the real numbers to determine whether every one of them that is F is also G? (I say *almost* equally puzzling because at least in mathematics there are prevalent proof strategies that obviate the need for any routine search procedures. The most obvious of these is proof by *reductio*. *Reductio* has no counterpart in possible-worlds semantics for belief-sentences; we do not establish an instance of $"(w)(DOX(w,S,@) \supset TRUE\text{-}IN(w,'p'))"$ by supposing that there is a doxastic alternative of @ for S in which the complement sentence is false and then deducing a contradiction.) The real problem is that in order to verify our possible-worlds formula we must have some direct or indirect way of telling which worlds are S's doxastic alternatives to this world @. The most obvious way of starting to tell this would be to find out what S believes, since the notion of a "doxastic alternative" is usually explained informally as that of a world compatible with what S believes, but this will not do for our purposes, for we are sworn to find out what S believes by first computing our truth-condition over the set of S's doxastic alternatives. No other way comes to mind; and so I do not see how our truth-condition can be "ultimate" in the way that our reply to the previous objection maintains.[22]

Notes

Introduction

1. His contribution to *the* theory of meaning *tout court* is what he presents in (1967b) and elsewhere; he conceives of "the theory of meaning" as being part of the philosophy of linguistics and hence part of the philosophy of science, so he assumes that his job is to provide the linguist with the beginnings of a coherent, sound, and productive methodology for semantics. As Platts observes (1979, p. 57), what is novel in Davidson's work is not the notion of truth-theoretic semantics *per se*, which goes back at least as far as the *Begriffschrift* and the *Tractatus*, but the idea that truth definitions can be provided for natural languages by empirical means and subject to empirical test.
2. Stephen Schiffer suggested this way of putting it, in conversation.

Chapter 1

1. Ontological commitments form an important subclass of such implications. Typically the canonical language will contain a formally specified stock of quantifiers and referring expressions; thus, the assignment of a particular SR to a target sentence shows us roughly which of the surface expressions contained in that sentence are understood as being syncategorematic and which (if any) are real referring terms.
2. I have always wondered about this plural. Why would a single sentence be said to have a "*set* of truth-conditions," unless it is ambiguous and must be assigned a truth-condition for each reading? I shall reserve the plural form hereafter for sentences that are ambiguous.
3. Richard Grandy has noted (1974 and in correspondence) that logical form in the Davidsonian sense is relative to one's choice of a logical theory for one's metalanguage. Thus, *if* logical form is a matter of fact to be discovered by linguistic semantics, the choice of an underlying logic is no trivial matter, and Harman's principle (2) must be neither wielded dogmatically nor flouted lightly. How is the choice to be guided? We try to mediate between the demands of semantic data and the claims of syntactic plausibility; ultimately, if all goes well, an underlying logic will be hit upon that affords an optimal fit. A further constraint is that formulas of the metalanguage must wear their truth-conditions on their sleeves (see chapter 3, note 19, and the Appendix).
4. For examination and defense of the notion of "robustness," see Wimsatt (1981).
5. Throughout its heyday, the term "Generative Semantics" was often taken to indicate acceptance of some syntactically substantive theses as well as methodological and metatheoretical views—for example, that morphemes of most of the different surface-grammatical categories, such as adjectives, derived nominals, prepositions, and most subordinating conjunctions, are underlying verbs (no surprise,

since a "verb" in underlying structure is a predicate, and predicates are by far the most prevalent type of expression in formulas of formal logic); that SRs contain no intensional operators; that lexical decomposition occurs (i.e., that lexical insertion can destroy syntactic structure); that lexical insertion takes place after transformations have already been applied to underlying SRs, so that there is no such thing as "deep structure" in the full sense that Chomsky originally intended; and that Ross's "Performative Analysis" is correct (much more on this later). As I understand the Metatheory, none of these claims is essential to it or even suggested by it.

6. Montague (1974), Cresswell (1973), Stalnaker and Thomason (1973), Dowty (1979), Partee (1973b, 1975), and many more.

7. Dowty points out that there is a distressingly lush proliferation of variations on Generative Semantics and Montague Grammar considered as instances of Universal Grammar and that it may be almost impossible to find grounds for choosing ultimately between them. (One might add that in general, each is particularly good at doing one thing, such as handling quantification or hyperintensionality or affording neat syntax in certain areas, but terrible at doing the things the others do well.) This fact may encourage fears (or hopes) of indeterminacy.

8. It is tempting to regard Montague Grammar and Generative Semantics as notational variants, once the latter has been stripped of the inessential features mentioned in note 5 and of any fancied commitment to extensional logic. There is an issue of directionality of transformations (Zwicky (1972); and see Dowty's comments (pp. 27ff.)); indeed, the view that transformations are better seen as "semantic interpretation" rules than as generative devices is closely associated with the decline of the word "transformation." But at our level of abstraction, the question of directionality has only heuristic significance.

9. Someone might suggest that we take Convention T itself as an axiom schema for our theory. But such a schema would have nonfinitely many instances (one for each target sentence) and would neither contain nor need any recursive element. It is a mystery how all these instances could be learned, even though they are indeed schematized by Convention T (see chapter 2). Nor, obviously, would our schematic theory offer any insight into the ways in which the meanings of complex sentences depend on those of their parts.

Some philosophers have occasionally doubted the probity of the idea that speakers have "infinite competence" or a "potential infinity of output." It is important to see that the Chomsky-Davidson-style argument does not really depend on the notion of nonfiniteness. Recursion in each case is virtually demanded by the fact that speakers can understand extremely long and *novel* sentences almost instantaneously at first hearing. How would a behaviorist who held that linguistic competence is acquired piecemeal through conditioning account for a hearer's immediate grasp of such a sentence as the following?

> He pulled at his lip and watched Peggy teaching Dinah to play the strange and sinister girl-children's game of the marshes, which looked like an elaborate version of mud-pies but was in fact a ritual to prevent the ghosts of one's eventual husband's female ancestors from sucking one's spirit away when one slept in the corner of his hut where once they too had slept. (Peter Dickinson, *The Poison Oracle* (Pantheon Books, 1974), p. 155)

10. Platts ((1979, p. 56); cf. McDowell (1976)) sees circularity here; "translation" in "translation of s into the metalanguage" has to mean *correct*, i.e., *meaning-preserving* translation; if the notion of a T-sentence presupposes that of sameness

of meaning, it can hardly be a substantive theoretical discovery or hypothesis that a theory whose job is to spit out T-sentences can serve as a theory of meaning. (Following McDowell, Platts sketches (p. 62) a characterization of "theories of meaning" in terms of the interaction of meaning with propositional attitudes that could independently be *found* to be satisfactorily instantiable by theories of truth.) I do not see this apparent circularity as vicious, for two reasons: (i) T-sentences are points of empirical contact in more ways than one. Speakers' intuitive judgments of sameness of meaning are among our data, and accordingly T-sentences in the strong "translation" sense may be counted as data even when we acknowledge explicitly that sameness of meaning is presupposed; so the rhetorical question would remain, of what over and above a truth theory is needed to account for those data. (ii) We shall find ample reason in chapters 2 and 3 for abandoning the "translation" requirement in any case and attenuating our notion of a "T-sentence" in a regrettable but unavoidable way.

11. There is some question whether a theory that states its truth-conditions in terms of possible worlds should be taken to meet the spirit of Davidson's requirements; this is taken up in the Appendix.

12. Notice: it is crucial that the translator provide his derivation. Davidson is not simply reading "is true iff" as "means that" (as he was once tempted to do), transforming the theory of truth into a theory of meaning by executive fiat. It is the *whole* truth theory that tells us what individual sentences mean.

> [What] we can learn from a theory of truth about the meaning of a particular sentence is [not] contained in the biconditional demanded by Convention T. . . . [I]t is brought out rather in the *proof* of such a biconditional, for the proof must demonstrate, step by step, how the truth-value of the sentence depends upon a recursively given structure. (1970, p. 22)

The meaning of a sentence, then, is determined not merely by that sentence's truth-condition, but by the way in which that truth-condition fits together with those of other sentences in a systematic theory. Some objections to Davidson's program seem plausible only when one ignores this fact, e.g., the objection that Davidson has no way of making his theory of English pair a particular sentence, rather than any other sentence having the same truth-value, with its own quote-name. Why will a Davidsonian theory entail " 'Snow is white' is true iff snow is white," rather than " 'Snow is white' is true iff grass is green"? The answer is that we cannot see how the latter biconditional, though true, could fit into a simple and systematic recursive truth definition for the language as a whole. Reeves (1974) offers the more trenchant example of a permutation based on a pair of coextending predicates: Why will a Davidsonian theory entail " 'John is cordate' is true iff John is cordate" rather than " 'John is cordate' is true iff John is renate"? A quick answer is that despite their sameness of extension, "cordate" and "renate" make different contributions to some contexts in which they can appear, such as modal, counterfactual, and propositional-attitude environments; thus, a truth theory must distinguish them somehow, either by positing a hidden reference-shifting operator inside intensional constructions, by relativizing predicates' extensions to possible worlds, or in some other special way. Granted, it is hard to imagine any such expedient that does not involve serious technical and philosophical difficulties; I discuss some of these in the Appendix. Note that the Metatheory is not itself committed to extensionalism of any sort.

13. Actually, there is one peculiar type of construction that seems to stand in the way; I have called attention to it in Lycan (1979a). But it is an oddity that need not detain us here.

14. In (1970, pp. 21–22), (1967b, pp. 456–57), (1973a, pp. 84–85).

15. Some theorists incline toward the view that logical forms for a language are written in that language or in a somewhat more formal idiom specific to it. Harman himself takes this line (1973a, 1973b), against those who regard underlying structures as being written in a neutral formal language, such as the one that McCawley (1972a) calls "Logos," and who assume universal semantic representation.

16. I feel considerable ambivalence as to just how fortuitous such a coincidence would be. On the one hand, "logical form" and "deep structure" are highly technical terms of respectively very different theories designed to perform entirely different tasks (the former to solve logical puzzles, the latter to figure in a formal axiomatization of the predicate "grammatical"); so their coincidence would come as quite a shock, however pleasant, and would need to be argued very powerfully. On the other hand, it would be almost as surprising if syntax and semantics were totally separate in their mechanisms, since it seems absurd to suppose that syntactic structure is not a key factor in determining how the meanings of complex expressions depend on those of their parts.

  The Metatheorists' distinctive emphasis on fitting semantics together with syntax is due primarily to Harman; Davidson himself has shown little interest in this aspect of the program.

17. Perhaps Russell had at least one sort of metaphysical ground in mind, since he sometimes spoke of *abbreviation* in this regard (e.g., he sometimes expressed his theory of proper names by saying that (logically improper) names "abbreviate descriptions"). This is psychologically very implausible when taken in full generality, but insofar as a process of abbreviation is one possible type of syntactic transformation, Russell was perhaps anticipating Harman's main contribution to the Metatheory. (On the abbreviation of descriptions, see Lycan (1984a).)

  It is time to acknowledge a common neologism. Current writers sometimes speak as if "logical forms" are *formulas* of our canonical idiom; an SR correctly assigned to a sentence would be that sentence's "logical form." Originally a sentence's logical form was an abstraction—a kind of form or structure it had that contrasted with its surface-grammatical form. In this original sense, an SR correctly assigned to a sentence would merely *share* that sentence's logical form (though its own surface-grammatical form would coincide with the logical form in question). I shall try to stick to the original sense hereafter, but little harm will be done if we occasionally fall into the standard equivocation.

18. Davidson concedes, perhaps too hastily, that "[t]he ideal of a theory of truth for a natural language in a natural language is unattainable," but he adds,

  > The question then arises, how to give up as little as possible, and here theories allowed by Convention T seem in important respects optimal. . . . It is only the truth predicate itself (and the satisfaction predicate) that cannot be in the object language. (1973, p. 82)

19. See also van Fraassen (1970) and some of the other papers in Martin (1970). Further reason is perhaps provided by Richard Routley's recent work on inconsistent but "paraconsistent" theories ((1980, p. 294); cf. Routley (1979) and Arruda (1979)).

Chapter 2

1. It should be easy to see how even an absurdly simple truth theory, such as the following, already yields an infinity of T-sentences.

Base clauses
Den('a') = Van.
Den('b') = Wilfrid.
Den('c') = Roderick.
⌜Fn⌝ is true for any name *n* iff Den(*n*) is a philosopher.
⌜Gn⌝ is true for any name *n* iff Den(*n*) is a poet.
Recursive clauses
⌜∼S⌝ is true for any sentence S iff S is not true.
⌜S₁ & S₂⌝ is true for any sentences S₁ and S₂ iff S₁ is true and S₂ is true.

2. For example, see Nolt (1977). This suggestion bears a number of possible implementations. The most obvious of these is (again) to take Convention T itself as an axiom schema; each T-sentence would then be provable by virtue of being an axiom. But obviously this, unassisted, would violate Davidson's finiteness constraint.

3. That the notion of "tacit knowledge" or otherwise nonoccurrent belief is a vexed one, I willingly if sorrowfully admit; see Lycan (1985).

4. This criticism was first called to my attention by John Nolt and Steven Humphrey. Stich has noticed it also (1976); his terms "T-sentence" and "T*-sentence" parallel my terms "pure T-sentence" and "impure T-sentence," and he distinguishes appropriately between Davidson's *"advertised* truth theories" and Davidson's *"delivered* truth theories." (See also Tennant (1977).)

Harman (in correspondence) has made an ingenious reply to this criticism (I develop it here at some risk of distorting his intention): Consider an impure T-sentence such as " 'John walked in the street' is true iff there is an event *e* such that *e* is a walking and . . . ," and suppose that this T-sentence does in fact correctly capture its target sentence's logical form. Suppose also that our canonical metalanguage contains enough of our target language (English) that we can grammatically form the biconditional (M) "John walked in the street iff there is an event *e* such that *e* is a walking and. . . ." Given that our theory of the sentence "John walked in the street" is correct, it seems to follow that (M) is a *logical truth* of our metalanguage. Now, our earlier impure T-sentence when conjoined with (M) yields the pure T-sentence we are seeking (" 'John walked in the street' is true iff John walked in the street"), by transitivity of the biconditional; thus, if (M) is a logical truth, our impure T-sentence alone entails its pure counterpart after all, and Davidson's theory of action sentences does have the "empirical bite" he claims for it.

My objection to this move is to note that the sense in which it shows Davidson's theory to be testable is a weaker sense than that in which as philosophers of science we want to require that theories be testable. Of course we want theories to entail observation sentences, and Harman has shown that *if Davidson's theory is true* it entails the relevant observation (T-)sentences. But the reason we want theories to entail observation sentences is that we want to be able to *derive* the observation sentences from the theory and then look to see whether they are true. We want theories to be "testable" in the bare sense of entailing observation sentences because we want actually to test them. So it is not enough that a theory entail observation sentences; the observation sentences must be derivable from the theory in what is for us an independently reliable way. This feature is just what is lacking in the foregoing account. For even if (M) is in fact a logical truth of our metalanguage, we could not know that it was, or even know that it was true, without either already knowing that the theory we are testing is true or already having performed some Davidsonian truth-theorizing on our metalanguage (supposing still that the metalanguage contains expressions of ordinary English such as "walked" as well as their technical counterparts such as "is a walking"); so we could not derive our pure T-sentence from Davidson's theory of action sentences unless we had already done (and justified) the relevant truth-theorizing.

5. It would also account for my feeling that Harman's criticism of possible-worlds semantics (1972b, sec. 7) has some merit, since the truth-conditions provided by a semantics based on a lush intensional logic are far less "pure" than—i.e., are far more different in superficial structure from their target sentences than—are those provided by a relatively extensional theory couched in a more conservative logic. What Harman's criticism would come to, then, is that the possible-worlds semantics is less testable than the more conservative theory would be, for what that is worth. Much more is said on this in the Appendix.

6. I see no reason, either empirical or a priori, for thinking that Davidson's "Kicked," "At," et al. have been introduced to us in metalinguistic terms of the sort Stich describes. There is at least some evidence in favor of my conceptual-stretching-via-grammatical-distortion account, in the form of precedent: we have learned other technical terms in varieties of technical English in that way (such as the terms "mass" or "event" in modern physics, or the term "class" in logic), and we can appreciate this without having a detailed view (based on a satisfactory theory of conceptual change) of exactly how the stretching works.

7. For a catalogue, see Lycan (1974).

8. In his trivialization argument, Martin invokes a "Translator" that merely takes the troublesome constructions of the target language onto the equally troublesome expressions of the home language and then produces T-sentences by purely mechanical orthographic rearrangement. His counter-truth-theoretic idea is that somehow we are to translate the difficult constructions of Alien into the correspondingly difficult constructions of English and come to understand them in virtue of this and our preexisting tacit mastery of English.

But although metaphrase translation of this sort does provide us with Alien words that make the same contributions to sentences of Alien as our corresponding words do to sentences of English, it does nothing to explain *how* either the Alien or the English words make the contributions that they do make, or exactly what contributions those are. Martin's proposal is of no help at all to the semantic *theorist* (Davidson has somewhat obscured the fact that his interests are in part theoretical interests, by using the radical-translation scenario so often as his model). We can learn what we want to know about English only by "translating" English sentences into a clear, disambiguated language that contains no problematic features such as opacity. (This is why possible-worlds semantics is felt to be so illuminating.) And we cannot perform *this* sort of translation without doing precisely the truth-theoretic-*cum*-syntactical job that Davidson urges us to do. For that matter, it is doubtful that Martin's "Translator" could pair sentences of Alien reliably with sentences of English unless it employed a syntax and a truth theory too.

9. Stich anticipates this sort of objection on pp. 220–221. He replies, first, that if a truth theory confines its predictions just to felt implications and the like, "then the theory might plausibly be viewed as no more than a theory of semantic intuition." But, he asks rhetorically, "[w]hy should a theory of semantic intuition be built by mapping object language sentences to sentences in a canonical language which admits of a truth theory?" Further, Stich complains, his "Wahr" example illustrates that showing how the semantic properties of "regimented" canonical formulas

(SRs) depend on the semantic properties of their parts does not suffice for showing how those of "unregimented" target sentences depend on those of *their* parts. Thus, a truth theory that delivers only impure T-sentences will fail at the very task that Davidson considers most important for a theory of meaning to perform.

To both of these points, I rejoin (again) that Stich ignores the crucial role awarded by the Metatheory to syntax. An approved semantics contains a grammar that *details* the mapping from target language to metalanguage and vice versa, and details it precisely in terms of the basic syntactic categories of the metalanguage that mirror the categories of the metalanguage's semantic primitives. Thus, the theory is considerably more than a theory of semantic intuition; it contains an entire syntax and thereby predicts all the target sentences' interesting syntactic properties as well. The answer to Stich's question of why we should adopt Davidson's format even for a theory of semantic intuition is a counterquestion: What competing format is there that satisfies as many of our preanalytical adequacy conditions as well as Davidson's does?

10. Indeed, if we wanted to adhere to *Quine's* methodological canons for linguistics, we would have a great deal of trouble with the foregoing task. As Parsons remarks, Davidson displays enormous sympathy with Quine's canons and thereby lets himself in for this trouble. I shall argue in chapter 9 that Davidson cannot reasonably be paying more than lip service to Quine's qualms and must reject Quine's central doctrines, if he has not abandoned the Metatheory.

11. Hintikka considers his case to be a counterexample, not just to theories of meaning that entail instances of Convention T, but to the principle of compositionality itself (the principle that the meaning of an expression is determined by the meanings of its component expressions taken together with the operation whereby they are combined). As Hintikka remarks, this principle is a commonplace (indeed, a happily chanted credo) of truth-conditional approaches since Frege, particularly Davidson's and Montague's. Hintikka sees "no valid *a priori* reason why meanings should be buildable by such step by step processes from the inside out" (p. 210); presumably he would reject the usual argument based on our ability to understand long, novel sentences on the grounds that the argument overlooks the alleged "interplay" between semantic elements and surface-grammatical environment.

Hintikka has pursued his rejection of compositionality in fashioning his current game-theoretic alternative to truth-based semantics ((1974, 1976); see also Saarinen (1979)).

12. Hintikka observes, correctly, that if we are to assign a formal interpretation and thereby a truth-value to a surface clause containing "any," we have to look at that clause's grammatical environment. But it does not follow that the meaning of the entire clause in which the clause occurs is not determined by the meaning of the clause, the meaning of the sentence's other semantic elements, and the compositional operation in force. The reason our interpretation of the surface clause can vary with surface-grammatical environment is that its superficial structure may reflect any of a number of different possible underlying semantic elements or compounds, and surface-syntactic environment may determine which. Of course the meaning of the containing sentence is not determined solely by the surface constituents themselves and the meanings they *would* have had had they occurred in isolation; it is determined by the meanings of the semantic elements that underlie their occurrences in the containing sentences. (Thus, if I understand Hintikka's argument on pp. 210–11, it equivocates on the notion of a "part" of a sentence.)

Chapter 3

1. Davidson himself brought up the example of "I am not speaking now" as a difficulty for his account, in his lectures at the 1971 Council for Philosophical Studies' Summer Institute in the Philosophy of Language, but he did not see the present ambiguity.
2. Montague (1968, 1972), Scott (1970), Lewis (1972), Kaplan (1977).
3. Lewis (1972, appendix). However, Lewis later despairs of a complete list (1980).
4. Colloquial English, for example, is shot through with restricted quantifiers ("No students allowed"; "Everybody ought to have a maid"; "You can bring anything you want to the exam"; "Nobody believes that"). It could be argued that *every* quantifier of any natural language is a restricted quantifier, even without the aid of Lewis's view (1970, 1973) that quantifiers that range only over actual objects are *eo ipso* restricted quantifiers. Note too that if any quantifier is to remain totally unrestricted, our metalanguage's set theory will have to be carefully tended lest paradoxical consequences should flow from the use of the universal set as a domain. (I am indebted to Michael Jubien for some discussion of this point.)
5. Like restricted quantifiers, hidden parameters are rife in English. Sometimes they are uncovered by substantive theories of the world: Harman argues (1975b) for a "society" parameter underlying moral predicates; Steven Boër and I (1975) discovered a teleological parameter in indirect-question clauses; relativity theory betrays a frame-of-reference parameter in even the most solid-seeming spatial and temporal terms such as "simultaneous."
6. In later work Lewis shows no inclination to take this line; following Cresswell (1972), he gives up relativizing truth to indices in the Montague-Scott sense and relativizes them simply to "contexts" *per se*, leaving it open which features of context are fixing the parameter in any given instance (1980). This vagueness may lead to trouble later on.
7. In this he follows Scott Weinstein (1974). For Weinstein (crudely summarized), a context or utterance-occasion determines a sequence of objects, viz., the sequence of things demonstrated by the demonstratives occurring within the utterance in question, in the order in which they occur. The utterance itself is true (false) iff the sentence-type of which it is a token is true (false) relative to the sequence determined by the context (i.e., iff that sequence satisfies the open sentence that we would obtain by replacing the demonstratives in the utterance by successively numbered free variables). A T-sentence directed upon a particular utterance is conditional in form, generated by the axiom that says in effect, "If u is a utterance of S and x is the sequence of objects respectively picked out in the context by the demonstratives contained in S in the order in which they occur, then u is true iff x satisfies the result of replacing the demonstratives in S with matching free variables" (cf. Weinstein's (5), p. 62). A noteworthy advantage of this formulation is that the technical term "picked out" occurs, here, not in the actual truth-condition assigned to the utterance in question, but in an apparently harmless sort of prologue. Unfortunately, Weinstein stops here, applying his method only to demonstrative pronouns and not to any of the other deictic devices we have mentioned; so we do not know how he would treat trick sentences such as "I am not speaking now" and "I do not exist," or how he would handle tense and other more subtle deictic elements.
8. The phrase "the object which is y" here translates a special notation of Burge's involving square brackets. The purpose of the special notation, Burge says, is to ape the surface-syntactic behavior of demonstratives in English and thus (in our

terms) to promote purity. I shall ignore it here, since the purity in question is gained only at the cost of "full explicitness" of the sort I urge in the Appendix, and since purity in this particular respect does not affect the concerns of this chapter. Burge's device may still point toward a useful syntactic hypothesis.

9. Harman made appeal to assignment functions in his lectures at the 1971 Council for Philosophical Studies' Summer Institute in the Philosophy of Language; but he proposed to relativize truth directly *to* assignments, which smacks of the Montague-Scott approach in that it treats indexical elements essentially as free variables (provided no restriction is placed on the admissibility of assignment functions) and therefore masks the role of contexts themselves in fixing determinate truth-values for particular utterances.

Cresswell (1972) adopts a way of representing the dependence of extension on context that seems very similar to mine. "Contexts" are construed as propositions stating facts about particular uses of sentences, and functions are defined from such propositions to the extensions of the various sorts of indexical terms (p. 139). Cresswell's method doubtless surpasses mine in rigor; mine is simpler.

10. I call this biconditional a "truth theorem" rather than a T-sentence because, though provable in our truth theory, it is not a T-sentence; as a result of semantic ascent, its right-hand side is not a purported logical equivalent of its target sentence. The theorem will *yield* the T-sentence we want, as soon as our pragmatics feeds it context-bound premises of the form "$\alpha('I,' C) = x$" and "$\alpha('now,' C) = t$."

11. Thus, α captures what Kaplan (1977) calls the "character" of an expression, as well as specifying the expression's content; here α tells us what (whom) "I" denotes on an occasion, and our pragmatic rule for computing α tells us how and why "I" denotes that person.

12. Geis (1970) and elsewhere.

13. We may well wonder whether *present* tense is indexical in that way. Two options leap to mind: (a) Unlike any other tense, present is simply a lexicalization of an underlying occurrence of "now," "now" here denoting as always a time interval of contextually determined length. (b) Present tense is grammatically parallel to past and the other tenses; it is derived from a similar quantificational construction, such as "$(\exists t)(\text{OVERLAPS}(t, \text{now}) \& \ldots)$," where t ranges over time intervals and "now" rather narrowly designates the time of utterance. Option (a) has the virtue of not requiring tendentious syntax, a leap of faith, or whatever to turn a quantificational structure into a surface tense marker; option (b) allows present tense to be a tense rather than another thing. Since tendentious syntax or some surrogate will be needed for each of the other tenses anyway (see below), (a)'s advantage seems pointless; so of the two I prefer (b). Further options appear once one considers intensional treatments of tense and/or the positing of tenseless, truth-valueless propositions as arguments of tense operators. (Cf. Dowty (1979), Kamp (1971).)

14. See Brinton (1977) and Burge (1973). However, I shall propose a competing strategy for dealing with context-bound descriptions in chapter 8.

15. The SRs in question here reveal an interesting ambiguity in the notion of our having "syntactic evidence" for a hypothetical assignment of logical form. There may be syntactic traces strongly indicating the hidden presence of reference to and quantification over "times," without this evidence pointing toward any plausible syntactic *history* or derivation connecting our SR to the target surface structure. Where this uncomfortable sort of situation leaves us with respect to Harman's principle (5) is unclear. (Cf. also the related SRs assigned to indicative conditionals in Lycan (1984b).)

16. Consider the verb "go." "Go" is deictic in that it cannot normally be used to describe its subject's approaching the speaker; thus, "Donald went into 1879 Hall" implies that the speaker is outside 1879 Hall (or at least that the speaker is speaking relative to a chosen vantage point that is outside 1879 Hall). Our method of assignment functions suggests that we should account for this implication by relativizing the truth of such a sentence to a *place* or "vantage point" considered as an object, and (further) that we should construe the sentence as containing a hidden parameter which in context denotes that spatial object. On this approach, we would have to suppose that the sentence's SR contained not only the spatial parameter in question but also a rather elaborate predicate relating the path of the subject's motion to the chosen vantage point, and, as before, we would have to suppose that all this hidden apparatus was somehow lexically fused into the single verb "go" or "went." This is awful.

  Some speakers, I have found, do not hear "Donald went into 1879 Hall" as false when the speaker is inside 1879 Hall. If their intuitions are correct, then allegedly deictic verbs of this type are not after all indexical in the sense of giving rise to contextual fluctuations of truth-value, and they need not affect our policy for handling deixis in writing T-sentences. The felt implication generated by the verb "go" would have to be accounted for in some other way, then, since there is certainly something wrong with the speaker's selection of that verb if the speaker's vantage point is inside 1879 Hall. One possible and attractive explanation of this is based on the theory of "lexical presumption" that I shall present in chapter 5.

17. Other tense operators can shift time also. Nor is time the only shiftable feature of context: *place* can be shifted by operators such as "somewhere"; *standards of precision* can be shifted by operators such as "roughly" and "strictly speaking"; etc. Lewis adds that *world* can be shifted by modal operators; this of course presupposes his view that actuality is an indexical property, which I reject (Lycan (1979b, secs. VI and VII)).

18. In (1980) Lewis himself disclaims any intention of pursuing the "ambitious goal" of finding a psychologically real syntax, and so presumably he is unconcerned to find any "determinate relation in nature" that connects logical form to surface structure. But it is this goal that I *envision* pursuing, whether or not Lewis is right in doubting that "it is worthwhile to pursue it in our present state of knowledge."

19. Richard Grandy has reminded me of the possibility of "taking tense logic seriously as logic" by writing our truth clause for ⌜PAST S⌝ as "Past(S is true)." This would flout Harman's principle (2), but then any choice to do tenses without tense logic would require extra postulates, thereby infringing on principle (3). My main objection to this proposed brute appeal to tense logic is that if Wallace's Problem is to be avoided (see the Appendix), further structure would have to be discovered in the metalinguistic predicate "Past," which discovery would render "Past" unsuitable for use in our final truth definition.

20. A possible objection here is that "thoughts" need not be explicitly represented in the brain—as little formulas somehow written in cerebral ink—in order to be thoughts. ("Brain writing" hypotheses have come under vigorous attack in recent years, in the works of Dennett (1975), P. M. Churchland (1979), P. S. Churchland (1980a), and others.) Perhaps not all thoughts are explicit representations, but it would be rash to conclude from this that the thoughts that directly underlie overt speech and hearing are not explicit representations (cf. Lycan (1981b)).

21. See Rosch (1973, 1975, 1977). Lynne Rudder Baker has protested to me that informants are simply unreliable on matters of this sort and that we ought not to take their classifications at face value. With regard to some theoretical issues in linguis-

tics I share this general sentiment (I shall manifest it lavishly in the next chapter), but in this case I see little ground for explaining away the informants' intuitions. For example, there seems no reason to suspect that when an informant classifies cat's-cradle neither clearly as a game nor clearly as a nongame, but as "sort of" a game, the informant is blind to some hidden determinate fact of the matter.

22. For example, the legal concept of *perjury* does not admit of degrees (even though in practice a judge has some leeway regarding severity of sentence). Suppose a witness knowingly gives some testimony that is true only to degree .52. Has the witness committed perjury? Should the witness go to jail?

23. See Zadeh (1965, 1971), Goguen (1969), and Sanford (1974, 1975, 1976). Lakoff also begins to explore the relation between fuzziness and semantic presupposition; I shall obviate the need for such exploration in chapter 4.

24. Lakoff's example is the expression "sort of." He contends that "sort of" is "in part . . . a deintensifier in that it shifts the curve to the left and makes it less steep," but that "it also drops off sharply to zero on the right."

> The values for 'sort of tall' are greatest when you are of intermediate height. If you are of less than intermediate height, then the values for 'sort of tall' are greater than those for 'tall'. But above intermediate height the values for 'sort of tall' drop off sharply. If you're really tall, you're not sort of tall. (p. 471)

My intuitions run against this. I do not hear "Wilt the Stilt is sort of tall" as *false* (true to degree 0), but as ironic understatement. Thus, I think that sentence is true, semantically speaking; what is wrong with uttering it in nonironic contexts is just that the utterer is in a position to make a much stronger statement, such as "Wilt the Stilt is very tall," and thus is violating Grice's Maxim of Strength (see chapter 4).

25. In the course of Lakoff's article the term "hedge" quickly acquires a technical use. In ordinary English a "hedge" is an expression that shifts truth-values *upward;* one "hedges" or qualifies one's claims in order not to be accused of overstatement or of outright falsehood. English contains "antihedges" as well, in this sense, such as "very" and "strictly speaking" and "and I use the term advisedly." Hedges and antihedges alike are called "hedges" in our new, broad technical sense.

26. Lakoff raises the question of whether a less fine-grained continuum of degrees of class membership might not serve our purposes (pp. 462–63, 482–83):

> After all, human beings cannot perceive [a real-valued continuum of] . . . distinctions. Perhaps it would be psychologically more real not to have an infinity of degrees of set membership, but rather some relatively small number of degrees, say the usual 7 ± 2. (p. 463)

But Lakoff puts forward several convincing reasons for staying with the real-valued representation.

27. However, if Hilary Putnam's (1975) theory of natural-kind terms is correct, matters may not be as complicated as Wittgenstein would have had us believe. It may be that a thing is a bird iff that thing satisfies a precise zoological criterion, and a thing is a vegetable iff that thing satisfies a precise genetic criterion determined by botanists.

28. Such a term would be assigned a list of "paradigm features," the features possessed by any *normal* or *typical* instance of the term. Thus, "game" would be assigned the list "Activity carried on for amusement; rule-governed; admits of winning and losing; competitive; involves moving of ritually designated counters, tokens, or other apparatus; . . . ." Perhaps the features on the list would be assigned some crude relative weights. An object's degree of membership in the

class of games would then be determined by its closeness to this paradigm—by the number of listed features it has, the degrees to which it has them, and their combinations.

29. Cf. Wallace's remark (1975, p. 54) that "[n]o more fundamental change can be made in a theory than changing the number of argument places of one of its key concepts."

Actually, a third option is suggested by some remarks of Davidson's:

> As long as ambiguity does not affect grammatical form, and can be translated, ambiguity for ambiguity, into the metalanguage, a truth definition will not tell us any lies. The trouble, for systematic semantics, with the phrase 'believes that' in English is not its vagueness, ambiguity, or unsuitability for incorporation in a serious science; let our metalanguage be English, and all *these* problems will be translated without loss or gain into the metalanguage. (1967b, p. 461)

The idea is that vagueness can simply be reproduced without comment on the right-hand sides of our T-sentences; a T-sentence that assigns a vague truth-condition to a vague target sentence "will not tell us any lies." Though we have seen in chapter 2 that Davidson's suggestion directed specifically toward ambiguity will not do, it is more plausible in the case of mere vagueness.

More plausible, but unsatisfactory. The trouble, as Richard Garner has noted in some unpublished writings, is that T-sentences are tokened in context but quote their target sentences out of context. Suppose our truth theory cranks out " 'France is hexagonal' is true iff France is hexagonal." The left-hand side of this biconditional is presumably truth-valueless, since no context or standard of strictness has been specified; but the context in which the whole T-sentence is tokened may be one in which its right-hand side is counted as unequivocally true or as unequivocally false, either of which possibilities would falsify (or neuter) the T-sentence as a whole.

30. There is even a distinctive gesture that indicates a nonabsolute degree of truth. One holds one's hand in the horizontal plane, palm down with fingers slightly spread, and oscillates it slightly about the axis determined by the middle finger.

31. Unless I have misunderstood Crispin Wright's argument (1976) for the deep incoherence of vague predicates, the present point rebuts it. Addressing the use of "degree semantics" against Sorites puzzles, Wright insists that speakers be able to tell when the application of a vague predicate is *"on balance* justified" and then reiterates a Sorites argument against the latter predicate. But we should either reject this requirement on grounds of genuine indeterminacy or reject the inductive principle that if we are "on balance justified" in applying a predicate satisfied to degree n, then we are "on balance justified" in applying it when it is satisfied to degree $n - \epsilon$.

32. It might be thought that, once we have fixed our context parameter C, the "reading" parameter is automatically fixed as well, since a speaker at a time has only one reading in mind. This is typically (though not invariably) so, and perhaps accordingly we might replace "R" itself by a functional expression such as "R(C)"; but there is no temptation to try to subsume our disambiguating operation under the assignment function α, since disambiguation is not a matter of assigning denotata to elements in logical form, but of choosing one of a set of logical forms in the first place.

33. As in the case of the "reading" parameter, one might think of subsuming L under α, since context presumably determines the language being spoken. But telling

what language is being spoken is not in any way a matter of computing the denotatum of some referring element in logical form.

Chapter 4

1. The example and the term were coined by Geis and Zwicky (1971).
2. Karttunen's subsequent writings have displayed much more sophistication in these matters (Karttunen (1974), Karttunen and Peters (1975, 1979)).
3. By "S_1 necessitates S_2" I mean simply that if S_1 is true, then S_2 must also be true. (S_1 *entails* S_2 iff: S_1 necessitates S_2 and if S_2 is false then S_1 must also be false.) Boër and I have identified this simple notion with van Fraassen's relation of the same name (Boër and Lycan (1976)). Martin (1979) charges us with having missed one or more of the subtleties of the latter; rather than trying to sort this out, I shall stick with the simple notion here.
4. For example, Lakoff (1972), who announces his conclusion that ". . . in certain cases [sic] the presupposition relation is transitive. . . . [But] transitivity of the presupposition relation fails in [other] cases" (pp. 574, 576), and Davison (1973a), who goes on to couch her discussion entirely in terms of regulative felicity-conditions on speech acts. Happily, this phenomenon has occurred less frequently since the early 1970s.
5. Thus, I deplore the appearance in print of a *Syntax and Semantics* volume (No. 11; Oh and Dineen (1979)) entitled *Presupposition*. In their preface the editors remark,

> Although PRESUPPOSITION may not be accepted by all readers of—or even all contributors to—this volume as the proper term for referring to the full range of phenomena discussed herein, one could observe at the conference held at the University of Kansas in April, 1977, that leading figures and newcomers alike found it the most nearly acceptable cover term. (p. xi)

No doubt; *competitors* for the title of "cover term" do not leap to mind. What is regrettable is that there should be any such "cover term" at all playing any significant role in linguistic theory. Imagine a group of chemists who coin a single term that applies exactly to the following things: halogens, silicon compounds, protons, colloidal suspensions, and elements studied by Mendeleev—and then go on to try to state significant generalizations using that term.

Gazdar (1979a) and Bach and Harnish (1979) are fully appreciative of this point and supportive of thesis (I), but they do not join me in trying to stamp out the use of the word "p*************."
6. However, see Harman (1975b).
7. For some reason, Martin (1979, p. 236) writes, ". . . since the roots of presupposition theory lie in the logical tradition and since it is there that the most developed theories of presupposition exist, any serious critique of semantic presupposition must be understood as an attack on the formal idea." This seems to me squarely wrong; certainly it is a breathtaking *non sequitur*. To deny of a natural language such as English that it exemplifies a certain formal idea is in no way an attack on the integrity of the formal idea itself.
8. I hope it is clear that when in this chapter I use the term "truth-valueless," the only sort of truth-valuelessness that I am at pains to impugn is that which is supposed to be occasioned by the failure of an extrinsic, contingent assumption about the world, i.e., that which can strike an otherwise perfectly meaningful and understandable sentence in virtue of the falsity of some other sentence. Nothing I say here conflicts with our earlier discussions of indexicality and vagueness, nor does it bear on any issue of literal truth *vs.* metaphorical truth or the like.

9. As I read the *Tractatus*, this denial is a corollary of §5.551:

> Our fundamental principle is that whenever a question can be decided by logic at all it must be possible to decide it without more ado.
>
> (And if we get into a position where we have to look at the world for an answer to such a problem, that shows that we are on a completely wrong track.)

Wittgenstein uses these principles to argue that logically proper names denote ultimate simples.

10. For a much fuller discussion of the issues involved here, see *MSP*, secs. 3.2 and 3.7.

11. This is very curious if true; "internal" and "external" are such overtly spatial terms that I cannot imagine how one could use them without having scope at least tacitly in mind.

I am grateful to Martin for lengthy and fruitful correspondence on this and related topics, despite the abuse I shall continue to heap on him in this chapter.

12. At least Boër and I are in good company; Martin has the same misconception of Russell's concerns: "Even Russell's theory of existential presupposition is formulated by negation in secondary occurrence which is the classical version of 3-valued internal negation" (p. 32). Russell, a stalwart champion of bivalence, would have been considerably startled to hear that he held a "theory of existential presupposition," if "presupposition" there means semantic presupposition.

13. Nor does the proliferation of lexical ambiguities stop with "not": on Martin's theory certain sentence operators such as "know" and "report" are called ambiguous between factive and nonfactive readings (p. 279). (Jerry Sadock has made a similar suggestion to us in correspondence.) Martin and Sadock admit that (23c), for example, has a reading on which (23c) does not necessitate Sam's being a Martian, but they claim that (23c) *also* has a reading on which (23c) does necessitate that and on which (24c) is a contradiction. I cannot hear (24c) as a contradiction, no matter how hard I try.

Martin adds,

> Methodologically, of course, the multiplication of senses beyond necessity is undesirable, and presupposition theory would become irrefutable if every alleged cancellation [of an alleged necessitation] was explained by hypothesizing a new sense. [Just so!—WL] But a few such ambiguities, especially that of negation, seem perfectly reasonable. (pp. 279–80)

They seem anything but reasonable to me.

14. He goes on to make a stronger claim than this: that the existence of "an intuitively recognizable difference" between two subclasses of nontruths "*alone* is adequate justification for tri-valent semantics" (p. 254, italics mine). Far from agreeing with this, I cannot see that the existence of such a difference even *suggests* the positing of a third truth-value. ("Within the class of even numbers there are two intuitively recognizable subclasses, viz., the class of even numbers divisible by 3 and the class of even numbers indivisible by 3; therefore, we should not speak just of odd and even, but of odd, even, and neuter.")

15. In support of this general picture of the singular terms in question, see also Devitt (1974), Stampe (1974), and Bell (1973).

16. It is unclear to me how often this kind of situation actually occurs. It is very tempting to maintain that when vacuous names occur in ordinary English, they do so attributively (see Boër (1978)), but this ignores cases of vacuous names in common use that are not known by anyone to be vacuous. More on this in note 18.

17. I owe this way of putting the point to Boër.

18. Plantinga (1978), Stalnaker (1979a), and others have sought middle ways between Millianism and Russellianism. Both Plantinga and Stalnaker fail, I believe (see Austin (1983); Lycan (1980b, 1984a)). Indeed, for purely formal reasons it is much harder than is generally recognized even to formulate a middle way, though I believe I have succeeded in (1984a). I do not have a worked-out account of vacuous names, but I stick to the position that a nonattributive name is semantically meaningless even though it may still play a vivid cognitive role for an individual speaker. (That cognitive role and truth-conditional meaning are strikingly independent of each other is a main theme of (1984a).)
19. This section is largely reprinted from *MSP*.
20. However, for what I take to be the reason for this lack of success, see Lycan (1970).
21. There is a related fallacy that has ensnared many a theorist: that of supposing that the term "infelicitous" *by itself* carries explanatory weight. Not infrequently a linguist, attempting to explain the felt unacceptability of uttering some sentence, observes that the utterance "would be infelicitous" and lets it go at that. But this "explanation" is tautologous. For Austin (cf. (1962, p. 14 and chaps. XI and XII)), the word "infelicitous" was expressly designed to be an umbrella term that covers all the indefinitely many ways in which an utterance in a context might be defective (recall, as I have noted above, that *falsity* is one common form of infelicity). Thus, to reply "It's infelicitous" when asked what is wrong with some particular utterance is simply to repeat that there is something wrong with it. If a theorist is to make any explanatory headway, he must say what *specific sort* of infelicity, whose mechanism is antecedently understood, is causing the problem.
22. Karttunen sees the relevance of three-valued logic in section 10 of (1973), but rejects it as modelling "presupposition" in English; evidently then he is *not* talking of semantic presupposition. However, he returns to three-valued logic in Karttunen and Peters (1979). See also Soames (1979b).
23. Katz (1979) also emphasizes that "the projection problem" is merely a special case of the compositionality question.

Chapter 5

1. Chiefly Lakoff (1969, 1972). See also Fillmore (1969) and Langendoen (1971). This chapter is largely reprinted from chapter 5 of *MSP*.
2. "Relative grammaticality" of the sort alleged here, like semantic presupposition, is a property of *sentences*. But there ought to be some interesting systematic relation between *speakers* and the "presuppositions" of the sentences they utter; it is natural to invoke a notion of "speaker's presupposition" and say that a speaker "presupposes" in this new sense all the presuppositions (old sense) of the sentence he utters. Yet this relation between a speaker and a presupposed sentence or proposition is annoyingly difficult to spell out; see section 2.3 of *MSP*. I shall not try to make any further progress on it here.
3. Horn argues for related conclusions concerning "only"; I think these are easier to explain away in terms of quantificational structure. Warner (1982) argues that "even" makes a substantive truth-conditional contribution to sentences in which it occurs.
4. Data of this sort were first called to my attention by Jonathan Schonsheck in an unpublished note.
5. He also offers examples concerning selectional restrictions, and some that depend on claims about coreference and identity; but I find these far less convincing than those I have listed.

6. Of course, this is not to say that sentences could have meanings at all in the absence of speakers who use them in certain ways in certain situations.

7. See McCawley (1968), Ross (1970), Lakoff (1972), Sadock (1975). These authors have defended a very strong syntactic thesis, usually called "the Performative Analysis," that has striking and anomalous semantic repercussions. I shall discuss and disparage this strong version of my present claim in chapter 6 (see also Boër and Lycan (1980)); a very minimal and harmless version will serve my purpose here.

8. The point as it stands is uncontroversial, but in chapter 6 I shall remark on one possible theoretical reason for doubting it.

9. Cresswell (1973, pp. 235–36) seems to endorse a similar proposal for his own brand of grammar, for he remarks on the "elegance" of incorporating "use-dependent acceptability principles" and notes that such principles can be generalized to include beliefs as well.

10. Actually, there is a relatively useless alternative reading of (5a) and (10) according to which what Jane did instead of going to the dentist was to *make a decision,* one that may or may not have been carried out.

11. Thus, I think the "subjunctive mood" has been misclassified by traditional grammarians; it is not a *mood* at all. However, I am ignoring one noteworthy bit of evidence against my present theory of counterfactual presumption: the fact that counterfactive force can be suspended in discourse of a certain sort (see *MSP*, sec. 3.8).

12. Since failure of a semantic presupposition would affect truth-value, semantic presuppositions would have to be encoded in logical form, either by the introduction of Bochvar-inspired multivalued recursive clauses in our truth definition or by some other, more mysterious means. But the failure of a lexical presumption characteristically does not affect truth-value; a sentence's lexical presumptions go beyond what is encoded in its logical form.

13. "The presence of a conversational implicature must be capable of being worked out; for even if it can in fact be intuitively grasped, unless the intuition is replaceable by an argument, the implicature (if present at all) will not count as a CONVERSATIONAL implicature; it will be a CONVENTIONAL implicature" (Grice (1975, p. 50)).

14. One slight embarrassment to this hypothesis, or at least to this hypothesis as made by me, is that I would dispute Grice's account of the one example he gives. It is natural (and I think etymologically sound) to suppose that the word "therefore" is a demonstrative roughly synonymous with "for that reason" or "on that ground." If so, then "He is an Englishman; he is therefore brave" does entail (though perhaps does not assert) that the subject's being an Englishman is the (or a) reason for thinking he is brave, and it *is* (however strictly speaking) false when that consequence is false. (Kempson (1975, pp. 213–14) and Warner (1982) also attack Grice on this point.) But Grice does not understand "therefore" in this way, so my disagreement with him over its interpretation does not affect my contention that conventional implicature as exemplified by Grice's sentence on *his* understanding is reducible to lexical presumption.

Gilbert Harman has pointed out to me that my treatment of conventional implicature as *lexical* ignores the possibility that a sentence might conventionally implicate something in virtue of some structural feature rather than in virtue of the appearance of a particular lexical item. Indeed, we shall see something like this happen in chapter 7. If need be, I think my notion of lexical presumption can easily be generalized.

Chapter 6

1. L. Jonathan Cohen anticipated this analogue, I think, in section II of (1964). (Cf. also Katz (1980, chap. 2).) Boër and I first discussed it in "A Performadox in Truth-Conditional Semantics" (1980), from which the first two sections of the present chapter are also drawn.

2. Lewis himself is not committed to that conclusion, since he rejects the Performative Analysis. My point is that anyone who accepts the Performative Analysis *and* accepts Lewis's account of the truth-conditions of performative sentences is committed to it. Lewis himself remarks:

   > Hence I do not propose to take ordinary declaratives as paraphrased performatives (as proposed in Ross, 1970) because that would get their truth-conditions wrong. If there are strong syntactic reasons for adopting Ross's proposal, I would regard it as semantically a version of the method of sentence radicals, even if it employs base structures that look exactly like the base structures employed in the method of paraphrased performatives. (1972, pp. 210–11)

3. These facts are explicitly recognized by Lakoff in writings subsequent to (1972); see particularly (1975).

4. Further, the suggestion that reason-adverbials of this type make no truth-conditional contribution belies certain clear paraphrase relations of a sort that I shall discuss in section 4.

5. The reason for that vulgar display was pedagogical: we had found that almost invariably, when philosophers or linguists were first confronted with the Performadox, they immediately responded, "Oh, oxfeathers! There's not even a *prima facie* paradox here; the 'solution' 's obvious! What's going on is plainly that *p!*" The trouble, needless to say, is that a different suggestion always replaced "*p.*" And, needless to say, all the immediately proposed "obvious" solutions were easily seen to be inadequate. The Performadox took a bit of getting used to.

6. "I state that P" at least implicates "P," by the Cooperative Principle. (Of course, one cannot usually be held legally responsible for mere implicatures.)

7. An energetic start has been made by Schiffer (1972). See also Ginet (1979).

8. Thus, sentences can be true$_2$ even when they are not being used to make assertions. We need the notion of "truth$_2$" in order to define that of "entailment$_2$" (S_1 *entails*$_2$ S_2 =$_{def}$ If S_1 is true$_2$, then S_2 must also be true$_2$).

9. Sadock writes,

   > . . . we should no more expect worthwhile intuitive answers from the man on the street (or even from the logician or linguist on the street) to questions like, 'Is the proposition expressed by this sentence true$_1$ or false$_1$?' than we should expect worthwhile intuitive answers even from physicists to questions like, 'How many electrons are there in the ink in this sentence?'. (p. 3)

10. This is not to say that we *always* have sharp and clear intuitions about truth$_1$ (even given all the facts of a situation). We have seen in the case of "semantic presupposition" that intuition can balk for pragmatic reasons even when the facts are in.

11. I admit that *if the Performative Analysis is correct,* the notion of truth$_2$ captures our intuitions about ordinary declaratives fairly well. Nondeclaratives also provide some support for Sadock's claim: interrogatives and imperatives are not heard by laymen as having truth-values, even though such sentences do have (semantic) truth-values, presumably because they are not used to make assertions.

12. "A speaker who utters a sentence S asserts P if (1) S conventionally designates a proposition Q which entails$_1$ *that I assert P* and (2) that I assert P is true$_1$" (Sadock (1979, p. 9); my italics replace a special notation of his).
13. I now therefore renounce my preference in "PTS" for Cresswell's Tolerated Method.
14. However, the demonstrative connection affords no improvement in the case of our tendentious reason-adverbials containing asserted conjuncts.
15. The Performative Analysis has come in for some telling syntactic criticism, some of it based on the same sorts of adverbial constructions that trouble us here; see Gazdar (1976) and Mittwoch (1977). Alternative accounts of Ross's data may be found in Anderson (1971), Fraser (1971), and Matthews (1972).
16. In fact, so far as I can see, this last claim (the core of the Performative Analysis) is not even supported to any great extent by the existence of sentences containing dangling adverbials, contrary to what has been argued by Lakoff (1972) and Sadock (1974). The dangling adverbials are strong indicators of performative verbs underlying *those sentences in which they appear.* But there is no obvious reason to go on to posit performative verbs underlying all the other declaratives that there are, save perhaps for a somewhat presumptuous "simplicity" argument to the effect that if some declaratives reflect structures containing hidden performative prefaces, then we may as well say that all declaratives do.
17. The same point holds for interrogative pairs such as "Are there edible mice?"/"I ask you whether there are edible mice" and imperative pairs such as "Bring the General his beach toy"/"I order you to bring the General his beach toy."
18. For example, see Baker (1970) and the references therein.

Chapter 7

1. This is objectionable in each of two ways. First, I do not see how anyone could show that it is not merely true, but part of the meaning of the word "sincere" that (e.g.) a speaker's request is sincere only if that speaker assumes that the hearer is able to perform the act requested. Second, the invocation of a term such as "sincere" as an object-language predicate is at best odd, given the natural assumption that the conversational and speechacty reasoning that figures in a case of implicating is carried out in the speaker's and hearer's metalanguage. Luckily, nothing in Gordon and Lakoff's essential program seems to depend on the sincerity-conditions' actually being taken as meaning postulates, except that the invocation of such explicitly speechacty material obviates our calling Gordon-Lakovian explanations (purely) *Gricean.*
2. "Meaning" here is obviously intended to include force. Since "meaning" as a philosophers' and linguists' term of art has no fixed use, Gordon and Lakoff are entitled to stipulate this if they like. But we must remember that for them "meaning" includes more than just logical form properly so called. Unfortunately, they also slip into using "logical structure" in a similar way, and that usage does engender methodological confusion on their part: the "logical structures" to which their "conversational postulates" apply are not logical forms alone, but logical forms *along with* the performative prefaces that operate on them; this feature is essential to Gordon and Lakoff's explanatory scheme, since the question of indirect force is at least on its face a question of speech-act theory, not of implicature *per se.* This is why I remarked in note 1 that Gordon and Lakoff take Grice's name in vain.

3. Searle himself notes later (Generalization 7, p. 81) that an indirect commissive may be performed by two of the same means by which Generalization 2 assures us indirect directives may be performed.

4. Searle also admits that there are various problems about indirect speech acts that his theory does not resolve, and in order to handle them he suggests a few natural additions to the apparatus constructed so far. As I have noted, he conjectures that there are conventions "of usage" (e.g., of politeness) that create a preference for one syntactic form over another, synonymous one. He further suggests (pp. 76–77) that there may be a Gricean conversational maxim to the effect that we ought to speak "idiomatically" unless there is some special reason not to do so (though it is not clear just what is meant by this). To account for the peculiarity of sincerity-conditions noted in Generalization 3—viz., that they are the only felicity-conditions that cannot be *queried* by a speaker as a way of performing an indirect directive—he points, quite plausibly, to the abnormality of asking others about one's own mental states or of baldly ascribing such states to others when addressing them (p. 77). Finally, he raises but does not resolve an issue that will soon return to vex us: Why does what is superficially a question, "Why don't you ϕ?," behave *syntactically* so much like an imperative?

   Fraser (1975) extends Searle's conservative approach to sentences that embed explicitly directive illocutionary verbs inside modal expressions. Costa (1979) and Bach and Harnish (1979) augment the approach by suggesting in some detail that indirect speech acts are in effect cases of "generalized" implicature. Jerry Morgan (1978) argues that the implicature is more strictly conventional than that, as I shall discuss below.

5. To take just one simple example: Georgia Green (1975) and J. R. Ross (1975) both point out that if the standard indirect forces of utterances were to be explained solely in conversational terms, then those indirect forces ought to be preserved through substitution of logical synonyms. There are plenty of counterexamples to this consequent:

   (i)   a. Why don't you shut up?
          b. How come you don't cease producing utterances?

   (ii)   a. Can you get me a Grant's?

          b. $\left\{ \begin{array}{l} \text{Are you able} \\ \text{Do you have the} \left\{ \begin{array}{l} \text{ability} \\ \text{capacity} \end{array} \right\} \\ \text{Is it possible for you} \end{array} \right\}$ to get me a Grant's?

   (iii) a. I want you to sign here.
          b. Among my desires at the moment is that you affix your signature at this spot.

So far, so good, but it is misleading of Green and Ross to take Gordon and Lakoff at their neologistic word in characterizing their approach as (purely) "conversational" in the first place. Gordon and Lakoff themselves concede in effect that their transderivational constraints are special and needed *over and above* "conversational principles" such as (GL-1). More importantly, our failure of substitutivity *salva* indirect force is very likely due to two facts pointed out by Searle in raising the same point: first, that Gordon and Lakoff's "conversational postulates" are *not* purely conversational, but mobilize speechacty factors that would never be expected to preserve substitution of logical synonyms; second, that there seems to be some conventional element involved in individual indirect speech acts that prefers some particular forms of words over some of their own logical equivalents. On the latter point, see especially Morgan (1978), which I shall discuss at length below.

6. A "whimperative" (Sadock (1970)) is a sentence that has interrogative surface mood features and intonation but normally exercitive force; thus, the uttering of a whimperative with its usual force constitutes an indirect speech act.

7. This point may be what Peter Cole is getting at on p. 272 of (1975).

8. For that matter, is a *locutionary* switch required? Van der Auwera (p. 36) suggests the rhetorical question as a counterexample.

9. This is not to deny that the function of some speech acts is to communicate information—e.g., *informing*. But speech-act theory is the study of performances of certain sorts and the conventional and institutional settings in which they are conducted, whereas Grice's theory of conversation is a theory of perlocutionary effect and of acquiring information by reasoning, and in its purest form not a study of *conventional* matters at all.

10. Failure to recognize the obvious possibility of multiple forces has led to much philosophical error. For example, Strawson himself seemingly committed the "speech act fallacy" (this term is due to Chisholm) in his classic paper "Truth" (1950b), when he noted that such expressions as "That's true" are used in acts of agreeing or concurrence, and then presumed to infer that they were not literal predications. In like manner many people seem to have become ethical emotivists straightway upon noticing that moral judgments are used to condemn, to praise, and to urge.

11. Costa (1979) and Bach and Harnish (1979) also use the metaphor of "short-circuiting."

12. Searle (1975, p. 69) seems to disagree for cases like (11). But I think he would have to concede (40)–(44). Bach and Harnish pursue their "radical pragmaticist" strategy so far as to echo their treatment of the Performadox by simply denying that sentences like (40)–(44) are grammatical.

13. Actually, (42) may instead be an instance of elliptical parataxis, of the sort discussed in chapter 6. The reason-adverbial may modify a suppressed performative preface that literally describes the foregoing utterance of (42a) as being a request.

14. No direct comparison is possible for this case, since the sentence that most straightforwardly has the direct force and content that (44) has indirectly (viz., "The soufflé is delicious") contains no sentential operator and so cannot be tested for slifting at all. As next best, I am using the explicit performative "I tell you that the soufflé is delicious."

15. Given the fairly rich variety of "telltale" devices that distinguish speech-act types from each other (see particularly Sadock (1974) and Davison, for abundant data), we must conclude that syntax individuates speech acts—particularly "impositives"—very finely. The question of why English singles out just the much smaller class of underlying mood markers it does is a fascinating one.

16. Interestingly, the prototheory at which we have arrived still bears some similarity to Gordon and Lakoff's original logicogrammatical account, since it posits simultaneous computation on a sentence's literal underlying structure *and* direct and apodeictic grammatical indication of the indirectly conveyed force. The important difference is that our prototheory denies that any genuine conversational reasoning occurs, and hence that Type-3 indirect force is conveyed by implicature.

17. I am grateful to Alice Davison for her generous discussion of the last two chapters.

Chapter 8

1. A fourth source of resistance to the computational paradigm is eliminativist-tending skepticism about folk psychology and about functionalist theories generally; see particularly P. S. Churchland (1980a, 1980b), P. M. Churchland (1981, 1983), Churchland and Churchland (1983), and Stich (1983). I have laid the foundations for a full-scale defense against these doxastophobes in Lycan (1981b, 1981c).

2. In its most simple form, the object will be a function from sequences of noise- and mark-types to SR-types-on-assignments or, if you like, to structured sets of possible worlds.

3. Lakoff and Johnson are perfectly aware of this (pp. 198–99), but they have further objections to press, which I shall take up below. They claim in particular that to view a language as a big set is to ignore "human understanding" (p. 184) and thus to leave out the most important element of meaning; but I think they underestimate the power of the sort of pragmatics I have begun to sketch in chapter 3, as does perhaps Ziff (1969).

4. Except that if the "executive order of Nature" is all there really is, sets must ultimately be expendable. But this is a problem for any philosopher anywhere.

5. Russell would not have tolerated demonstrative reference to something whose existence is inferred rather than known by acquaintance. Russell aside, I am uncomfortable with the idea that *all* descriptions involve ostension; it is hard to find ostension, except by courtesy, in "the first woman to become President of the United States."

6. Brinton astutely points out that even in "perfect," uniquely individuating descriptions it is not the definite article that does the individuating, but the meanings of the predicates in the description's matrix together with facts about the world.

7. Strawson did not say whether a speaker who tokens a sentence containing an empty description thereby makes a truth-valueless statement or rather makes no statement at all.

8. I thank Parke Godfrey for the comparison.

9. An SR-type along with an assignment is very like what Garner (1972, p. 210) calls a "locution." Garner warns on Austin's behalf against taking locutions as primary truth-bearers, but he appeals to an assumption or two of Austin's that I do not share.

10. Austin held that illocutionary acts were the primary truth-bearers (see Garner (1972)); I reject this, of course.

11. See Perry (1977, 1979) (cf. Lycan (1981c, 1984a)). See Ziff (1972b) and Garner (1972) on the outrageous multiplicity of everyday referents for that innocent-seeming phrase.

12. An SR-type together with an assignment is very close to what Garner in some unpublished papers calls a "pure statement," a "something that is just and simply true or false." But it is not what Austin called a "pure constative," viz., an utterance-event-token having purely assertive illocutionary force and no other illocutionary force. (The Metatheory *per se* says nothing about illocutionary force at all.) What I would call the locutionary content of a sentence is considerably more of an abstraction from the "total speech situation."

13. I am much indebted to Richard Garner for years of wrangling over the issues raised in this section.

14. A more subtle appeal to "scenarios" is made by John Haugeland (1979).

15. Some of Lakoff and Johnson's remarks suggest the idea that there is actually no such thing as a purely literal expression, that every word of English is metaphorical to some degree. That idea I take to be false on pain of regress. If there is one thing that seems indisputable about metaphorical meaning, it is that such meaning is derivative; an expression could not be used metaphorically if it did not first have a literal meaning that is the basis of the metaphor. Of course, it is possible that all the original literal ancestors are extinct.

16. One marginal excuse for this is that metaphor is largely (though I grant not entirely) a function of lexical meaning rather than sentential structure, and it is the latter rather than the former that concerns me in this book.

17. As in the case of metaphor, there is a temptation to think of ambiguity as an occasional oddity or surd standing out against the univocity that characterizes normal linguistic practice. And, as in the case of metaphor, one must not yield to that temptation; for virtually no well-formed sentence of English is entirely unambiguous. My colleague Paul Ziff is particularly well skilled at seeing bizarre but entirely genuine readings of what to ordinary people seem like perfectly straightforward sentences.

18. See Lycan (1984c), Dennett (1983), and the references contained therein.

Chapter 9

1. Of course, this is all loose talk; it would take several volumes on the philosophy of science to spell it out. Here I am only remarking on appearances.

2. Harman (1967), Davidson (1973b, 1973c, 1974, 1975), etc. In the past decade, Harman has leaned increasingly away from Quinean skepticism, Davidson increasingly toward.

3. Cf. Quine's earlier remarks (p. 386) on "fitting" and implicit guidance, and Stich (1972).

4. This view of "logical forms," in combination with Harman's suggestion that SRs or logical forms are *thoughts*, fits neatly with Quine's claim that ascriptions of thoughts or beliefs to human subjects are likewise indeterminate (for an explanation of the connection, see Harman (1969)).

5. Quine's reasons for this belief seem to rest on his indeterminacy doctrine. I shall take this up briefly later on.

6. Kalke (1969), Stich (1968), Putnam (1978a).

7. See, e.g., Dowty (1979), Geis (1974), and Partee (1973a).

8. Something of the sort occurs in Burge (1973).

9. The would-be Quinean Metatheorist could avoid this last criticism by accepting a principle of language-replacement: "When ordinary language can be replaced, without detriment and with gain in elegance, by the relevant canonical talk, it ought to be so replaced for the purposes of serious theorizing." This is a plausible dictum; and the reconstructed Metatheorist could reinstate Davidson's defense of events by arguing as follows: Davidson's semantic arguments have shown that event-mentioning sentences of first-order logic are the best all-purpose paraphrase of action sentences. So we can replace the latter by the former. If we can replace the latter by the former, we ought (according to the aforementioned principle) to do so. If we ought to do so, then we ought to speak exclusively (at least when doing serious theorizing) in Davidson's idiom, and therefore we ought to accept at least some sentences of that idiom. This will involve our accepting some (regimented) sentences that quantify over events; therefore, we ought to believe in events.

I am persuaded by this argument, barring my earlier objections to talk of "the best all-purpose paraphrase" of a single English sentence. But the argument rests on a considerably stronger methodological assumption than is required by Davidson's orthodox version, viz., on the cited principle of language-replacement, which is controversial.

10. This position is suggested by Davidson's remarks in (1967b, pp. 309, 320) and (1970, p. 186). In (1976, pp. 40–41) he explicitly denies that a theory of truth is a theory of meaning.

11. (1967b, pp. 312–13), (1973b), and elsewhere.

12. Hintikka (1969a) challenges this bold assumption.

13. In no way do I mean to rule out the possibility of there being distinct but *noncompeting* truth theories for the same language. Such theories might both be true. For example, if indeed there are or could be cultures that mobilized "alternative conceptual schemes," their respective truth theories for English might differ accordingly; one might analyze ordinary English in terms of material objects, another in terms of processes, and another in terms of goggleshoops. It might be that all are correct; on my view, there are material objects and there are processes and (I am strongly inclined to think) there are goggleshoops as well, these terms being drawn from different individuative schemes overlaid onto space-time. I do not think it is only what is *invariant* in the three truth theories that can be said to be correct.

14. The foregoing sections of this chapter are a slightly expanded version of part of Lycan (1976). I am indebted to Professors Quine, Davidson, and Harman, and to Stephen Stich, for helpful discussions and correspondence on the relation between truth-theoretic semantics and the indeterminacy doctrine.

15. Here too I am grateful to Harman and to Professor Quine, as well as to W. D. Hart.

16. Harman (1969) tends to blur them. In fact, he seems to run whatever may be meant in these passages together with the underdetermination thesis (pp. 15, 21).

17. Those who are puzzled by the notion of an "infinite totality of possible data" will find it fairly well explained in Quine (1970a, p. 179).

18. Charles Landesman (1970) has made this point independently. Michael Friedman (1975) enforces a related distinction.

19. Quine has conceded this point (in conversation); but he adds that determinacy of translation over and above any observational fact of the matter amounts to the existence of propositions, and he has argued independently against the latter.

   The trouble with this approach is that Quine's most powerful and systematic argument against propositions is that based on the indeterminacy thesis ("If there were propositions, there would be a fact of the matter about translation"). But if the nonexistence of propositions is a cornerstone of the defense of the indeterminacy thesis itself, this argument is vitiated on grounds of circularity. One must rely on the independent metaphysical arguments that Quine has provided (1960, chap. VI); and I doubt whether these rather thin considerations by themselves would convince many philosophers to abjure talk of meaning *tout court*.

20. See Harman (1969) for clear and extended elaboration on this point.

21. I doubt that the distinction made here (mainly for rhetorical reasons) corresponds to that harmless one made in (1960) between "observation sentences" and other kinds; it is more like the traditional positivistic one. (But cf. Boorse (1975).)

22. It might be well at this point to anticipate two bad objections to the argument "from above."

   First: It may look as if Quine is merely saddling the field linguist with a Skinnerian psychology and methodology. It is tempting to reply that, since this program results in the counterintuitive claim (III), we ought to give up on the behaviorist program rather than on meaning. Harman (1969) replies at some length to this response, but it is well to mention a further consideration that Quine (1974) advances: The field linguist in particular is a "behaviorist ex officio"—whether or not behaviorist psychology is the best psychology, his evidence is *de facto* limited to behavioral evidence. It will not help to invoke neurological considerations, either, because in order to have established the relevant neurological theory, we would already have to have correlated brain-states with meanings or at least with beliefs, and Quine's point is precisely that that is what we cannot do in the first place; in order for neurological findings to come into play at all, some radical translation would already have to have been done.

Second: One might object that a bilingual has privileged access to a correct translation manual, since he can simply introspect which expression of Native corresponds to an expression of English. But why does the objector look upon introspection as anything more than an alternative way of assessing analytical hypotheses? Quine argues persuasively (1960, pp. 71, 74) that the bilingual must have "helped himself with analytical hypotheses" all along the way in any case, and that, whether or not the bilingual has privileged access to them, they are still indeterminate. See also Rorty (1972, pp. 449–50).

23. No one whom Quine has convinced of (III) should balk at this, however absurd it may sound. If I ask myself what my word "rabbit" refers to, the answer will of course be, "Rabbits! Not rabbit-stages, or process-rabbits, or parts of the Great Rabbit, or anything else." But this answer is in English, and it presumes a correlation between a word ("Rabbit") of the language about which I asked the question and a word ("Rabbit") of the metalanguage in which I answered it. And this is just to make another analytical hypothesis, the homomorphic one.

Quine's way of softening the apparent absurdity of indeterminacy-at-home is hard to grasp (see (1968, pp. 48ff.)). M. C. Bradley (1969) has criticized it, but his conclusion seems to be merely, as his title indicates, that on Quine's view we can never know what we ourselves mean (if I understand Bradley correctly, he reads Quine as trying to avoid this consequence by talking in the passage cited about the relativization of reference to a background language), that Quine has therefore failed to avoid this consequence, and therefore that Quine's view is absurd. But Quine does not shirk the consequence at all. True, if we cannot know even what we ourselves mean, then there is no such thing as meaning; but this is precisely what Quine believes.

I think Quine means the relativity of my terms' reference to background language to be quite an obvious point: *of course* when I ask myself what a word of mine refers to, I must ask in a metalanguage (since I must mention the word in question) and thus am forced to raise the question of whether that metalanguage contains the object language or only appears to do so, i.e., the question of whether the object language is to be translated homophonically or heterophonically by a subset of the sentences of the metalanguage. Much is made of this point in Wallace (1972).

24. This one has been emphasized to me by Nick Georgalis and also by Robert Kirk, to both of whom I am indebted for illuminating correspondence on this topic.

25. Bradley (1976) sees a separate indeterminacy argument directed against the operation of parsing itself.

26. I think Ziff (1970) misses this point.

27. There is a related peculiarity regarding observation terms (also pointed out by Bradley (1976)): Quine's occasional talk of "*degrees*" of indeterminacy. Observation sentences, though indeterminate, are "less" indeterminate than more theoretical

ones (cf. (1970, p. 181n) and (1969b, p. 312), *inter alia*). I can make very little sense of this. *Underdetermination* certainly comes in degrees. But how can it be a question of degree whether or not there is a fact of the matter? It would seem that either there is a fact of the matter or there is not. Perhaps what Quine means is something weaker than what he appears to be saying, such as: (a) underdetermination comes in degrees (conceded); (b) the *obviousness* of indeterminacy comes in degrees (as it surely does, the degrees corresponding to the degree of theoreticity; that is why the number-theory/set-theory case is so plausible, as compared to the "gavagai" case); or (c) some sentences, but not others, involve more than one indeterminacy—their indeterminacy is compound. I am inclined to think that Quine means all three of these suggestions, particularly (c). As sentences get more theoretical, they are subject to more different indeterminacies, even though all are indeterminate in at least one way at the outset. (This fact may well explain (b). And cf. (1968, p. 67).) So far as the main point, (III), is concerned, if my interpretation here is right, the talk of "degrees" of indeterminacy is quite misleading.

28. For an excellent discussion of Davidson's abandoning of reference realistically construed, see Sterelny (1981); also, Devitt (forthcoming, chap. 10).

29. Quine explicitly acknowledges this in (1970), where he remarks that the examples were

> aimed not at proof but at helping the reader to reconcile [by illustration] the indeterminacy of translation imaginatively with the concrete reality of radical translation. The argument for the indeterminacy is another thing. . . . (p. 182)

30. Landesman (1970), Rosenberg (1967), and Friedman (1975) have raised much the same question effectively. Stephen Leeds (1973) offers an interesting discussion of the point, but I cannot survey it here.

Sometimes Quine seems to emphasize the *fundamentalness* of physics. In lectures he has said that "no fact of the matter" means "no *physical* fact of the matter," no fact making any difference to the ultimate subatomic particles and their motions. Certainly no syntactic or semantic hypothesis either entails anything about quarks and gluons or is deducible from any statement about quarks and gluons. But the same is true of any psychological hypothesis, any biological hypothesis, any law of auto mechanics, and any ordinary statement about tables and chairs. Quine may want to say that biology, auto mechanics, and furniture nevertheless *supervene on* microphysics (fix the microphysics and you have fixed the hearts, lungs, carburetors, valve lifters, and sofas), whereas semantics continues to float freely overhead; but this last is precisely what Quine's opponent denies. If semantics is part of a largely functionalist psychology, then it too supervenes on microphysics. Two worlds cannot differ psychologically without differing microphysically.

31. If you are having trouble tearing yourself away, see Lycan (1971a). For pursuit of Quine on number theory and set theory, see Lycan and Pappas (1976), but do not believe what we said there in labored exegesis of Quine's materialism.

32. Harman has suggested to me that much of Quine (1960) can be read as an *ad hominem* against Carnap. In this case, if we attribute Quine's behavioristic view of language to Carnap, we find that the *ad hominem* succeeds; the consequences of the behavioristic view for Carnap's other claims about synonymy, analyticity, and so on are dire.

33. Quine remarks (1960, pp. 220–21) that (III), the indeterminacy thesis, is of a piece with Brentano's contention that intentional idioms are irreducible to nonintentional ones. This is exegetically, historically, and theoretically interesting, especially since Quine does tend to regard the indeterminacy thesis as tantamount to denying mentalism and Cartesian dualism (see (1968, pp. 186–87) and Harman

(1967, 1969)), and since intentionality has often been taken to characterize the mental. But it is not immediately obvious why Quine identifies his view with Brentano's.

The following argument, or something like it, may suffice: If belief-statements are not reducible to nonintentional statements, then beliefs are not reducible to sentential attitudes. And if beliefs are not reducible to sentential attitudes, then, since anything over and above sentential attitudes is inscrutable to the field linguist, beliefs are inscrutable to him and thus to the empirical method in linguistics and psychology. But if so, we shall need a "separate science" in order to get at them. (Quine, of course, goes on to conclude that they need not be gotten at, there being no fact of the matter, and thus that it would be otiose for us to begin trying to construct an "autonomous science of intention.") So the irreducibility thesis implies at least the "separate science" and underdetermination theses, if not indeterminacy outright. Now we must argue for the converse: If there is no fact of the matter concerning translation, there is none concerning belief-statements, except relative to a translation manual (cf. Harman (1969, p. 16)). But if there is no fact of the matter concerning belief-statements, and there is one concerning sentential-attitude ascriptions, then the former are not reducible to the latter. The indeterminacy thesis therefore implies the irreducibility thesis.

Chapter 10

1. See Putnam (1975), Fodor (1980), Stich (1978), Burge (1979), and Lycan (1981c); also, Schiffer (1981b) and McGinn (1982).
2. Putnam (1978b, 1978c), Dummett (1978a), other essays in (1978c), and (1973, 1975, 1976). McGinn (1982) joins me in assimilating Dummett's qualms to methodological solipsism.
3. I have argued in (1981c) and (1984a) that belief ascriptions are pragmatically ambiguous and do have solipsistic readings as well as their more easily perceived semantical-content readings. However, (i) the ambiguity claim is controversial, and (ii) it is nonsolipsistic truth-conditions that are the topic of the present discussion in any case.
4. CRS goes back at least as far as Wilfrid Sellars (1963 and elsewhere). Its most vigorous defender at present is the renegade Harman (1974, 1975a, 1982). It has affinities with what Artificial Intelligence researchers call "procedural semantics"; see Johnson-Laird (1977), Fodor (1978), Woods (1981), Wilks (1972, 1982), and Ringle (1982).
5. Soames (1979b) proffers a competing picture of translation between English and the language of thought—a sort of shallow lexical translation, such as one might make using a Danish-Flemish dictionary if one knew neither Danish nor Flemish save for some purely syntactic features of each. (Soames notes that such a translation might be done either by applying a series of grammatical transformations to the string being translated and in the process substituting lexical items of the new language for those contained in the original string, in the manner of Generative Semantics, or by imitating the recursive translation procedure devised by Montague in "PTQ.") This suggestion is nicely solipsistic, since any translation method consisting purely of syntactic rearrangement plus lexical switching can be contained entirely within a speaker's head, and no appeal is made to reference or truth. But (unless I have misunderstood him) Soames does not address the question I have just put to Harman, viz., that of what the "translation" is to preserve. If we are given no answer to this, no constraints are put on the system of "syntactic"

transformations, and so the positing of them plays as yet no explanatory role in connecting sentences of English to speakers' and hearers' propositional attitudes. (For all we know, any English sentence might be related "syntactically" to any formula of the language of thought.) Again, the obvious constraint to impose is preservation of truth-condition, though Soames or a CRS theorist may resist this. Concerning such resistance, read on.

6. Incidentally, I am prepared to admit a narrow notion of "meaning"—"conceptual" or computational or solipsistic meaning—and I do not doubt that this notion would be captured, from speaker to speaker, by some version of CRS. (However, see note 10.)

7. Harman is well aware of Twin Earth cases and the like, and he makes an attempt to accommodate them (1982, sec. 3.2). He proposes to relativize the functional role of a concept to a "normal context," the "content" of the concept now being determined by role together with context rather than by role alone. Our "context" is Earth; Twin Bill's is Twin Earth. (Of a spontaneously created person who comes into being in outer space with ostensible memories and beliefs about an Earthlike environment, Harman says it is "quite arbitrary what we say" about the content of that person's concepts—we could take that person's "normal context" to be either Earth or Twin Earth, whichever we liked. This seems quite wrong to me. I would say that the fortuitous person's concepts simply do not refer; on my view it is a fact that the person's thoughts are about neither Earth nor Twin Earth. After all, the person is the moral equivalent of an Evil Demon victim.) We might add here, following Stephen White (1982), that although functional role fails to determine reference, it does determine functions from "normal contexts," or (as White treats them) contexts of acquisition, to referents.

But I do not see that Harman's modification blunts the nonsolipsistic drive of my earlier arguments. Even though functions from "normal contexts" to things in the world may correspond to items that are securely within speakers' heads, they play no behavior-explanatory role themselves, *in propria persona*. As Loar puts it (1982, p. 280), they are not themselves constituents of functional roles. They seem to add nothing to the picture already provided by functionalist psychology, and have no point unless they point toward a different sort of semantic description and explanation.

8. Field (1972, 1977), LePore (1982), Loewer (1982), Loar (1981), McGinn (1982), Schiffer (1981b, 1982), Devitt (forthcoming). Schiffer is skeptical of the uniqueness of a reliability-maximizing assignment of truth conditions to the formulae of a person's language of thought; I assume he is equally skeptical in the case of a person's public language. But for reasons that will emerge I believe the two languages should be treated very differently with regard to motivation of their respective semantics.

9. I owe this point to Kim Sterelny; cf. his (1983).

10. Again (cf. note 6 and McGinn (1982)), I am willing to concede a solipsistic notion of meaning, "meaning-for-S-at-t" perhaps, which might be identified with conceptual role. As I will argue at greater length in chapter 11, it is fruitless to bicker over what aspect of human linguistic activity is most properly *called* "meaning." Here I am concerned only to insist that there is *a* sense, and a standard and important sense, in which meaning determines truth-conditions.

It may be replied (as it was recently by Devitt in a conversational moment of devil's advocacy) that although this is so and although the arguments of this chapter have (easily) succeeded in showing that CRS is inadequate to capture the meanings of the sentences of public natural languages, I have done nothing to

show that *the whole package deal* comprised of truth, meaning, propositional attitudes, communication, assertion, and the rest is worth its weight in quarks and
gluons. It is currently fashionable (and, I grant, true) to observe that these notions
are part of a large and inchoate folk theory that should be accepted by philosophers
only if its explanatory utility can satisfactorily be demonstrated.

I cannot produce the desired demonstration, but to do so is no part of my project
in this book. For present purposes (and on the basis of previous defenses (Lycan
(1981b, 1981c)), I am presupposing the integrity of the propositional attitudes and
the truth of the commonsense view that human subjects of such attitudes communicate with each other. I am also appealing to the sorts of data that are traditionally addressed by theories of meaning, and contending that truth-theoretic
semantics is the best such theory. My main contention here is only that if we drop
the notions of truth and reference, we drop that of linguistic meaning as well;
whether the most recently proposed sentencing and execution of meaning is a
good idea, I here leave for others to judge.

Thus, I think the issue of the probity of referential semantics for natural languages is quite separate from that of the probity of referential semantics for
propositional attitudes—and both, I take it, are separate from the question of the
psychological reality of syntax, since no issue of methodological solipsism arises
there. I have defended (1981c) what LePore and Loewer call a "dual aspect"
semantics for belief, recognizing both semantical and causal/computational features of belief states, but unlike some theorists (such as Field (1977) and McGinn
(1982)) I do not extend this duple treatment to public natural languages, precisely
because they are public.

11. We must here disregard people whose foreseeings are logically guaranteed, and
people whose malfunctioning introspectors keep "I foresee that I will marry Jane"
from being assertible even when the people do so foresee.

12. Brandom himself expresses diffidence about the centrality and about the robustness of the truth-like notion that is needed to subserve a theory of assertibility:
"From the point of view of the technical project of generating assertibility conditions, the notions of truth and of truth conditions are theoretical auxiliaries, to be
cut and pasted in whatever ways give us the nicest account of assertibility conditions" (p. 148). I take this to mean at least that Brandom would be happy with any
notion answering to Convention T (cf. our discussion in section 6 of chapter 9 of
"V-satisfaction" and the like) and with a "merely disquotational" as opposed to
"causal-explanatory" idea of truth, as current jargon has it. On the latter question I
have no firm opinion, particularly since I have seen no clear and complete explanation of the "merely disquotational" sense of 'true,' though I daresay the "prosentential" theory of truth due to Grover, Camp, and Belnap ((1975); cf. Brandom
(1981)) qualifies as the most promising explication of it to date. As for "causal-
explanatory": I am arguing in this chapter that truth and reference are explanatory,
in the sense of figuring importantly in explanations of generalizations regarding
speech communities; and the past fifteen years' work in the theory of reference has
convinced me that reference and hence truth are in large part causal notions. But I
know of no additional motivation for the conventional hyphen.

13. Readers who are fond of group organisms will see another way of looking at our
present setup: The game-room together with its occupants is itself an input-output
system, provided from outside with sense-data and eventually issuing responses.
The players inside the room are merely the homunculi who corporately constitute
the game-room's language of thought. The game-room thus construed as a single
organism speaks a private and solipsistic language if any; its terms refer only to the

objects that the player-homunculi can see, window-appearances being the functional equivalent of retinal hits. (This is because the assertion rules key only on properties of objects that are directly detectable by the players. For the same reason, Twin-Earth difficulties cannot arise.)

14. The reader may be reminded, pleasantly or unpleasantly, of John Searle's "Chinese Room" argument against machine intentionality (1980). Since elsewhere (1980a) I have urged that Searle's argument is a nonstarter, I must distinguish it from my own present complaint against CRS. Searle infers, from the single premise that *internally* a machine is only a formal manipulator of uninterpreted symbols, the conclusion that the machine's inner states must lack intentional content; this I take to be a glaring *non sequitur*, since "content" in the semantical sense is an "external" or wide property of states of organisms in any case. My own argument is rather that if our "conceptual-role" game consists only in the formal manipulation of symbols *and if* by hypothesis no wide semantical properties are generated thereby (with the environment's collusion), then the game does not constitute a language, nor its players' competence at it understanding of one.

15. ⌜Fa⌝ is V-true iff *a* V-satisfies F. A V-truth definition results when the move to V-satisfaction is not compensated by a corresponding move to V-reference.

16. See Devitt (1983) for a discussion of some of the relevant issues; also, for a more general treatment, Devitt (forthcoming). I side with Devitt on almost all points in this area. (I am also indebted to him for many hours of conversation on the topic of this chapter and for his comments on an earlier version of it.)

17. Crispin Wright alludes (1979, p. 283) to an Aristotelian Society audience "who seemed, by and large, to think that anti-realism could be nothing other than the Positivism of the Thirties." I would not accuse Dummett of unsubtlety or ham-handedness, but on the point of verificationism in particular I could not say how his view differs from A. J. Ayer's (save perhaps for eschewing sense-data).

18. But only roughly so, as Michael Devitt points out (1983, p. 96). Even in the most primitive teaching situations a good many theoretical assumptions are mobilized by both teacher and pupil; for the teacher rewards or punishes, strictly speaking, when *he thinks* P is or is not warrantedly assertible for the child, and the child's response over time is similarly mediated. Language-learning takes place amid a tumult of active theorizing about the world (cf. Quine's arguments against the view that an individual sentence has a verification-condition).

19. In response to a related argument of Strawson's, Dummett takes up the case of pain-behavior and pain (1978c, pp. xxxii–xxxvii). But I do not understand his discussion, at least not in relation to the simple point I have just made; he seems concerned to defend a view of Wittgenstein's against Strawson's criticism.

20. An instance of this argument is appealed to by John Pollock in (1967) and again in (1974). I discussed Pollock's use of the argument, somewhat ineffectually, in (1971b, pp. 112–13), not then seeing the objection I shall make here.

21. It seems to me that Brandom's point about the need for truth-conditions in sentential compounding, which was first made by Dummett himself, goes against the sort of verificationism that 3 seems to involve, and against the conclusion of the argument itself. For if meaning is not to be explained in terms of truth-conditions at all, and if assertibility is the key component of meaning, then why does even the simplest compounding of sentences into complexes "induce" truth?

In light of Dummett's verificationist tendencies, I find it also strange that he admits and even insists on the existence of meaningful but effectively undecidable sentences. But presumably "undecidable" would be defined in terms of classical, bivalent, and "face-value" truth (cf. our discussion of premise 8, above).

22. Dummett points out (1975, p. 120) that "[i]t would not be tolerable . . . to say that a theory of the motions of the planets was one that achieved the best possible fit with their observed movements, any discrepancy being due to mistakes on the part of the planets."

23. Soames points out several ways in which linguistic theories can aid and guide lower-level psychological theories of processing, as well.

24. In putting forward a distinct but similar argument, Soames seems to have a Generative Semantics format in mind, or at least one in which multiplicity of transformations is minimized in such a way that syntactic derivations become long and laborious. He compares theories of this type to axiomatizations of mathematical theories that minimize axioms and thereby make proofs much longer than the corresponding psychological processes could possibly be.

   Katz (1981) poses a piquant puzzle: Suppose we are visited by aliens who converse with us in what seems to be English (and let us also stipulate that the aliens' sentences have the same truth-conditions as ours). But we find through psycho-physiological examination that they produce surface structures from SRs in entirely different ways, i.e., by strikingly different processing (p. 89, slightly paraphrased into my jargon). Do the aliens speak English? Katz believes they do, and if his intuition is correct, then there is no fact of the matter about the grammar of English, or at least no psychological fact of the matter; neither a description of the alien processing nor a description of our processing would be a correct grammar of English to the exclusion of the other. To avoid this consequence one would have to deny that the aliens speak *English* strictly so called.

   This is a bullet I find myself willing to bite. Katz (or the reader) might incredulously wonder if I think the communicative coincidence between the aliens and ourselves is some kind of cosmic accident or miracle. But I think the case as Katz describes it *already* qualifies as miraculous or nearly so; if such a totally bizarre thing were to happen, I would say it was up for grabs.

25. Of course, a person does not lose tenure in a linguistics department for disclaiming responsibility to psycholinguistics. Linguists closely associated with Montague commonly disavow (as Montague did) any concern whatever with human wetware or even software. For them linguistics is simply a mathematical exercise and, even when considered as having anything at all to do with humans, instrumentalistically interpreted. That fact has no bearing on the ingenuity and brilliance of their work, but to me there seems ultimately little point in such an exercise.

26. Note, e.g., Hilary Putnam's disparaging remarks in his fifth John Locke Lecture (1978a) on the notion of "possibility in principle."

27. It is overwhelmingly plausible to think as well that the description will be couched in the vernacular of some logical theory, even if no currently existing logic is suited to the job, because the functional states that figure in thinking and interact with SRs must have articulate formal structures in order to play the distinctive causal roles they do, and their truth-conditions attach directly to those structures.

Chapter 11

1. See Fodor (1968), Dennett (1978b) Lycan (1981a), and Cummins (1983).

2. As we have seen in section 3 of chapter 7, the "illocutionary deflector" is a very black box indeed.

3. Richard Garner has remarked to me that it would be interesting to try to understand the Freudian slip in terms of our model. (For a persuasive depiction of Freud as homuncular functionalist, see Cummins (1983, sec. IV.3).)

4. I have gone on and on about functional hierarchies in (1981a). See also Mellick (1973).

5. Under the rubric "merely social" I have in mind defects such as rudeness, tactlessness, and obscenity.

6. In reality, to take this literally would be too big a job, because of the open-endedness of Grice's conversational maxims and the unlimited variety of local background knowledge that can figure in Gricean reasoning. Sterelny (1982) criticizes Grice's theory of implicature on this ground, and argues not implausibly against the inclusion of something like my "implicator" in our picture of the human speech center. I am not sure whether he would dispute my characterization of the relation between implicature and semantics.

7. On this issue, see Lycan (1981b, fn. 28; in press).

8. As I quaintly put it in (1979b), "[T]he term 'meaning' . . . floats freely on the surface of semiotic study as a whole, anchoring nowhere unless at someone's terminological whim" (fn. 9, p. 221).

9. Dummett and some of his followers seem to think it valuable to repeat at intervals that "a theory of meaning is a theory of understanding," as if that statement in itself were enough to suggest what is wrong with Davidson's program. In the sense in which I understand "understand," of course a theory of meaning is a theory of understanding, but tautologously so. Dummett evidently is using "understand" in a more restricted sense appropriate to solipsistic psychology.

Appendix

1. Wallace first mentioned the difficulty in (1972). Edwin Martin also noticed it in (1978); cf. McGinn (1980).

2. This option is suggested by (but is not quite the same as) Montague's treatment of "believes that" in (1973).

3. Notice that this truth-condition must be stated metalinguistically; the material-mode operator "It is true in w that" is nonextensional.

4. Recall Wallace's remark (p. 54) that "[n]o more fundamental change can be made in a theory than changing the number of argument places of one of its key concepts." And in (1973a) Davidson observes:

> Theories that characterize or define a relativized concept of truth (truth in a model, truth in an interpretation, valuation or possible world) set out from the start in a direction different from that proposed by Convention T. Because they substitute a relational concept for the single-place truth predicate of T-sentences, such theories cannot carry through the last step of the recursion on truth or satisfaction which is essential to the quotation-lifting feature of T-sentences. (p. 79)

In chapter 3 we found it necessary to relativize our truth predicate at least to a set of contextual parameters in order to deal with natural-language indexicality and vagueness. Davidson concedes later that "[t]ruth relative to a time and a person would seem to be in the same boat as truth in a model" (p. 85), but argues that the impurities introduced into T-sentences by such contextual parameters at least involve only concepts that

> we may hope to explain without appeal to notions like truth, meaning, synonymy or translation. The same cannot be said for truth in a model. (p. 85)

5. In fact, it is frequently obvious that the first truth-condition assigned is not adequate. For a classic example of a forceful objection to a first try, see Stine (1973). Ugly complications develop.

6. In Lycan (1979b) I catalogued some of the different moves available here.

7. See Plantinga (1974, chap. VII, sec. 4) and Lycan (1979b, pp. 308–11). (Cf. also Grandy (1974).) It should be emphasized that Montague and many other intensional logicians are delighted to stick to "pure" semantics, and positively disdain any search for the "facts in reality" that make sentences true or for "psychological reality," either one. Bear in mind that the criticisms I shall raise here and elsewhere are directed only against theorists who bend the methods of possible-worlds semantics to their own more ambitious purposes.

8. Christopher Peacocke (1978) and Anil Gupta (1978) have devised a clever way of bridging Wallace's gap; both seek to avoid the objection that a target sentence might have meant something other than what it does mean, by introducing truth predicates flagged for real-world meaning. This strategy may work for the alethic modalities (though I have some doubts about it even there), but it does not extrapolate to belief operators unless we make some adventitious assumptions about the nature of belief, such as an analogue of the S_4 axiom for it. (For a comprehensive and wider criticism of Peacocke's and Gupta's papers, see LePore and Loewer (1984). Related points about model- as opposed to truth-theoretic semantics are made in LePore (1983).)

9. If any Fregean account of opacity is correct, including, say, Hintikka's theory in (1969c), then further analysis may reveal only a systematic shift in the reference of terms occurring within the scope of nonextensional constructions, as one finds, uncontroversially, in the case of direct quotation. But the systematicity of this reference-shift at least would have to be accounted for, even though it introduces pragmatic considerations of reference-determination that call for a weakening of our notion of compositionality.

10. See Sellars (1967, 1969, 1973, and elsewhere). Davidson's well-known paratactic analysis of indirect discourse (1969) is actually a version of Sellars's theory, but is vulnerable to an objection that does not apply to Sellars's own version (see Lycan (1973a)).

11. In outline, the derivation is as follows:

1. "Jones believes that Fa" is true iff $(\exists x)$ (BELIEVE(Den("Jones"),x) & Sat($^{\ulcorner}$·Fa·$^{\urcorner}$, x)). (Instance of our Sellarsian belief clause)

2. Den("Jones") = Jones.

3. Sat($^{\ulcorner}$·Fa·$^{\urcorner}$, x) iff ·Fa·(x). (Lemma)

Therefore,

4. "Jones believes that Fa" is true iff $(\exists x)$ (BELIEVE(Jones,x) & ·Fa·(x)). (From 1,2,3)

(4) is an only mildly impure T-sentence.

The proof of the lemma 3 is long and tricky, owing to the delicacy of the use/mention moves involved, the difficulty of manipulating Sellars's funny demonstrative, and the interpenetration of the two; it requires the use of the demonstrative apparatus developed in chapter 3 and calls for several additional assumptions. (I am not even quite sure that the proof is sound. If it is not, then I think we must revert to our possible-worlds-style competitor.)

I am indebted to Anil Gupta for discussion of lemma 3 and for his very instructive comments on an earlier draft of this chapter.

12. Even if our Sellarsian approach works out in the end, there may be more constructions in English and other natural languages that fit neither into Tarski's original

paradigm nor into that paradigm augmented to accommodate nonextensional sentence operators. For example, English may contain a grammatically basic category of predicate modifiers, and it may not be clear how recursive clauses may be written for such modifiers in such a way as to yield T-sentences. Considering the trouble we have taken over belief clauses, the prospect is a depressing one.

So much the worse, one might think, for all this preoccupation with Convention T. Working semanticists do not aim constantly at proving T-sentences; in fact, it is quite rare that anyone ever takes the trouble to prove one. Could we not construct a fully compositional theory of English without T-sentences and without tears? Why not just assign a Fregean intension to each morpheme (paying close attention to syntax) and not worry about extensions at all? We would end up with a theory that assigned a "thought" or proposition to each English sentence, these propositions being made out of properties or concepts or what have you. The meaning of a target sentence would be given simply by the intension it expressed; Convention T need not be mentioned (or used).

But the idea of a "property" or a "concept" without an extension is bizarre. If our Fregean senses *have* extensions (even though we are not moved to delineate them), and particularly if we construe intensions as functions from worlds to whatever and there is a layer of extensions at the bottom (notably the values of functions from worlds to sets of individuals), then the base clauses of a truth definition will be available and so, *via* the recursive clauses, will be the T-sentences. (If I understand him correctly, Cresswell (1974, appendix) makes much this same point.)

13. Personally I favor the strategy advocated by Plantinga (1974) and independently by Castañeda (1974), of building up "nonexistent possibles" set-theoretically out of (actual) properties and other intensional objects; I have offered a preliminary defense of this strategy in Lycan (1979b, sec. XII).
14. Chiefly in conversation. He credits the term to C. B. Martin.
15. Armstrong (1980) offers a more explicit version of this argument.
16. I emphasize again that neither Montague nor any other "pure" semanticist need take any notice of this.
17. On the denotation of singular terms, see Kripke (1972) and Devitt (1981); on satisfaction, at least for natural-kind terms, see Putnam (1975) and Boër (1984).
18. I am indebted to Jim Waldo for illuminating discussion of the matters to be taken up in the remainder of this section.
19. For example, Cresswell's extremely powerful intensional abstractor (1973) allows the formation of many ungrammatical strings of English words; Cresswell relies on an unformulated filtering device to stem this excessive generative capacity. It is this device, a black box so far, that in effect serves as his grammar.
20. Interestingly, this is not Montague's own choice (in (1973) Montague understands "believes that" simply as relating its subject to a proposition); it is originally due to Hintikka (1962).
21. In fact, there is a simple set of rewriting rules that connects the two and that has some generality. Let us replace the logical form's antecedent by a restriction class on the quantifier, thus:

(i) $(w)(\text{TRUE-IN}(w, \, 'p'))$.
       $\epsilon \, \text{DOX}_s$

Truth-conditions can be obtained for any number of other nonextensional operators simply by varying the restriction class: we could let it be the class of S's epistemic alternatives ("S knows that p"), the class of S's visual alternatives ("S sees that p"), the class of biologically possible worlds ("It is biologically necessary that p''), the class of all worlds ("It is logically necessary that p''), etc. The rewriting rules are, simply:

(ii)   Given (w)(TRUE-IN(w, $'p'$)),
             ϵ R$_i$

a. If "i" is replaced by a name, front the name; if "i" is null, write "It is" at the head of the clause.

b. Insert whatever replaces "R" immediately after the fronted name or "It is," and lexicalize it appropriately ("believes that" for "DOX," "logically necessary that" for null R, etc.).

c. Erase everything else except "p."

Of course, this set of rules answers to nothing in standard syntax, nor does it help to explain any syntactic properties of the relevant surface structures in English.

22. I have given a related argument against David Lewis's modal realism in Lycan (1979b, pp. 294–96). For discussion of still further obstacles to the folding of possible worlds into psychology, see Partee (1979a, 1979b).

References

Alston, W. (1963). "Meaning and Use." *Philosophical Quarterly* 51. Reprinted in Rosenberg and Travis (1971).

Anderson, S. (1971). "On the Linguistic Status of the Performative/Constative Distinction." Bloomington, Ind.: Indiana University Linguistics Club Publications.

Armstrong, D. M. (1980). *The Nature of Mind and Other Essays.* Ithaca, N. Y.: Cornell University Press.

Armstrong, D. M. (1983). *What Is a Law of Nature?* Cambridge: Cambridge University Press.

Arruda, A. (1979). "A Survey of Paraconsistent Logic." In *Proceedings of the Fourth Latin-American Logic Conference.* Amsterdam: North-Holland.

Atlas, J. (1975). "A New Principle for Linguistic Semantics: Do Not Multiply Scope Ambiguities beyond Necessity." Presented at the Fifth International Congress of Logic, Methodology and Philosophy of Science, London, Ontario.

Austin, D. (1983). "Plantinga's Theory of Proper Names." *Notre Dame Journal of Formal Logic* 24.

Austin, J. L. (1950). "Truth." *Aristotelian Society Supplementary Volume* 24.

Austin, J. L. (1961). "Performative Utterances." In *Philosophical Papers.* Oxford: Oxford University Press.

Austin, J. L. (1962). *How to Do Things with Words.* Oxford: Oxford University Press.

Bach, K., and M. Harnish (1979). *Linguistic Communication and Speech Acts.* Cambridge, Mass.: MIT Press.

Baker, C. L. (1970). "Notes on the Description of English Questions." *Foundations of Language* 6.

Bar-Hillel, Y. (1964). "The Present Status of Automatic Translation of Languages." In F. L. Alt, ed., *Advances in Computers, Vol. 1.* New York: Academic Press.

Bell, J. M. (1973). "What Is Referential Opacity? *Journal of Philosophical Logic* 2.

Block, N. (1981). "Psychologism and Behaviorism." *Philosophical Review* 90.

Bochvar, D. A. (1939). ["On a Three-Valued Logical Calculus and Its Applications to the Analysis of Contradictions."] *Matématičéskij Sbornik* 4.

Boër, S. (1978). "Attributive Names." *Notre Dame Journal of Formal Logic* 19.

Boër, S. (1984). "Substance and Kind: Reflections on the New Theory of Reference." In Shaw (1984).

Boër, S., and W. G. Lycan (1973). "Invited Inferences and Other Unwelcome Guests." *Papers in Linguistics* 6.

Boër, S., and W. G. Lycan (1975). "Knowing Who." *Philosophical Studies* 28.

Boër, S., and W. G. Lycan (1976). *The Myth of Semantic Presupposition.* Bloomington, Ind.: Indiana University Linguistics Club Publications.

Boër, S., and W. G. Lycan (1980). "A Performadox in Truth-Conditional Semantics." *Linguistics and Philosophy* 4.

Boorse, C. (1975). "The Origins of the Indeterminacy Thesis." *Journal of Philosophy* 72.

Bradley, M. C. (1969). "How Never to Know What You Mean." *Journal of Philosophy* 66.

Bradley, M. C. (1976). "Quine's Arguments for the Indeterminacy Thesis." *Australasian Journal of Philosophy* 54.

Bradley, M. C. (1977). "Mind-Body Problem and Indeterminacy of Translation." *Mind* 86.

Brandom, R. (1976). "Truth and Assertibility." *Journal of Philosophy* 73.

Brandom, R. (1981). "Anaphoric Reference and Indirect Description." Ms., University of Pittsburgh.

Brandom, R. (1983). "Asserting." *Noûs* 17.

Brinton, A. (1977). "Definite Descriptions and Context-Dependence." *Noûs* 11.

Burge, T. (1973). "Reference and Proper Names." *Journal of Philosophy* 70. Reprinted in Davidson and Harman (1975).

Burge, T. (1974). "Demonstrative Constructions, Reference and Truth." *Journal of Philosophy* 71.

Burge, T. (1979). "Individualism and the Mental." In P. French, T. Uehling, and H. Wettstein, eds., *Midwest Studies in Philosophy*. Vol. 4: *Studies in Metaphysics*. Minneapolis: University of Minnesota Press.

Butler, R. J., ed. (1966). *Analytical Philosophy, First Series*. New York: Barnes and Noble.

Carnap, R. (1947). *Meaning and Necessity*. Chicago: University of Chicago Press.

Cartwright, R. (1966). "Propositions." In Butler (1966).

Castañeda, H.-N. (1974). "Thinking and the Structure of the World." *Philosophia* 4.

Chomsky, N. (1957). *Syntactic Structures*. The Hague: Mouton and Co.

Chomsky, N. (1965). *Aspects of the Theory of Syntax*. Cambridge, Mass.: MIT Press.

Churchland, P. M. (1979). *Scientific Realism and the Plasticity of Mind*. Cambridge: Cambridge University Press.

Churchland, P. M. (1981). "Eliminative Materialism and the Propositional Attitudes." *Journal of Philosophy* 78.

Churchland, P. M. (1982). "Is *Thinker* a Natural Kind?" *Dialogue* 21.

Churchland, P. S. (1980a). "Language, Thought and Information Processing." *Noûs* 14.

Churchland, P. S. (1980b). "A Perspective on Mind-Brain Research." *Journal of Philosophy* 77.

Churchland, P. M., and P. S. Churchland (1983). "Stalking the Wild Epistemic Engine." *Noûs* 17.

Clark, R. (1970). "Concerning the Logic of Predicate Modifiers." *Noûs* 4.

Cohen, L. J. (1964). "Do Illocutionary Forces Exist?" *Philosophical Quarterly* 14. Reprinted in Rosenberg and Travis (1971).

Cole, P. (1975). "The Synchronic and Diachronic Status of Conversational Implicature." In Cole and Morgan (1975).

Cole, P., ed. (1978). *Syntax and Semantics*. Vol. 9: *Pragmatics*. New York: Academic Press.

Cole, P., and J. L. Morgan, eds. (1975). *Syntax and Semantics*. Vol. 3: *Speech Acts*. New York: Academic Press.

Cooper, R., and T. Parsons (1976). "Montague Grammar, Generative Semantics and Interpretive Semantics." In Partee (1976).

Costa, M. (1979). "How to Close a Window with Words." Ms., University of South Carolina.

Cresswell, M. J. (1972). "The World Is Everything That Is the Case." *Australasian Journal of Philosophy* 50.

Cresswell, M. J. (1973). *Logics and Languages*. London: Methuen.

Cresswell, M. J. (1974). "Adverbs and Events." *Synthese* 28.

Cummins, R. (1983). *The Nature of Psychological Explanation*. Cambridge, Mass.: Bradford Books/MIT Press.

Davidson, D. (1965). "Theories of Meaning and Learnable Languages." In *Proceedings of the 1964 International Congress for Logic, Methodology, and Philosophy of Science*. Amsterdam: North-Holland.

Davidson, D. (1967a). "The Logical Form of Action Sentences." In N. Rescher, ed., *The Logic of Decision and Action*. Pittsburgh: University of Pittsburgh Press.

Davidson, D. (1967b). "Truth and Meaning." *Synthese* 17. Reprinted in Rosenberg and Travis (1971); page references are to the latter.

Davidson, D. (1969). "On Saying That." In Davidson and Hintikka (1969).

Davidson, D. (1970). "Semantics for Natural Languages." In Visentini *et al.* (1970). Reprinted in Davidson and Harman (1975); page references are to the latter.

Davidson, D. (1973a). "In Defense of Convention T." In H. Leblanc, ed., *Truth, Syntax and Modality*. Amsterdam: North-Holland.

Davidson, D. (1973b). "On the Very Idea of a Conceptual Scheme." *Proceedings and Addresses of the American Philosophical Association* 47.

Davidson, D. (1973c). "Radical Interpretation." *Dialectica* 27.

Davidson, D. (1974). "Belief and the Basis of Meaning." *Synthese* 27.

Davidson, D. (1975). "Thought and Talk." In Guttenplan (1975).

Davidson, D. (1976). "Reply to Foster." In Evans and McDowell (1976).

Davidson, D. (1977). "Reality without Reference." *Dialectica* 31. Reprinted in Platts (1980).

Davidson, D. (1978). "What Metaphors Mean." *Critical Inquiry* 5. Reprinted in Platts (1980).

Davidson, D. (forthcoming). "A Nice Derangement of Epitaphs." In a *Festschrift* for H. Paul Grice, ed. by R. Grandy and R. Warner.

Davidson, D., and G. Harman, eds. (1972). *Semantics of Natural Language*. Dordrecht: D. Reidel.

Davidson, D., and G. Harman, eds. (1975). *The Logic of Grammar*. Encino, Calif.: Dickenson.

Davidson, D., and J. Hintikka, eds. (1969). *Words and Objections: Essays on the Work of W. V. Quine*. Dordrecht: D. Reidel.

Davison, A. (1973a). *Performatives, Felicity Conditions, and Adverbs*. Doctoral dissertation, University of Chicago.

Davison, A. (1973b). "Words for Things People Do with Words." In *Papers from the Ninth Regional Meeting of the Chicago Linguistic Society*. Chicago: University of Chicago Department of Linguistics.

Davison, A. (1975). "Indirect Speech Acts and What to Do with Them." In Cole and Morgan (1975).

Davison, A. (1983). "Linguistic or Pragmatic Description in the Context of the Performadox." *Linguistics and Philosophy* 6.

Dennett, D. C. (1975). "Brain Writing and Mind Reading." In Gunderson (1975). Reprinted in Dennett (1978b).

Dennett, D. C. (1978a). "Artificial Intelligence as Philosophy and as Psychology." In Dennett (1978b).

Dennett, D. C. (1978b). *Brainstorms*. Montgomery, Vt.: Bradford Books.

Dennett, D. C. (1983). "Cognitive Wheels: The Frame Problem of AI." Ms., Tufts University.

Devitt, M. (1974). "Singular Terms." *Journal of Philosophy* 71.

Devitt, M. (1981). *Designation*. New York: Columbia University Press.

Devitt, M. (1983). "Dummett's Anti-Realism." *Journal of Philosophy* 80.

Devitt, M. (forthcoming). *Realism and Truth*. Princeton, N. J.: Princeton University Press.

Donnellan, K. (1966). "Reference and Definite Descriptions." *Philosophical Review* 75. Reprinted in Rosenberg and Travis (1971).

Dowty, D. (1979). *Word Meaning and Montague Grammar*. Dordrecht: D. Reidel.

Dreyfus, H. (1979). *What Computers Can't Do*. Revised edition. New York: Harper Colophon Books.

Dummett, M. (1959). "Truth." *Proceedings of the Aristotelian Society* 59. Reprinted in Dummett (1978c); page references are to the latter.

Dummett, M. (1973). *Frege: Philosophy of Language*. London: Duckworth.

Dummett, M. (1975). "What Is a Theory of Meaning?" In Guttenplan (1975).

Dummett, M. (1976). "What Is a Theory of Meaning, II." In Evans and McDowell (1976).

Dummett, M. (1978a). "The Philosophical Basis of Intuitionistic Logic." In Dummett (1978c).

Dummett, M. (1978b). "The Philosophical Significance of Gödel's Theorem." In Dummett (1978c).

Dummett, M. (1978c). *Truth and Other Enigmas*. Cambridge, Mass.: Harvard University Press.

Evans, G., and J. McDowell, eds. (1976). *Truth and Meaning*. Oxford: Oxford University Press.

Field, H. (1972). "Tarski's Theory of Truth." *Journal of Philosophy* 69. Reprinted in Platts (1980).

Field, H. (1975). "Conventionalism and Instrumentalism in Semantics." *Noûs* 9.

Field, H. (1977). "Logic, Meaning, and Conceptual Role." *Journal of Philosophy* 74.

Fillmore, C. (1969). "Types of Lexical Information." In F. Kiefer, ed., *Studies in Syntax and Semantics*. New York: Humanities Press.

Fillmore, C. (1975). *The Santa Cruz Lectures on Deixis*. Bloomington, Ind.: Indiana University Linguistics Club Publications.

Fillmore, C., and D. T. Langendoen, eds. (1971). *Studies in Linguistic Semantics*. New York: Holt, Rinehart and Winston.

Fodor, J. A. (1968). "The Appeal to Tacit Knowledge in Psychological Explanation." *Journal of Philosophy* 65.

Fodor, J. A. (1978). "Tom Swift and His Procedural Grandmother." *Cognition* 6. Reprinted in *RePresentations* (1981); Cambridge, Mass.: Bradford Books/MIT Press.

Fodor, J. A. (1980). "Methodological Solipsism Considered as a Research Strategy in Cognitive Psychology." *Behavioral and Brain Sciences* 3.

Fodor, J. A., T. Bever, and M. Garrett (1974). *The Psychology of Language*. New York: McGraw-Hill.

Fodor, J. A., J. D. Fodor, and M. Garrett (1975). "The Psychological Unreality of Semantic Representations." *Linguistic Inquiry* 6.

Fodor, J. D. (1982). "How Can Grammars Help Parsers?" Delivered at the Conference on Syntactic Theory and How People Parse Sentences, Ohio State University, May, 1982.

Fraser, B. (1971). "An Examination of the Performative Analysis." Bloomington, Ind.: Indiana University Linguistics Club Publications.

Fraser, B. (1975). "Hedged Performatives." In Cole and Morgan (1975).

Frazier, L. (1979). *On Comprehending Sentences: Syntactic Parsing Strategies*. Bloomington, Ind.: Indiana University Linguistics Club Publications.

Frazier, L., and J. D. Fodor (1978). "The Sausage Machine: A New Two-Stage Parsing Model," *Cognition* 6.

Frege, G. (1879). *Begriffschrift, eine der Arithmetischen nachgebildete Formelsprache des reinen Denkens.* Halle: L. Nebert.

French, P., T. Uehling, and H. Wettstein, eds. (1979). *Contemporary Perspectives in the Philosophy of Language.* Minneapolis: University of Minnesota Press.

Friedman, M. (1975). "Physicalism and the Indeterminacy of Translation." *Noûs* 9.

Garner, R. (1971). " 'Presupposition' in Philosophy and Linguistics." In Fillmore and Langendoen (1971).

Garner, R. (1972). "On Saying What Is True." *Noûs* 6.

Garner, R. (1975). "Davidson, Truth and Meaning." Ms., Ohio State University.

Gazdar, G. (1976). "On Performative Sentences." *Semantikos* 1.

Gazdar, G. (1979a). *Pragmatics: Implicature, Presupposition, and Logical Form.* New York: Academic Press.

Gazdar, G. (1979b). "A Solution to the Projection Problem." In Oh and Dineen (1979).

Geach, P. (1965). "Assertion." *Philosophical Review* 74. Reprinted in Rosenberg and Travis (1971); page references are to the latter.

Geis, M. (1970). *Adverbial Subordinate Clauses in English.* Doctoral dissertation, Massachusetts Institute of Technology.

Geis, M. (1974). "Two Theories of Action Sentences." *Ohio State University Working Papers in Linguistics* 18.

Geis, M., and A. Zwicky (1971). "On Invited Inferences." *Linguistic Inquiry* 2.

Ginet, C. (1979). "Performativity." *Linguistics and Philosophy* 3.

Goguen, J. A. (1969). "The Logic of Inexact Concepts." *Synthese* 19.

Gordon, D., and G. Lakoff (1975). "Conversational Postulates." In Cole and Morgan (1975).

Grandy, R. (1973). "Reference, Meaning and Belief." *Journal of Philosophy* 70.

Grandy, R. (1974). "Some Remarks about Logical Form." *Noûs* 8.

Green, G. M. (1975). "How to Get People to Do Things with Words." In Cole and Morgan (1975).

Grice, H. P. (1957). "Meaning." *Philosophical Review* 66. Reprinted in Rosenberg and Travis (1971) and in Steinberg and Jacobovits (1971).

Grice, H. P. (1961). "The Causal Theory of Perception." *Aristotelian Society Supplementary Volume* 35.

Grice, H. P. (1968). "Utterer's Meaning, Sentence-Meaning, and Word-Meaning." *Foundations of Language* 4.

Grice, H. P. (1969). "Utterer's Meaning and Intentions." *Philosophical Review* 78.

Grice, H. P. (1975). "Logic and Conversation." In Davidson and Harman (1975) and in Cole and Morgan (1975); page references are to the latter.

Grice, H. P. (1978). "Further Notes on Logic and Conversation." In Cole (1978).

Grover, D., J. Camp, and N. Belnap (1975). "A Prosentential Theory of Truth." *Philosophical Studies* 27.

Gunderson, K., ed. (1975). *Minnesota Studies in the Philosophy of Science.* Vol. 8: *Language, Mind, and Knowledge.* Minneapolis: University of Minnesota Press.

Gupta, A. (1978). "Modal Logic and Truth." *Journal of Philosophical Logic* 7.

Guttenplan, S., ed. (1975). *Mind and Language.* Oxford: Oxford University Press.

Hare, R. M. (1952). *The Language of Morals.* Oxford: Oxford University Press.

Harman, G. (1967). "Quine on Meaning and Existence, I." *Review of Metaphysics* 31.

Harman, G. (1968). "Three Levels of Meaning." *Journal of Philosophy* 65.

Harman, G. (1969). "An Introduction to 'Translation and Meaning,' Chapter Two of *Word and Object.*" In Davidson and Hintikka (1969).

Harman, G. (1972a). "Deep Structure as Logical Form." In Davidson and Harman (1972).

Harman, G. (1972b). "Logical Form." *Foundations of Language* 9. Reprinted in Davidson and Harman (1975); page references are to the latter.

Harman, G. (1973a). "Against Universal Semantic Representation." Presented at Performadillo (University of Texas Conference on Pragmatics), Austin.

Harman, G. (1973b). *Thought*. Princeton, N. J.: Princeton University Press.

Harman, G. (1974). "Meaning and Semantics." In Munitz and Unger (1974).

Harman, G. (1975a). "Language, Thought, and Communication." In Gunderson (1975).

Harman, G. (1975b). "Moral Relativism Defended." *Philosophical Review* 84.

Harman, G. (1982). "Conceptual Role Semantics." *Notre Dame Journal of Formal Logic* 23.

Haugeland, J. (1979). "Understanding Natural Language." *Journal of Philosophy* 76.

Hausser, R. L. (1973). "Presuppositions and Quantifiers." In *Papers from the Ninth Regional Meeting of the Chicago Linguistic Society*. Chicago: University of Chicago Department of Linguistics.

Heringer, J. (1972). "Some Grammatical Correlates of Felicity Conditions and Presuppositions." *Ohio State University Working Papers in Linguistics* 11.

Hintikka, J. (1957). "Quantifiers in Deontic Logic." *Societas Scientiarum Fennica, Commentationes Humanarum Literarum* 23.

Hintikka, J. (1961). "Modality and Quantification." *Theoria* 27.

Hintikka, J. (1962). *Knowledge and Belief*. Ithaca, N. Y.: Cornell University Press.

Hintikka, J. (1969a). "Behavioral Criteria of Radical Translation." In Davidson and Hintikka (1969).

Hintikka, J. (1969b). *Models for Modalities*. Dordrecht: D. Reidel.

Hintikka, J. (1969c). "Semantics for Propositional Attitudes." In J. W. Davis, D. Hockney, and W. K. Wilson, eds., *Philosophical Logic*. Dordrecht: D. Reidel. Reprinted in Hintikka (1969b).

Hintikka, J. (1974). "Quantifiers and Quantification Theory." *Linguistic Inquiry* 5. Reprinted in Saarinen (1979).

Hintikka, J. (1975a). "A Counterexample to Tarski-Type Truth-Definitions as Applied to Natural Languages." *Philosophia* 5.

Hintikka, J. (1975b). *The Intentions of Intentionality*. Dordrecht: D. Reidel.

Hintikka, J. (1976). "Quantifiers in Logic and Quantifiers in Natural Languages." In S. Körner, ed., *Philosophy of Logic*. Oxford: Blackwell. Reprinted in Saarinen (1979).

Hockney, D., W. Harper, and B. Freed, eds. (1975). *Contemporary Research in Philosophical Logic and Linguistic Semantics*. Dordrecht: D. Reidel.

Horn, L. (1969). "A Presuppositional Analysis of 'Only' and 'Even'." In *Papers from the Fifth Regional Meeting of the Chicago Linguistic Society*. Chicago: University of Chicago Department of Linguistics.

Johnson-Laird, P. (1977). "Procedural Semantics." *Cognition* 5.

Kalke, W. (1969). "What Is Wrong with Fodor and Putnam's Functionalism." *Noûs* 3.

Kamp, J. A. W. (1971). "Formal Properties of 'Now'." *Theoria* 37.

Kanger, S. (1957). *Provability in Logic*. Stockholm: Almqvist and Wiksell.

Kaplan, D. (1977). *Demonstratives*. Ms., University of California, Los Angeles.

Karttunen, L. (1971). "Implicative Verbs." *Language* 47.

Karttunen, L. (1973). "Presuppositions of Compound Sentences." *Linguistic Inquiry* 4.

Karttunen, L. (1974). "Presupposition and Linguistic Context." *Theoretical Linguistics* 1.

Karttunen, L., and S. Peters (1975). "Conventional Implicature in Montague Grammar." In *Proceedings of the First Annual Meeting of the Berkeley Linguistics Society.* Berkeley: University of California Press.

Karttunen, L., and S. Peters (1979). "Conventional Implicature." In Oh and Dineen (1979).

Katz, J. (1972). *Semantic Theory.* New York: Harper and Row.

Katz, J. (1979). "A Solution to the Projection Problem for Presupposition." In Oh and Dineen (1979).

Katz, J. (1980). *Propositional Structure and Illocutionary Force.* Cambridge, Mass.: Harvard University Press.

Katz, J. (1981). *Language and Other Abstract Objects.* Totowa, N. J.: Rowman and Littlefield.

Keenan, E. L. (1971). "Two Kinds of Presupposition in Natural Language." In Fillmore and Langendoen (1971).

Kempson, R. (1975). *Presupposition and the Delimitation of Semantics.* Cambridge: Cambridge University Press.

Kintsch, W. (1974). *The Representation of Meaning in Memory.* New York: Wiley and Sons.

Kripke, S. (1959). "A Completeness Theorem in Modal Logic." *Journal of Symbolic Logic* 24.

Kripke, S. (1963). "Semantical Analysis of Modal Logic I." *Zeitschrift für mathematische Logik und Grundlagen der Mathematik* 9.

Kripke, S. (1965). "Semantical Analysis of Modal Logic II." In J. Addison, L. Henkin, and A. Tarski, eds., *The Theory of Models.* Amsterdam: North-Holland.

Kripke, S. (1971). "Identity and Necessity." In M. Munitz, ed., *Identity and Individuation.* New York: New York University Press.

Kripke, S. (1972). "Naming and Necessity." In Davidson and Harman (1972).

Kripke, S. (1975). "Outline of a Theory of Truth." *Journal of Philosophy* 72.

Lakoff, G. (1969). "Presuppositions and Relative Grammaticality." In W. Todd, ed., *Philosophical Linguistics,* Series I. Evanston, Ill.: Great Expectations.

Lakoff, G. (1971). "On Generative Semantics." In Steinberg and Jacobovits (1971.)

Lakoff, G. (1972). "Linguistics and Natural Logic." In Davidson and Harman (1972).

Lakoff, G. (1973a). "Hedges: A Study in Meaning Criteria and the Logic of Fuzzy Concepts." *Journal of Philosophical Logic* 2. Reprinted in Hockney, Harper and Freed (1975); page references are to the latter.

Lakoff, G. (1973b). "Notes on What It Would Take to Understand How One Adverb Works." *Monist* 57.

Lakoff, G. (1975). "Pragmatics in Natural Logic." In E. L. Keenan, ed., *Formal Semantics of Natural Language.* Cambridge: Cambridge University Press.

Lakoff, G. (1982). "Experiential Factors in Linguistics." In Simon and Scholes (1982).

Lakoff, G., and M. Johnson (1980a). "Conceptual Metaphor in Everyday Language." *Journal of Philosophy* 77.

Lakoff, G., and M. Johnson (1980b). *Metaphors We Live By.* Chicago: University of Chicago Press.

Lakoff, R. (1971). "If's, And's, and But's about Conjunction." In Fillmore and Langendoen (1971).

Lambert, K., ed. (1970). *Philosophical Problems in Logic.* Dordrecht: D. Reidel.

Landesman, C. (1970). "Skepticism about Meaning." *Australasian Journal of Philosophy* 48.

Langendoen, D. T. (1971). "Presupposition and Assertion in the Semantic Analysis of Nouns and Verbs in English." In Steinberg and Jacobovits (1971).

Langendoen, D. T., and H. Savin (1971). "The Projection Problem for Presuppositions." In Fillmore and Langendoen (1971).

Leeds, S. (1973). "How to Think about Reference." *Journal of Philosophy* 70.

Leeds, S. (1978). "Theories of Reference and Truth." *Erkenntnis* 13.

LePore, E. (1982). "Truth and Inference." *Erkenntnis* 17.

LePore, E. (1983). "What Model-Theoretic Semantics Cannot Do." *Synthese* 54.

LePore, E., and B. Loewer (1981). "Translational Semantics." *Synthese* 48.

LePore, E., and B. Loewer (1983a). "Absolute Truth-Theories for Modal Languages as
Theories of Interpretation." Ms., Rutgers University/University of South Carolina.

LePore, E., and B. Loewer (1983b). "Three Trivial Truth Theories." *Canadian Journal of
Philosophy* 13.

LePore, E., and B. Loewer (1984). "Dual Aspect Semantics." Ms., Rutgers Univer-
sity/University of South Carolina.

Lewis, D. (1969). *Convention.* Cambridge, Mass.: Harvard University Press.

Lewis, D. (1970). "Anselm and Actuality." *Noûs* 4.

Lewis, D. (1972). "General Semantics." In Davidson and Harman (1972).

Lewis, D. (1973). *Counterfactuals.* Cambridge, Mass.: Harvard University Press.

Lewis, D. (1975). "Languages and Language." In Gunderson (1975).

Lewis, D. (1980). "Index, Context and Content." In S. Kanger and S. Öhmann, eds.,
Philosophy and Grammar. Dordrecht: D. Reidel.

Lewis, D. (1983). "Individuation by Acquaintance and by Stipulation." *Philosophical
Review* 92.

Liberman, M. (1973). "Alternatives." In *Papers from the Ninth Regional Meeting of
the Chicago Linguistic Society.* Chicago: University of Chicago Department of
Linguistics.

Loar, B. (1981). *Mind and Meaning.* Cambridge: Cambridge University Press.

Loar, B. (1982). "Conceptual Role and Truth-Conditions." *Notre Dame Journal of Formal
Logic* 23.

Loewer, B. (1982). "The Role of 'Conceptual Role Semantics'." *Notre Dame Journal of
Formal Logic* 23.

Lycan, W. G. (1970). "Hintikka and Moore's Paradox." *Philosophical Studies* 21.

Lycan, W. G. (1971a). "More on the Reasons for Indeterminacy of Translation." Ms.,
University of North Carolina.

Lycan, W. G. (1971b). "Noninductive Evidence: Recent Work on Wittgenstein's 'Criteria'." *American Philosophical Quarterly* 8.

Lycan, W. G. (1973a). "Davidson on Saying That." *Analysis* 33.

Lycan, W. G. (1973b). "Inverted Spectrum." *Ratio* 15.

Lycan, W. G. (1974). "The Case for the Modified Davidsonian Analysis of Action-
Sentences." Handout, University of North Carolina.

Lycan, W. G. (1976). "Reality and Semantic Representation." *Monist* 59.

Lycan, W. G. (1979a). "Semantic Competence and Funny Functors." *Monist* 62.

Lycan, W. G. (1979b). "The Trouble with Possible Worlds." In M. Loux, ed., *The Possible and the Actual.* Ithaca, N. Y.: Cornell University Press.

Lycan, W. G. (1980a). "The Functionalist Reply (Ohio State)." *Behavioral and Brain
Sciences* 3.

Lycan, W. G. (1980b). "Thoughts on Stalnaker's Semantics for Belief." Ms., University
of North Carolina.

Lycan, W. G. (1981a). "Form, Function, and Feel." *Journal of Philosophy* 78.

Lycan, W. G. (1981b). "Psychological Laws." *Philosophical Topics* 12.

Lycan, W. G. (1981c). "Toward a Homuncular Theory of Believing." *Cognition and
Brain Theory* 4.

Lycan, W. G. (1984a). "The Paradox of Naming." In Shaw (1984).

Lycan, W. G. (1984b). "A Syntactically Motivated Theory of Conditionals." In P. French, T. Uehling, and H. Wettstein, eds., *Midwest Studies in Philosophy*. Vol. 9. Minneapolis: University of Minnesota Press.

Lycan, W. G. (1985). "Tacit Belief." In R. J. Bogdan, ed., *Belief*. Oxford: Oxford University Press.

Lycan, W. G. (in press). "Epistemic Value." *Synthese*.

Lycan, W. G., and G. Pappas (1976). "Quine's Materialism." *Philosophia 6*.

McCawley, J. (1967). "Meaning and the Description of Languages." *Kotoba no Uchū* 2, Nos. 9–11. Reprinted in Rosenberg and Travis (1971).

McCawley, J. (1968). "The Role of Semantics in a Grammar." In E. Bach and R. T. Harms, eds., *Universals in Linguistic Theory*. New York: Holt, Rinehart and Winston.

McCawley, J. (1972a). "A Program for Logic." In Davidson and Harman (1972).

McCawley, J. (1972b). "Syntactic and Logical Arguments for Semantic Structures." Bloomington, Ind.: Indiana University Linguistics Club Publications.

McDowell, J. (1976). "Truth Conditions, Bivalence, and Verificationism." In Evans and McDowell (1976).

McDowell, J. (1981). "Anti-Realism and the Epistemology of Understanding." In Parret and Bouveresse (1981).

McGinn, C. (1980). "Operators, Predicates and Truth-Theory." In Platts (1980).

McGinn, C. (1982). "The Structure of Content." In A. Woodfield, ed., *Thought and Object*. Oxford: Oxford University Press.

Martin, E. A. (1972). "Truth and Translation." *Philosophical Studies* 23.

Martin, E. A. (1978). "The Psychological Unreality of Quantificational Semantics." In C. W. Savage, ed., *Minnesota Studies in the Philosophy of Science*. Vol. 9: *Perception and Cognition*. Minneapolis: University of Minnesota Press.

Martin, J. (1975). "A Many-Valued Semantics for Category Mistakes." *Synthese* 31.

Martin, J. (1979). "Some Misconceptions in the Critique of Semantic Presupposition." *Theoretical Linguistics* 6.

Martin, R. L., ed. (1970). *The Paradox of the Liar*. New Haven, Conn.: Yale University Press.

Matthews, P. H. (1972). Review of Jacobs and Rosenbaum, eds., *Readings in English Transformational Grammar*. *Journal of Linguistics* 8.

Matthews, R. (1975). "Recognizing and Understanding Indirect Speech Acts." Presented at the American Philosophical Association (Eastern Division) meetings, December, 1975; abstracted in the *Journal of Philosophy* 72.

Mellick, D. (1973). *Behavioral Strata*. Doctoral dissertation, Ohio State University.

Mittwoch, A. (1977). "How to Refer to One's Own Words: Speech-Act Modifying Adverbials and the Performative Analysis." *Journal of Linguistics* 13.

Montague, R. (1968). "Pragmatics." In R. Klibansky, ed., *Contemporary Philosophy: A Survey*. Florence: La Nuova Italia Editrice. Reprinted in Montague (1974).

Montague, R. (1970). "English as a Formal Language." In Visentini *et al.* (1970). Reprinted in Montague (1974).

Montague, R. (1972). "Pragmatics and Intensional Logic." In Davidson and Harman (1972). Reprinted in Montague (1974).

Montague, R. (1973). "The Proper Treatment of Quantification in Ordinary English." In J. Hintikka, J. Moravcsik, and P. Suppes, eds., *Approaches to Natural Language*. Dordrecht: D. Reidel. Reprinted in Montague (1974).

Montague, R. (1974). *Formal Philosophy* (ed. by R. Thomason). New Haven, Conn.: Yale University Press.

Morgan, J. L. (1969). "On the Treatment of Presupposition in Transformational Grammar." In *Papers from the Fifth Regional Meeting of the Chicago Linguistic Society.* Chicago: University of Chicago Department of Linguistics.

Morgan, J. L. (1977). "Conversational Postulates Revisited." *Language* 53.

Morgan, J. L. (1978). "Two Types of Convention in Indirect Speech Acts." In Cole (1978).

Munitz, M., and P. Unger, eds. (1974). *Semantics and Philosophy.* New York: New York University Press.

Nolt, J. (1977). "Harman's Criticism of Operator Theories of Adverbs." Ms., University of Tennessee.

Oh, C.-K., and D. A. Dineen, eds. (1979). *Syntax and Semantics.* Vol. 11: *Presupposition.* New York: Academic Press.

Parret, H., and J. Bouveresse, eds. (1981). *Meaning and Understanding.* Berlin: Walter de Gruyter.

Parsons, K. (1973). "Ambiguity and the Truth-Definition." *Noûs* 7.

Parsons, T. (1972). "Some Problems Concerning the Logic of Grammatical Modifiers." In Davidson and Harman (1972).

Partee, B. (1973a). "Some Structural Analogies between Tenses and Pronouns in English." *Journal of Philosophy* 70.

Partee, B. (1973b). "Some Transformational Extensions of Montague Grammar." *Journal of Philosophical Logic* 2. Reprinted in Hockney, Harper, and Freed (1975) and in Partee (1976).

Partee, B. (1975). "Montague Grammar and Transformational Grammar." *Linguistic Inquiry* 6.

Partee, B., ed. (1976). *Montague Grammar.* New York: Academic Press.

Partee, B. (1979a). "Montague Grammar, Mental Representations, and Reality." In French, Uehling, and Wettstein (1979).

Partee, B. (1979b). "Semantics—Mathematics or Psychology?" In R. Bauerle, U. Egli, and A. von Stechow, eds., *Semantics from Different Points of View.* Berlin: Springer-Verlag.

Peacocke, C. (1978). "Necessity and Truth Theories." *Journal of Philosophical Logic* 7.

Perry, J. (1977). "Frege on Demonstratives." *Philosophical Review* 86.

Perry, J. (1979). "The Problem of the Essential Indexical." *Noûs* 13.

Plantinga, A. (1974). *The Nature of Necessity.* Oxford: Oxford University Press.

Plantinga, A. (1978). "The Boethian Compromise." *American Philosophical Quarterly* 15.

Platts, M. (1979). *Ways of Meaning: An Introduction to a Philosophy of Language.* London: Routledge and Kegan Paul.

Platts, M., ed. (1980). *Reference, Truth and Reality.* London: Routledge and Kegan Paul.

Pollock, J. (1967). "Criteria and Our Knowledge of the Material World." *Philosophical Review* 76.

Pollock, J. (1974). *Knowledge and Justification.* Princeton, N. J.: Princeton University Press.

Putnam, H. (1965). "Brains and Behaviour." In R. J. Butler, ed., *Analytical Philosophy, Second Series.* Oxford: Blackwell.

Putnam, H. (1966). "Dreaming and 'Depth Grammar'." In Butler (1966).

Putnam, H. (1975). "The Meaning of 'Meaning'." In Gunderson (1975).

Putnam, H. (1978a). *Meaning and the Moral Sciences.* London: Routledge and Kegan Paul.

Putnam, H. (1978b). "Realism and Reason." In Putnam (1978a).

Putnam, H. (1978c). "Reference and Understanding." In Putnam (1978a).

Quine, W. V. (1960). *Word and Object*. Cambridge, Mass.: MIT Press.

Quine, W. V. (1968). "Ontological Relativity." *Journal of Philosophy* 65. Reprinted in *Ontological Relativity and Other Essays* (1969); New York: Columbia University Press.

Quine, W. V. (1969a). "Reply to Chomsky." In Davidson and Hintikka (1969).

Quine, W. V. (1969b). "Reply to Hintikka." In Davidson and Hintikka (1969).

Quine, W. V. (1970a). "On the Reasons for Indeterminacy of Translation." *Journal of Philosophy* 67.

Quine, W. V. (1970b). "Philosophical Progress in Language Theory." *Metaphilosophy* 1.

Quine, W. V. (1972). "Methodological Reflections on Current Linguistic Theory." In Davidson and Harman (1972).

Quine, W. V. (1974). *The Roots of Reference*. LaSalle, Ill.: Open Court.

Reeves, A. (1974). "On Truth and Meaning." *Noûs* 8.

Reis, M. (1974). "Further *and*'s and *but*'s about Conjunction." In *Papers from the Tenth Regional Meeting of the Chicago Linguistic Society*. Chicago: University of Chicago Department of Linguistics.

Ringle, M. (1982). "Artificial Intelligence and Semantic Theory." In Simon and Scholes (1982).

Rorty, R. (1972). "Indeterminacy of Translation and of Truth." *Synthese* 23.

Rosch, E. (1973). "On the Internal Structure of Perceptual and Semantic Categories." In T. E. Moore, ed., *Cognitive Development and the Acquisition of Language*. New York: Academic Press.

Rosch, E. (1975). "Cognitive Representations of Semantic Categories." *Journal of Experimental Pschology: General* 104.

Rosch, E. (1977). "Human Categorization." In N. Warren, ed., *Advances in Cross-Cultural Psychology*. Vol. 1. London: Academic Press.

Rosenberg, J. F. (1967). "Synonymy and the Epistemology of Linguistics." *Inquiry* 10.

Rosenberg, J. F., and C. Travis (1971). *Readings in the Philosophy of Language*. Englewood Cliffs, N. J.: Prentice-Hall.

Ross, J. R. (1970). "On Declarative Sentences." In R. Jacobs and P. Rosenbaum, eds., *Readings in English Transformational Grammar*. Waltham, Mass.: Ginn and Co.

Ross, J. R. (1975). "Where to Do Things with Words." In Cole and Morgan (1975).

Routley, R. (1979). "Dialectical Logic, Semantics and Metamathematics." *Erkenntnis* 14.

Routley, R. (1980). *Exploring Meinong's Jungle and Beyond*. Canberra: Australian National University Research School of Social Sciences Philosophy Department Monograph No. 3.

Russell, B. (1905). "On Denoting." *Mind* 14.

Russell, B. (1918). "The Philosophy of Logical Atomism." Reprinted in R. C. Marsh, ed. (1956). *Logic and Knowledge*. London: Allen and Unwin.

Ryle, G. (1938). "Categories." *Proceedings of the Aristotelian Society* 38.

Ryle, G. (1949). *The Concept of Mind*. London: Hutchinson.

Saarinen, E., ed. (1979). *Game-Theoretical Semantics*. Dordrecht: D. Reidel.

Sadock, J. (1970). "Whimperatives." In J. Sadock and A. Vanek, eds., *Studies Presented to Robert B. Lees*. Champaign, Ill.: Linguistic Research, Inc.

Sadock, J. (1974). *Toward a Linguistic Theory of Speech Acts*. New York: Academic Press.

Sadock, J. (1975). "The Soft, Interpretive Underbelly of Generative Semantics." In Cole and Morgan (1975).

Sadock, J. (1979). "The Performadox." Ms., University of Chicago.

Sanford, D. (1974). "Classical Logic and Inexact Predicates." *Mind* 83.

Sanford, D. (1975). "Borderline Logic." *American Philosophical Quarterly* 12.

Sanford, D. (1976). "Competing Semantics of Vagueness: Many Values versus Super-Truth." *Synthese* 33.

Schiffer, S. (1972). *Meaning.* Oxford: Oxford University Press.

Schiffer, S. (1981a). "Indexicals and the Theory of Reference." *Synthese* 49.

Schiffer, S. (1981b). "Truth and the Theory of Content." In Parret and Bouveresse (1981).

Schiffer, S. (1982). "Intention-Based Semantics." *Notre Dame Journal of Formal Logic* 23.

Scott, D. (1970). "Advice on Modal Logic." In Lambert (1970).

Searle, J. (1969). *Speech Acts.* Cambridge: Cambridge University Press.

Searle, J. (1975). "Indirect Speech Acts." In Cole and Morgan (1975).

Searle, J. (1980). "Minds, Brains, and Programs." *Behavioral and Brain Sciences* 3.

Sellars, W. (1963). "Some Reflections on Language Games." In *Science, Perception, and Reality.* London: Routledge and Kegan Paul.

Sellars, W. (1967). *Science and Metaphysics.* London: Routledge and Kegan Paul.

Sellars, W. (1969). "Language as Thought and as Communication." *Philosophy and Phenomenological Research* 29.

Sellars, W. (1973). "Reply to Quine." *Synthese* 26.

Shaw, J. L., ed. (1984). *Analytical Philosophy in Comparative Perspective.* Dordrecht: D. Reidel.

Simon, T., and R. J. Scholes, eds. (1982). *Language, Mind, and Brain.* Hillsdale, N.J.: Lawrence Erlbaum Associates.

Smiley, T. J. (1960). "Sense without Denotation." *Analysis* 20.

Soames, S. (1979a). "Linguistics and Psychology." Ms., Princeton University.

Soames, S. (1979b). "A Projection Problem for Speaker Presuppositions." *Linguistic Inquiry* 10.

Soames, S. (1979c.) "Why Semantic Theories of Natural Languages Are Not Psychological Theories of Understanding." Ms., Princeton University.

Soames, S. (1984). "Semantics and Psychology." In J. Katz, Ed., *The Philosophy of Linguistics.* Oxford: Oxford University Press.

Sosa, E. (1970). "Propositional Attitudes *De Dicto* and *De Re.*" *Journal of Philosophy* 67.

Stalnaker, R. (1972). "Pragmatics." In Davidson and Harman (1972).

Stalnaker, R. (1974). "Pragmatic Presuppositions." In Munitz and Unger (1974).

Stalnaker, R. (1978). "Assertion." In Cole (1978).

Stalnaker, R. (1979a). "Semantics for Belief." Ms., Cornell University.

Stalnaker, R. (1979b). "Thoughts." Ms., Cornell University. Incorporated into chapter 1 of *Inquiry* (1984); Cambridge, Mass.: Bradford Books/MIT Press.

Stalnaker, R., and R. Thomason (1973). "A Semantic Theory of Adverbs." *Linguistic Inquiry* 4.

Stampe, D. W. (1974). "Attributives and Interrogatives." In Munitz and Unger (1974).

Stampe, D. W. (1975). "Meaning and Truth in the Theory of Speech Acts." In Cole and Morgan (1975).

Steinberg, D. D., and L. A. Jacobovits, eds. (1971). *Semantics: An Interdisciplinary Reader.* Cambridge: Cambridge University Press.

Stenius, E. (1967). "Mood and Language-Game." *Synthese* 17.

Sterelny, K. (1981). "Davidson on Truth and Reference." *Southern Journal of Philosophy* 19.

Sterelny, K. (1982). "Against Conversational Implicature." Ms., Australian National University.

Sterelny, K. (1983). "The Language of Thought Revisited." Ms., Australian National University.

Stich, S. (1968). *Grammars, Psychological Theories, and Turing Machines*. Doctoral dissertation, Princeton University.

Stich, S. (1972). "Grammar, Psychology and Indeterminacy." *Journal of Philosophy* 69.

Stich, S. (1976). "Davidson's Semantic Program." *Canadian Journal of Philosophy* 4.

Stich, S. (1978). "Autonomous Psychology and the Belief-Desire Thesis." *Monist* 61.

Stich, S. (1983). *From Folk Psychology to Cognitive Science*. Cambridge, Mass.: Bradford Books/MIT Press.

Stine, G. (1973). "Essentialism, Possible Worlds and Propositional Attitudes." *Philosophical Review* 82.

Strawson, P. F. (1950a). "On Referring." *Mind* 59. Reprinted in Rosenberg and Travis (1971); page references are to the latter.

Strawson, P. F. (1950b). "Truth." *Aristotelian Society Supplementary Volume* 24.

Strawson, P. F. (1964). "Intention and Convention in Speech Acts." *Philosophical Review* 73.

Tarski, A. (1956). "The Concept of Truth in Formalized Languages." In *Logic, Semantics, Metamathematics* (tr. by J. H. Woodger). Oxford: Oxford University Press. Excerpted in Davidson and Harman (1975).

Tennant, N. (1977). "Truth, Meaning, and Decidability." *Mind* 86.

Thomason, R. (1973). "Semantics, Pragmatics, Conversation, and Presupposition." Presented at Performadillo (University of Texas Conference on Pragmatics), Austin.

Thompson, S. A. (1971). "The Deep Structure of Relative Clauses." In Fillmore and Langendoen (1971).

Ulm, M. (1978). "Harman's Account of Semantic Paradoxes." *Studies in Language* 2.

van der Auwera, J. (1980). *Indirect Speech Acts Revisited*. Bloomington, Ind.: Indiana University Linguistics Club Publications.

van Fraassen, B. (1966). "Singular Terms, Truth-value Gaps, and Free Logic." *Journal of Philosophy* 63.

van Fraassen, B. (1970). "Truth and Paradoxical Consequences." In Martin (1970).

Visentini, B., *et al.* (1970). *Linguaggi nella Societá e nella Tecnica*. Milan: Edizioni di Communitá.

von Stechow, A. (1981). "Presupposition and Context." In U. Mönnich, ed., *Aspects of Philosophical Logic*. Dordrecht: D. Reidel.

von Wright, G. H. (1951). *An Essay in Modal Logic*. Amsterdam: North-Holland.

Waismann, F. (1965). *The Principles of Linguistic Philosophy* (ed. by R. Harré). New York: St. Martin's Press. Excerpted in Rosenberg and Travis (1971).

Wallace, J. (1972). "On the Frame of Reference." In Davidson and Harman (1972).

Wallace, J. (1975). "Nonstandard Theories of Truth." In Davidson and Harman (1975).

Wallace, J. (1979). "Only in the Context of a Sentence Do Words Have Any Meaning." In French, Uehling, and Wettstein (1979).

Warner, R. (1982). "Discourse Logic and Conventional Implicature." *Studia Anglica Posnaniensia* 14.

Weinstein, S. (1974). "Truth and Demonstratives." *Noûs* 8. Reprinted in Davidson and Harman (1975); page references are to the latter.

White, S. (1982). "Partial Character and the Language of Thought." *Pacific Philosophical Quarterly* 63.

Wilks, Y. (1972). *Grammar, Meaning and the Machine Analysis of Language*. London: Routledge and Kegan Paul.

Wilks, Y. (1982). "Some Thoughts on Procedural Semantics." In W. Lehnert and M. Ringle, eds., *Strategies for Natural Language Processing*. Hillsdale, N.J.: Lawrence Erlbaum Associates.

Wilson, D. (1975). *Presuppositions and Non-Truth-Conditional Semantics*. New York: Academic Press.

Wimsatt, W. C. (1981). "Robustness, Reliability, and Overdetermination." In M. Brewer and B. Collins, eds., *Scientific Inquiry and the Social Sciences*, San Francisco: Jossey-Bass.

Wittgenstein, L. (1921). *Tractatus Logico-Philosophicus* (English edition tr. by D. F. Pears and B. McGuinness (1961). London: Routledge and Kegan Paul.

Wittgenstein, L. (1958). *Philosophical Investigations*. Oxford: Blackwell.

Woodruff, P. (1970). "Logic and Truth-Value Gaps." In Lambert (1970).

Woods, W. (1981). "Procedural Semantics as a Theory of Meaning." In A. Joshi, B. Webber, and I. Sag, eds., *Elements of Discourse Understanding*. Cambridge: Cambridge University Press.

Wright, C. (1976). "Language-Mastery and the Sorites Paradox." In Evans and McDowell (1976).

Wright, C. (1979). "Strawson on Anti-Realism." *Synthese* 40.

Zadeh, L. (1965), "Fuzzy Sets." *Information and Control* 8.

Zadeh, L. (1971). "Quantitative Fuzzy Semantics." *Information Sciences* 3.

Ziff, P. (1960). *Semantic Analysis*. Ithaca, N. Y.: Cornell University Press.

Ziff, P. (1969). "Natural and Formal Languages." In S. Hook, ed., *Language and Philosophy*. New York: New York University Press. Reprinted in Ziff (1972a).

Ziff, P. (1970). "A Response to 'Stimulus Meaning'." *Philosophical Review* 79. Reprinted in Ziff (1972a).

Ziff, P. (1972a). *Understanding Understanding*. Ithaca, N. Y.: Cornell University Press.

Ziff, P. (1972b). "What Is Said." In Davidson and Harman (1972). Reprinted in Ziff (1972a).

Zwicky, A. (1972). "Remarks on Directionality." *Journal of Linguistics* 8.

Index

348   Index